CHICAGO
Aviation

CHICAGO
Aviation
An Illustrated History

David M. Young

NORTHERN

ILLINOIS

UNIVERSITY

PRESS

DeKalb

© 2003 by Northern Illinois University Press

Published by the Northern Illinois University Press, DeKalb, Illinois   60115

Manufactured in the United States using acid-free paper

All Rights Reserved

Design by Julia Fauci

Library of Congress Cataloging-in-Publication Data

Young, David, 1940 Sept. 22–

Chicago aviation : an illustrated history / David M. Young.

   p.   cm.

Includes bibliographical references and index.

ISBN 0–87580–311–3 (alk. paper)

1. Aeronautics—Illinois—Chicago—History. I. Title.

TL522.I4 Y66 2003

629.13'09773'11—dc21

2002033803

Contents

Lake Michigan

Wisconsin

Kenosha

Waukegan

Waukegan

Woodstock

Palwaukee

Schaumburg   O'Hare

Dupage

Geneva

Aurora
Municipal   Wheaton

Meigs

Chicago

Midway

Gary
Municipal

Lewis-Lockport

Joliet   Lansing   Gary

Indiana

RSWEITZER

1989 Chicago Area Public Airports
⊕ Air Carriers
⊗ General Aviation Airports

Preface

• Aviation is the newest of the transportation modes, its history dating back only a century and falling entirely within the period in which the photographic and print media were able to record its development. We can only guess at what the first sailing ship on the Great Lakes, the 1679 *Griffon,* might have looked like, but most aircraft have been definitively documented on film and in print. There are photographs and eyewitness accounts of Octave Chanute's glider experiments of 1896, Augustus Herring's compressed-air–powered hang glider of 1898, and Pop Dickinson's ill-fated *American Defender* of 1912.

The business of commercial transportation is such that new developments are rarely confined to one location for very long, and aviation is no exception. A good idea is almost never kept secret for more than a few years, even during a war, when secrecy is a goal. An improved, swivel-axle freight wagon developed in one city traveled with a load of goods to another city and was quickly copied by the residents there, who were looking for something more efficient than a two-wheel oxcart. The canal lock, making possible waterborne commerce over uneven terrain, spread from Italy to northern Europe and finally to the New World, culminating in the Panama Canal, which links two oceans.

The development of aviation was an international effort from the start. The French may have been dominant in ballooning before the advent of powered flight, but experiments with heavier-than-air machines by Otto Lilienthal in Germany, Louis Mouillard in Egypt, and Samuel Pierpont Langley and Octave Chanute in the United States were conducted almost simultaneously in the late nineteenth century. Equally important, the information on their successes and failures was shared, largely through the efforts of Chanute. When the brothers Orville and Wilbur Wright decided to try their hand at building a flying machine, they contacted both Langley in Washington and Chanute in Chicago for information.

Such was the international competition and interest in flying that the Wright brothers' success in 1903 was within a few years eclipsed by the accomplishments of aviation pioneers in Europe who quickly built better airplanes while the Wrights squabbled with various American inventors over their patent rights. There was also a synergy between military and civil aviation almost from the beginning of controlled flight. During World War I, the American government adopted military aircraft of European design for its air fleet, and surplus planes were converted to non-military uses after the war, when a market developed for purely commercial aircraft. Conversely, in the 1930s, the United States developed the DC-3 for the commercial market, and that plane was converted to military use during World War II. The DC-3, in turn, led to a long line of American-built commercial aircraft that dominated the world's skies until the 1970s, by which time European plane builders with Airbus figured out that economics was as important a component of the civil aircraft industry as was aeronautical technology.

Chicago's role in aviation also changed over the years, often very rapidly. Octave Chanute's presence made the city a center of aviation research between 1890 and 1903, although it was more of a clearing house for information than a place where airplanes were invented. Then, after the city briefly became an aeronautical backwater, in 1910 the Aero Club of Illinois was formed to promote the sport by a group of wealthy flying enthusiasts. Until World War I intervened, the Aero Club made the Chicago area one of the world's aviation centers by staging giant air shows and building Cicero Field, Chicagoland's first airport in the modern sense of the word.

Chicago's role in aviation changed again after World War I. For many of the same geographic reasons that the city had become a maritime and railroad hub earlier, it now became the principal midcontinental aviation nexus, first for air mail and a few years later for the developing commercial airline system. Municipal/Midway and O'Hare airports successively became the busiest in the world in terms of the volume of aircraft and passengers. Airplanes built in Los Angeles; Seattle; and Toulouse, France, came to Chicago to swap passengers. This is a role the city still plays early in the twenty-first century, as is underscored by the political controversy over the building of a third airport and the expansion of O'Hare.

★ ★ ★ ★

This book builds upon several earlier works about early Chicago aviation, including one published in the 1950s and another, written by the late Neal Callahan and me, that came out in 1981. Because the literature on local aviation is sparse, this work relies on primary sources such as the files of the now-defunct Aero Club of Illinois in the Chicago Historical Society collections; newspaper clippings; government reports; the writings of such pioneers as Octave Chanute; and interviews of aviation old timers like Matty Laird, Al Spoorer, Sinny Sinclair, and Don Lockwood. It also uses the notes and documents accumulated during both my tenyear stint as the principal aviation writer for the *Chicago Tribune* in the 1970s and 1980s and subsequently as a business writer for the newspaper.

The book would not have been possible without the help of a number of people. The project was suggested by Martin Johnson, my editor at Northern Illinois University Press, to coincide with the hundredth anniversary of powered flight. Simine Short, a glider buff and self-made expert on Chanute, freely contributed photographs

and Chanute documents. She also read portions of the manuscript and made a number of suggestions. Chris Lynch, whose family business was at Midway Airport for more than half a century, willingly provided photographs and information on that airport. Marjorie Kriz, now retired from the Federal Aviation Administration, shared her research on early Chicago aviation and the Aero Club of Illinois. Her late boss Neal Callahan stimulated my interest in aviation. He collected photographs and made available information he had gathered in interviews with many of the brave young men who had taken to the air in earlier times, most of whom are now long gone. He and I also rummaged around the runway side of O'Hare, where we looked at the instrument landing systems, and visited the O'Hare and Midway towers and the TRACON and ARTCC air traffic control centers.

Officials of the Illinois Division of Aeronautics in Springfield provided considerable data on the issue of reliever airports, in which the state took a prime role, and Dick Adorjan of the Illinois Department of Transportation opened doors to enable me to peruse the state's files on the third airport issue. Ed Slattery and his successors at the National Transportation Safety Board in Washington, including most recently Alan Pollock, were always helpful in providing that agency's and its predecessors' reports on air crashes as well as some subsidiary information that did not always show up in the official reports. Langhorne Bond, FAA administrator under President Jimmy Carter, was never too busy to provide deep background on the politics of aviation, with some nuances not always obvious to the public.

Over the years, Mark Michaelson and Joe Hopkins of United Airlines arranged for access to that carrier's archives, for time in cockpit simulators, and for the jumpseat tickets that enabled me to experience first-hand how the big planes are flown. Art Jackson and his successors at American Airlines and Jerry Cosley and Larry Hilliard at TWA were similarly helpful, as were officials of British Airways who arranged for a cockpit flight in the supersonic Concorde, and of Air France who let me do the same on several of their 747s so I could understand the nuances of air traffic control spoken in several languages. Officials of McDonnell-Douglas in St. Louis and Long Beach, California; Lockheed in Burbank, California; Boeing in Seattle; and Airbus Industries in Toulouse, France, gave me tours of their plants and made executives available for interviews. At a British Aerospace factory in Wales, I got to crawl over their antique aircraft collection, including my favorite, the World War II Mosquito, and received explanations of the subtleties of the "supercritical wing."

On the general aviation side, Bill Howell, one of the last private airport operators in Chicagoland, explained the economics and operations of small airports and took me up in his Stearman biplane to see how they used to fly in the good old days. Matty Laird spent an entire day with me explaining what aviation was like during its golden age in Chicago. Various officials of Kenosha, Waukegan, DuPage, Palwaukee, and Lewis-Lockport airports gave me tours and explained how those reliever airports work. DuPage even arranged for chopper rides so I could "shoot" approaches over residential areas near the airport to get a better understanding of environmental issues as they impact airport expansion plans.

Various *Chicago Tribune* editors provided encouragement and endured my sometimes arcane whims during my long career at that newspaper, none more so than Bernie Judge, the *Tribune*'s former city editor who always seemed to find money in the budget to allow me to do such things as watch flight attendants conduct emergency drills at the Eastern Airlines school in Miami; take a trip on the world's smallest airline, based in Kirksville, Missouri; and rent a ferrying TWA 707 in Kansas City to do a whimsical story on what it would be like to be the only passenger on a commercial jet. (The up side was that the attendant handed me a cup of coffee at the aircraft door, the pilot came back and sat in the seat next to me to personally convey the flight information instead of making an announcement over the public address system, and they didn't lose my luggage.) Mary Jane Grandinetti of the transportation section of the paper was always willing to listen to ideas for stories on less-well-known aspects of aviation and often published them. Terry Brown, Owen Youngman, and John McCarron, the bosses of the business department, encouraged me to write on the economics of aviation—a factor that determines the fate of many an airplane, airport, and airline.

The late Robert McKane, a World War II navy pilot assigned to Glenview for much of that conflict, read an early version of the manuscript and offered some helpful suggestions. Bob Rockafield, a retired newspaper executive, read the finished manuscript and offered many corrections, suggestions, and comments.

An illustrated history relies heavily on photographs, and I had considerable help from a variety of sources, including Chris Lynch and Simine Short, whom I mentioned earlier. The Chicago Historical Society allowed me to peruse its extensive collection. Barbara Hanson, archivist at United Airlines, was extremely helpful with that carrier's collection, as was Ben Kristy at American Airlines' C. R. Smith Museum. Tom Hill, curator at the Octave Chanute Aerospace Museum in Rantoul, Illinois, spent the day with me perusing that institution's collection. Robert Zielinsky allowed me access to his scrapbook of historical photos. David Phillips, an architectural photographer, generously provided some old photos from his collection. Randy Sweitzer did the maps.

CHICAGO
Aviation

Chicago at the Dawn of Powered Flight

• When Wilbur Wright, the more determined of the two Wright brothers of Dayton, Ohio, decided in 1900 to seek some advice on how and where to test an as-yet-unpowered flying machine, he wrote to the same place almost everyone else in the world consulted on the subject of aviation—Chicago. This was the home of Octave Chanute, the retired railroad civil engineer who had made aviation his avocation and in the process established himself as the world's leading scholar on the topic even before he organized an international symposium on flight in 1893. He had transformed his home into the global clearing house for data on the successes and failures of would-be aviators and their machines.

Augustus Herring summoned Chanute by overnight lake packet from Chicago because he needed a credible witness for his attempt to fly in a powered hang glider on October 11, 1898, on the beach near St. Joseph, Michigan. A few years later, the Wright brothers invited Chanute to watch their glider and controlled-flight experiments near Kitty Hawk, North Carolina. Such was his reputation that he could spread the word of their successes to an astonished European scientific community.

At the time Wilbur Wright first wrote Chanute on August 10, 1900, no one in the world had conducted a controlled flight in a heavier-than-air machine, although Chanute and the Wrights were convinced it was just a matter of time. Chanute, who had conducted his own gliding experiments from the dunes along Lake Michigan beaches south of Chicago in 1896, proffered the advice that if the Wrights were serious they should experiment from a sand dune and make any long flights over water. Wind was crucial to early aviators, who needed it to attain sufficient air speed for flight, and the U.S. Weather Bureau's wind tables showed that

in September, the month the Wrights had free from their bicycle business to experiment, Chicago was indeed, as its reputation stated, the nation's windiest city. But the secretive Wilbur Wright was wary of the press attention that had plagued Chanute during his 1896 experiments on the Indiana beaches and decided on the remote location near Kitty Hawk on North Carolina's outer banks—the sixth windiest location in the United States.[1]

As a result, Chicago was not the site of a flight by a powered heavier-than-air machine until 1909, when the Wright brothers' rival, Glenn Curtiss, put on an exhibition. That flight so impressed a group of wealthy Chicagoans that they formed a club that was to dominate the city's aviation community for the better part of the next decade. It was the golden age of aviation in the Windy City. A succession of spectacular international air shows and the building of what was then the nation's finest airport established Chicago as one of the world's aviation centers. But aviation had no single capital from which all innovation emanated; once word of the Wright brothers' success spread, tinkerers and daredevils around the world rushed to their workshops and farm pastures to begin building and flying all sorts of contraptions.

World War I changed all that. Governments in Europe and America took control of the new flying machine for its military potential and built thousands of airplanes and trained pilots to fly them. The aviation clubs declined in influence and importance as huge numbers of war-surplus aircraft and trained pilots abruptly became available to attempt all sorts of commercial ventures. The barnstorming flying exhibitions that had drawn crowds to county fairs and metropolitan air shows in the prewar years continued as a way for pilots to make a living, but with diminished importance, so the pilots began to dust crops and haul people and products for a living. The newspapers that had so aggravated Chanute and the Wrights used airplanes to quickly haul photographs from major news events to their home presses, and some companies hired planes to haul parts between factories. But the most important single consumer of aviation in the postwar era was the U.S. Post Office Department, which was always looking for newer and faster ways to move the mail.

Even before the war ended, the post office had established an experimental air mail service, and because the Windy City was along the transcontinental postal route between New York and San Francisco, it became a hub for service throughout the Midwest. It was a role that continued through the twentieth century. Early airplanes didn't have the range to overfly Chicago, and by the time bigger and longer-range planes were developed, Chicago had attained critical mass as a connecting center for passengers, parcels, and mail.

Eventually, airline economics dictated that the city remain the nation's midcontinental hub, as it had in the railroad and, to some extent, the maritime eras. It was simply not practical from a financial standpoint to have direct flights connecting every city in the country, so millions of passengers were, and still are, hauled to Chicago to change planes. The businessman from Omaha bound for Boston, the little old lady from Buffalo on her way to visit her sister in El Paso, the surfer traveling from California to his home in Akron, and the congressman on his way back to his district in Iowa—all had to negotiate themselves and their baggage between gates at either Midway or O'Hare airports in Chicago. Eventually the international carriers discovered the advantage of the Chicago hub and began scheduling flights there to pick up and discharge passengers flying from or bound elsewhere; this was a factor in the Boeing company's 2001 decision to relocate its corporate headquarters from Seattle to Chicago.

Maintaining its position as the nation's most important midcontinental hub in the face of strong competition from other cities required Chicago to conduct an almost continuous program of airport expansion and improvement during the twentieth century, first at Municipal/Midway Airport and later at O'Hare International Airport. Beginning in 1912 and continuing for most of the century Chicagoans could brag they had the world's busiest airport, whether it was Cicero Field, Municipal, or O'Hare. But the volume of flights at those airports, especially O'Hare, inevitably gave rise to complaints about noise, pollution, and congestion. As Chicago's first century in the age of powered flight ended, the metropolitan area was debating whether to expand O'Hare or to build a new, third airport in farm fields in a remote south-suburban exurb.

The third-airport debate could hardly have been anticipated back in 1855 by a crowd of onlookers who had gathered in a semirural clearing just west of the Chicago River to watch the city's first aviation event—a balloon ascension. Chicago, barely twenty years old at the time, had become one of the nation's busiest ports by virtue of the Great Lakes and its new canal connection to the Mississippi River, and it was in the middle of a railroad-building boom that within a few years would make it the nation's uncontested rail capital as well. Yet the transportation technology that would transform the languorous trading post of forty or fifty souls in 1830 into a major metropolitan center within the span of a single human lifetime was already in transition. The two-hundred-ton sailing schooner would slowly yield to the five-hundred-foot steel steamer capable of carrying ten thousand tons of cargo, and the railroads were driving the overland freight wagon into extinction, although the dray horse would still be the principal motive power for the distribution of goods from the railroad freight house and dock as late as 1903. At that time primitive motor trucks relying on the same internal-combustion technology as the airplane were beginning to appear, primarily as small package-delivery vehicles.

The railroad's rise to ascendancy in Chicago had been particularly abrupt by historical standards. The city's railroad industry started in 1848 with a single ten-mile line westward and within six years had grown to ten railroads with three thousand miles of track in all directions, successively rendering the overland dray, the stagecoach, and the steamboat obsolete. The expansion of the city's railroad plant and of the volume of trains it handled continued through the end of the nineteenth century.

The automobile's appearance was a different proposition. Although two horseless carriages were displayed at the 1893 Columbian Exposition in Chicago, the new vehicle didn't make an impression on the public until the 1895 *Times-Herald* race showed it was a practical device. Between then and the end of the century, no fewer than twelve companies in the Chicago area began building automobiles, and by 1908 there were 5,475 autos registered within the city limits of Chicago.

Railroads and five-hundred-foot steamships required enormous capital investment far beyond the capability of individual entrepreneurs, but a primitive automobile could be built by almost any-one in a shed behind the house, and many were. All that was required was a formerly horse-drawn wagon, an internal combustion engine, and a few bicycle parts to serve as a drive train linking the engine to the wheels. Because much of the technology required to power road vehicles and flying machines is similar, though airplanes are far more complicated machines, some of the same people who invested in early automobiles and motorcycles, like seed merchant Charles Dickinson, wound up trying to build airplanes.

The newfangled flying machine was not a particularly useful transportation device for pragmatic Chicago. Some of the more farsighted aviation pioneers predicted that airplanes had a future as weapons of war, but the primitive craft of the early twentieth century could barely carry two people safely aloft, and they seemed incapable of filling the heavens with commerce as Alfred Lord Tennyson had predicted as early as 1842 in *Locksley Hall*. Some of the aviation pioneers, the Wright brothers and Glenn Curtiss in particular, were trying to make money building and exhibiting airplanes, but early aviation in Chicago and elsewhere was primarily a sport, as was ballooning. Clubs were formed to promote both sports, and public flying exhibitions and air races were held. From these modest beginnings grew the nation's premier air transportation center.

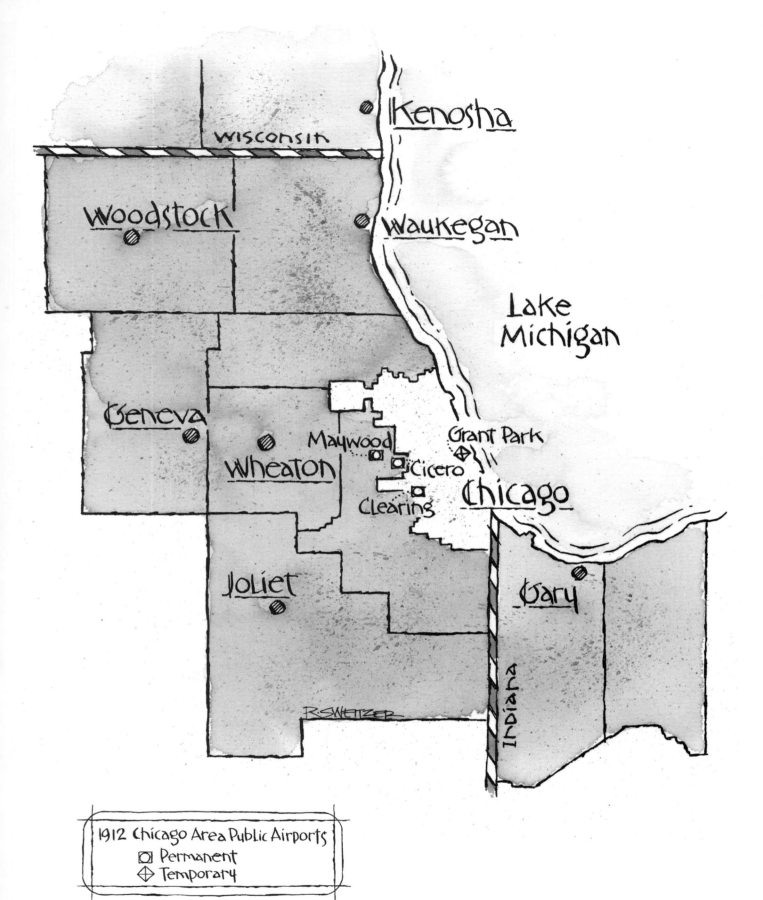

Wisconsin

Kenosha

Woodstock

Waukegan

Lake
Michigan

Geneva

Maywood

Grant Park

Wheaton

Cicero

Chicago

Clearing

Gary

Joliet

Indiana

R. SWEITZER

1912 Chicago Area Public Airports
◻ Permanent
◈ Temporary

The Balloons

Balloon ascensions in the nineteenth and early twentieth centuries were exciting events that drew large crowds. This ascension occurred in Springfield in 1890. The patches on the gas bag indicate that it had suffered some damage in prior flights. (Illinois State Historical Library)

• On a windy Independence Day in 1855, a large crowd gathered at a field at Peoria and Randolph Streets on Chicago's West Side to watch the latest innovation come to their frontier town, which was barely a quarter of a century old. The telegraph had arrived a few years earlier, enabling Chicagoans to send to New York messages that would have taken a month to deliver by post. Puffing steam locomotives capable of racing across the landscape at thirty miles an hour, thrice the speed of stagecoaches, had come to the city in 1848, the same year a canal was completed, connecting the city to New Orleans via the Mississippi River.

The crowd in 1855 was attracted by the spectacle of flight—a man taking to the air in a balloon. Silas M. Brooks, a thirty-year-old barnstorming aeronaut, was scheduled to conduct the city's first aerial ascension. Pumping hydrogen into the gas bag had taken most of the day, but by 3:30 P.M. he was ready to take off on what was scheduled to be a short flight over the city; the danger of landing in Lake Michigan a mile to the east precluded anything more adventurous for the former musician and band leader. Brooks had made his first ascension in a balloon barely two years earlier and in the weeks prior to his Chicago venture had lost two balloons in accidents.

As Brooks dumped ballast from the basket beneath the balloon *Eclipse* and the ground crew released the ropes, the crowd cheered. The elation was short lived, however, as was the flight. Shortly after becoming airborne, Brooks realized a strong west wind threatened to carry him out over the lake, and he frantically vented gas from the balloon, which then caught on some telegraph wires along the Michigan Southern Railroad right-of-way, sending Brooks and his gondola tumbling onto the tracks. The balloon, relieved of its ballast, suddenly shot skyward and drifted riderless out over Lake Michigan. Brooks later recovered the air bag but found it had been too severely damaged for further flight. He went to Rockford, Illinois, and assembled another balloon, the *Comet,* beneath which he performed in other Illinois cities for several years and, after 1860, in the East.[1] A few years later, Lake Michigan would prove deadly to more-skilled balloonists Washington Harrison Donaldson and John Wise.

As new and exciting as Brooks's balloon and ascension had been in antebellum Chicago, men and women had been riding in balloons for almost seventy years by the time he took up flying. Chicago was still an uninhabited marsh in a remote corner of the Great Lakes when humanity's con-quest of the air began in France in 1783, when two groups of experimenters almost simultaneously developed balloons and began sending people aloft in them. Within months ballooning had become a craze, not only in France and much of Europe, but also in the remote United States, then in the process of winning its independence from Great Britain.

The Origins of Ballooning

The first recognized balloon flight was made on June 4, 1783, in provincial Annonay, France, when the brothers Jacques-Étienne and Joseph-Michel Montgolfier sent aloft a smoke-filled paper bag, assuming it rose because smoke had lifting properties. They soon discovered that heated air, not smoke, gave balloons their lift. News of their accomplishment spread across France, and Professor Jacques-Alexander-César Charles in Paris began designing his own balloon after concluding that gas provided better lift than hot air. His flight the following August 27 in Paris was arguably more influential than that of the Montgolfiers. An enormous crowd that included Americans John Quincy Adams and Benjamin Franklin, as well as Étienne Montgolfier, watched the hydrogen-filled balloon ascend until it disappeared from sight. It finally burst and fell to earth fifteen miles from the launch site.[2]

It was Franklin who provided perhaps the most prescient and certainly the most widely quoted remark of the day. When another spectator opined that the balloon was little more than a useless toy, Franklin replied: "What is the use of a new born babe?" Franklin enjoyed considerable prestige and influence in France, and the remark was widely circulated. The ascension was the birth of something new.[3]

Not to be outdone, Étienne Montgolfier, the following September 19 at Versailles, sent one of his hot-air balloons aloft with a duck, a sheep, and a rooster. The ascension was witnessed by Louis XVI. A month later, on October 15, a Montgolfier balloon

Early airships consisted of little more than a skeleton covered with fabric. They came in a variety of shapes, although the cigar-shaped gas bag very quickly became accepted as the most aerodynamic. (Illinois State Historical Library)

heated by burning straw and tethered to the ground for safety carried human passengers aloft for the first time, to an altitude of two hundred feet. One of them, Francois Pilatre de Rozier, made a five-mile free flight in a Montgolfier balloon a month later and an ascension to 11,700 feet in 1784. He also had the dubious distinction of becoming the world's first aeronautical fatality a year later when his balloon, inflated by the volatile combination of hot air and hydrogen gas, exploded near Boulogne on an attempted thirty-seven-mile crossing of the English Channel. An assistant died with him.[4]

Less than a year after Paris went balloon crazy, the fad crossed the Atlantic Ocean to America, where Peter Carnes began working on balloons in Philadelphia. He sent an unmanned balloon aloft on a tether several times in Baltimore on June 24, 1784, before a thirteen-year-old boy named Edward Warren stepped out of the crowd and volunteered to go up in it, becoming the first person in the New World to fly.[5]

Balloons were put to perhaps their most practical use in America in the nineteenth century during the Civil War, when the Union Army assembled an aerial corps that included many of the nation's most famous aeronauts, men like John Wise, John Steiner, John la Mountain, and Thaddeus Lowe, and used it for reconnaissance. It was largely disbanded in 1863 when the generals running the Army of the Potomac lost interest in aerial reconnaissance, but the military and commercial potential of flight intrigued at least one foreign observer in America during the war. Count Ferdinand von Zeppelin, the German who in the twentieth century built that nation's fleet of rigid airships, which were used to bomb England and provide trans-Atlantic transport, attributed his interest in lighter-than-air flight to a balloon ride Steiner gave him on August 29, 1863, in St. Paul, Minnesota.[6]

There was little commercial utility to ballooning before and after the Civil War, however. About the only way for someone to make a living at it was by barnstorming across the country giving exhibitions and rides. As the novelty of watching people and balloons ascend on short hops began to wear thin, aeronauts increasingly had to resort to long-distance flights or acrobatic stunts, such as parachuting from a balloon or hanging from a trapeze beneath one, to draw paying crowds or patrons willing to sponsor the events.

Balloonists were forced to take other jobs in the off-season. Silas Brooks, who retired briefly to work in a St. Louis museum the year after his Chicago flop, by 1858 was once again making ascents in Illinois, but without much financial reward. After his July 3, 1858, ascension in Jacksonville, a newspaper in Springfield suggested the community take up a collection to subsidize his scheduled flight a few days later in the latter city, and later yet he was charging five dollars a head for tethered ascensions and twenty-five dollars—a considerable sum in those days—for short flights in Hartford, Connecticut. He retired after a serious accident in 1894 and died in a poorhouse in 1906 at age eighty-one. Brooks at least died of natural causes. Many of the barnstormers that roamed America in the nineteenth century playing county fairs and city parks were less fortunate. Some of the aeronauts were outright daredevils.[7]

Chicago's First Aerial Fatalities

Washington Harrison Donaldson, an acrobat and trapeze artist, arrived in Chicago twenty years after Brooks as a flying advance man for P. T. Barnum's famous Roman Hippodrome. Donaldson's task was to whip up enthusiasm for the coming circus by drawing large crowds to a series of balloon ascensions. Although there had been several previous balloon flights in Chicago, including one by Donaldson in 1872, the novelty of flight was still sufficient to draw large crowds to watch him dangle from a trapeze suspended from a balloon. Donaldson, a protégé of famed aeronaut John

Wise, had many successful ascensions to his credit and a number of narrow escapes. In 1872, he crashed into a smokestack seventy-five feet above the ground in Columbus, Ohio, and later that year, unable to properly deflate his balloon upon landing in Chillicothe, Ohio, he was nearly dragged to his death on the ground. A few days later, during another ascension in Chillicothe, he struck a building, and the next month he tore a gas bag while attempting to land. He gained altitude too quickly on another flight, causing the hydrogen in his gas bag to expand and tear the netting supporting his trapeze. In yet another incident in Ironton, Ohio, he was swept away by high winds. In 1873 he attempted a trans-Atlantic flight from New York, but it ended in Connecticut 2,600 miles short of its destination.

In retrospect, Donaldson's 1875 flight in Chicago, his 139th ascension, was doomed from the start. It was his original intention to take several passengers on a hop across Lake Michigan—a feat never before attempted—but unfavorable winds on July 14 delayed the ascension. Donaldson actually got aloft with several passengers on board but was forced to return hastily to earth. The next day winds and rain from the southwest whipped up whitecaps on the lake, and it was discovered that someone had inadvertently introduced air into the balloon's hydrogen-filled bag, reducing its lift capacity. Donaldson decided to make the trip anyway, but with a lighter load. The original plan had been to take two newspaper reporters, James Maitland and Newton S. Grimwood, on the trip, but they were forced to draw lots for the lone available space. Anticipating that he would be gone for several days and would land somewhere in Michigan, Grimwood borrowed ten dollars from another reporter to pay for his return trip by train. Grimwood had little reason to think that anything would go wrong, despite the novelty of flight, because Donaldson had already survived 138 balloon ascensions all over the United States.

With Donaldson and Grimwood in the basket, the balloon rose slowly from Dearborn Park at Randolph Street and Michigan Avenue in the late afternoon and drifted slowly on a breeze toward the northeast over Lake Michigan. A large crowd watched the balloon grow smaller and smaller until it disappeared in the distance. It was the last anyone would see of Donaldson. Newspaper accounts of the time stated that just before dusk several persons aboard a lumber schooner thirty miles off the Evanston shore noticed a balloon perilously close to the surface of the water. When they sailed to its assistance, the balloon unexpectedly gained altitude as if it suddenly had been lightened of all ballast, and it soared away to the northeast. Grimwood's body was discovered in the lake on August 16 near Grand Haven, Michigan, his watch stopped at 11:20, presumably six hours and twenty minutes after the flight began, and his life jacket was badly torn. The few notes he had taken on the trip were found on his body, but they gave no indication of what had gone wrong.[8]

Donaldson was presumed to have been lost in the lake, although his body and the balloon were never recovered. Persons who contended that they had seen him after the 1875 disaster kept popping up for years. One account published in the *New York Times* twenty-one days after the balloon's disappearance and twelve days before Grimwood's body was found quoted a "reliable gentleman" as having seen Donaldson alive and well in Algonac, Michigan, a week after the balloon left Chicago. Another, much later, report quoted a man named Richard Dobson, of Marion, Indiana, who said he had seen Donaldson several years after the event making a balloon ascension in Scotland. Still another account stated that years later some fishermen discovered on a remote island near Norway the badly deteriorated body of a man who had on a ring bearing the inscription "Wash.D." Some lumberjacks in Michigan were also reported to have discovered a skeleton entangled in rope web-

bing similar to the type used to support the gondola of a balloon; however, the men had been lost at the time of the discovery and were unable to lead authorities back to the site.[9]

It was not long before Lake Michigan claimed two other aeronauts. Four years after Donaldson's disappearance, John Wise, then seventy-one, attempted a long-distance flight from St. Louis in a balloon called *Pathfinder*. He took off in the late afternoon of September 28, 1879, and was seen floating over the Illinois cities of Alton and Carlinville. A railroad engineer reported that he saw the balloon at 11:30 that night, floating out over Lake Michigan at Miller, Indiana. Neither Wise nor the balloon was ever seen again, although the body of his passenger washed up down the shore in Indiana on October 24.[10]

Despite the accidents and threat of the lake, Chicago in the early twentieth century was something of a center of balloon and airship activity appropriately enough based around a South Side amusement park. White City, at 63rd Street and South Parkway (now Martin Luther King Drive), had opened to the public in 1905 with a boardwalk, a roller coaster called the Scenic Railway, a Ferris wheel, and assorted other amusements. Sometime prior to the park's public opening, aeronaut Horace B. Wild had established his balloon base there. In 1903 he built the first of his fourteen airships, a primitive blimplike craft powered by a Curtiss gasoline-fueled motorcycle engine that turned a pair of paddles that functioned as an air screw. Between 1903 and 1910, when he turned his attention to heavier-than-air machines, Wild performed frequent ascensions at White City to delight the crowds. The amusement park also was used as one of the launch sites for the First International Aerial Race in 1908. Long-distance balloon races had become popular as an activity of wealthy sportsmen early in the twentieth century after the newly invented airplane began to draw away aeronauts like Wild, Alberto Santos Dumont, and Lincoln Beachey.[11]

Early airships used the cigar-shaped gas bag for improved aerodynamics and typically were powered by a small gasoline engine that turned an airscrew, or propeller. Here aeronaut Horace B. Wild floats above Chicago in 1907 in his *Sky Buggy*. The hose in Wild's right hand controls the release of hydrogen to enable the airship to descend. The cable tethering the vehicle to the ground for safety purposes can be seen beneath Wild.

After 1910, Wild abandoned airships for aeroplanes. For a time he was active in both the Aeronautic (also spelled Aeronautique) Club of Chicago and the Aero Club of Illinois, and he participated in the 1911 and 1912 air shows in Chicago. He formed the International Aircraft Company, at 105 South LaSalle Street, to build planes, but like so many aviation pioneers he proved to be more of a daredevil than a businessman. He was arrested in 1917 for impersonating an army captain, apparently while trying to sell stock in his company, and again in 1920 for receiving stolen government property. He died in 1940 in New York.[12]

On July 4, 1908, a crowd estimated at 150,000 gathered at White City and Jackson and Washington Parks to watch nine balloons begin a race to Canada in an attempt to break the world ballooning distance record of 872 miles then held by the German craft *Pommera*. The size of the crowd was not surprising; balloons were still a local novelty in 1908 and the airplane had yet to make an appearance in Chicago. Although the Wright brothers had first flown a heavier-than-air machine in 1903, they remained secretive about their invention for years while the battle over their patent rights was fought out in the courts. Curtiss drew a big crowd when he made the first aeroplane flight in

Chicago the next year, but that exhibition also included a dirigible piloted by Captain Thomas Baldwin.[13]

The largest balloon in the 1908 race, and by some accounts the largest in existence at the time, was the twenty-one-thousand-pound *Chicago,* owned by Charles O. Coey, president of the Aeronautic Club of Chicago. The *Chicago* finished third, flying 542 miles from Chicago to Atwood, Ontario, in fourteen hours and forty minutes. The *Fielding San Antonio,* owned by Dr. F. J. Fielding and flown by E. E. Honeywell, won the race by traveling 786 miles to Sheffort, Quebec, in twenty-three hours and fifteen minutes.[14]

Ballooning continued at White City for more than a decade after the 1908 race despite the appearance of and competition from the airplane. However, the crash of the blimp *Wingfoot* in 1919 put an end to the popularity of the sport there. The hangar, which had been converted to a roller rink sometime after the 1919 disaster, was itself destroyed by fire in 1925. The amusement park never recovered from the damage the fire caused to the former hangar and other buildings, and it was ultimately a victim of the Great Depression. It closed in 1934.[15]

Chicago didn't have another international balloon race of the magnitude of the 1908 event until the Century of Progress world's fair of 1933, when the Gordon Bennett Cup races were held. Those annual balloon contests had started in 1906 after New York newspaper publisher Gordon Bennett, who later also established airplane races named after himself, donated the necessary trophy to an international ballooning organization. They continued until just before World War II. The September 2, 1933, Bennett race attracted aeronauts from Germany, Denmark, Belgium, France, Poland, and the United States despite bad weather that turned the race into an adventure for two crews.

The balloon of Ward T. Van Orman, the Goodyear company aeronaut, almost crashed into Lake Michigan, dunking him and his aide in the basket before regaining altitude. Then Van Orman encountered a squall over Canada that tossed the balloon around for six hours before it finally crashed at fifty-five miles an hour in a remote forest in Quebec, became hung up in the trees, and left the crew dangling twenty-five feet above the ground. After they finally got down, they hiked fourteen days through dense forest until they attracted attention by cutting a telephone line and waiting for a lineman to investigate. The adventure was good only for second place; the Polish crew set down even farther into the wilderness.[16]

The Century of Progress was also the site of another ballooning mishap. The U.S. Army had begun experimenting with high altitude research balloons in the 1920s at its balloon school at Scott Field, near Belleville, Illinois, and on November 4, 1927, Captain Hawthorne C. Gray had set a world altitude record of 42,470 feet but died in the open gondola after his oxygen supply ran out. Auguste Piccard, in Belgium in 1931, introduced the pressurized gondola to protect aeronauts against such danger, and the organizers of the Century of Progress invited his brother, Jean Felix Piccard, to attempt a new record at the Chicago fair. Jean Piccard designed an aluminum gondola for the balloon *Century of Progress.* Its ascent from Soldier Field was scheduled for August 4, 1933, but pilot Tex Settle had problems from the start.[17]

A balky gas valve almost caused cancellation of the flight, but Settle was concerned that venting hydrogen in Soldier Field in the presence of a large crowd would be dangerous, so he decided to take off. The flight had to be aborted a few minutes later, and the balloon crashlanded on the Chicago, Burlington & Quincy Railroad tracks just south of Union Station at 14th and Canal Streets. *Century of Progress* was not a total failure, however. It was salvaged and, ascending from the Goodyear-Zeppelin company facility in Akron, Ohio, three months later, set an

Powered airships were developed almost simultaneously with heavier-than-air craft. Balloonist Thomas Scott Baldwin's airship SC-1 was acquired by the Army Signal Corps in 1908. (Illinois State Historical Library)

altitude record of 61,237 feet. The gondola was ultimately donated to Chicago's Museum of Science and Industry.[18]

From Balloons to Airships

It wasn't long after balloons were developed that aeronauts began to look for mechanical methods of propulsion, as well as more aerodynamic shapes. There was general agreement that a cigar-shaped balloon was the aerodynamic solution, but propulsion systems proved to be a problem for most of the nineteenth century. The aeronauts in the first flight across the English Channel in 1785 carried oars for aerial rowing, which proved to be useless. Steam engines were too heavy and required too much fuel and water for the lift capability of balloons. Henry Giffard, a French engineer, reduced the weight of one steam engine to one hundred pounds, but it was not

powerful enough except in the lightest winds. Other inventors tried manual power, hydrogen-fueled engines, and even electric motors. The development of the gasoline engine by Gottlieb Daimler in 1885 eventually solved the problem. The first dirigible flight using a Daimler engine was in 1888, but it took a decade for aerialists to adequately refine the invention. Alberto Santos Dumont, a wealthy Brazilian living in Paris and probably the most famous aeronaut of his time, was finally able to make a seven-mile circle around Paris's Eiffel Tower in a gasoline-powered airship in 1901.[19]

The culmination of the efforts to build a powered airship was the development of the giant rigid-frame dirigible. Even before World War I, Count Ferdinand von Zeppelin's company had become so dominant in the industry of building airships that his name was applied to the giant craft that later circumnavigated the globe. Zeppelin began experimenting with his first airships at approximately the same time the Wright brothers were experimenting with fixed-wing airplanes, and for more than a decade the two creations were rivals as military and commercial aircraft. Airplanes quickly established themselves as superior military weapons, but it was not until the 1930s that it was clear that they were better commercial vehicles as well. Zeppelins were making trans-Atlantic flights with sizeable passenger loads long before airplanes were capable of doing so.

Some Zeppelins had envelopes, to hold the gas, that at 800 or more feet in length and 135 feet in diameter exceeded in size the hulls of most ocean-going ships of the time (see table 1). Despite their size, they were capable of speeds exceeding seventy miles an hour and had a range of more than 8,000 miles with as many as seventy-two passengers aboard.[20]

The Zeppelins overcame to some extent, though not entirely, the nemesis of aerialists since the invention of the hot-air balloon—wind. One of the reasons John Wise had decided to start his fatal flight in 1879 was that the wind had increased to the point that he was afraid his inflated balloon would be damaged if it remained on the ground. During his first ascension in Chicago in 1872, Washington Donaldson had narrowly escaped death when the wind suddenly picked up and his balloon drifted out over the lake, but he was rescued by a passing vessel. Zeppelins could not operate in windstorms, but they could fly in winds that would keep balloons on the ground.

Aerialists very early determined that there were risks inherent with both methods used to inflate balloons and give them lift. Until the U.S. Navy developed propane heaters for hot-air balloons after World War II, most such balloons required an open fire to heat the contents of the gas bag to give the vehicle lift, and there was always the risk that sparks would ignite the bag's fabric. Hydrogen provided superior lifting properties, but it is an extremely volatile gas and contributed to scores of aerial accidents, including the *Hindenburg* disaster in 1937. Hydrogen was also difficult and expensive to manufacture in the eighteenth century

Table 1—Development of Transportation Vehicles, 1912–1936

Vessel	Type	Year Built	Length (feet)	Speed (mph)	Passenger Capacity
Titanic	Ocean liner	1912	882	28	2,603
Pilgrim	Blimp	1925	105	50	2
B-247	Airplane	1933	51	189	10
M10,000	Streamliner	1934	200	90	116
DC-3	Airplane	1935	64	192	21
Hindenburg	Airship	1936	804	84	72

Sources: Christopher Chant, *The Zeppelin: The History of German Airships from 1900 to 1937* (London, 2000), 111; Enzo Angelucci, *World Encyclopedia of Civil Aircraft* (New York, 1982), 205, 214; Zenon Hansen, *The Goodyear Airships* (Bloomington, Ill., 1977), 10; John H. White Jr., *The American Railroad Passenger Car* (Baltimore, 1978), 2:612–20.

Dirigibles were still competitive with airplanes on long-distance service in the 1930s, when they provided the only transoceanic passenger flights. The *Graf Zeppelin,* shown here over Buckingham Fountain in Grant Park, visited Chicago in 1929 during its successful circumnavigation of the globe. (Chicago Historical Society)

when ballooning began; initially it was made on-site by running diluted sulfuric acid over iron filings, and somewhat later by forcing steam over iron filings in a tube. In the nineteenth century, cheaper gases that were manufactured from coal and were used to light homes became available for balloonists. At the time, helium was unknown.[21]

Hydrogen was the favored gas for commercial and military airships until after World War I, when a disaster in Chicago caused the industry to look for a safer alternative. The Goodyear company, which specialized in blimps, and the Zeppelin company, which was famous for its giant, rigid-frame dirigibles, joined forces after the war to build airships in the United States. Blimps have envelopes that collapse when deflated, but in dirigibles the gas bags are concealed within a rigid metal skeleton that has an outer skin for aerodynamic purposes. *Airship* is a generic term for all such lighter-than-air craft. The American tire company's original blimp project had begun before the war at White City in Chicago, the only facility anywhere near Goodyear's corporate operations in Akron with a hangar large enough to accommodate such airships. Construction on Goodyear's new airship hangar at Wingfoot Lake, near Akron, was not yet completed in May 1917 when the navy ordered some blimps for coastal patrol, so both the B. F. Goodrich and the Goodyear Tire and Rubber Companies were forced to use White City for the final assembly of components fabricated in Akron.[22]

The White City hangar was not quite large enough to accommodate a completed airship, so a trench was dug along the centerline of the building to permit the observation cars to be attached below the gas bag. The crew sent from Akron completed its work on the first blimp, the B-1, and on May 29, 1917, the craft began its flight to Akron to be turned over to the navy. Goodyear transferred its blimp production to Akron when the new hangar was completed there, and Goodrich took over the White City facility, building five navy B-ships there from September 1917 through June 1918. Then that company, too, transferred its operations to Akron.[23]

When the war ended and Goodyear decided to build commercial blimps, its Wingfoot Lake hangar was still in use for the navy program, so the company once again leased the White City building for final assembly. The commercial blimp design had evolved from the navy's B types with two major improvements: the envelope was segmented into compartments, or ballonets, to maintain the shape of the envelope during the expansion and contraction of the gas due to temperature and altitude variations, and the propellers were mounted tractor-style in front of the two Gnome engines instead of pusher-style in the rear, as was the practice on some airships. The new blimp had an open gondola, like its predecessors, and a gas bag filled with 95,000 cubic feet of volatile hydrogen, the standard element then used to inflate airships.[24]

When Goodyear officials decided to build commercial blimps, they were aware of the dangers of hydrogen; indeed, Zeppelin's *LZ4* dirigible had exploded and burned on the ground near Stuttgart, Germany, on August 5, 1908, killing many persons, and the *Schwaben (LZ10)* had exploded and burned on June 28, 1912, killing thirty-nine passengers and crew members. The risks involved in the use of hydrogen might have been acceptable in military operations during World War I,

when Zeppelins were used to bomb England, but as Goodyear discovered in 1919 in Chicago, such risks were not acceptable in peacetime commercial airships. Inert helium, which had first been identified spectroscopically in 1868 but had not been isolated until 1895, was safer because it would not burn, but in 1919 it was still too expensive to use in blimps. Helium at that time cost $125 per thousand cubic feet, compared with five dollars for hydrogen.[25]

The Wingfoot Disaster and Its Aftermath

As in the case of the navy blimp earlier, the components for the *Wingfoot,* as the new blimp was to be called after the company logotype, were manufactured in Akron and shipped to Chicago, where crews completed assembly of the $100,000 vehicle at White City and inflated it with hydrogen in time for its scheduled maiden flight on July 21, 1919. Pilot John A. Boettner climbed into the ten-passenger car with mechanics Henry Wacker and Carl (Buck) Weaver, and Army Colonel Joseph C. Morrow, an observer, and started the engines just after 9:00 A.M. The *Wingfoot* rose slowly and headed north for Grant Park in what turned out to be an uneventful flight. The airship was then moored in Grant Park for a while to allow the crowd gathered there to look it over, and just before noon Boettner took off for a trip north along the lakeshore to Diversey Avenue, returning to Grant Park at about 3:00 P.M. without a hint of trouble.[26]

About an hour later, Boettner and his crew were ready to return to White City for the night. They brought along as passengers Earl Davenport, the publicist for White City, and William G. Norton, a photographer for the *Chicago Herald and Examiner,* who apparently wanted to take some aerial photographs of the Loop. So instead of proceeding down the lakeshore, Boettner flew west over the Loop. Boettner said later that he was flying at approximately

The blimp *Wingfoot Express*, Goodyear's first commercial airship, was shown to the public at Grant Park on its maiden flight before it crashed into a Loop bank. The craft had been fabricated in Chicago. (Chicago Historical Society)

forty to forty-five miles an hour at 1,200 feet when he felt heat from a fire: "Looking back [at the tail], I saw shots of fire on both sides of the rear of the bag. I watched the flames for a couple of seconds before I said anything to the other fellows. Knowing the ship was finished, I yelled, 'Over the top, everybody.' As I yelled I felt the frame buckle, but by this time they were beginning to slide over the sides."[27]

The *Wingfoot* was completely in flames within seconds and plunging downward toward the Illinois Trust and Savings Bank building on the northwest corner of La Salle Street and Jackson Boulevard. The bank had closed for business for the day, but scores of employees were still inside completing their

accounting of the day's transactions. The flaming *Wingfoot* crashed through the skylight on the roof of the building and onto the main business floor, and the gasoline from its fuel tanks exploded upon impact. Thirteen people died in the disaster—ten bank employees, who burned to death in the fire or were crushed by falling debris, and three of the airship's passengers. Twenty-eight bank employees were injured. Surprisingly, two of the blimp crew survived without serious injury. Boettner had parachuted safely onto the roof of a nearby building, as had Wacker. However, Weaver was killed after his parachute caught fire from the blimp, and he fell through the skylight and into the inferno below.[28]

Goodyear's *Wingfoot Express,* which caught fire and crashed through the skylight of a Loop bank on its maiden series of flights in 1919, suffered Chicago's first aeronautical disaster. The hydrogen-filled blimp is shown here in the air above Grant Park prior to the disaster (lower right). The Field Museum and Illinois Central 12th Street (Roosevelt Road) station can be seen on the horizon. The center photo shows the damage inside the bank, where ten bank employees were killed by the explosion, fire, and falling debris. The crowd that gathered after the disaster hampered rescue efforts (upper right). The photograph shows firefighters removing a body by ladder from the bank roof. (Chicago Historical Society)

All of the blimp's passengers were killed. Norton lost control of his parachute and slammed into a nearby building. He died the next day while asking, according to newspaper legend, whether the photographs he made had been saved. Davenport, the only person to ride the car down, died when he was impaled on the bank roof.[29]

Even before the fire had been extinguished, Cook County law enforcement officials had begun an investigation of the incident. Boettner was arrested on the scene, and State's Attorney Maclay Hoyne ordered the arrest of sixteen other Goodyear employees for possible criminal prosecution. Coroner Peter Hoffman impaneled a special jury and took them to the scene. In an emergency meeting that night, just six hours after the crash, the City Council drew up a resolution instructing the corporation counsel to draft an ordinance that would give the city control of airships and airplanes flying in airspace within its corporate limits.

Boettner and the other Goodyear employees taken into custody were never brought to trial because there was no evidence to indicate that a crime had been committed. William C. Young, head of Goodyear's aeronautics department, later

The giant German dirigible *Graf Zeppelin* visited the Century of Progress fair in Chicago in 1933 on one of the 505 flights to various parts of the world, covering more than a million miles between 1929 and 1935. (David R. Phillips Collection)

gave the opinion that static electricity in the air or, more probably, hot oil that spewed onto the gas-filled envelope was the probable cause of the fire. Boettner at first suggested static electricity, but later theorized that sparks from the engine that had blown back against the envelope were the cause.[30]

After the disaster and the resulting political furor, Goodyear decided to use nonflammable helium to inflate its airships. Improvements in the process used to isolate helium and increased demand for it from the military and from Goodyear resulted in a decrease in its price to less than twenty dollars per thousand cubic feet. That was still four times the price of hydrogen, but in the opinion of the nation's

airship community, the added cost was justifiable because of the increased safety. However, helium was unaffordable for sport balloonists, a factor that contributed to the decline of that pastime until propane heaters appeared in the 1950s.[31]

With the shift of the last of Goodyear's operations from White City to Akron following the *Wingfoot* disaster, Chicago became a spectator to the airship. The 776-foot *Graf Zeppelin* appeared briefly in Chicago's skies twice, in 1929 during her around-the-world cruise and again in 1933 during the Century of Progress exposition along the lakefront. Two of Goodyear's blimps, *Puritan* and *Reliance*, were based at the fair to give visitors sightseeing rides.[32]

The zeppelin *Hindenburg* perished in a

spectacular ball of flame on May 6, 1937, at Lakehurst, New Jersey, when the hydrogen used to inflate her caught fire, probably from static electricity. Thirty-five of the ninety-two persons on board were killed. The disaster is credited with dooming the dirigible, but most nations had abandoned their rigid airship programs long before. Great Britain had dropped its program in 1930 following the crash during a rainstorm of its *R-101* dirigible near Beauvais, France, and the United States followed suit in 1935 following the aerial breakup of the *Macon.* The airships were simply too slow, too clumsy, too expensive to build, and because of their giant size, too difficult to handle to remain competitive amid the rapid advances in airplane technology after about 1925.[33]

The operating penalty imposed by helium because of its inferior lifting properties—it has 92 percent of the lift of hydrogen—was almost as severe: the *Hindenburg* was capable of carrying seventy-two passengers on a trans-Atlantic voyage when inflated with hydrogen, but only forty when filled with helium. It was not helium's cost but its availability that ultimately doomed the *Hindenburg,* however. The United States had a world monopoly on helium and for strategic reasons refused to part with any.[34]

U.S. Navy dirigibles had been inflated with helium from the beginning, but it didn't save them from disaster. Three of the navy's four rigid airships were destroyed when they crashed during or as a result of bad weather. The *Shenandoah,* which in 1923 had cost an astounding $2.2 million to build and an additional $211,500 to inflate with helium, broke up in midair during a squall over Ohio in 1925, killing fourteen of the forty on board. The *Akron,* built in 1931, crashed in a storm over the Atlantic near her Lakehurst base in 1933, taking seventy-three of her crew of seventy-six to their graves. The *Macon,* built in 1933, suffered a structural failure and crashed during rough weather

over the Pacific Ocean in 1935, but only two of the eighty-three crewmen were killed. That was the final straw for the United States. The surviving dirigible, the *Los Angeles,* was scrapped in 1939 after a fifteen-year career in which she made 331 flights.[35]

However, helium-inflated blimps continued to be popular in the United States, both in naval and commercial service, long after the dirigible disappeared. Airship historian Peter W. Brooks estimates that more than nine hundred "pressure airships," as blimps and their kin are officially known, were built in the United States in the first ninety years of the twentieth century, although over the same span more than 1.5 million airplanes were built. The navy phased out its blimp program in 1962, but commercial blimps were popular as advertising vehicles through the end of the century as companies such as Goodyear and Fuji used the airships to promote their products at sporting and other public events. The blimps, operating initially from Midway Airport but later from DuPage Airport thirty-five miles west of the Loop, also served as airborne platforms for television cameras recording such events as professional golf matches and football games.

Sport ballooning suffered a precipitous decline after the 1930s: a census in 1959 showed that there were only fourteen airworthy balloons in the United States. The high cost of the gasses necessary to inflate the balloons was a factor in their decline, as was the inherent risk of ascending in them—a liability that increased as the sky filled with airplanes. However, the last few decades of the twentieth century marked the revival of the hot-air balloon. In the 1950s the navy adapted propane burners to heat balloons used for scientific research, and it wasn't long before amateur aeronauts were taking to the skies again. While balloon rallies were held almost annually in the western suburbs of Chicago, they are now most frequently held in rural

Despite the increased dominance of airplanes over airships in the 1930s, blimps
were unusual enough to attract the attention of crowds
at Chicago's Century of
Progress fair in 1933. (David
R. Phillips Collection)

areas around the nation to avoid the
heavy airplane traffic common to metropolitan areas.[36]

More than a century ago, before airplanes had been invented and when balloons were still relatively uncommon in
Chicago's skies, a semi-retired civil engineer who had made a name for himself
building railroads began to systematically
ponder the problem of manned flight. The
man was Octave Chanute, and his twenty
years of investigations into the peculiari-

ties of flight made him perhaps the world's
leading authority on aviation. In his August 1, 1893, opening address to the Third
International Conference on Aerial Navigation in Chicago, Chanute predicted the
ultimate commercial failure of the great
airships that had yet to be developed by
enterprises like Zeppelin and Goodyear.
On the subject of flying machines he was
somewhat less pessimistic: there was a
chance for commercial success, but only in
the distant future.

Octave Chanute

• Balloons were one of several devices in the nineteenth century that whetted humanity's desire to follow birds into the air. In such scattered places as Algeria; Egypt; Australia; Germany; England; Washington, D.C.; Chicago; and San Diego as the century progressed, individual experimenters, usually operating independently, began to tinker with heavier-than-air machines, gliders for the most part although a few machines were powered. The designs were borrowed from a wide range of sources, everything from avian anatomy to railroad bridges. In the final decades of the nineteenth century, these inventors' efforts increased substantially and began to attract the attention of the scientific community, which in turn began to conduct seminars on how to apply engineering technology to solve the problem of flight, and finally, as the century closed, to conduct experiments, putting the theories to practical tests. Their collective efforts culminated, on a cold, windswept beach on the Outer Banks of North Carolina on December 17, 1903, in the world's first controlled flight in a powered machine.

The specific chain of events that led to the Wright brothers' triumph had been set in motion more than a decade earlier, as

Chanute poses on the Indiana dunes in 1896 with the multiplane glider he designed. The machine was unsuccessful. (National Air and Space Museum, Smithsonian Institution)

Samuel Pierpont Langley was one of the many early experimenters in aviation. Between 1890 and 1903 he tested powered and unpowered airframes from a house-boat-mounted catapult on the Potomac River near Washington, D.C. (Christopher Lynch Collection)

much by a succession of technical seminars organized by and around Octave Chanute as by any experiments with heavier-than-air machines. In the last quarter of the nineteenth century, Chanute, for whom aviation was never anything more than an avocation, published what amounted to humanity's accumulated knowledge of flying to that time. He compiled information on aviation experiments the world over and published it; corresponded with, encouraged, and even financed experimenters; conducted some experiments of his own with gliders; and organized and spoke at seminars on the engineering problems of aviation. Chanute's 1894 book, *Progress in Flying Machines,* is probably the single most influential work on aviation ever published.

Chanute, who as far as can be determined probably never flew in a machine himself, was indisputably Chicago's most

important aviation figure and the only one to rank among the world's most important aviation pioneers. Historian Tom D. Crouch probably puts Chanute's work in the best perspective: "More than any other figure, Chanute was responsible for propelling American aeronautics from folk technology to the status of an engineering discipline. In so doing he set in motion a chain of events that led to the triumph of Dec. 17, 1903."[1] It was Chanute whom the Wright brothers appealed to for encouragement in their darkest hour, when they were still obscure bicycle makers in Dayton, Ohio. It was Chanute who finally carried the word of their triumph to an astounded Europe.

A decade before that first flight, he had been instrumental in organizing and was the keynote speaker at the Third International Congress on Aerial Navigation, one of many technical meetings held in conjunction with Chicago's Columbian Exposition of 1893. In his remarks, he traced the developments in flight since the Second International Conference on Aerial Navigation in Paris in 1889, which he also had attended. He also made some predictions. "Success, when it comes," he said of heavier-than-air machines, "is likely to be reached through a process of gradual evolution and improvement, and the most that can we can hope to accomplish at present is to gain such knowledge of the general elements of the problem as to enable us to judge the probable value of future proposals, both as mechanical or as commercial enterprises." He was more pessimistic about the future of dirigibles: "The attainment of . . . moderate speeds requires very large and therefore costly balloons, which carry very few passengers and it is clear that while such craft may be justified by the exigencies of war, they cannot compete commercially with existing modes of transportation."[2]

These musings may seem bland by modern standards, but for the conservative civil engineer who had been concerned about being publicly ridiculed for his view that humanity was capable of building a flying machine, they were quite a significant leap forward. Despite Chanute's esteemed reputation among scientists and the pioneers of flight worldwide, it had taken considerable effort for Albert Francis Zahm, a fellow aviation enthusiast and professor of physics at Notre Dame University, to persuade Chanute to chair and speak at the 1893 Columbian Exposition conference in his home town. A similar conference in Buffalo, New York, in 1886 had been an unmitigated disaster when the principal speaker, recruited by Chanute, had been hooted off the stage.[3]

The Chicago conference, which was covered by the national press, proved to be so successful that Chanute came out of the closet and became an active promoter of aviation for the remaining seventeen years of his life, rather than simply a scholar discussing the achievements of others. The year after the Chicago convention, a series of twenty-seven articles summarizing the aviation experiments that had been conducted around the globe to that date, which had been published by Chanute's friend M. N. Forney in the *Railroad and Engineering Journal* in New York beginning in October 1891, was published in book form for the general public to see. This was Chanute's *Progress in Flying Machines.* Within a few years he was actively sponsoring glider flights on the sand dunes along the Indiana shore of Lake Michigan with machines he had helped to design.

Early Life

Chanute was not so much a Chicagoan as he was a citizen of the world. By the time he was born in Paris, on February 8, 1832, the first child of history professor Joseph Canut, people had been flying in balloons for nearly half a century and Sir George Cayley (1773–1857) had already experimented with manned gliders and methods of providing them with propulsion. The elder Canut emigrated to the United States in 1838 to become a vice president of Jefferson College in Louisiana, sixty-four miles north of New Orleans, and took his six-year-old son along. Young Octave changed his surname to Chanute after he had become thoroughly Americanized and attained the majority age of 21.[4]

Chanute led a sheltered life in Louisiana: he was tutored at home in French, Greek, and Latin, and his father did not allow him to play with other boys. Before leaving the house, the father often locked his son in the library, with books as his only companions. Octave's daughter recalled that Chanute's childhood isolation caused him trouble with English slang for the remainder of his life: "I remember once he asked us what a 'four flusher' was. I fancy that he had never played cards."[5]

After the family moved to New York City in 1844, Chanute's isolation finally ended. He learned English and entered school, and he decided on a career in engineering. In those days only a handful of institutions, including the United States Military Academy at West Point, offered engineering degrees, so a common way to learn the profession was on the job. In 1849, the seventeen-year-old Chanute went to Sing Sing (now Ossining), just north of New York City, and asked the engineer who was building the Hudson River Railroad for employment. Told that no job was available, Chanute offered to work for free. That sufficiently impressed the engineer, who put Chanute to work as a volunteer chainman on a surveying crew—the lowliest job available. Chanute performed so well that within two months he was on the payroll at $1.12 a day. After four years, the industrious young man became the division engineer in charge of terminals and maintenance of way at Albany; he was the man responsible for keeping the tracks and yards in shape.[6]

Octave's father had returned to France in 1850, and without any family in the New York area Chanute decided to follow the railroad action west. At that time the Midwest was the site of considerable railroad building as new lines fanned out across Illinois. He first moved to Joliet to help build sections of the Chicago & Alton Railroad, then to Peoria as chief engineer of the Peoria & Oquawka (later the Toledo, Peoria & Western), assigned to build that line 112 miles to the Indiana border.

New railroad construction was put on hold during the Civil War, and early in the conflict he was forced to visit his mother in Confederate-held New Orleans to settle her mother's estate, which was in jeopardy of being seized by the French government unless she claimed title to it before the statute of limitations expired. It was a relatively easy matter getting permission to pass through the Union lines below Cairo, Illinois, but once he was in the South Chanute was arrested several times and threatened with execution as a spy.[7]

He talked his way out of the situations, reached New Orleans, got his mother's power of attorney to save her estate, and began the long trip home. The confederate commander at Bowling Green, Kentucky, refused to give him a pass through the lines to return to the North. Chanute's daughter related the exchange as her father recalled it to her years later:

"Then he asked, 'General what would you do were you placed in my position?'

"The general answered, 'I would run the blockade Sir.' Father said, 'Then you advise me to do it?'

"'No sir, I forbid your doing it.'"[8]

Chanute promptly hopped a stagecoach with a group of "Jewish drummers" (salesmen) who were headed north, and when pickets stopped the vehicle to demand passports, Chanute waved in their faces the power of attorney written in French and covered with official seals. The ploy worked; he was back in Peoria ten days after leaving New Orleans.[9]

Chanute held a succession of railroad jobs following the war. He later helped to build the stock yards in both Chicago and Kansas City; the first bridge over the Missouri River; and sections of the Chicago, Burlington & Quincy and Union Pacific Railroads. It was during this time that Chanute honed engineering skills in bridge building—learning about stress analysis, truss design, the strength of materials, and the effects of winds on structures—that would come in handy later in designing airframes.

Engineering Studies

Chanute's professional reputation was so secure by 1873 that he was appointed chief engineer of the ailing Erie Railroad in New York, a line plagued with poor planning, bad management, and the depredations of assorted robber barons. Chanute's appointment followed Jay Gould's ousting from control of the railroad, and despite continued financial shenanigans by Gould's successors, Chanute somehow managed to get the Erie converted to standard gauge and its main line improved with double track.

During his ten-year tenure in New York, Chanute increasingly became involved in activities of the American Society of Civil Engineers. There he chaired one of the society's technical committees studying the feasibility of a mass transit system for New York City. Despite some opposition from New York's Tammany Hall political machine and assorted special interest groups, Chanute and his friend M. N. Forney put together a plan for elevated railway lines that became the basis for New York's rapid transit system.

The stress and public pressure from working on the railroad and the transit plan so exhausted Chanute that he took his family on a four-month vacation to Europe, delighting in pointing out to his own young children the sights in Paris he remembered from his boyhood. He also discovered that some of his professional colleagues there had become intrigued with the possibilities of flight. He returned to New York and resumed his post at the Erie for another eight years. Then in 1884 he retired from active railroading, moved back to Kansas City, and founded an engineering consulting firm and eventually a company specializing in wood preservation. The latter enterprise resulted from an American Society of Civil Engineers committee assignment of finding ways to prevent wood trestles and crossties from rotting prematurely. By immersing himself in this engineering problem in the same way he would later immerse himself in aviation, Chanute became an expert on wood preservation, and his expertise became widely known in the industry. In 1889 he moved to Chicago to better oversee his Chicago Tie Preserving Company. The business was lucrative enough that he

Some of Chanute's earliest glider tests in 1896 were with the Otto Lilienthal–designed monoplane. (National Air and Space Museum, Smithsonian Institution)

found he had enough time and money on his hands to indulge his long-standing interest in aviation.

Up to this point in his life, Chanute had not publicly exhibited any interest whatsoever in flying machines. In fact, it is not entirely certain when the problem of flight captured his imagination. Biographer Pearl I. Young and Chanute researcher Simine Short both concluded that he became interested in the topic and casually began accumulating reports and articles in his private collection sometime before 1860. Articles on aerial navigation in his personal scrapbooks date back as far as 1852. However, Crouch concluded after examining Chanute's correspondence and papers in the Library of Congress that Chanute's serious interest dated from his European trip of 1875.[10]

By the end of the following decade, Chanute had accumulated enough information on aerial navigation to be able to speak publicly with authority, although he did so only reluctantly for fear of ridicule. When he and a friend, Robert H. Thurston, head of Cornell University's Sibley College

of Mechanical Engineering, organized the program for the mechanical engineering section of the American Association for the Advancement of Science convention in Buffalo, New York, in 1886, they invited an amateur ornithologist to discuss birds in flight and to test the reaction of their colleagues to the subject of aeronautics. The talk turned out to be a disaster when the ornithologist, Israel Lancaster, who had spent much of his life on a farm in Illinois but had later moved to the South, was unable to demonstrate his flying models, or effigies as he called them. He was laughed off the stage. Chanute had confined his opening remarks to the opinion that flight was an interesting research topic, the solution to which was some years in the future.[11] About the only positive outcome of the event was that one attendee, Samuel Pierpont Langley, director of the Allegheny Observatory, left the meeting determined to investigate the feasibility of manned flight. Though Langley never attained success like that of the Wright brothers, his later experiments established him as one of the nation's aviation pioneers.

Chanute's assistants tested hang gliders in 1896 on the Lake Michigan dunes in Indiana. The biplane with cruciform tail proved to be the most successful model.

It was Chanute's old friend Forney, who had merged the *American Railroad Journal* and *Nostrand's Engineering Magazine* into the *Railroad and Engineering Journal* and was looking for fresh material for the new magazine, who in the wake of the Buffalo fiasco persuaded Chanute to undertake an intensive study of aviation and write a series of technical articles on the topic. While conducting his research, Chanute visited Paris during the 1889 Second International Conference on Aerial Navigation and presented a paper on the physical basis of aerodynamics. The paper was so well received that he decided later in the year to accept an invitation to the American Association for the Advancement of Science convention in Toronto, where he discussed the technical possibilities of manned flight. That paper also was enthusiastically received by his colleagues.[12]

A year later, when his friend Robert Thurston invited him to address the engineering students at Cornell, Chanute, though still conservative, was somewhat more optimistic about the future of heavier-than-air aviation. He began his remarks with a disclaimer: "Until quite recent years, the possible solution of the last transportation problem remaining for man to evolve—that of sailing safely through the air—has been considered so nearly impracticable that the mere study of the subject was considered as an indication of lunacy."

And he ended his speech on a positive note:

> If we are to judge the future by the past, such improvements are likely to be won by successive stages, each fresh inventor adding something to what has been accomplished before; but still, when once a partial success is attained, it is likely to attract so much attention that it is not impossible that improvements will follow each other so rapidly that some of the present generation will yet see men safely traveling through and on the air at speeds of 50 to 60 miles an hour.[13]

By then, Chanute also had concluded that to sustain flight a successful airplane would have fixed wings, or "aeroplanes," as opposed to birdlike flapping wings. For propulsion, it would have an "airscrew," or propeller, driven by a lightweight gasoline engine.[14]

Progress in Flying Machines

Forney dutifully serialized Chanute's talk in five issues (July–November 1890) of *The Railroad and Engineering Journal,* and the following year began publishing in the same magazine the twenty-seven-article serial that became Chanute's epic *Progress in Flying Machines*. In it, Chanute was even more optimistic about the potential success of flying machines; the *if* of flight had become a *when*. "The first apparatus to achieve a notable success will necessarily be somewhat crude and imperfect. It will probably need to be modified, reconstructed, and readventured [tested] many times before it is developed into a practical shape." Airplanes would eventually fly at 100 to 150 miles an hour, he then predicted, and their first practical application would be in war.[15]

The articles made Chanute the world's most recognized authority on the subject of aviation. The Columbian Exposition conference in 1893 and the publication of *Progress in Flying Machines* in book form expanded his prestige: he had been known to a relatively small but worldwide group of engineers, and now he had captured the attention of the general public. It was after this 1893 conference that it occurred to Chanute that he would have to conduct experiments of his own to test the theories that he and others had not yet proven.

He had been experimenting with model gliders and corresponding with Otto Lilienthal, a German who had been testing manned gliders and was the first person to demonstrate that a person could sail through the air by dangling from an airframe in a manner now common with hang gliders. Lilienthal used the method of shifting his body to maintain stability in flight, and Chanute was not certain that it was a practical method, especially when it came time to power the airframe. Chanute's conclusion was that powered and unpowered flying machines had to be self-stabilizing, or capable of maintaining equilibrium in flight, and that he would have to build and test gliders himself to find a better system of maintaining stability. That led to a series of experimental flights in Indiana before the end of the nineteenth century.[16]

Although he had been thinking about building a glider as early as 1892 and had corresponded with both Lilienthal in Germany and Louis Mouillard in Egypt, another glider experimenter, Chanute didn't begin work in earnest on his own machines until December 1895. That was when he and former Langley associate Augustus M. Herring, a bright but sometimes volatile young engineer with an interest in aviation, began building glider models as a prerequisite to creating full-scale machines.

One of their models, and the subsequent full-scale gliders based on it, was similar to Lilienthal's batlike, mono-winged machine, which Herring had already tested. Another was based on a ladder kite, so named because it looked something like a stepladder, with many wings piled one atop the other, which Chanute, in his quest for equilibrium, had found was stable in gusty winds. The multi-wing glider was designed by Chanute with four pairs of biplane wings set one behind the other along a central frame. The wings were mounted on pivots so they could swing forward or back when hit by a gust, stabilizing the aircraft in flight. Springs pulled the wings back into their normal positions after the gust had passed.[17] The airframe fuselage was pure Chanute—a bridge-style truss based on a design used on countless railroads. The truss design gave the frame great strength without commensurate weight.

The idea behind Chanute's preoccupation with the pivoting wings, and with a pivoting tail on a later machine, was that they would provide an automatic stabilizing mechanism for a pilot hanging from the glider and too preoccupied to pull levers or turn wheels to keep the machine on an even course in flight. Today pilots control their powered aircraft and maintain stability by means of such devices as hydraulically powered rudders, horizontal stabilizers on the tail, and ailerons on the wings. On a hang glider, the principal method of control is the pilot's shifting of the body, a technique that does not always allow the glider to regain stability quickly enough to save the pilot in gusty weather.

The 1896 Glider Tests

On June 22, 1896, Chanute, Herring, and William A. Avery, a carpenter who had been enlisted to build the gliders, secretly established their camp at a place called Miller Station that was along the dunes at the south end of Lake Michigan to avoid any public notice of what they were doing. Miller is now a park in Gary, Indiana, but in 1896, before Elbert Gary built his steel mill nearby, it was an isolated area used mainly by naturalists and hunters of waterfowl.

The group first tested the Lilienthal machine by running down the dunes into the face of a lake breeze, then leaping into the air. Herring and others made two hundred hang glides with it, one as long as 116 feet, before concluding that the 36-pound craft was too difficult to operate in the wind. By way of contrast, Orville Wright's first powered flight in 1903 was only 120 feet long.[18]

Chanute's attempt to keep his tests secret lasted barely twenty-four hours. A *Chicago Tribune* reporter, apparently tipped off by the Miller Station agent, showed up on June 23. A story headlined "Men Fly in Mid Air" appeared on page one the following day.[19]

The multi-wing glider, which Chanute called *Katydid,* did not perform as well as he had hoped. The wings of the purely ex-

perimental machine were numbered and could be shifted around to test different configurations. The original wing arrangement (four sets in front and two in the rear) proved to be inefficient, so the configuration was changed several times. After a few tests, the crew reduced the number of wings from twelve to eight on June 25 and shifted them to different configurations thereafter. Ultimately about two hundred glides were made, the longest being 82 feet.[20]

On July 4, Chanute and his staff returned to Chicago to digest what they had learned and to prepare for a second round of tests. Chanute wrote that he was convinced that "more had been learned during the two weeks of experiment with full-sized

models than had been previously acquired during about seven years of theoretical study and experiments with models."[21]

Back in the workshop in Chicago, Chanute and Herring once again reconfigured the *Katydid,* this time by stacking the wings vertically. They also built an entirely new glider, a triplane later modified to a biplane configuration, that was to prove the most influential machine they would test. Unlike the wings of the *Katydid,* the wings of the new machine were held rigidly in place by a truss; the tail was designed to give slightly in order to keep the aircraft stable when it was hit with gusts of wind. Herring achieved this flexibility by means of a universal joint.

Credit for the design of the "two-surface

The most bizarre of the gliders, and the least successful, was designed by William Paul Butusov and tested by the Chanute group in 1896. It was so cumbersome it had to be launched from a trestle. Butusov nicknamed it "Albatross" although it more resembled a bat. (National Air and Space Museum, Smithsonian Institution) machine," as it became known from Chanute's diary entries, was the subject of a later dispute between the two men. Even though Chanute gave Herring full credit for the design of the tail, Herring claimed that the machine was an outgrowth of a kite he had tested on the dunes in June 1896 and that Chanute's only contribution was the decision to incorporate superimposed biplane wings.[22]

Despite learning of the August 9, 1896, death of Lilienthal in a gliding accident in Germany, Chanute decided to proceed with a second round of tests in Indiana later that month. To avoid publicity, Chanute and his assistants, which by then included glider buff William Paul Butusov, chartered a boat to carry their four gliders to a new, more remote site on the dunes on August 21, 1896. They picked a place called Dunes Park about five miles east of Miller Station. The ploy failed: the new tests were on the front page of a Chicago newspaper by August 27, and on September 8 Chanute noted in his diary that a reporter from one newspaper was complaining about being scooped by a reporter from another publication.[23]

The reporters were principally interested in a glider designed by Butusov that looked like a cross between a Beluga whale and a giant bat. Appropriately named *Albatross*, the machine was so cumbersome that it had to be launched from a trestle built on the site. It was heavily damaged in an unmanned flight in late September, by which time Chanute and Herring had concluded it would never fly.[24]

A storm delayed flying for several days in August, but once the weather improved, the performance of the new Chanute-Herring machine quickly eclipsed everything else. Herring and Avery flew the glider as a triplane on August 29 but found it unstable. They removed the lower set of wings and flew it as a biplane on August 31. In the face of a fifteen-mile-an-hour northerly wind, Herring was able to make one hop of 97 feet. Within a few days Avery and Herring were flying for 253 and

239 feet while they dangled beneath the glider, and on September 11 Herring made a fourteen-second glide of 359 feet in the teeth of a twenty-two-mile-an-hour wind. The longest flight of the rebuilt multi-wing Chanute machine was Avery's 188 feet, also on September 11.[25] Because of deteriorating weather—some early autumnal gales on Lake Michigan—the group decided to break camp on September 26 and return to Chicago to digest what they had learned.

Herring's refusal to help with the Butusov machine so he could spend his time flying the Chanute-Herring glider had created ill will among the others, and on September 14 Chanute had accepted his resignation. The two men maintained an on-again-off-again relationship for years. Herring invited Chanute back to the Indiana dunes in September 1897 to watch him test another copy of the Chanute-Herring biplane glider. On September 5, Herring made a 600-foot flight in the machine, thoroughly impressing Chanute. The positive impression didn't last for long. Herring took a job in St. Joseph, Michigan, and attempted with intermittent success to find other sponsors to finance his dream of building a powered aircraft, and on October 10 and 22, 1898, he made hops of 50 and 73 feet in a biplane glider powered by compressed air that operated two propellers. Unfortunately, the weather calmed and he was unable to duplicate his first flight after summoning Chanute from Chicago to be his expert witness. Chanute left convinced that Herring was a failure.

With the experiments completed and conclusions in hand, Chanute then prepared to share his findings with the world, first in a paper read to the Western Society of Engineers, which was later published in the organization's journal. He had no illusions that his experiments alone would lead to flight, but continued to hold the belief that it would be an evolutionary process to which many men would contribute and in which his role would be one of "advancing the question a little."[26]

Association with the Wright Brothers

That article and Chanute's 1894 book may have advanced the question even more than he realized at the time. In May 1900 he received a letter from Wilbur Wright, a bicycle shop owner in Dayton, Ohio, who explained that he and his brother, Orville, were experimenting with gliders and had read *Progress in Flying Machines*. Wright told Chanute that he planned to experiment further with a glider that used a system of wing warping for control and asked where the winds would be favorable for such tests. Chanute, always trying to encourage young experimenters, wrote back that San Diego, California, or Pine Island, Florida, would be preferable but that any number of locations along the Atlantic Coast would suffice.[27]

The brothers then wrote the U.S. Weather Bureau to determine where the average winds were the strongest in August and September, two of the few months each year they could spare from their bicycle business. Bureau officials sent back a summary of 120 sites for August and September 1899, which indicated that Chicago had the strongest average velocities at 16.2 miles an hour, but on the basis of Chanute's experience with the press in 1896, Wilbur had already decided against any site near an urban area. He chose Kitty Hawk, North Carolina, which had an average velocity of 13.4 miles an hour. Relatively strong winds, of course, were necessary for gliders to stay aloft.

On August 10, Wilbur wrote Chanute again, this time for advice about where to obtain long pieces of spruce to build the glider's wings. Those two exchanges began a long correspondence between the men that over the next eleven years amounted to 435 letters as well as various meetings. Although the relationship became strained at times, the Wrights considered Chanute one of their few friends and confidants.

When the Wrights returned to Dayton from Kitty Hawk in October 1900 after con-

ducting their initial glider experiments, they quickly wrote Chanute with the details. He was intrigued, especially with the flights in which the pilot rode in a prone position to reduce drag instead of dangling from the glider as had been the practice to that day. Chanute wanted to mention their experiments in a magazine article he was preparing for *Cassier's Magazine*, but the brothers were reluctant for him to divulge any details about their glider. Ultimately, Chanute sent them a portion of the manuscript containing a one-paragraph summary that mentioned the use of a prone pilot; the article published seven months later was the first public mention of the Wright brothers' experiments.[28]

Chanute visited the brothers in Dayton on June 26–27, 1901, and they invited him to their planned glider experiments in Kitty Hawk later that summer. He showed up on August 5 to learn that the Wrights were disappointed that the tests with a new machine were not going as well as tests had gone the previous year with a machine they had abandoned on the beach. They returned to Dayton later that month, contemplating whether to abandon their quest to fly, but Chanute intervened and asked Wilbur to address the prestigious Western Society of Engineers in Chicago.

The speech to an enthusiastic gathering of seventy members of the society and a long chat with Chanute afterward in his Chicago home revived Wilbur's spirits. Chanute was convinced that despite the problems in 1901, the Wrights had already progressed beyond anything else that had been done. In the spring of 1902, Chanute spread their name far and wide with magazine articles published as far away as Europe. The publicity irked the secretive Wrights.[29]

Thus began a period of strained relations between the three men that would last until Chanute's death. The situation was aggravated on October 4, 1902, when Chanute showed up at the brothers' camp in Kitty Hawk with Herring and a copy of their 1896 glider in tow. Chanute left the

One of Chanute's most unusual looking test gliders was the multiplane machine later dubbed the *Katydid*. It employed as many as twelve wings, which could be stacked, as shown in this Museum of Science and Industry model, or attached tandem-style the length of the aircraft. (Simine Short)

camp on October 15 and went to Washington, where he convinced Langley he should see what the Wrights were doing. However, the Wrights refused to extend an invitation to their potential rival, citing the lateness of the season.

Disenchantment with the Wright Brothers' Secrecy

It was Chanute's April 3, 1903, speech to the Aero-Club de France, a group of balloonists in Paris, that was to cause the greatest friction. Although Chanute did not reveal the details of their wing-warping technique for maintaining stability in flight or any other technical details of the machine, the speech had an enormous impact on the French, who realized that for the first time they had fallen behind in the quest to fly. The idea that some American amateurs were about to conquer the skies with a heavier-than-air machine offended Gallic sensibilities; after all, they had led

the world in aeronautical technology since the Montgolfiers.[30]

The Wrights in turn were offended by the insinuation that they were Chanute's pupils, that he had subsidized them and that in 1900 he had provided them with the details of wing warping developed by Mouillard in Egypt. The warped wing was a precursor of the aileron. To his death Chanute apparently believed wing warping predated the Wrights and that their contribution was to successfully refine it.

In his speech, Chanute had referred to the Wrights by using the phrase "dedicated collaborators," which was widely interpreted in French aeronautical circles as meaning he considered the brothers to be his disciples. Whether the comment was intentional, innocent, or misinterpreted, it caused the secretive Wrights to become increasingly disenchanted with Chanute, although not to the point that they were willing to sever relations. The situation did not improve any when the brothers learned that a French publication, *L'Aerophile,* had printed a picture of the Wrights' 1901 glider, misidentifying it as a "Chanute machine."[31]

Despite the deterioration of their relationship, the Wrights invited Chanute back to Kitty Hawk in late 1903 to watch their attempts to fly with a powered machine. Chanute arrived on November 6 but found the weather so cold and windy that he left a week later—a full month before the Wrights finally flew their airplane. Chanute, then 71, was at his Chicago home at 1138 North Dearborn Street on Thursday, December 17, when he received the historic news by telegraph from Katharine Wright, the fliers' sister:

"The boys have done it."

Once they succeeded, the Wrights became preoccupied with obtaining their patents and protecting the commercial value of their invention. Chanute, as always, viewed the invention of the airplane as an evolutionary process in which the Wrights took the final step. In a paper read before the mechanical engineering section of the American Association for the Advancement of Science meeting in St. Louis two weeks after the Wrights' first flight, Chanute was already speculating in a professorial manner about the future of the airplane:

Flying machines promise better results as to speed, but yet will be of limited commercial application. They may carry mail and reach inaccessible places, but they can't compete with the railroads as carriers of passengers or freight. They will not fill the heavens with commerce, abolish customs houses, or revolutionize the world, for they will be too expensive for the loads which they carry, and subject to too many wind contingencies. Success, however, is probable.[32]

Although he visited the Wrights in Dayton in early 1904 and continued to correspond with them, alerting them in September 1907 that onetime balloonist Albert Santos-Dumont had made a 726-foot flight in the airplane *14-bis* in Paris, Chanute didn't see an airplane fly until September 1908, when he attended a public exhibition by Orville Wright at Fort Myer, Virginia. He was present on September 17 when Orville crashed, injuring himself and killing his passenger, Army Lieutenant Thomas E. Selfridge, the first fatality in an airplane crash in the United States. Chanute, who stayed to help and advise Katharine Wright during her brother's convalescence, correctly surmised that the crash had resulted from a broken propeller.

Chanute, shown seated at left, encouraged the Wright brothers and visited them at their camp in Kitty Hawk but was not present on December 17, 1903, when they made their first successful powered flights.

Octave Chanute two years
before his death in 1910.
(Octave Chanute Aerospace
Museum)

Chanute and the brothers continued to bicker by letter until early 1910, when Wilbur suggested they bury the hatchet. "We prize too highly the friendship which meant so much to us in the years of our early struggles to see it worn away by uncorrected misunderstandings," Wilbur wrote Chanute on April 29, 1910. The old man replied a few days later that he had been ill and would write after returning from a trip to Europe.[33]

Chanute, by then a widower, was already contemplating the end and was planning to visit a spa in Europe to help him recover his health. The previous year he had given away his models and the lantern slides he used to illustrate his lectures and had divided his estate among his four surviving children. Shortly after replying to Wilbur's letter, he left with his three daughters for Europe. There his conditioned worsened, and he was hospitalized in Paris. He finally returned to Chicago with a nurse attending him on the trip. He died in his home on November 23, 1910.[34]

The family telegraphed the Wrights, and Wilbur caught the night train for Chicago. His written tribute appeared a few months later:

If he had not lived, the entire history of progress in flying would have been other than it has been, for he not only encouraged the Wright brothers to persevere in their experiments, but it was due to his missionary trip to France in 1903, that the Voisins, Bleriot, Farman, De Lagrange, and Archdeacon were led to take the revival of aviation studies in that country, after the failure of Ader and the French government in 1897 had left everyone in despair. . . .

His private correspondence with experimenters in all parts of the world was of great volume. No one was too humble to receive his share of time. In patience and goodness of heart he has rarely been surpassed.[35]

Chanute lived long enough to see the airplane come to Chicago, in 1909, but not the great flying spectacles that were to dominate aviation until World War I. The war provided the airplane a grisly utility, creating an instant market for both aircraft and people to fly them. In the years between Chanute's final illness and the war, Chicago became a center for aviation exhibitions and a place where young aviators could learn how to fly.

3
The Flying Machine Comes to Chicago

• Like the automobile a decade earlier, the flying machine arrived in Chicago abruptly. The Columbian Exposition of 1893 displayed three hundred horse-drawn carriages and only two automobiles. By the turn of the century, only seven years later, there were enough cars on Chicago's streets that the city was compelled to regulate them, and by 1908 there were 5,475 horseless carriages registered. The city's first public demonstration of an airplane didn't occur until 1909, but two years later Chicago both staged an air show that drew international attention and huge crowds and opened its first permanent airport.

The sputtering flying machines delighted crowds, as balloon ascensions had done earlier. The crowd at Chicago's 1908

balloon race was estimated as high as 150,000. Two years later a flying exhibition in suburban Cicero drew 25,000 persons. Later that year a crowd of 200,000 turned out in Chicago's Grant Park to watch the first confirmed heavier-than-air flight over the city, the previous ones having all been in the suburbs.[1]

As a practical matter, flying exhibitions were the only way for both aviators and the builders of the machines they flew to make money in the first decade of the airplane's existence. The armies of several nations had expressed an interest in airplanes as a machine for military reconnaissance, which is why the Wrights demonstrated their machine in Fort Myer, Virginia, in 1908, but that market would not develop

Although Europeans were building high-speed monoplanes shortly after 1910, the open pusher biplane remained popular at U.S. air shows. Lincoln Beachey's aircraft being pushed along the track at the Illinois State Fairgrounds in Springfield was an evolutionary successor to the craft the Wrights had flown at Kitty Hawk eleven years earlier. (Illinois State Historical Library)

Flying contraptions came in a variety of shapes and forms in the early days of aviation, like this experimental powered tetrahedral kite from Alexander Graham Bell's Aerial Experiment Association. The bank of more than two thousand cells was intended to give the aircraft lift. The engine was mounted in the rear to push the aircraft. (Christopher Lynch Collection)

until the war clouds gathered in Europe prior to World War I.

Chanute and the Wrights had debated the possibility of flying exhibitions as a source of income soon after the brothers first flew in 1903. During his January 22, 1904, visit to Dayton, the old man suggested the brothers enter their airplane in an aeronautical meet at the St. Louis Exposition, a world's fair scheduled for later in the year, but they demurred. About $200,000 in prizes were being offered, and Chanute spent $1,400 to have Avery rebuild one of his biplane gliders to enter. Ultimately, Avery made forty-six flights in the glider in St. Louis between September 23 and October 26, 1904.[2] As late as 1910 Chanute was still chiding the brothers, who by that time were actively entering competitions, for their failure to do so earlier: "I told you . . . that you were making a mistake by abstaining from prize-winning contests while the public curiosity was so keen, and by bringing patent suits to prevent others from doing so."[3]

As soon as the news of the Wrights' airplane spread, newspaper publishers across the country began offering large prizes to aviators to perform feats. William Randolph Hearst offered $50,000 for a coast-to-coast flight, and James Gordon Bennett established the international air races named after him. In Chicago, J. C. Shaffer, publisher of the *Chicago Evening Post,* offered $1,000 to anyone who could fly between Chicago and New York; and H. H. Kohlsaat, publisher of the *Chicago Record Herald,* offered a $10,000 prize for a somewhat less ambitious flight between Chicago and Springfield, Illinois. Shaffer then raised his offer to $25,000. It was Kohlsaat who in 1895, as publisher of what was then called the *Chicago Times-Herald,* had introduced the spectacle of the horseless carriage to the American public by sponsoring an auto race between Chicago and Evanston with $3,500 in prizes.[4]

Soon after Chanute spread the word of the Wrights' first flight, adventuresome young men around the world scrambled to emulate them, a phenomenon that similarly had occurred in Chicago after the 1895 *Times-Herald* automobile race. Within five years of that event, twenty-two com-

panies had popped up in Chicago to manufacture autos, and a dozen actually got
their vehicles into production. However,
building an airplane that could be safely
flown was a considerably more complicated undertaking than mounting a gasoline engine on the rear of a buggy and at-
taching it with a bicycle chain to the axle.
That didn't stop tinkerers from trying. Despite the continuing presence in Chicago
of Chanute and a couple of his disciples,
people who could dispense sound technical advice, early aviation seemed to attract
young men who could best be described as
daredevils—balloonists, race drivers, and
motorcyclists. It also seemed to attract a
fair number of devotees with limited technical backgrounds and only a faint idea of
the laws of flight.[5]

Early Airplane Builders

Events in Chicago were no exception to
what was happening elsewhere. In the six
years after the Wrights' first flight in Kitty
Hawk, the motley handful of tinkerers in
Chicago who tried to emulate their accomplishments met with very limited success.
Only one of the twelve inventors who obtained patents on aeronautical devices between 1900 and 1910 is believed to have
produced an airplane capable of even a
modest flight.

Typical of the aeronautical inventors of
that day was James F. Scott, a scenic artist
by trade who was low bidder on a government contract to develop an airplane. Although he knew nothing about the technology of aviation, his bid had appeared
among those of such qualified applicants
as the Wright brothers and Herring when
the U.S. Army received proposals in early
1908 to build an airplane and deliver it
within 185 days to Fort Myer for testing.
Scott submitted a bid of $1,000 for a
multi-wing aircraft, but soon realized he
could not build it for anywhere near that
price. Nor could he raise any more than
the 10 percent deposit the army required
with each bid, in Scott's case $100.[6]

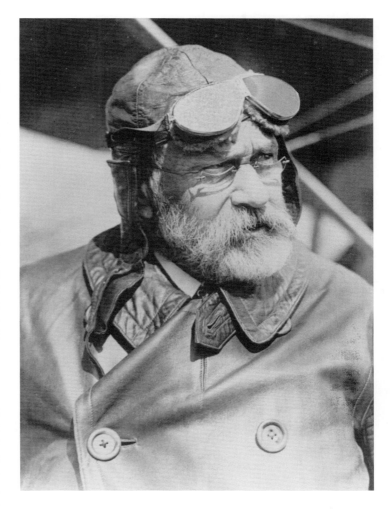

In light of the U.S. Patent Office's original reluctance to grant protection to
Chanute's glider and to the Wrights' wing-
warping technique, some of the devices
they approved a few years later were laugh-
able. Frank M. Mahan, president of the
Lindgren-Mahan Fire Apparatus works in
Chicago, was granted a patent on July 23,
1907, for a combination airplane-dirigible.
There is no record it was ever built. Brothers George and Robert Anderson, coal deal-
ers in Chicago, supposedly built an am-
phibious aircraft, and Robert A. Moore
designed and built for the U.S. Army's
competition in 1908 an aircraft with three
propellers powered by a single engine (the
original Wright machine had two props operating off a single engine) and wings filled
with gas chambers to keep it afloat in the
event of an aquatic landing.[7]

Charles (Pop) Dickinson was
a wealthy Chicago seed
company owner who be-
came intrigued with the new
technology of internal combustion engines and eventually invested in both automobiles and airplanes. An
acquaintance of Octave
Chanute, he became active
in and eventually directed
the Aero Club of Illinois.

Pilot Art (Smash Up) Smith, who frequented Cicero Field, poses for the camera as his crew readies his Mills biplane for the starting of the engine. Planes of the time lacked brakes, so crews often had to hold the plane to keep it from moving until the engine developed sufficient power for flight. (Illinois State Historical Library)

Balloonist Horace B. Wild attempted to repeat Albert Santos-Dumont's success in France in making the transition from dirigibles to heavier-than-air machines, but he proved to be more adept with hot air. He claimed as early as 1907 to have made flights in an aeroplane using six-thousand-revolution-per-minute gyroscopes, a dubious claim considering the state of the art of aviation at the time. The next year he was supposedly building an airplane, and by 1910 he owned a plane and was planning to fly it in shows, but it was damaged in an accident before it could be publicly exhibited.[8]

Perhaps the most successful of Chicago's aerial tinkerers in the first decade of flight was Carl S. Bates. He had begun dabbling in aviation at age fourteen on a farm near Cedar Lake, Iowa, where he

made a man-carrying kite and built and flew a Chanute-style glider in 1898. He came to Chicago in 1903 to study at the Armour Institute of Technology, and under Chanute's guidance he tried to build a powered multi-wing plane in his own shop, but it was unsuccessful. For a while he settled on developing and building gasoline engines, but in 1908 he built a smaller copy of a Glenn Curtiss airplane with a front horizontal and rear vertical rudder and ailerons near the wingtips, and powered by a ten-horsepower, air-cooled engine. Because he lacked money for a magneto, he wired a battery to the engine.

Bates tried the aircraft on some short hops in late 1908, but the battery proved insufficient to keep the engines running. Chanute heard of his plight and bought him a magneto, which Bates then tested in some unsubstantiated flights, one of which he claimed was 460 yards (1,380 feet), long, near Daytona Beach, Florida. By April 1909 he was back in Chicago building airplanes with a small group of investors who included James Scott and race driver Ray Harroun, an eventual winner of the Indianapolis 500 auto race.[9]

When airplanes finally arrived in Chicago beginning in 1909, they were from elsewhere. The first documented flight in the area was on October 16, 1909, when Glenn Curtiss flew a biplane for a quarter of a mile over the infield at Hawthorne Race Track in west-suburban Cicero. Curtiss had won the Gordon Bennett Cup the previous year in France, and the Cicero flight was part of a national tour to demonstrate his airplane. High winds had prevented him from flying on October 15, and the winds continued the next day, but he decided to try a flight in late afternoon to avoid disappointing the large crowd that had gathered. The flight lasted only forty seconds and attained an altitude of only sixty feet, but it launched Chicago into the air age.[10]

On July 5 of the following year, Eugene Ely and J. C. (Bud) Mars, two members of the Curtiss flying exhibition team, put on a brief flying exhibition before a crowd of 25,000 at Hawthorne following regularly scheduled motorcycle races. A strong northeast wind prevented them from attempting anything more complex than brief straightaway flights over the infield.[11]

The Early Exhibitions

Two months after the exhibition by Ely and Mars, Walter P. Brookins, a twenty-one-year-old aviation buff the Wrights had hired and trained as a pilot in 1910 when they finally decided to take Chanute's advice and get into the aerial exhibition business, made the first confirmed flight over Chicago itself. Brookins, who had come to Chicago to try to claim Kohlsaat's $10,000 prize for flying from there to Springfield, decided to present a free exhibition on Sep-

tember 27, 1910. A crowd estimated at 200,000 jammed into Grant Park as he made several flights in a Wright pusher as a tune-up for the Springfield trip. In the terminology of the time, a pusher was an airplane with the propeller mounted behind the pilot to push the aircraft; a tractor plane was one with the propeller in front.[12]

The following day Brookins took *Chicago Record Herald* reporter Grover F. Sexton on a seven-minute flight over Grant Park. Sexton was the city's first recorded airplane passenger. He described his flight as "a very pleasant experience, like riding in an automobile on a perfectly smooth road. . . . The earth just seemed to drop out from under us."[13]

The Springfield flight occurred September 29 and was Chicago's first of several aviation spectacles that captured the attention of the city's press and public until World War I put a temporary end to exhibition flying. The event was considered so important that Wilbur Wright himself came up from Dayton to watch and to inspect the airplane before it took off. Chanute was ill at the time in a Paris hospital. The program called for an Illinois Central Railroad train carrying newsmen and dignitaries to meet the plane in Springfield. Brookins would fly above the railroad, a common navigational practice in the years before aerial navigation aids were developed. Despite thirty-minute-long fuel stops in downstate Gilman and Mount Pulaski, Brookins made the flight in five hours and forty-nine minutes, ten minutes less than the train.[14]

Brookins's takeoff from Chicago had been witnessed by many aviators from around the nation, who had arrived in town to participate in the *Chicago Evening Post*'s Chicago–New York race scheduled to begin October 1. The group included Ely; Curtiss; Augustus Post, secretary of the Aero Club of America; and Blanche Scott, of Rochester, New York, one of the earliest women fliers.

The New York race was doomed from the start. Originally the rules had called for aircraft to fly in both directions, with the first one completing the trip in either direction winning the $25,000 purse put up jointly by the *Chicago Evening Post* and the *New York Times*. However, Curtiss and the Wrights pointed out that pilots starting from New York would have to buck headwinds but those leaving from Chicago would have the advantage of tail winds. As a result, Chicago was designated as the sole starting point. There were other restrictions that required pilots and machines to be prequalified, to conduct test flights of at least an hour's duration in the week prior to the race, and to make the 800-mile trip within 168 hours, including ground time for refueling, repairs, and sleep.

The promoters had hoped to attract scores of fliers from around the globe, but the difficulty of such a long race in primitive planes with their balky engines, not to mention the relative inexperience of pilots who for the most part had flown only in local exhibitions, caused many aviators, including all of the amateurs from the Chicago area, to drop out before the race began. Those pilots who stayed treated Chicagoans to a series of spectacular exhibitions at Hawthorne and argued in their hotel rooms at night over the final regulations. The three surviving pilots—Ely, J. A. D. McCurdy, and Charles F. Willard—were concerned that they were risking their lives and machines on a winner-take-all race. The promoters then decided that only one plane would make the trip, and the pilots drew lots to determine which one.[15]

The plan was to have the plane fly to the fairgrounds at LaPorte, Indiana, where a large crowd awaited it. The course was marked with large white cloths painted with black arrows, and the roofs of several cars of a special train following his route were painted white for easy identification. From LaPorte the plane was to continue to a golf course in South Bend, Indiana.

Ely won the lottery. Decked out in a fancy, yellow French flying suit, he took off from Hawthorne at 4:30 P.M. on October 9 while McCurdy and Willard circled the field in their planes in a salute. He made only nine miles in ten minutes before a clogged fuel line forced him down at 85th Street and Honore Avenue. He then damaged his front landing-gear wheel while trying to take off, forcing his sponsor, Curtiss, to race to the scene in a car with a replacement. By the time the repairs were complete, it was too dark to fly.

Ely finally got off the ground the next day, but the hop ended in a ditch three blocks away. He was able to get airborne again after more repairs, but that flight lasted only thirty minutes before engine trouble forced him to make an emergency landing in a slough near East Chicago, Indiana. In two days he had flown only about twenty miles. Curtiss's crews worked through the night to make the necessary repairs, but the plane was only able to proceed another nineteen miles eastward before the engine quit and Ely was forced to crash land. At that point he gave up, abandoning the airplane to Curtiss's crews and boarding a train to Cleveland.[16]

The Problem with the Wrights

Several weeks after the failed race, wealthy Chicago industrialists Harold F. McCormick and Charles Dickinson decided to visit New York to watch the Belmont Air Show, the nation's first aviation extravaganza. They were sufficiently impressed with what they saw that McCormick began a few months later to privately discuss with other local aviation enthusiasts the idea of staging in Chicago a show more spectacular than what he had seen in New York. Undaunted by the earlier *Chicago Evening Post* fiasco, they planned the event for the following year.

At the March 6, 1911, meeting of the board of directors of the Aero Club of Illinois at the Chicago Athletic Association, McCormick proposed that the club organize and sponsor such an air show later the same year. The suggestion prevailed, then the directors adjourned to Grant Park to determine whether it would be a suit-

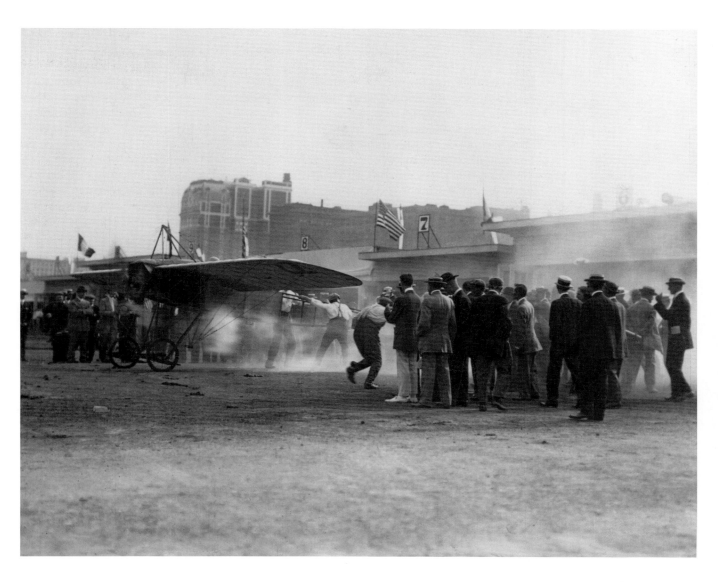

able site. The huge, 319-acre park, built on filled land between downtown Chicago and Lake Michigan, was large enough to accommodate a big crowd and a temporary airport. Much of the actual flying could take place over the lake.[17]

The organizers had enough clout to secure the use of Grant Park for such an event. Their principal problem was raising enough money to finance the prizes that would be necessary to attract well-known aviators from throughout the world. McCormick and James E. Plew invited almost every prominent businessperson in Chicago to a fundraising dinner on April 6 at the Blackstone Hotel to hear famed balloonist Augustus Post speak and show

lantern slides of the 1910 Belmont show. McCormick made his pitch for donations at the dinner.[18]

The results of the solicitation were disappointing, and a few weeks later McCormick began sending hundreds of solicitation letters to businesspeople and prominent Chicagoans who had not attended the Blackstone dinner. McCormick, who had been interested in aviation since watching Santos-Dumont perform in a balloon in 1901 in Paris, then became the show's principal financial backer, advancing the Aero Club $45,000 in cash and putting up a personal bond for $80,000 in prize money.[19]

The other major problem McCormick

The 1911 International Air Show at Grant Park sponsored by the Aero Club of Illinois attracted huge crowds. The public was still intrigued by the newfangled flying machines, like this monoplane warming up. (David R. Phillips Collection) faced in 1911 was the Wright brothers' unwillingness to participate. Their difficulty in obtaining a patent from 1903 to 1908 was a factor that contributed to their reluctance to publicly display and share information about their machines, and that reluctance was the source of much of the friction between them and Chanute. Once the famous patent—number 821,393—was granted, the Wrights then had to go to court to enforce it against other aviators, including Glenn Curtiss, who had developed their own airplanes during the Wrights' 1903–1908 period of silence. Once the court ruled, it gave the patent a broad interpretation, holding that it covered not only the brothers' wing-warping mechanism, but ailerons as well.[20]

On January 10, 1910, the Wrights had gotten a favorable ruling from Judge John R. Hazel of the Federal District Court in Buffalo against Curtiss and the Herring-Curtiss Company, but the decision was held in abeyance pending an appeal. The Wrights had claimed in their complaint that Curtiss's *June Bug,* although it was equipped with ailerons instead of using wing warping, was an infringement on their patent. In effect, they wanted all airplanes, regardless of the type of control surfaces they used, covered by the patent. The final decision on the issue by the U.S. Court of Appeals wasn't handed down until January 13, 1914.[21]

The possibility that the Aero Club would be forced to pay the Wrights a license fee to hold their air show so concerned the organization that it sent a delegation to Dayton on April 14, 1911, to discuss the financial arrangements. The delegation, consisting of McCormick and John T. McCutcheon, *Chicago Tribune* cartoonist and early aviation promoter, found that the Wrights were adamant: they wanted $10,000 to license the meet and financial guarantees for every Wright pilot who appeared in it. They did give the two Chicagoans free plane rides during the visit.[22]

Orville Wright's comments, as reported by McCormick, were blunt:

He very openly stated there were three things he wanted: First, to prevent foreign aviators from coming to America. Second, to get as much money out of the meet as possible. Third, to support his patents. He stated that our meet was a detriment to them rather than a gain. He stated he did not care whether aviation in America was helped or not. He stated he would now sue every aviator they could afford to and their only reason for not doing so was that it cost too much money.[23]

To shield themselves personally from the possibility of a lawsuit by the Wrights, the members of the Aero Club formed the International Aviation Meet Association (IAMA), a nonprofit organization that would be legally responsible for the event. James E. Plew, the White Motor Car dealer in Chicago who in 1909 opened a dealership to sell Curtiss airplanes and who succeeded Chanute as president of the Aero Club, became the president of the IAMA as well. McCormick served on the new organization's executive committee, and Dickinson was a general committee member. McCormick promptly proposed that to protect itself in case the Wrights used their patent to drive away other aviators and monopolize the meet, the IAMA should require that a certain number of aviators be entered before any of the $80,000 in prize money could be awarded.[24]

The greatest concern was getting foreign aviators to participate on the Wrights' home turf. Such internationally known fliers as Earle Ovington, Thomas Baldwin, and T. O. M. Sopwith had expressed interest in participating in the Chicago meet but were concerned about finances. Ovington wanted a $6,000 guarantee, and Sopwith was willing to come for a $5,000 guarantee plus the option of giving rides at $100 per flight. Campbell Wood, secretary of the Aero Club of America, opined that foreign aviators would cost $2,000 to $8,000 apiece, an average bond of $4,500 per aircraft, and some sort of indemnity by IAMA against legal action by the Wrights.[25]

The brothers promptly fired off a letter to IAMA warning that any patent infringements would be dealt with in court, "as the parties exhibiting machines and holding meets where infringing machines are exhibited become themselves infringers."[26] But sentiment was beginning to turn against the Wrights, and meet officials in Chicago were considering ignoring their threats. Bernard Mullaney, general manager of the proposed meet, described the Wrights' position as a "dog in the manger policy which should not be encouraged" and urged other aviation organizations in the United States to band together and come up with some sort of cooperative defense. By the summer of 1911 the dispute between Chicago and the Wrights had attracted national attention, and the brothers were publicly criticized by aviation organizations in several states. Finally, on July 28, the Aero Club of America sanctioned the event, by then less than a month in the future.[27]

Under McCormick's influence, the Aero Club of Illinois decided to resist the Wrights' demands, although they were aware that the refusal to pay the licensing fees was a gamble. They desperately needed the Wrights' planes and pilots to make the meet a success and correctly guessed the prizes were so attractive that the Wrights could not boycott the event even if they didn't go to court to stop it. The Aero Club also correctly surmised that the Wrights would have a better chance in court suing the pilots and aircraft companies instead of the nonprofit IAMA. Most of the fliers in the meet ultimately bowed to the $100-a-day licensing fee to take a chance on winning part of the IAMA's big prize purse. The Wrights finally filed a patent infringement suit against IAMA on August 7, 1911—five days before the meet began—but never pursued the case although the organization had set aside $10,000 in a special escrow account to cover any damages assessed by the courts.[28]

Speed races in the early days of flying were often held on closed oval courses over which the pilots made a number of laps around pylons, in the style of auto races. The date and location of this race is uncertain, but the photograph was probably taken in 1912 at Clearing or Cicero Field. (David R. Phillips Collection)

Although there had been an aviation fatality earlier in suburban Cicero, one of Chicago's first occurred on August 15, 1911, when St. Croix Johnstone crashed in the lake off Grant Park in front of a huge crowd at an air show. Efforts by members of the Life Saving Service to rescue him from the wreckage were unsuccessful. (Joshua Koppel Collection)

LIFE SAVERS IN A VAIN EFFORT TO RECOVER ST CROIX JOHNSTONE'S BODY AUG. 15, 1911.

$80,000 in Prizes Lures Fliers

The Aero Club and IAMA took a hard line on the guarantees being demanded by the more famous aviators. The organizations decided there would be no guarantees other than a $250-per-aviator stipend to cover expenses. They believed that the $80,000 purse would lure the world's best fliers. The decision proved correct: even the Wrights sent a team.

Meanwhile, IAMA continued to arrange the logistics of the ambitious exhibition. Seats were built for 63,000 spectators, and the runway and 1.33-mile race course was designed and prepared by James S. Stephens, an Aero Club member. The club had to procure a large amount of castor oil to lubricate the airplane engines, and ominously, in view of what would transpire in Europe within a few years, they marked out the shape of a battleship hull on the ground that aviators could bomb with bags filled with flour. Hangars were built in the park, and Pinkerton agents were hired to guard the planes. The federal government cooperated by transferring the cutter *Tuscarora,* normally stationed in Milwau-

kee, to Chicago for water rescues. It also sent a detachment of troops from north-suburban Fort Sheridan for crowd control; an artillery unit from Fort Riley, Kansas, to man signal guns; and a Signal Corps unit to provide wireless service.

The city's newspapers promoted the event heavily, and IAMA spent more than $19,000 on advertising and publicity. The *Chicago Tribune* carried a special supplement on August 8 explaining what was about to take place, detailing the status of aviation to that day, and even speculating on the possibility of space travel. William B. Stout, an aviation buff who would go on to greater fame by overseeing the design of the Ford Tri-Motor and the futuristic M10,000 streamliner train, covered the meet for the *Tribune.*[29]

Many businesses in the city conducted promotions. Hotels along Michigan Avenue overlooking the park advertised the view from their rooms and quickly sold out for the week; Marshall Field & Company, the department store, printed daily programs and displayed two airplanes the week of the meet. The location of the meet undoubtedly contributed to its success: Grant Park is adjacent to Chicago's central business district and easily accessible by the city's elevated transit system, commuter railroads, and intercity passenger trains. Never before had an aviation meet of such magnitude been held in the downtown area of one of the world's major cities.

Grandstand and general admission tickets on sale in the Auditorium Theater, hotels, and downtown stores went for fifty cents to two dollars, depending on the location of the seats, and automobile parking cost one dollar. The show began at 3:30 P.M. each day, and many businesses let their employees out early to watch the day's events, which started with a flight-duration contest. It was followed by a race on a three-and-a-half-mile course over the lake at 4:30 P.M., biplane passenger-carrying races at 5:30 P.M., altitude competition at 6:00 P.M., and cross-country flying at 7:00 P.M. Before the events began each day, many of the pilots earned pocket money by giving Chicagoans plane rides for several hundred dollars apiece.[30]

Such airplane rides were more akin to wing walking. There were no jump seats. Tribune cartoonist McCutcheon, who took two rides as a passenger at the Chicago show, recalled his ride earlier in the year in Dayton:

> I sat on the lower wing of the biplane, with my feet on a small bar below and clung to the struts. I think the pressure of my grip must show to this day. The pilot sat beside me with two control levers in his hands. The engine was suspended above us and two big propellers, connected by chains, were behind us, between the two wings. It was extremely primitive, crude and awkward, but it did go up, and after ten or fifteen minutes came safely down.[31]

The Meet Opens

The intended publicity and unintended attention caused by the Wright dispute did their job. For nine days in August 1911, the world aviation community turned its attention to Chicago. Several hundred thousand persons were on hand in the Grant Park area on Saturday, August 12, 1911, to watch what was to that time the largest extravaganza in the brief history of aviation. Opening day provided its share of thrills, none of them fatal, and kept the crowds coming back for more.

Because of frequent malfunctions on the primitive and fragile aircraft, pileups were common, although the relatively slow flying speed of the airplanes of that day meant that few crashes were fatal. On opening day, Arthur Stone crashed in his Queen Bleriot monoplane when a wing hit the ground during a steep turn at low altitude, flipping the plane on its back. Stone was unhurt. Frank Coffyn and two passengers in his Wright biplane escaped injury when he made a forced landing and struck another plane sitting on the field, and James Martin overshot a landing in his Bristol Farman biplane and hit a fence.

After its engine was started, Rene Simon's Moisant went out of control on the ground, hitting a tree. Because propeller governors, the hydraulically powered devices that control the pitch of propellers and permit pilots to "feather" their props, had not yet been developed, the aircraft of the day had to be restrained by chocks and ground crews after the engines were started to prevent them from running away. Conversely, upon landing pilots had to shut off their engines and coast to a stop because the airplanes had no brakes.

The winners on opening day included Earle Ovington, who defeated Britain's Sopwith in the speed races by flying twenty miles in twenty-three minutes and fifty-two seconds—an average speed of about just over fifty miles an hour. Howard Gill won the altitude contest by climbing to 4,980 feet in his Wright biplane, and Calbraith P. Rogers, who would be killed in a crash less than a year later in Long Beach, California, won the endurance contest by staying airborne for two hours, fifty-five minutes, and thirty-three seconds.

The next day, Sunday, an estimated

Pilot J. D. McCurdy posed for a photographer in his pusher (rear mounted propeller) biplane before taking off to perform in the 1911 International Aviation Meet. The ground crews had to restrain the airplane after the engine was started because it had no brakes. The engine was shut off upon landing. (Joshua Koppel Collection)

J. A. D. McCURDY - BIPLANE

400,000 persons jammed into downtown Chicago to try to watch the meet, but some spectators could get no closer than State Street, in the middle of the city's mercantile district two blocks west of the park. Traffic on nearby streets was halted when wagon drivers and motorists temporarily abandoned their vehicles to get a closer look. Spectators crowded onto bridges over the Illinois Central Railroad right-of-way on the western edge of the park, lined the tops of buildings along Michigan Avenue, hung out hotel windows, climbed lamp posts, and perched atop signs to get a better view.

Some of the pilots responded to the crowd with daredevil antics. Lincoln Beachey, one of the most famous stunt pilots of his time, who sometimes flew decked out in a pinstriped suit and tie and at other times dressed as an old woman, dived from one thousand feet, skimmed over the tops of cars on Michigan Avenue, and made turns at such low altitudes that his wheels touched the ground. Boston aviator Harry Atwood visited the meet on Monday, August 14, as a scheduled stop on his successful 1,266-mile cross-country flight from St. Louis to New York City in an effort to claim a $10,000 prize. He

made it to New York on August 25.

The other aviators on the third day of the Chicago meet continued to lead a charmed existence despite five accidents. Rene Simon was skimming over the lake when the engine of his Moisant failed, and he was forced to glide to a crash landing in the water. Hugh A. Robinson, who at the time was airborne in the only flying boat at the meet, a Curtiss hydro-aeroplane, landed and taxied to the downed pilot—conducting perhaps the first air-sea rescue in history. Simon, clinging to Robinson's boat, refused to leave the scene until a tugboat attached lines to the Moisant and towed it to shore. Later the same day, Lee Hammond was saved by a rescue boat more than three miles out in the lake after a loose wire fouled his propeller. He was able to leap from the plane into the water just before it crashed.

As long as they escaped injury or death, crashes didn't seem to bother the pilots of the day. Ovington was back in the air in a Bleriot fifteen minutes after he crashed his Curtiss on a turn. However, the luck of the aviators ran out the next day, August 15, when the meet suffered its only two fatalities. William R. Badger, a twenty-seven-year-old pilot from Pittsburgh, was trying to top a stunt by Beachey. He attempted a three-hundred-foot dive and waited until he was only twenty feet off the ground to attempt to pull out of it; his body was crushed in the wreckage.

Two hours later, Chicagoan St. Croix Johnstone, twenty-six years old, crashed in his monoplane in the lake and drowned. Another pilot said the plane seemed to have exploded at 1,600 feet before diving straight into the water. Robinson, who was again aloft in his flying boat at the time, attempted another air-sea rescue. He landed near where Johnstone's plane had disappeared into forty feet of water and waited anxiously for the downed pilot to free himself and bob to the surface. He stood by until divers freed the body trapped in the wreckage. The accident was witnessed from the air by McCutcheon, who had been offered an airplane ride by Orville Wright and was flying above the field with pilot Frank Coffyn when the accident occurred. McCutcheon recalled later that he watched transfixed as an ambulance sped across Grant Park toward the lake, where Johnstone's plane could still be seen just below the surface. The surviving aviators flew an extra day after the official

end of the meet to raise money for Johnstone's widow.[32]

The two deaths brought an immediate outcry that the remainder of the meet should be cancelled. Dr. Stuart Johnstone, father of the dead aviator, issued a public appeal to stop the "carnage," but IAMA officials decided to continue, contending that many aviators had come long distances to participate and that the meet was important to increase humanity's knowledge of aviation. The remainder of the meet was completed without another fatality, although mishaps continued to occur.

The Windy City Problem

Probably the biggest single problem to aviators was the wind. The airplane of that day was little more than a lightweight glider powered by a gasoline engine and capable of an average speed of slightly more than fifty miles an hour. The Wright Company forbade its pilots to fly in strong winds, but Beachey and Eugene Ely, both flying Curtiss aircraft, got their planes into the air on at least one day when no one else would attempt flying.

A strong wind from the west proved to be the most troublesome for pilots. The

For a few weeks in 1911, Chicago was the center of aviation in the world as pilots and planes performed at the International Aviation Meet show in Grant Park. (Joshua Koppel Collection)

American aircraft, like these biplanes at the 1911 air show, had not advanced much beyond the original Wright machines of a decade earlier, but sleek and fast European monoplanes appeared at the show. World War I—still three years in the future—would result in substantial improvements in aircraft and their performance. (Chris Lynch Collection)

tall buildings to the west of Grant Park made takeoff into such a headwind impossible, and because the lake was immediately to the east, pilots had insufficient room to build the necessary speed for a takeoff with a tail wind. Even today pilots prefer to take off into a wind to gain sufficient air speed to get airborne because lift is provided by the speed of the wings passing through the air, not by the ground speed of the plane. The aircraft of that earlier day also had great difficulty taking off with a cross wind, making north-south operations hazardous any time the west wind exceeded a few miles an hour.

The tall buildings and gusting winds around them almost resulted in a disaster on the second day of the meet when an unexpected gust caused J. J. Frisbie's plane to brush a statue atop the 250-foot Montgomery Ward building. Frisbie, who injured his hand in the collision, temporarily lost control of the plane, which spiraled downward for a few seconds before he was able to regain control with his uninjured hand and land safely.

Beachey was undoubtedly the star of the show; with his powerful custom Curtiss bi-

plane he won more prize money ($11,667) than any other aviator using a single aircraft, although Sopwith, who used three planes, was the largest individual money winner ($14,020). Among the airplane builders, the Wright Company team collectively won $16,029, but the upstart Curtiss team won $27,291. The Moisant team won $8,143. The least fortunate aviator was L. Leckowicz, who won only sixty cents for getting his Queen monoplane into the air for eighteen seconds.

Beachey set a world altitude record of 11,642 feet on the last day of the meet, breaking the French-held international record of 11,152 and establishing a mark that would not be exceeded for three years. The method was typical of what pilots at that time did to set altitude records: Beachey used every drop of fuel in his tanks to get his plane as high as possible, then when the engine conked out, he glided back to earth. It took an hour and forty minutes for the small engine, working at full throttle, to pull Beachey's plane upward more than two miles above the earth. The downward glide to a safe landing lasted only twelve minutes.

STONE STARTING TRIP ENDING IN ACCIDENT SAT AUG 12
INTERNATIONAL AVIATION MEET CHICAGO AUGUST 1911

Arthur Stone flew a Queen 50 monoplane for more than an hour during the 1911 air show. Note the bracing and wires to support the wing. (Joshua Koppel Collection)

WRECK OF STONE'S MONOPLANE INTERNATIONAL AVIATION MEET CHICAGO 1911

The slow speeds of airplanes and low altitudes at which they were flown in the early years of aviation meant many pilots walked away from crashes. Arthur Stone survived the crash that destroyed his monoplane during the 1911 air show. (Joshua Koppel Collection)

Two other world records were set in the meet. On August 19 Sopwith and Simon, both flying planes built by Frenchman Louis Bleriot, set a record for climbing—500 meters (1,634 feet) in three minutes and twenty-five seconds. The final record, set on the same day, was for two-man duration (endurance) flying. G. W. Beatty, of the Wright team, carried a passenger aloft in his biplane for three hours and forty-two minutes. Ten American records were also set in the meet, five of them by Sopwith. (See appendix A for aviators' winnings and records.)

In some cases a record was set one day only to be eclipsed later in the meet. Coffyn set a three-man duration record on opening day, only to be eclipsed by Sopwith the next day; a few hours later, Beachey topped them both. The Wright team's Phil O. Parmalee set an American altitude record of 10,837 feet only to have Beachey top it with a new world record on the last day of the meet.

Although the meet was hailed by the public and the aviation community as a great success, it was a financial failure. Despite receiving $145,635 in revenue from tickets, programs, and advertising, the International Aviation Meet Association lost $64,109 on the event. Two months after the meet ended, IAMA assessed its guarantors $75,000 to cover the operating loss and the escrow account that had been established in the event IAMA lost its court case to the Wrights.

In addition to $102,938 in prizes and expenses paid to the participating aviators, the association spent $17,551 getting Grant Park ready for the show; $37,770 for grandstands and hangars; $3,087 for bands and entertainment for the crowds; $753 for field hospitals; $20,390 in administrative expenses, primarily in salaries for the staff; and $19,267 for advertising and publicity.[33]

Although there was some dissent among members of the parent Aero Club of Illinois, the meet established that private organization as the dominant force in aviation in Chicago—a position it would hold for more than a decade during the formative years of flying. Absent any government interest in aviation, the club of rich men established the rules of the air, built the airports, promoted the industry, and taught young newcomers how to fly.

The Aero Club

The Aero Club of Illinois is unique in Chicago history—an association of individuals varying in social status, from high school students to wealthy magnates, whose occupations spanned the spectrum from auto mechanic to corporate executive. Their common bond was flying, and their organization dominated early aviation in Chicago like nothing before or since. Although the aeronauts—the balloonists—had their own association early in the century, the Aero Club *was* aviation in Chicago after 1910. The club operated the only public airport, trained the pilots, and set the rules for flying. It also staged air shows—spectacles that drew public attention and attracted young persons interested in flying.

At that time, flying was a sport. There was no commercial aviation, although a few far-sighted souls tried to make a go at air freight. Young persons who wanted to fly bought an airplane from Curtiss or the Wrights if they had the resources to do so, or, like Emil (Matty) Laird, they built their own. Other early Aero Club members of

Katherine Stinson was one of the women aviation pioneers who learned to fly at the Aero Club in Chicago. (Christopher Lynch Collection)

limited means worked as mechanics or pilots for those who could afford airplanes. Some young aviation enthusiasts simply hung around the handful of flying fields and picked up what knowledge they could by watching or volunteering to help. Aviation in the years before World War I was an informal community that encouraged the curious to join.

The Aero Club and the facilities it built at its airport in west-suburban Cicero acted as a magnet for young men and women from across the United States who wanted to learn to fly. In 1912, Katherine Stinson, a member of the aviation family that later gained fame, came to Chicago at age twenty-one from her native Mississippi to learn to fly, as did Chance M. Vought, a New Yorker who was studying engineering and later went on to found the firm that built some of the most famous U.S. military aircraft. Glenn L. Martin, another aviation company founder, used Chicago as his base in the years before World War I.[1]

In most parts of the nation, almost anyone who wanted to see an airplane fly or to ride in one had to wait until the county fair was held each year and some barnstormer came along offering rides for whatever the local market would bear. In Chicago, grandfathers and their grandchildren could simply take the Metropolitan Douglas Park elevated train to the Aero Club airport in Cicero any weekend the weather was good and watch club members practice their maneuvers. If they were lucky, they could talk a pilot into taking them up.

Aviation in its earliest years was dominated by the wealthy; some of the same people who had the means to buy automobiles in the years before Henry Ford introduced the affordable Model T in 1908 also bought airplanes. Among Aero Club members, James E. Plew was a White auto dealer; Harold F. McCormick's International Harvester Company built automobiles between 1906 and 1911, then the firm decided to concentrate on motor

trucks; and Charles Dickinson was one of the founders and backers of the Chicago Motocycle Company, which built cars with names like Caloric and Fostler between 1902 and 1905 before disappearing from the auto scene.[2]

Glenn Curtiss had suggested the possibility of an aero club when he met with some aviation enthusiasts after his 1909 flying demonstration, and they didn't take long to get the proposal into the air. The group met February 10, 1910, and officially the club came into existence. The venerable but ailing and largely absent Octave Chanute was elected the club's first president, and the other officers included Plew, who was Curtiss's agent in Chicago as well as an automobile dealer; Harold McCormick, one of Chicago's richest socialites as well as vice president of International Harvester, which was run by his brother; and Victor Lougheed, a recent migrant from California and member of the family that founded the Lockheed Corporation. Dickinson, owner of a local seed company, was also a member.[3]

Harold F. McCormick

Although the spectacular air show of 1911 obscured almost everything else the Aero Club did that year, its most important accomplishment was to build a permanent public airport at which aviators could practice and train. The air show was the impetus for the airport, and McCormick was the man and the money behind both. Until he unexpectedly dropped from the flying scene just before World War I, the heir to the Cyrus McCormick reaper fortune succeeded Octave Chanute as the single most important individual in aviation in Chicago.

McCormick was as unlikely an aviation pioneer as Chicago has had. He was a dominant socialite, member of one of the city's patrician families, and he spent as much of his time as possible in Europe. He used his wealth to establish aviation in

Chicago, and at age thirty-nine he attempted to learn to fly after secretly designing and building his own airplane.

He was born May 2, 1872, the son of Cyrus Hall McCormick, inventor of the mechanical reaper and founder of the company that became International Harvester. The elder McCormick was one of the industrialists who made his fortune by harvesting the vast prairie that stretched for a thousand miles west of Chicago. Young Harold McCormick received all the benefits of his father's wealth. He attended Princeton University, where he played football, and soon after his graduation in 1895 he married Edith Rockefeller, the daughter of oil magnate John D. Rockefeller. For many years the McCormicks ruled Chicago society, lavishing money on their favorite causes. Harold and Edith were benefactors of Chicago Grand Opera, the city's first resi-

dent company, which opened its doors in 1909. Altogether they gave an estimated $5 million to the opera. Among their other contributions, they also financed the McCormick Institute for Infectious Diseases.[4]

Harold McCormick's interest in aviation dated from 1901, when he was visiting Paris shortly after the death of his eldest son, John Rockefeller McCormick, and saw Santos-Dumont circle the Eiffel Tower in a dirigible to collect a 100,000-franc prize. He later wrote to an intermediary asking him to obtain from Santos-Dumont a photograph or drawing of the balloon. The aeronaut refused.[5]

McCormick's interest in aviation was rekindled in Chicago eight years later when he was in the crowd with Chanute and Dickinson when Curtiss made his demonstration flight in Cicero and later suggested forming an aero club. McCormick also

Lincoln Beachey was perhaps the most famous stunt flyer in America in the years before World War I. Dressed in a suit, or sometimes as an elderly woman, he thrilled crowds at Chicago's 1911 international air show. (Christopher Lynch Collection)

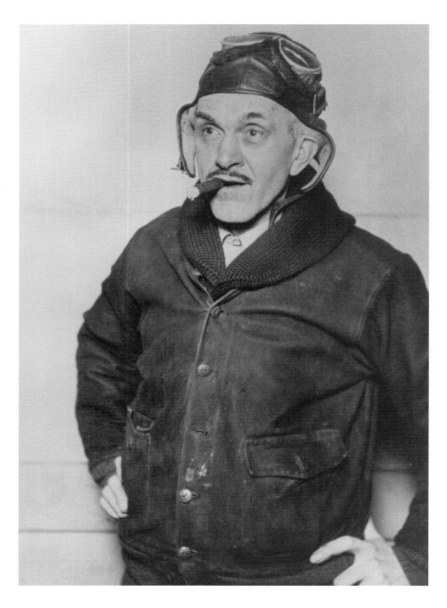

Henry (Pop) Keller was a product of the Aero Club's flight school in 1912. He was killed in a crash in 1928 at Ashburn Field while teaching someone else how to fly.

came a pilot and aeronautical engineer for Max Lillie's aviation school in 1913 at Cicero Field, and edited *Aero & Hydro,* an early aviation weekly. Within a year Vought was off on his own designing and later building airplanes.

Two months prior to the 1911 air show, Aero Club members decided it might be a good idea to have an aerodrome where aviators, especially local fliers, could practice for the meet. McCormick stepped up and loaned the club 180 acres he owned in Cicero. The land would eventually be developed, but at the time it was vacant.[6]

McCormick, meanwhile, had secretly designed and built his own airplane, intending to test it at the site of the new Cicero airport before it opened to the public. The machine looked something like an umbrella with a hole in the center and was powered by an engine mounted in front. Because he didn't want any publicity, probably for fear of ridicule, he took the aircraft to Cicero Field in the wee hours of the morning of July 2, 1911, to fly it. His attempt at secrecy was no more successful than Chanute's had been in 1896; a newspaper reporter-photographer team trailed him, and the story and a picture were in print the next day.[7]

The plane was too difficult to turn for practical aerial operation, and its engine proved balky when Charles F. Willard, one of the entrants in the air show, came to Chicago to test it. McCormick finally ordered the plane dumped in Lake Michigan after a year and a half of work costing $50,000 failed to correct the problems. It was such an embarrassment to him that when *Aero Magazine* editor Percy Noel wrote for a photograph, Grover Sexton, Aero Club secretary and a friend of McCormick, wrote back: "The only way I know of that I could get a picture of Mr. McCormick in his machine would be to chloroform him and call out the National Guard."[8]

McCormick succeeded Plew as president of the Aero Club for 1912, but the following year turned his attention to hydroplanes, as seaplanes were called in those days. Even

accompanied Dickinson in late October 1910 to the Belmont aviation meet in New York. He was elected an officer of the Aero Club of Illinois when it was formed in early 1910 and was the driving force behind the 1911 air show in Chicago.

It was in 1910 that McCormick also hired Chance Vought, a twenty-year-old engineering student, to work at International Harvester, and interested that young protégé in aviation. Vought went to Dayton to learn to fly at the Wright school, be-

before his flap with the Wright brothers in 1911, McCormick had been friendly with Glenn Curtiss, possibly the nation's leading builder of seaplanes. He and fellow North Shore resident Logan A. (Jack) Vilas had bought their own flying boats from Curtiss in 1913, and McCormick at least occasionally used his for the twenty-five-mile commute between work and his home in Lake Forest. McCutcheon, in his autobiography, recalled answering the phone in his studio one day to discover McCormick on the other end of the line:

> "Hello, John. How would you like to ride home with me in my new plane this afternoon?"
>
> "Great Scott! How long have you had a plane?"
>
> "I just got it. It's a Curtiss. I flew in it for the first time this morning."

McCormick built a hangar on the Lake Michigan beach below his house and hired a pilot to fly the plane. The more adventuresome Vilas took flying lessons from Curtiss.[9]

McCormick's plane was a tractor type with the one-hundred-horsepower engine in front pulling the aircraft and a range of about four hundred miles. It was short-lived. Pilot Maximilian Theodore Liljestrant, or Max Lillie as he was commonly known around Chicago, crashed it into the lake off Clarendon Beach on July 15, 1913, when it was swamped by a high wave during takeoff. He was uninjured but told reporters he wouldn't give fifteen cents for what was left of the airframe. However, the engine, worth $2,000, was salvaged.[10]

McCormick immediately bought a replacement, hired pilot Charles C. Witmer to fly it for him, and prodded the Aero Club to organize a seaplane endurance meet over the Great Lakes later that year. His last fling in aviation was in 1914 when he, Plew, and Bion J. Arnold announced that they planned to start a commuter airline in May of that year using seaplanes to ferry passengers between various North Shore suburbs and Grant Park and the South Shore Country Club. Lake Shore Airline, which had two seaplanes, was intended to be a profit-making venture charging a steep twenty-eight-dollar round-trip fare between Lake Forest and downtown Chicago on four daily scheduled circuits. However, Chicago's irregular weather, especially the crosswinds, made a shamble of schedules, and the airline disappeared before the end of the year.[11]

After 1914, McCormick's interest in aviation began to wane. Despite the war, he and his wife spent most of their time in Europe from 1915 to late 1918, when he reluctantly assumed the presidency of International Harvester Company upon the retirement of his brother Cyrus. His duties as chief executive of that firm and his domestic troubles apparently left little time for aviation, for he never attempted to get back into Aero Club activities, although he didn't bother to officially resign from the club until 1922.[12]

Assorted romantic associations gave McCormick a great deal of unwanted notoriety and did in his first marriage. It got worse: press reports of the day say he was duped out of considerable money by a young woman who claimed she was the daughter of the Sultan of Turkey. The publicity and his divorce from Edith in 1921 caused him to resign as the president of International Harvester. The following year he married Ganna Walska, a Polish opera singer; they divorced in 1931. Seven years later he met and married a California woman and spent much of the rest of his life in that state. He died on October 16, 1941.[13]

McCormick's abrupt departure from aviation didn't leave a vacuum at the Aero Club. Engineer Bion J. Arnold served as the club's president in 1913, then power passed to another wealthy Chicagoan interested both in flying and the marvels of the motor age—Charles Dickinson, or "Pop" as he later became known to the following generation of aviators.[14]

Pop Dickinson

Although he was not as well known as some of his contemporaries, Charles Dickinson was probably the most important promoter of aviation in Chicago following the death of Chanute. He was the ultimate aviation buff. For the quarter century from 1910 to his death in 1935, Dickinson was a constant presence in the aviation community, financing projects that otherwise would not have been undertaken, helping barnstorming pilots who were down on their luck, encouraging young people to take to the air, and constantly promoting flying; yet his principal claim to fame in the newspapers of the day was that he was the nation's oldest pilot.

Surprisingly, Dickinson's four major aviation ventures were all bitter disappointments, but after each collapsed he returned to the flying fields to try something else. After his racing plane failed to get off the ground in the 1912 Gordon Bennett race, Dickinson turned his attention to financing the development of Ashburn Field so aviation in Chicago could continue to have a base of operations. When he failed to convince Chicago's political establishment to buy Ashburn as the municipal airport, he attempted to start an airline service between Chicago and New York using Ashburn as a base. After that failed, he tried his hand at a government contract for air mail service between Chicago and Minneapolis–St. Paul in competition with a consortium that included some of the wealthiest and most powerful men in the city. That failed, and Dickinson turned to airplane racing.

Despite his failure to establish a commercial airline, Dickinson used his wealth and influence to keep Chicago's fragile young aviation community alive until the development of the air mail routes in the next decade made aviation a commercially viable industry. There is no way of determining how much of his money he poured into aviation, but it is certain that he got very little financial return on the investment. Like Chanute before him, Dickinson found aviation an all-encompassing avocation to which he devoted the last part of his life.

He was born on May 28, 1858, the youngest of six children, in a small cottage on State Street where the Carson Pirie Scott & Company department store now stands. His father, Albert, had founded the Dickinson Feed and Seed Company in 1855. After it was destroyed in the Chicago fire of 1871, the family rebuilt it into one of the largest companies of its kind in the world. It was the success of the seed company that permitted Dickinson to invest heavily in aviation ventures.[15]

Young Dickinson studied medicine for a while, as did his sister, Frances, who became an eye surgeon. However, Dickinson did not find medicine to his liking and instead went into the family business with his older brother. He was intrigued by the new technology of automobiles and in 1902 founded the short-lived Chicago Motocycle Company. (*Motocycle* was an early term for automobile.) It is not known when he first developed an interest in aviation, but he was present with Chanute and McCormick on October 15, 1909, when Glenn Curtiss urged the formation of an aero club in Illinois.

His serious involvement in aviation dates from 1910 and the death of wife, Marie, whom he had married in 1897. The couple had been childless. The next year, Dickinson sold the family house at 603 N. Dearborn Street and moved its contents into a warehouse and himself into a suite in the Blackstone Hotel overlooking Grant Park. For the remaining twenty-five years of his life he lived first in the Blackstone and later in the Union League Club.

A Quaker, Dickinson neither smoked nor drank, although his associates said he was not a church-going man. He always wore identical business suits, and he operated his seed company more progressively than most businesses of that day. The company had a free employee cafeteria and medical department, and during hard times Dickinson gave his employees interest-free loans with which to buy homes. When his brother retired as president of the company, Dickinson assumed control with the title of vice president, leaving the title of president unfilled in deference to his brother.

Dickinson disliked driving automobiles, liked train travel, and loved airplanes. He was almost continuously at Cicero Field after 1910, and the men who remembered him there said that despite his stature as one of the city's moneyed elite, he was not afraid to get his hands dirty helping to work on a flying machine. He apparently took his first plane ride when he went up with Calbraith P. Rogers in Chicago on August 27, 1911, several days after the international air show ended.

While other Aero Club members prepared for the 1912 air show, Dickinson was given the task of finding an American entry for the Gordon Bennett Race, also to be held that year in Chicago. That meant raising the money to build an airplane to represent the United States under Aero Club sponsorship, and Dickinson's efforts were plagued with trouble almost from the beginning. Because the 1911 air show had lost money, Dickinson could find few persons willing to invest in a plane that had to be designed and built from scratch in order to compete with the more advanced European monoplanes that were expected to be entered. The Europeans, after lagging behind the United States in aviation for nearly a decade, had made considerable progress in building swift monoplanes for racing. Americans had concentrated mainly on the slower but more reliable biplanes.

After unsuccessfully soliciting for funds for the plane, Dickinson pledged his own financial support to the project and on June 22—less than four months before the race was to be held—ordered a racer based on a design submitted by Norman Prince. The specifications called for an airplane capable of flying at 115 miles an hour to compete with the French entries in the race. It proved impossible to put the racer

together on such short notice. The Gnome engine was delivered late. It was attached to the airframe, and the airplane was hurriedly shipped to Chicago, where it arrived only a few days before the race. It had not even been test flown. Considerable bickering over the plane's airworthiness and which pilot should fly it ensued, and on September 2 Dickinson gave up and announced that in the interest of safety he was withdrawing it from the race.

He shrugged off that fiasco and launched into several other aviation projects. One of his favorite activities was to be flown over the city, often by pilot Max Lillie, scouting for future airport sites. At the time, McCormick's interest in aviation was waning, and it was obvious to Dickinson that it was only a matter of time before the Aero Club would have to find a replacement for its base at Cicero Field, which McCormick owned. Dickinson realized that the airplane would play an important role in Chicago commerce, and he looked for airport sites in remote areas, away from residential development, that would provide room for expansion as aviation grew in importance. He became convinced that the Lake Calumet area on the far South Side was the perfect site for an airport and seaplane base.

Much of Dickinson's time in the years before World War I was spent promoting aviation. After his election as Aero Club president, he persuaded the club to start a youth program in Chicago high schools. Matty Laird was one of the products of that program. Like many aviation pioneers, Dickinson also realized that aviation had a military application and urged Congress to form an air force.

Dickinson became preeminent in Chicago aviation in 1915 when McCormick, by then spending most of his time in Switzerland, began selling off Cicero Field to developers. Dickinson promptly bought the site for Ashburn Field and paid for the building of runways, hangars, access roads, a bunkhouse for pilots, and a well for water. Once Ashburn was in operation, Dickinson tried to convince the U.S. government to establish an air base there and the city to develop it as a major airport. That project, too, ended in failure.

Although military units were twice stationed at Ashburn Field in World War I, the government ultimately built Chanute Air Field in Rantoul as its major installation in northern Illinois. Chicago was moderately interested in the possibility of a municipal airport until the *Wingfoot* blimp disaster in 1919. Attempts by Dickinson after World War I to interest the U.S. Post Office Department in using Ashburn as a base for its fledgling air mail service also failed, although the field was used as a maintenance facility for air mail planes using Grant Park. In the early 1920s, when the post office was looking for a facility to replace Grant Park, it chose not Ashburn, but Checkerboard Field in west-suburban Maywood. A few years later, when the commercial airlines began carrying the mail, they chose Chicago's new Municipal Airport, later renamed Midway. Ashburn continued as a general aviation field of diminishing importance until it was sold to developers in the early 1950s.

Dickinson's Early Airlines

In 1919, Dickinson became interested in the possibility of establishing a commercial airline. The development of larger airplanes and more powerful engines during World War I raised the possibility that commercial service was feasible, but as the early airline entrepreneurs learned, the aircraft of that time were still not sufficiently reliable to win the public's confidence, and there was little market for air freight. Dickinson's 1919 venture was a case of an airline ahead of its time. Alfred W. Lawson, a former professional baseball player, self-taught aeronautical engineer, and at the time a resident of Milwaukee, had built the first American large-cabin commercial transport plane, which weighed seven tons

fully loaded, could carry twenty-four passengers, was powered by two four-hundred-horsepower Liberty engines, and had a ninety-four-foot wingspan. Although the aircraft was seriously underpowered, Dickinson believed that it had sufficient potential for him to support Lawson in his attempt to establish a passenger airline between Chicago and New York City.[16]

The plane left Ashburn Field on August 31, 1919, on the maiden demonstration flight of the newly formed Lawson Airline Company with pilot Charles Cox at the controls and Chicagoan Ralph Diggins in the navigator's seat. When Cox arrived in Toledo at the end of the first leg of the flight, he discovered that the designated landing field was covered with debris. On his third attempt to land the plane, he brushed a tree, damaging a wing, but there were no injuries to anyone aboard the plane. He was finally forced to land in a farm field several miles away.

The plane was repaired and continued on to New York and Washington before returning to Milwaukee. The demonstration trip of two thousand miles took from August 27 to November 7. The plane had made various publicity stops, including six days each in New York and Washington; had been grounded in Indianapolis for ten days because of rain; and had sustained damage during a crash landing in Connellsville, Pennsylvania, after which the aircraft had to be dismantled and shipped to Dayton, where it was overhauled. Realizing the plane needed more power, Lawson built an even larger aircraft, but it crashed on its first flight in Milwaukee in May 1921, and after that he was unable to continue in the business.[17]

Undaunted by the Lawson failure, Dickinson in 1923 tried again to start an airline between Chicago and New York. On July 26, he became the first passenger to travel at night between the two cities. With pilot Eddie Stinson at the controls and mechanic Art Gray on board, Dickinson left Ashburn in a single-engine, all-metal

Matty Laird, at right; Pop Dickinson, center; and Alfred O. Sporrer were three of Chicago's most important aviation pioneers. Laird built planes, Dickinson ran the Aero Club of Illinois and financed it with his own money, and Sporrer was a pilot.

Junkers at 11:00 P.M. and made Curtiss Field in Garden City, New York, at 8:30 the next morning. The flight was to demonstrate the feasibility of overnight service. Late that year, Dickinson announced that his New York airline would begin carrying passengers the following May 1.[18]

"I'll probably spend a great many thousands of dollars this summer in starting this line," Dickinson said in announcing the nonstop night service. "I may never make a cent out of it, but I don't care. If I can prove that such a line can be operated from Chicago and thereby put this city on the map as a center of American aviation, I will be satisfied. I have lived 65 years now, and I have been playing with airplanes for 14 years, and my only wish is to see Chicago become the center of American flying."[19]

Nothing more was heard of the proposed airline until May 2, 1924, when Dickinson telephoned several Chicago newspapers from New York to announce that it had made its first trip. He and pilot Elmer Partridge had completed the maiden flight from Ashburn to Garden City in eight hours and fifteen minutes with a lunch stop in Cleveland. He told the newspapers that he and Partridge were canvassing Manhattan that night for passengers for the return trip and that the new airline had bought three French-built Breguets from Tony Yackey. The planes were ready for service.

Unfortunately, the public was not yet ready for the rigors of flying, especially when the available alternatives were the comfortable Broadway and Twentieth Century Limited trains. The airplanes of the day were unheated and cramped. Thus Dickinson's newest venture quickly failed.

It was another two years before the awarding of government air mail contracts to private airlines made commercial aviation feasible, and then only for carrying freight. When that happened, Dickinson was ready. He outbid the well-financed National Air Transport (NAT) on a government contract for air mail service between Chicago and Minneapolis after being told

by a NAT official in a pre-bid conference that he would never get the contract.

Unfortunately, not only was the new airline undercapitalized, but Dickinson had submitted a bid too low to enable him to recover costs. However, he hired some of the nation's finest pilots, including his old friends Elmer Partridge and Ervin E. Ballough; bought some airplanes from his protégé Matty Laird; and proceeded to launch the venture on June 6, 1926. It was a disaster from the start. Partridge was killed when he crashed in a storm just after takeoff from Minneapolis for Chicago, and most of the other pilots were forced down by high winds and clouds of dust. After a succession of labor troubles and other mishaps left him with only one available pilot, the old man gave up on August 17 and folded the airline.

He then shrugged off his third failure at starting an airline and turned his attention to airplane racing, a fad that was then sweeping the country. Dickinson bought two powerful Laird Commercials, which Ballough and Charles (Speed) Holman flew for him. In 1927, Ballough and Dickinson finished second in a cross-country race between New York and Spokane, Washington, which was won by Holman. The next year Ballough and Dickinson finished second in the National Air Races in Los Angeles, and in January 1929 they set a new record time of nine hours and fifty-nine minutes between Miami and Chicago.

Dickinson finally obtained a government-issued pilot's license on September 21, 1930, at age seventy-two, although he had been flying as early as February 13, 1921, when he made a solo flight after taking lessons from Partridge at Ashburn Field. In his final years, Dickinson spent much of his time pursuing an unusual hobby with James Organisciak, a Catholic priest—collecting tickets on inaugural flights of new airlines in the then rapidly expanding airline industry. Before he died, he had collected thirteen airline tickets bearing the number one, indicating an inaugural flight.

On September 2, 1935, he was stricken with a fatal heart attack while in New York to see a cardiovascular physician for treatment. Seven days later, his friends Al Sporrer and Ervin Ballough honored his wishes by emptying an urn containing his ashes from George Horton's airplane five hundred feet over Lake Michigan near Grant Park.

The Future Plane Builders

The Aero Club also included a number of members who were somewhat lower on the social scale than McCormick and Dickinson but who went on to greater success in aviation. They included the brothers Victor and Allan Loughead, airplane builder Matty Laird, and William B. Stout, a designer of airplanes, automobiles, and trains.

The Loughead half brothers Victor and Allan were more typical of the rank-and-file members of the Aero Club in its earliest years. Allan went on to greater fame as a founder of the Lockheed Corporation, one of the nation's major airplane builders, but Victor, a hotheaded writer, was the one who got them started in aviation. He had left their native California and moved to Chicago to work at Plew's White Steam automobile dealership. Plew had decided to sell planes as well as cars and got Victor hooked on aviation. In 1909 he sent the young writer, who that year produced his first book on aviation, *Vehicles of the Air,* to Glenn Curtiss's Hammondsport, New York, factory to buy an airplane. He also sent Victor to San Francisco to acquire the rights to a tandem glider designed by the enigmatic glider pioneer James F. Montgomery; Plew hoped to mount an engine on the airframe and create a saleable airplane.[20]

While in San Francisco, Victor convinced his younger brother Allan, who was working as an auto mechanic, to move to Chicago to work on Plew's two aircraft. Victor became a charter member and officer of the Aero Club of Illinois when it was formed, and Allan later joined the club to learn to fly. Allan's first flight at the controls occurred when George Gates, who had home-built an airplane roughly modeled on a Curtiss, needed an extra hand to operate the aileron controls and took the younger Loughead brother along.

When Plew withdrew from the aircraft sales business following the crash of one of his planes, Allan went to work for another car dealer, Sam Dixon, as an instructor and pilot for his International Aeroplane Manufacturing Company of Chicago at twenty-five dollars per week. He then became a county fair exhibition pilot, typically receiving 25 percent of the gross receipts, which were guaranteed to be a minimum of $500 per day. However, he decided to build his own airplanes and returned to California to go into partnership with his other brother, Malcolm.

Victor, meanwhile, was raising a furor in the Aero Club in Chicago. In 1911 he irked the Wrights in Dayton when he visited them to debunk the results of some glider flights that exceeded in duration those of Montgomery. Back in Chicago, he promptly got into a dispute with McCormick over the planned international air show. On the day the air show opened, Victor angrily resigned his membership in the Aero Club, apparently dissatisfied with the choice of Bernard Mullaney as the meet's full-time director. "The meet itself," he protested, "under the guise of a non-profit-paying corporation, has been turned into a salary-disbursing organization, and its management vested in the hands of a man with the tact of a Missouri mule, whose only claim to the special knowledge desirable for the place inheres in the fact that he has a pull with the city administration and was a notorious local politician out of a job."[21]

Victor continued to bum around Chicago for a while, in 1912 publishing his second aviation book, *Airplane Designing for Amateurs,* before returning to California. There he managed to get into a dispute with his two half brothers that they were unable to reconcile.[22]

This Speedwing and other racing planes were built at Ashburn Field by Matty Laird in the late 1920s. Like many early aviators, Laird learned to fly at the Aero Club's Cicero Field.

William B. Stout (1880–1956) was a young mechanical engineer originally from Quincy, Illinois. He had become interested in airplanes as a boy in 1894 and, after the turn of the century, had corresponded with Chanute. The old man, always willing to encourage potential aviators, loaned Stout some glider models for a speech on aviation he gave in 1907 in Minneapolis. By 1912, Stout was in Chicago, having talked his way into a job as the automotive and aviation editor of the *Chicago Tribune*.[23]

Stout also joined the Aero Club of Illinois and proposed that that organization publish on a semimonthly basis an official club bulletin to be called *Aerial Age*. The club liked the idea, and McCormick financed the project. The first issue, published in June 1912, contained an article by Stout proclaiming "Chicago—World's Flying Capital." The article warned that America was lagging behind the Europeans in developing airplanes for military uses. *Aerial Age* developed into an early, but short-lived, magazine about flying.[24]

Like so many of the young aviation enthusiasts who flocked to Chicago in the years before World War I, Stout decided that his future was elsewhere. He wanted to be an engineer designing transportation machines, and in 1914 he took a job as chief engineer and new-car designer for an automobile company interested in manufacturing cyclecars, inexpensive automobiles cobbled together from motorcycle parts—a fad vehicle of the time. Two years later he moved to Packard Motor Car Company in Detroit, and when the company started an aviation division, he was asked to become its chief engineer.

When America finally entered the war, Stout helped the government design the Liberty engine. However, he became disillusioned when the War Department, which was preoccupied with biplanes, ignored a triangular-winged monoplane he had designed. Stout had eliminated all external bracing, such things as the struts and wires typical of biplanes of the time, in favor of internal bracing within the wing itself. He later designed a bat-winged plane that some aviation historians have described as a precursor of the flying wing. Later, after leaving government service, he built an all-metal airplane—a concept pioneered by Germany's Junkers after World War I. He called it the "Air Sedan." Most planes of the time consisted of a wooden skeleton with a fabric cover.[25]

With Henry Ford's backing, Stout later established a freight airline between Detroit and Grand Rapids, Michigan, and after Ford bought the company, Stout helped design the famous Ford Tri-Motor, America's first successful commercial pas-senger airliner. In 1932 he also designed, for Chicago's Pullman Company, America's first aerodynamic, self-propelled streamliner—the Rail Plane. It was followed the next year by a three-car articulated streamliner built for the Union Pacific Railroad, called the M10,000.[26]

Women in the Air

Not all the daredevils who came to Chicago were men. At a time when women's suffrage was gaining momentum in the United States, a handful of prospective aviatrices, as women fliers were often called at the time, took to the skies in flying machines to show an enthralled American public that they could be every bit as good as men at being pilots. Some of them too died horrible deaths in crashes. The young women pilots were akin not so much to the two venerable campaigners

The *American Defender* was the custom monoplane Pop Dickinson financed to represent the United States in the 1912 Gordon Bennett race in Chicago. It was delivered late and was scratched from the race because there was insufficient time to test it.

for women's equality Elizabeth Cady Stanton and Susan B. Anthony as they were to Nellie Bly (née Elizabeth Cochrane), the newspaper reporter who in the late nineteenth century proved she could survive in what was then a man's profession by feigning insanity to get a story from inside a New York asylum and made a globe-circling trip by train and ship in seventy-two days. The aviatrices put their lives on the line with daredevil stunts as dangerous as anything attempted by Lincoln Beachey.[27]

Chicagoan Julia Clark, who had learned to fly at Glenn Curtiss's school, was killed when her plane crashed during an exhibition in Springfield, Illinois, on June 17, 1912, after being warned by Andrew Drew that she was too inexperienced to fly. Bessie Coleman, perhaps the first black woman pilot, was killed April 30, 1926, when she fell more than a mile from an open cockpit as her airplane went out of control during a parachuting exhibition in Florida. Coleman had worked as a manicurist in Chicago to finance flying lessons in France in 1920 because local flying schools did not accept blacks of either gender. She barnstormed across the nation for six years as a pilot and parachutist before her death.[28]

Katherine Stinson became the first of her family to fly when at twenty-one years of age she left her home in Canton, Mississippi, and came to Chicago in 1912 to enroll in Max Lillie's flying school at Cicero Field. By some accounts, she hoped to use earnings from aviation to finance her study of music in Europe, but she became hooked on flying. On July 19, 1912, she became the fourth woman in the United States to receive a pilot's license.[29]

Within a month she was already barnstorming around the Midwest. It wasn't long before she began setting records: she became the first woman to fly U.S. mail when on September 23, 1914, she carried a sack of letters aloft while performing at the Montana State Fair in Helena, and on July 18, 1915, at Cicero Field, she became the first woman to perform a loop-the-loop manuever. She set long-distance record with a flight of 610 miles in late 1917, then eclipsed it on May 23, 1918, with a flight of 783 miles between Chicago and Binghamton, New York, carrying some mail. The eleven-hour, thirteen-minute flight, which ended when she ran out of fuel, also set a record for duration.[30]

Like most barnstormers of the day, she had to engage in a bit of showmanship. Just as Lincoln Beachey, the most famous exhibition pilot of his day, often flew in a suit and tie and sometimes dressed as a grandmother, Katherine Stinson, who was popularly described as the "Flying Schoolgirl" because of her diminutive, five-foot height and girlish appearance, appeared publicly in skirts and a tam-o'-shanter, although she wore trousers when flying. She was a natural pilot, and like Beachey she had some favorite crowd-pleasing stunts. "She used to fit Roman candles on the wings of her airplane, when she made exhibition flights at state fairs. In many of the exhibitions at night, she would come down after the fireworks display in the middle of a half-mile track with only a burning tar barrel to indicate how she was to land."[31]

Despite her flying skills, she, like other women aviators, was refused an appointment to the Army's air wing in World War I, and as a result she spent the war driving an ambulance in Europe. However, her success as a pilot attracted her younger siblings, and one by one Edward A. (Eddie), Marjorie (Madge), and Jack B. Stinson all took to the air with her—the "Flying Stinsons" as they collectively became known. The family moved to San Antonio, Texas, in 1915 and opened their own airport and flying school. Eddie and Jack eventually formed a company in Dayton and later relocated to Detroit to manufacture airplanes. Eddie died in Chicago in 1932 from injuries received when the aircraft he was demonstrating to a potential customer ran out of fuel over Lake Michigan and hit a flag pole while he was trying to make a crash landing near the Jackson Park golf course.[32]

By then, Katherine Stinson had retired from flying. She had contracted tuberculosis in 1920 and after a long recovery had married a former World War I pilot in 1928. They moved to New Mexico, where he practiced law and served on the bench and she became an architect. After long lives, they died within three months of each other in 1977.[33]

★ ★ ★ ★

Perhaps the most important reason Chicago was able to attract talented aviators from across the nation was not the spectacles the Aero Club sponsored, but its first-rate airport and attendant flying school and support facilities. The greatest names in flying, people like Lincoln Beachey, T. O. M. Sopwith, and Walter Brookins, might visit Chicago once or twice a year to make some money in one of the city's aerial extravaganzas. However, most of the aviators who came to the Windy City in the years before World War I—the Katherine Stinsons,

Chance Voughts, and Glenn Martins—were attracted by its aviation facilities.

There were few truly public airports in those years. Most flying fields, including those of the Wrights and Glenn Curtiss, were privately owned by the men who conducted their business there. They might accept aviation tenants so long as it didn't interfere with their businesses. But anyone could come to the Aero Club's airport in west-suburban Cicero and learn to fly or fix airplanes, chat with pilots and mechanics, build their own airplane, or just hang over the fence and watch the brave young men and women test their flying machines. The club, true to the legacy of its first president, Octave Chanute, encouraged any and all to come and learn about the wonders of the flying machine. The club's professed goal in those years was to encourage and raise the public's interest in aviation, a phenomenon that for so many years had been the secret of the Wrights despite Chanute's efforts to bring it to the attention of the world. On most days, the adventure cost only a nickel—the price of an elevated train ride from the Loop to Cicero.

Chicago as a Growing Air Center

• The development of aviation from a sport to a business was the result of two functions over which the government held a monopoly—national defense and mail delivery. Commercial aviation would probably have developed eventually, but World War I greatly accelerated the process. Prior to 1914 the principal source of income for most people in aviation was barnstorming—exhibition flying—and even airplane builders had to resort to it to make ends meet. Quite simply, the airplane needed a commercial market if it were to develop into anything more than a curiosity or a toy of the rich.

The war speeded the development of larger, faster, and more reliable airplanes, vehicles that could be adapted to aerial commerce once the hostilities ended. The war also forced the government to train thousands of pilots and mechanics, young men who discovered that flying was a far more adventurous career than driving a tractor on the family farm and that fixing airplanes was more interesting than tinkering with automobile engines in the local garage.

The second requisite for the development of commercial aviation was a large and stable market for its services. The railroad industry in America reached its apex in 1916. By that time, more than a quarter of a million miles of track were in use, and the railroads dominated intercity freight and passenger traffic like no industry before or since. For residents of most communities in the first quarter of the twentieth century, even for those of the suburbs of major cities, the only link with the outside world was by train. By then the railroads had put most of America's other common carriers—the canals and river steamboats—out of business: they so dominated the transportation system that the federal government was forced to nationalize them temporarily when they choked on military traffic during World War I. Thereafter, the railroad system slowly began to contract as motor vehicles began to take away business in the short-haul markets, although inroads could not be made into the railroads'

long-haul business until the government built a better road system. The intercity highway system in 1918 consisted of a network of poorly connected and largely unmarked dirt roads, for the most part built and maintained by municipalities, townships, and counties to serve the farm-to-market trade.

The principal requisite for weapons of war, whether they be rifles or airplanes, is performance, but commerce demands reliability above all else in its vehicles. In the industrial age, a person or parcel must arrive safely and on schedule. Airplanes in 1918 were still largely unreliable curiosities, grounded in bad weather and at night. Because of their limited lift capacity, they could never be a factor in the haulage of such bulk commodities as iron ore and coal, and they could not compete with railroads in price for most merchandise freight. A wealthy man in 1925 might have been able to ship a belatedly purchased antique chair from New York to Chicago by air in time for his wife's birthday, but his company could not afford to ship its annual production of sofas by anything but rail. For the most part, he was also unwilling to ship himself by air to attend day-long sales conferences in the Windy City.

Thus the only potential market for commercial aviation immediately after the Great War ended was among entities that needed to reliably transport small parcels with high value. As a practical matter, the only enterprise with deep enough pockets to create and nurture a postwar market for air freight was the government. The U.S. Post Office Department, with congressional support and subsidies, could not only subsidize the new industry but also build the national system of airports and airways necessary to sustain a scheduled, all-weather aerial mail service.

It was inevitable that Chicago, which by virtue of its system of railroads and waterways had developed into the nation's dominant midcontinental transportation hub, would have a major role in any national air mail system. That became a reality within a few years of the end of the war.

Kenosha

Kenosha

WISCONSIN

Woodstock

Waukegan

Great Lakes

Lake
Michigan

Heath
Wilson
Cook County

Geneva
Pioneer
Maywood
Wheaton
Checkerboard
Municipal
Chicago
Ashburn

Joliet
Ford
Gary
Calumet

Indiana

R. Sweitzer

1928 Chicago Area Public Airports
Air Carriers
General Aviation Airports

The First Airports

GLENN CURTISS   HENRY FORD

• Chicago's early position of prominence in aviation was due in large part not only to the Aero Club's enthusiastic sponsorship of air shows but to its role in establishing first-class flying fields that in the years before World War I rivaled any airports on earth. The first airports were usually little more than pastures onto which aviators could fly their primitive machines with a minimum of obstructions. Except at some of the aviation spectacles, most early flights, the ones during which pilots learned and practiced their skills, rarely lasted more than a few minutes or got above a few hundred feet. All that was needed in the way of ground facilities was an unused barn or shed in which to store and work on the aircraft.

Thus the Wright brothers, once they completed their testing on the sandy but remote beaches of Kitty Hawk, looked around their hometown of Dayton for a suitable field where they could test and practice without making long trips to North Carolina. The site they selected was a one-hundred-acre cow pasture called Huffman Prairie alongside an electric interurban railway about eight miles from town. In one corner of the meadow they erected a wooden shed that looked like a

Seaplanes didn't require airports, although they did need bases on shore. They were popular in Chicago for a few years prior to World War I, but Lake Michigan's fierce storms and winter ice limited their use. Here seaplane builder Glenn Curtiss and automaker Henry Ford pose with one of Curtiss's flying boats. (Christopher Lynch Collection) motor car garage where they could build and store their airplanes.[1]

As the popularity of airplanes spread across the globe and rivals began to challenge the early Wright monopoly, flying fields similar to Huffman Prairie sprouted around major cities. Early pilots also used pastures and occasionally golf courses; the long fairways unobstructed by trees made suitable runways. For major exhibitions that drew large crowds, horse racing tracks with their substantial grandstands and large infields were converted into aerodromes for a day—as in the case of Belmont in New York and Hawthorne near Chicago—or large public parks were used. Chicago's lakefront Grant Park, with its relatively clear approaches to the north, south, and east, was especially suitable for air shows.

These were only temporary solutions; the growing aviation community needed permanent airports at which pilots could be trained and could practice, new aircraft mechanics could learn their trade, and tinkerers could experiment with the untested machines they had built. In the years after 1910, a sizable percentage of the airplanes that sputtered across America's skies were homemade, a phenomenon the Wrights' patent lawyers were helpless to stop.

It is not entirely certain when Chicago's first flying field came into existence, although Cicero Field was certainly its first full-service public airport. Carl S. Bates used a golf course in Washington Park in December 1908 to test his first airplane with a series of short hops. Later that month, he took the machine to White City Amusement Park at 63rd Street and South Park Avenue, where Joseph Beifeld, the principal investor in White City, had allowed balloonists to use the site even before it opened to the public in 1905. Beifeld paid to have ground leveled for a landing strip to allow Bates to test his machine. That aerodrome was where Wild, Scott, Bates, and Harroun got their start in flying heavier-than-air machines.[2]

By 1910, a small flying field was in operation at 65th Street and Major Avenue in the Clearing Industrial District just south of where Midway Airport now stands, and in April 1911 the Chicago School of Aviation started in business at 118th and Morgan streets in the West Pullman neighborhood not far from Lake Calumet. It later moved to Hawthorne Race Track in Cicero, but nothing much was heard of the operation thereafter.

The aerodrome at 65th and Major was in operation long enough to produce several aviators who later gained national recognition. Although there never were more than a handful of planes stationed on the field—one of them was the Curtiss machine owned by Plew—Benjamin B. Lipsner, the man who later organized the U.S. Air Mail Service, and famed pilot Rudolph W. (Shorty) Schroeder began their aviation careers there. It was also the field used by Otto Brodie, Chicago's first professional pilot. Brodie, a native of Wisconsin who had been hired by Plew as a demonstration driver for White automobiles, was sent by Plew to the Curtiss factory in Hammondsport, New York, in late 1909 to learn to fly after the auto dealer obtained the Curtiss airplane franchise in Chicago. Brodie then became the demonstration pilot for Plew's single plane; Schroeder was his mechanic.[3]

Chicago's first two airports worthy of that name were both Aero Club projects. With Harold McCormick's backing, in 1911 the club developed in west-suburban Cicero what was for a time one of the finest airports in the world. When McCormick lost interest in aviation and sold off Cicero Field for development, Pop Dickinson stepped in and financed Ashburn Field on what was then the remote Southwest Side of Chicago. For sport flying it was every bit as good as Cicero Field, although it proved to have limitations that proscribed its use as a commercial airport.[4]

Aviation was an entirely private business in the years before World War I. Federal, state, and local governments in the United States rarely had much to say about

Municipal Airport was built beginning in 1926 as an all-weather air mail facility with cinder runways in a relatively undeveloped area of Chicago's Southwest Side. The airport didn't have an appreciable number of flights for two years.

the aerial machines and the people who flew them, except when cities like Chicago banned aircraft from flying over their downtown areas. The Aero Club airports and other, smaller flying fields operated by private individuals around the metropolitan area served the small but growing aviation community until World War I forced the federal government to build air fields for the war effort. Chicago did not get involved in the airport business until the 1920s, when the city realized that for competitive reasons it would need an airport to handle the fledgling air mail business.

Cicero Field

The impetus for the development of the metropolitan area's first full-service public airport was the 1911 air show that the Aero Club was organizing. Club officials wanted a place where pilots could practice for the upcoming show, aviation enthusiasts could gather, and the club could con-

duct its activities. The Aero Club's biggest legacy to Chicago was Cicero Field, the place where many of the first generation of Chicago aviators learned their trade.

For a time the Aero Club claimed that Cicero Field was the busiest airport in the world—a title that eventually would be inherited by Municipal Airport, as Midway was originally called, and later by O'Hare International Airport. Between early March and October 19 of 1912, its second full year of operation, a total of 2,265 flights were made at Cicero Field, contrasted to 431,400 flights in 1959 at Midway, its busiest year in the propeller era, and 908,977 flights at O'Hare in the year 2000.[5]

For the three years of its existence, Cicero Field was one of the most complete flying facilities in the world. It was the site of Aero Club activities, various aeronautical manufacturing operations, flying schools, and periodic air shows that attracted as many as forty thousand spectators. It had its own station on the Metropolitan West

The earliest air mail pilots navigated strictly by sight, often flying above railroad tracks to keep on course. A beacon system was set up in the 1920s for night flying, and by the late 1920s, radio navigation stations were developed. These had the advantage of enabling pilots to fly when inclement weather obscured the beacons. This radio navigation station opened in Chicago in October 1929.

Side Elevated Railroad's Douglas Park line, and, as club members liked to boast, ample space for parking cars.[6]

It is not certain exactly when McCormick suggested that the 180 acres of vacant land he owned in Cicero could be used as an Aero Club airport, but with the 1911 air show scheduled for Grant Park well into the planning stages, the club officials on June 9 announced their intention to develop the airport on the McCormick land between 16th and 22nd Streets and 48th and 52nd Avenues.[7] The club's plan was to level the site for a single grass runway seven hundred feet wide and fifteen hundred feet long, although as a practical matter planes could take off and land in almost any direction. The airport was little more than an open field until the 1911 air show closed and the hangars and stands that had been erected in Grant Park were moved there, giving the new aerodrome sufficient facilities to handle about 250

planes. Equipment from the air show that couldn't be used at Cicero Field was sold.[8]

Although McCormick slipped out to Cicero in the early morning hours on July 2, 1911, to test fly his ill-fated umbrella plane, the airport did not officially open until July 4, with a balloon ascension and some exhibition flights by Dan Kreamer, H. W. Powers, Otto W. Brodie, and Allan Loughead. By then there were fifteen planes permanently stationed there.

A week later, on July 13, Kreamer became the Chicago area's first victim of a fatal airplane crash: he piled up his machine while trying to qualify for a pilot's license issued by the Aero Club. He had put the Curtiss biplane, owned by Plew, into a sharp turn at one hundred feet and spun into the ground at 7:18 P.M. He was rushed to St. Anthony de Padua Hospital, where he died about an hour and a half later, leaving a widow and two children. The crash, coming less than a month before the scheduled start of the 1911 air show, received front page treatment in all the Chicago newspapers the next day.[9]

An immediate result of the fatality was that the Aero Club began requiring legal waivers of all flyers who wanted to use the field; Dickinson signed his August 26, 1911. Despite the mishap, the airport remained a beehive of activity for the next month as pilots and planes arrived to practice for the upcoming air show. There was also a fair amount of practicing by amateurs and people learning to fly. For example, Harold (Kiddy) Karr, then a fifteen-year-old Crane Technical High School student but later the nation's first licensed naval aviator, began his aviation training in a glider that was towed into the air behind an automobile.[10]

After the air show, a field captain was hired to run the place through the end of the flying season on November 14. In 1912, its second season of operation, pilot Andrew Drew was hired as airport manager at forty dollars per week.[11] The field reopened in March 1912 when Max Lillie started his flying school there, and traffic increased daily, although the official public opening was not until May 30. A week before that official opening the field reported its busiest day to that time, with twenty-seven flights by pilots Lillie, Farnum Fish, DeLloyd Thompson, and Art (Smash Up) Smith. Lillie was well enough known that he attracted prospective pilots from across the nation, Katherine Stinson among them, and the school became so busy that by mid-1913 Lillie was forced to hire instructors to keep pace with the demand for flying lessons. However, the school did not survive Lillie's death during an exhibition in Galesburg, Illinois, in September 1913.[12]

The Aero Club liked to stage aerial extravaganzas to open the airport each season, and in 1912 it solicited the Curtiss Aeroplane Company's flying team for a four-day show on the Decoration Day weekend May 30–June 2. The team included Julia Clark, Horace Kearney, Farnum Fish, and Motohishi Kondo and was

guaranteed half the paid admissions—55 percent of the gate if the famous Lincoln Beachey performed. Flying exhibitions were barely four years old in the United States, and the stars were already commanding top dollar.[13]

The 1912 Air Shows

The hoopla of opening day at the airport was dampened somewhat by news of Wilbur Wright's death from typhoid fever in Dayton, but not enough to cancel activities planned by the rival Curtiss team. At the time of Wilbur's death, the Aero Club was embroiled in another patent controversy with Orville Wright over the use of airplanes at a succession of aerial extravaganzas planned for making Chicago the world's aviation capital for one month in September 1912, with international air meets intended to eclipse the 1911 show. The brothers, who had begun to win patent infringement suits against their rivals, had signed an agreement with the Aero Club of America on April 29, 1912, to get 30 percent of the winnings of all U.S. pilots at events sanctioned by that organization. The Wrights also wanted a 30 percent deposit posted in a New York bank by August 1, 1912, in return for allowing Chicago's international air meet to proceed the following month.[14] That agreement caused McCormick to again complain about the Wrights' tactics. On August 3, 1912, Orville Wright told Norman Prince, an Aero Club official who had traveled to Dayton to meet with him, that the Wright Company also might try to interfere with the Gordon Bennett race in Chicago because it was being held in conjunction with the air meet.[15]

The revelation caused another Aero Club member to complain to McCormick, "Judging from the above it looks to me as if first: that Orville Wright believes they have an unassailable patent on flying, and that the questions of construction detail and methods are of no consequence, or he is firmly of the opinion that there is only one way

Airplane racing was a lucrative way for pilots to augment their income in the 1920s and 1930s. Charles (Speed) Holman, at left, won $6,250 in prize money and a trophy, which he is shown accepting from cross-country race sponsor Russell E. Gardner on May 29, 1929, in St. Louis.

flying can be accomplished, and that is covered by the Wright Company patent."[16]

The dispute was finally resolved a week before the scheduled start of the international air meet when its Chicago organizers agreed to pay Wright's company $6,000 up front. In return, Orville Wright, who signed for his company, agreed not to sue the meet's organizers or participating pilots, American or foreign, for any patent infringements.[17] The settlement finally cleared the way for the Aero Club's ambitious plans for 1912. In addition to a sequel to the international air meet of the previous year, the club planned a "grand circuit" long-distance contest from Chicago to Kansas City, St. Louis, Indianapolis, Cincinnati, Dayton, and Detroit and hoped to stage a demonstration of the military capabilities of airplanes with a "Sham Aerial Attack by Night." The Aero Club also was negotiating for Chicago to be the host city for the Gordon Bennett Cup—an international speed race that had to be held over a large oval course. Cicero Field was deemed too small for the crowds expected at both the international air meet and the Gordon Bennett race, although it was suitable as the local airport for the grand circuit race.[18]

Gordon Bennett, the publisher of the *New York Herald,* had established automobile and yacht races years before and in 1906 added a balloon race. It was only a matter of time before airplanes became popular enough to have a race of their own, and in 1909 the first such Gordon Bennett Cup was held in Rheims, France, in conjunction with the international air meet there.[19] Because tradition dictated that the winning nation of one year got to host the race the next, American Charles T. Weyman's victory in the July 1, 1911, race in Eastchurch, England, flying a French-built Nieuport monoplane, meant the United States would host the race in 1912. The Aero Club of Illinois had applied to be the host city on July 8, 1911, slightly more than a week after Weyman's win.[20]

The Aero Club's plans for 1912 sounded almost too ambitious, and that turned out to be the case. The grand circuit race had to be cancelled after no pilots could be found to fly in it, the Gordon Bennett race was a disappointment, and the international air meet was not as spectacular as its predecessor had been in 1911. The grand circuit race was the first victim of reality. Soon after planning had started, McCormick, then president of the Aero Club, expressed doubt that any of the other cities involved would give the race adequate support, although his organization had pledged $25,000 in prizes. Stephens then suggested that the club had been pushing the envelope too far and that an 1,800-mile flight exceeded the capability of the vast majority of pilots; indeed, he contended, only four pilots in the nation had made any extended cross-country flights. Within a few weeks McCormick cancelled the grand circuit race, although he suggested a shorter race from Chicago to Dayton, Akron, and Detroit and back might be possible.[21]

The Gordon Bennett Race

The Aero Club was already mired in problems planning for the Bennett Cup. The club had made its official bid for the race on March 18 to the Aero Club of America, and within a week it was looking for a site. The Bennett Cup was run somewhat like the Indianapolis 500 auto race: the participants circled the racecourse until they reached the required number of laps, although in the aerial race the contestants were not all aloft simultaneously, and the pilot with the shortest measured flying time won. The club wanted a four-mile perimeter around which the planes could fly for thirty laps, or 120 miles, although the 1911 race in England had only been ninety-four miles.[22] At least two sites were being seriously considered—the north-suburban Skokie Valley area near Northfield, and the Clearing Industrial District, west of Cicero Avenue at approximately 71st Street on Chicago's Southwest Side. The Clearing site, which already had a small flying field, was finally selected because it would cost $5,000 less to lease and prepare.[23]

That was the easy part of the preparation. Selecting an airplane in which to compete against the favored French team turned out to be a nightmare as well as a commentary on the technical status of aviation nearly a decade after the Wrights first flew. By 1912, the French were once again the world's dominant aviators, having regained the status they had held in the ballooning era. The flying machine was invented in America, and a number of aviation historians blame America's aeronautical backwardness in the second decade of flight on the secrecy of the Wrights and the patent wars they carried on against other American aviators. The brothers' insistence on a percentage of the revenues of every American airplane flown commercially acted as a damper on aeronautical innovation in the United States, a particularly unfortunate situation because after 1910 the Wrights themselves ceased to be a significant factor in technological innovation.[24]

In any event, the Wright Flyer the Aero Club of Illinois considered buying in February 1912 for $5,000 was a considerable improvement over the Flyer No. 3 built in

1905. It now had landing wheels instead of skids and a more powerful engine, and the elevators had been moved from the front of the plane to the now traditional location on the tail. Despite the improvements, it was still a truss-winged biplane capable of speeds of only about fifty miles an hour. During the Bennett race, when Max Lillie took off on an exhibition flight in a Wright biplane and made three laps of the course at an altitude of 150 feet, he was lapped several times on each circuit by the two French pilots then in the air. Henry Woodhouse, who covered the event for *Flying,* a monthly bulletin published by the Aero Club of America, described Lillie's Wright Flyer as "so slow in comparison it seemed to be standing still."[25]

The new and formidable French racer of the time was a sleek, enclosed-fuselage monoplane called the Deperdussin monocoque. It was the first aircraft built specifically for high-speed flying. It was designed in early 1912 by Louis Bechereau (later designer of the famous SPAD VII pursuit plane used in World War I) for Armand Deperdussin's aircraft company, and early tests indicated it was capable of speeds in excess of one hundred miles an hour. The first major test of the Deperdussin was to be the Gordon Bennett race in Chicago, scheduled for later that year.[26]

Aero Club officials, including Dickinson, who headed the committee, knew there was no existing American airplane that could compete with the Deperdussin and decided to have one designed. Slightly more than four months before the scheduled race the club published an announcement of a design contest. The specifications broke with American tradition by stipulating that a monoplane was preferred. It had to be capable of flying 115 miles an hour.[27]

Norman Prince submitted the winning design for a sleek Curtiss-Burgess airframe powered by a 160-horsepower French Gnome engine. The $17,500 plane, which was financed largely from Dickinson's own pocket after he was unable to find other investors, was optimistically named the *American Defender.* The engine was slow in arriving from France, and when the assembled plane was delivered to Chicago a week before the scheduled start of the race, it was still untested. There was a squabble over who would fly the plane, then Stephens scratched it from the lineup for safety reasons.[28]

A major factor in Stephens's decision was the lack of a qualified pilot. Earle Ovington, one of the nation's best airmen, diplomatically answered an Aero Club inquiry by stating that he had given up flying because of his wife and child. He suggested that Lincoln Beachey was one of the few American pilots capable of handling a monoplane, but Beachey's status was uncertain because he had been suspended by the Aero Club of America for flying in an unauthorized meet. Ultimately, Dickinson picked Norman Prince to fly the *American Defender,* but the Aero Club of America selected a different team that included Glenn Martin, Paul Peck, and DeLloyd Thompson.[29]

The dispute was made moot when the plane was scratched. It never flew, although Dickinson put it on display for a few days at Cicero Field before moving it to a storage lot behind his seed company offices at 35th Street and California Avenue. There the *American Defender* rotted away amid junked cars.[30]

Because the British had declined to enter the race earlier, the *American Defender*'s withdrawal left the three French entries unopposed, and the crowds were modest. Only a few hundred persons, mainly aviators and newsmen, were on hand at 9:38 A.M. September 9 when Jules Vedrines took off in his 140-horsepower, Gnome-powered Deperdussin. He completed his thirty laps at an altitude of only sixty feet in one hour, ten minutes, and 56.85 seconds for an average speed of 105.5 miles an hour. By way of contrast, the New York Central Railroad's No. 999 steam locomotive, now on display in Chicago's Museum of Science and Industry, set a world speed record of

Early airplane factories, like the Laird plant at Ashburn Field shown in this 1931 photo, were relatively primitive operations. Laird's facility was essentially a carpentry shop for building the airframes and a machine shop for fabricating the mechanical components. The engines were manufactured elsewhere.

112.5 miles an hour in 1893 near Batavia, New York, and in 1919 Ralph De Palma set a land-speed record of 149.8 miles an hour in a gasoline-powered Packard motor car.[31]

The other two French pilots, Maurice Prevost in a Deperdussin and Andre Frey in a Hanriot (Nieuport), both aircraft with 100-horsepower Gnome engines, waited until the winds died after 4:00 P.M., by which time the crowd had grown to five thousand persons. By staying close to the ground at only forty feet and making tight turns at the pylons, Prevost was able to lap Frey twice, but was three minutes slower than Vedrines for the thirty-lap race.[32]

The 1912 International Meet

The international aviation meet that began a few days later in Grant Park was not as spectacular as the 1911 extravaganza and had a decidedly more local flavor. Possibly because Cicero Field had been pumping out graduates from its flight schools, but more probably because in 1912 the

Aero Club offered prizes of less than a third of what it had paid the previous year, sixteen of the forty-one registered pilots in the show were from Chicago. Still, the money was sufficient to attract the incomparable Lincoln Beachey, who once again dazzled the crowd by playing leap frog over locomotives on the adjacent Illinois Central Railroad, spiraling three thousand feet over the lake, and touching his wheels to another aircraft while both were flying. The final day of the meet he flew in a dress as "Mademoiselle Levaseur."[33]

Although the ten-day meet attracted crowds estimated at 100,000, somewhat smaller than those of the previous year, it was marred by accidents, high winds that caused flying to be suspended at least one day, and bickering between pilots and officials of the Aero Club. The wind caused most of the aviators to ground their planes on September 15 and the *Chicago Tribune* to ominously warn of the dangers of flying, citing statistics that there had been 182 deaths in aviation mishaps in

Curtiss-Wright Airport in Glenview was a busy but remote place in 1931. It was later acquired by the navy as a training base for pilots. (Illinois State Historical Library)

the period between 1890 and 1912.[34]

Howard Gill, a pilot from Baltimore, died on September 14 in a midair collision with George Mestache of Belgium while practicing at Cicero Field— Chicago's first dual-aircraft fatality. Six days later, at a coroner's inquest, Mestache claimed he had not wanted to fly because of the impending darkness but had been forced to by meet officials because "they had crowds out there and we must give them something for their money." He said he had consented to fly only if his would be the only machine in the air at the time.[35]

Albert J. Engel of Cleveland had to be rescued from his Wright hydroplane twice

on the same day, September 18: the first time when his engine failed during a take-off in choppy water off Clarendon Beach, and the second time when he became lost in a fog while flying to Grant Park and ran out of fuel four miles offshore. The next day Russian pilot Ignace Semeniouk was rescued from the lake after his radiator burst and he crashed.[36]

On September 20, the pilots threatened to strike if they weren't paid over-time for extra flights that meet officials had scheduled. Although that dispute was resolved, the Aero Club suffered another money-losing year despite attempts to trim its expenses by canceling competitions and reducing the purse at the surviving events. The club lost $3,579 in 1912 despite revenues of $84,546, an improvement over the $10,980 lost in 1911 on the international aviation meet alone (on revenues of $145,635). However, the losses both years clearly indicated that sport aviation was not going to be a profit-making proposition and that the fledgling industry could not survive without wealthy patrons or revenue from some commercial enterprise.[37] The club bowed to the inevitable in early 1913, announcing that it was putting its finances on a sounder basis and that in the future it would concentrate less on exhibitions and more on scientific and engineering development.

* * * *

One of the least publicized but most successful programs the Aero Club conducted, and one that survived its 1913 cutbacks, was the model-airplane club created to interest boys in flying. William B. Stout claimed the idea as his, based on a club he belonged to in St. Paul, Minnesota, before coming to Chicago. On January 23, 1912, The Aero Club of Illinois had mailed out letters to several high schools inviting teachers to attend an organizational meeting. The idea was to get students interested in aviation by having them build flying models, for the most part powered by wound rubber bands. Matty Laird credited the Chicago model club for getting him started in aviation.[38]

In 1915, Stout carried the idea to Detroit. At a meeting of the Detroit Society of Automotive Engineers in the Ponchartrain Hotel, he had four young Chicago modelers demonstrate their craft. "The youngsters flew their models from the speaker's table at the end of the room out over the audience and, with twisted rubber triggers, dropped paper 'bombs' on the crowd. The last model, a flying boat with floats, took off from a big meat platter full of water on the speakers table, and flew the length of the room."[39]

Seaplanes

The seaplane model demonstration was indicative of what was happening back in Chicago. If the Aero Club there couldn't afford to compete in the international air show business, it could at least become the world seaplane capital. The club's interest in flying boats happened to coincide with a similar shift in interest of its principal patron, Harold F. McCormick, who bought his first seaplane in the spring of 1913.[40]

At about the same time the Aero Club announced its change in direction for 1913, the magazine *Aero and Hydro* announced it would cosponsor with the club a seaplane contest in Chicago off Grant Park on July 5–7. A similar meet had been held on September 17–21, 1912, in conjunction with the international aviation meet, but the $1,000 prize had gone unclaimed. The 1913 seaplane meet was to have two parts—a race or "efficiency contest" over a closed course off Grant Park, followed by a long-distance race to Detroit.[41]

The club also considered establishing a hydroplane base on the North Side of Chicago to complement Cicero Field. The proposed Clarendon Beach hydroaerodrome, as it was called, was to include a clubhouse with "bungalows for resident aeroyachtsmen and members of the club" and some hangars moved from Cicero Field. There is no record that any of the structures were ever built.[42]

The so-called hydroaeroplane efficiency contest was to be something of a cross between the Gordon Bennett Cup and the popular yacht races on Lake Michigan. Contestants were required to make circuits of a two-mile course around the south breakwater at Chicago Harbor for an elapsed distance of ten miles, alternately taking off and landing at predetermined points. Anyone blowing a turn had to go back and successfully negotiate it. The judges were to communicate with pilots by means of signal flags—red indicating a foul, white indicating danger, and white with a red center indicating one lap to go. The long-distance race was similar to the auto reliability or endurance tours popular at the time: the first plane to get to Detroit via a circuitous route around Michigan's lower peninsula would win.[43]

The two contests drew some of the best seaplane pilots in the nation—Anthony Jannus in his Benoist, DeLloyd Thompson in a Walce, and Glenn L. Martin in his own plane. Logan A. (Jack) Vilas, a local pilot who had only recently learned to fly, also entered. Vilas, a friend and neighbor of Mc-Cormick, had bought a flying boat about the same time as McCormick and had gone to Curtiss's Hammondsport, New York, school to learn how to fly it. He then flew the plane back to Chicago, becoming the first aviator to fly across Lake Michigan.[44]

Vilas and a passenger, a Benton Harbor hotel manager along for the ride, took off from St. Joseph, Michigan, on July 1, 1913, and flew the sixty-four miles to Chicago in one hour and thirty-four minutes. For its time it was quite a feat, although the famed French flyer Roland Garros had flown 145 miles over water between Tunis and Sicily six months earlier, on December 18, 1912, and Farnum Fish had flown over Lake Michigan for ninety miles between Chicago and Milwaukee on May 25, 1912, but never out of sight of land.[45]

Vilas, who had only five hours of flying experience when he made his lake crossing, described the flight as "routine" to a newspaper reporter after landing off Grant Park. Thirty-five years later he recalled in an interview that several times he had lost sight of the shore because of the mist over Lake Michigan and was forced to navigate by watching the action of the wind against the water. He had an altimeter aboard but no compass. He had intended to fly the lake at about two thousand feet but eventually flew at five thousand feet because of the mist and updrafts. "Frankly I was scared. How did I know how that airplane would hold together up there in that thin air?"[46]

It was an auspicious start for his long and distinguished career as an aviation hobbyist and yachtsman. On June 7, 1914, Vilas conducted an air-sea rescue with his seaplane after another pilot, Anthony Stadleman, crashed into the lake off Clarendon Beach, and on June 22 he used his plane to show conservation officials near Trout Lake, Wisconsin, how airplanes could be used to spot forest fires. Later he headed the Civil Air Patrol in Illinois, and in 1942 he sponsored Willa Beatrice Brown, the first black person in the CAP. In 1962, United Air Lines named a Boeing 720 jetliner for Vilas to honor his contributions to aviation. He died on May 15, 1976, in Chicago.[47]

Although the long-distance contest was an impressive aviation event for its time, the hydroplane efficiency race that preceded it was a flop. On July 5, 1913, the flight trials for the lakefront efficiency race had to be postponed because of high winds, and two days later Glenn Martin, probably the most experienced seaplane pilot of the time, was involved in an accident in the lake off Van Buren Street. Martin had gotten his plane airborne to two hundred feet to test his steering apparatus, but he lost altitude and his forward pontoon clipped a motorboat wake and splintered. The plane turned a somersault and sank with Martin and his mechanic beneath it. Neither man was hurt, and Martin was able to not only salvage the seaplane but also fly it in the long-distance Great Lakes Race that began the next day.[48]

The first leg of the long-distance race—between Chicago and Michigan City—started poorly when only three of the seven planes entered were able to get airborne before a rainstorm and high winds put an end to any other attempts. The same storm forced Jannus into the lake off Gary, damaging his plane beyond repair. Walter Johnson saw the storm coming and landed early in Whiting, Indiana, to seek refuge. Only Beckwith Havens, carrying the owner of the Curtiss flying boat as a passenger, got to the intended Michigan City destination the first day.

Havens got into trouble on the second day, July 9, when he mistook South Holland, Michigan, for his intended destination of Macatawa Harbor and landed thirty miles short of where he was supposed to be. Then he had trouble getting his engine to full power for take off. While he dawdled, Roy M. Francis, who had been delayed a day by the storm in Chicago, flew into sight. Storms grounded the race on the third day, July 10, and only Glenn Martin got airborne July 11. Martin made the 152 miles to Macatawa in less than four hours, and after stopping for lunch, he nearly caught the other two aircraft near Pentwater, Michigan, before a floating log damaged a propeller and put him out of the race. High winds kept the surviving three planes on the ground on July 12 and 13, then Havens and his passenger got underway again the following day and made Detroit at 3:30 P.M. on July 18 to win the race. The 886-mile flight had taken a little more than ten days, but total flying time was about fifteen and a half hours—an average speed in the vicinity of sixty miles an hour.[49]

The Waning Aerial Spectacles

A few days after the long-distance race was completed, the Aero Club announced it would stage even more events the next year, but except for an appearance by Lincoln Beachey before crowds estimated at one hundred thousand in Grant Park on May 16–18, 1914, they didn't come to pass.[50] It was Beachey's last appearance in Chicago; his antics finally caught up with him on March 14, 1915, when he crashed into San Francisco Bay while performing before a crowd of fifty thousand and was killed.

The Aero Club's last big air show in Grant Park was held on March 9, 1915, when a boyish-looking Art (Smash Up) Smith from Fort Wayne, Indiana, substituted for Beachey and entertained the large crowd with thirty-two continuous loop-the-loops. He almost became a casualty during a night demonstration when one of the skyrockets attached to his wings exploded and burned a hole in a wing. "Smith shot up from Grant Park with a whirl and flash of light that made his machine look like a fireworks factory."[51]

By the end of 1913 Chicago was beginning its decline as a major international aviation center. The Aero Club was finding it increasingly difficult to finance the aerial spectacles, its principal patron was losing interest in the sport, and some of its best flyers had died in crashes or moved away. War clouds were gathering over Europe.

Harold F. McCormick's interest in aviation began to wane that autumn. In September he began to negotiate the sale of the land under Cicero Field. Although he remained on the Aero Club board as a director in 1914, the field's sale was completed early that year. James Stephens wrote the Grant Land Association, which was developing the property, to ask if the Aero Club could continue to use it as an airport. The association replied that it had every intention to go ahead with the development and would give the club twenty days notice before it had to clear out.[52]

Accidents had already claimed some of the mainstays at Cicero, and others had left Chicago to pursue aviation careers elsewhere. Andrew Drew was killed on June 12, 1913, when he crashed his well-known plane, the *VinFiz*, while performing in Lima, Ohio, and Lillie died three months later in a crash at Galesburg, Illinois. Stout, Vought, and Martin had left Chicago to design and build airplanes in other cities. When World War I began in Europe in 1914, the great pilots of Britain, France, and Germany enlisted in those nations' fledgling air corps rather than continuing their barnstorming in the United States. Many of the better American pilots also went to Europe to fight even before the United States became involved in 1917.

Cicero Field continued in existence for another two seasons. The airport's last major event was the Aero Club show on July 18, 1915, when several thousand spectators showed up to watch, among other

The continuous availability of good airports after 1911 enabled Chicago boosters to promote the city as an aero-nautical center.

CHICAGO
the
AERONAUTICAL
CENTER

feats, Katherine Stinson loop-the-loop. Her airplane, built in Elmer Partridge and Henry Keller's aircraft factory at Cicero, was powered by an engine salvaged from Beachey's wrecked plane and bought from his estate. The exodus from Cicero began shortly thereafter. In August of that year Partridge and Keller moved their factory and flight school to a new aerodrome at 87th Street and Pulaski Road. Matty Laird, another local plane builder, remained to work on his second airplane, his Anzani forty-five-horsepower machine called *Bone Shaker,* which he and Katherine Stinson would use for stunt flying for the next two years. On January 26, 1916, the Grant Land Association donated all the hangars and equipment at Cicero Field to the Aero

Club with the proviso that the club remove them. Laird was the last to leave on April 16, when he flew his other airplane, *Baby Biplane,* to Partridge-Keller Airport.[53]

Because neither the city nor state nor federal government had much interest in aviation or airports at the time, and would not until the nation became embroiled in World War I, it was left to the Aero Club to find a replacement for Cicero. Dickinson, who succeeded McCormick as the Aero Club's principal patron, began looking for another airport site soon after it became obvious Cicero was doomed. Within a year, both the army and navy were looking for airfields at which to train pilots for the war.

The Changes that War Brought

Probably because balloons were used for aerial reconnaissance from the middle of the nineteenth century, the flying machine was considered a potential weapon of war even before its invention. Chanute in 1894 warned of that possibility: "It has been suggested that the first practical application of a successful flying machine would be to the art of war, and this is possibly true."[1]

The Wrights, soon after they perfected their machine, tried in 1905 to sell one to the U.S. Army as a weapon or reconnais-sance vehicle, and three years later Army Lieutenant Thomas E. Selfridge had the dubious distinction of becoming the first person to die in an airplane accident, when the plane in which he was riding crashed during a demonstration flight with Orville Wright at the controls. Even the Aero Club of Illinois, a group devoted to the sport of flying, began early in its existence to promote the military possibilities of the airplane. As early as 1911, during the international air show, the club held a bombing exhibition in which pilots

Dutchman Anthony Fokker built pursuit planes for the Germans during World War I. After the war he transferred his skills to civil aviation and built what is considered the first successful passenger-carrying aircraft, which was much copied by other builders. The Fokker F-10 Tri-Motor is shown during its 1928 visit to Municipal Airport. (Illinois State Historical Library)

David Behncke, shown in the cockpit of a Dickinson airline plane in 1926, was the World War I pilot who successively operated Checkerboard Field, flew as an air mail pilot, and founded the Air Line Pilots Association.

tried to hit the form of a battleship marked on the ground in Grant Park with plaster balls filled with chalk or flour. The club intensified its lobbying as the war approached.[2]

When war finally came, the airplane was the new weapon in the arsenal, first as a reconnaissance vehicle, and somewhat later as a bomber. But the most famous airplanes of World War I were the pursuit planes, the fighters with names like SPAD, Fokker, and Sopwith, that were designed solely to destroy other airplanes. They were flown by daring young men like Roland Garros of France, Oswald Boelcke and Manfred von Richthofen of Germany, and Eddie Ricken-

backer of the United States, who became national heroes. Probably more important to commercial aviation in the long run was the development during the war of seaplanes and bombers capable of carrying of carrying reasonable payloads.

The greatest boon to commercial aviation once the hostilities ended were the thousands of airplanes that had been built for the war and quickly became cheap surplus property that the government sold off afterward, and the thousands of pilots and mechanics who had been trained from scratch. By late 1918, the aviation industry, which probably didn't have more than 1,000 employees prior to the war, employed more than 200,000 people. Because Chicago's small aircraft-building industry was largely devoted to sport flying and the U.S. military insisted on mass production of a few types of aircraft, the bulk of the wartime production was at the Wright factory in Dayton; the Curtiss plant in Buffalo; the Fisher Body facility in Detroit; and Standard Aero in New York. The unintended effect was to render Chicago a backwater for aircraft manufacture after the war ended.[3]

After the armistice, cheap warplanes and newly trained pilots were available for all sorts of commercial enterprises. The sudden surplus of planes and pilots was far greater than the sport and barnstorming market that had been Chicago's prewar staple could bear. It only remained for a patron with sufficient resources to find a market for the surplus fleet: that was the government and the U.S. Post Office Department.[4]

The war changed aviation permanently. The government assumed a greater and greater role in aviation, taking over systems like safety regulation, which had previously been handled by the flying clubs, and increasingly projects such as the building of airports. Thus commercial aviation and government almost from the start developed a symbiotic relationship. That reduced the role of private aviation organizations like the Aero Club of Illinois to that of booster groups and lobbyists for what became known as "general aviation"—the sport, corporate, and private-flying segments of the industry.

In the years immediately before World War I, the voices of the aviation enthusiasts in the Aero Club were among the few raised in favor of military aviation in an otherwise apathetic nation. In 1912, the club began lobbying Washington in favor of the military aviation bill then before Congress. Two years later the Aero Club, by then preoccupied with the hydroplane fad, suggested that the navy build a seaplane base in Chicago, and shortly thereafter the club wrote army officials in Washington to in-

quire about what would be required of civil aviation in the event of war. The club also appointed a technical committee on war comprising Lee Hammond, Harold McCormick, James Plew, and E. Percy Noel and took an inventory of available aircraft in the Chicago area. This was two months before the assassination of Austrian archduke Ferdinand in Sarajevo by a Serbian nationalist precipitated hostilities in Europe. As the war in Europe progressed, the Aero Club continued beating the drum for military aviation, suggesting that hydroplane patrols could have saved the ocean liner *Lusitania* sunk by a German submarine off the Irish coast in 1915.[5]

Many of the Aero Club leaders lent their names in 1915 to an organization called the National Aeroplane Fund, which lobbied for increased military spending on aviation, warning that the U.S. Army and Navy combined had at the time fewer than twenty aircraft available for war and little experience handling them, while Great Britain had 2,500 aircraft. The new organization urged a national subscription drive, similar to what France and Germany had held in 1912 and 1913, to raise money to buy planes.[6]

As the United States was drawn toward war, the Aero Club intensified its activities on behalf of military and naval aviation. It conducted a subscription drive to raise $20,000 for improvements to the new Ashburn Field to make it capable of handling a reserve aviation squadron. By September of that year, the Army Signal Corps affirmed the club's proposal for a "United States Central Aviation Reserve" and agreed to open a training center at Ashburn. By then, a few Chicago aviators were already in Europe flying for the allies as volunteers.[7]

The First of the Aces

The ace of the group was Norman Prince, a polo player and member of a prominent Boston family who was living and practicing law in Chicago when the war broke out. Before he moved to Chicago, Norman had decided to take up aviation against the wishes of his father, Frederick H. Prince, chairman of the executive committee of the board of Armour and Company, the Chicago meat packer. Under an assumed name, George Mannor, he went from Boston to Atlanta to obtain a pilot's license. His father promptly shipped him to a Chicago law firm in 1912, but he yearned to fly and quickly became involved in Aero Club activities. Later that year, Prince submitted the winning design for the *American Defender,* the plane that was built too late for the 1912 Gordon Bennett race, and in 1913 he showed up in Aero Club records as a member of the organization's legal committee.[8]

Soon after the war began, Prince and his brother, Frederick, volunteered their services as aviators to the French. Norman was one of the organizers of the famous *Escadrille Americaine,* later known as the Lafayette Escadrille. In the war, he flew with such skill that he became the first ace from the Chicago area, shooting down five German planes to win the designation and being shot down once. The French were sufficiently impressed with his combat record to promote him from sergeant to lieutenant and award him the Legion of Honor.

Perhaps his best-known adventure occurred in August 1916, when he inadvertently landed next to a German trench and was captured. Two German infantry officers then forced him at pistol point to fly a reconnaissance flight over French lines. He escaped when he noticed that neither German had fastened his seat belt; he promptly looped the loop, causing his passengers to fall to their deaths. Two months later, on October 6, he barely escaped death in a dogfight when a German pilot shot away part of a wing and some of the supporting wires on his airplane. Prince nursed the plane back to friendly lines.

Soon thereafter, he was detailed with his squadron to protect a French night flight of bombers in a raid against an arms factory in Oberndorf, Germany. He survived a dogfight against German planes attempting to defend the factory, but was wounded by anti-aircraft fire from the ground. Prince flew back to the French aerodrome, but he was severely injured when he crashed while attempting to land. He died a week later on October 15, 1916, in a hospital in Alsace—the third American aviator killed in the war.[9]

Despite the best efforts of aviation clubs, when World War I finally became impossible for the United States to ignore, the nation was characteristically unprepared and without an air force worthy of the name. If the European powers can be excused for their failure to recognize fully at the onset of hostilities the potential of the flying machine in war, the United States cannot; by the time Congress declared war on April 6, 1917, aviation had become an integral part of the conflict in Europe.

A few months after Congress acted, the United States agreed to a French request to build and equip an air force with 4,500 planes, 5,000 pilots, and 50,000 mechanics. At the time, America owned only about 100 military airplanes, and it was estimated that there were no more than 1,000 skilled aviators, civilian and military, in the country. Chicago's role in the conflict had begun slightly more than five months before Congress declared war, when on October 28, 1916, five military pilots were assigned to a makeshift air base at Ashburn Field and an air show was staged by the Aero Club to drum up enthusiasm.[10]

John T. McCutcheon, the cartoonist and aviation promoter, had enlisted in the army air service a few days before. He took his first flying lesson at Ashburn in a military biplane while a crowd of five hundred, some of whom had taken a Wabash Railroad train from the Loop, watched. McCutcheon, who covered World War I from both the German and French sides of the line, years later described himself as "a

A last vestige of the U.S. Air Mail Service, the federal agency that predated the commercial airlines, is its name carved above the door of a maintenance building that is now part of Hines Veterans Administration Hospital in Maywood. The building originally served as a mail center for Maywood Airport.

fellow who couldn't back a car out of a garage—let alone tune in correctly on a radio football game," and said he had never had any temptation to learn to fly.[11]

The installation at Ashburn Field was primitive even by 1916 standards: the four army aircraft had tents for hangars, and the five Signal Corps aviators, commanded by Captain Joseph C. Morrow, lived in smaller tents. Military pilots were so scarce that the installation's three principal flight instructors were civilians—Theodore Mac-Caulay, A. Livingstone Allen, and J. D. Hill. Allen was the only veteran of aerial combat in the group. Early in 1916 he had enlisted in the British Royal Flying Corps and spent three weeks directing artillery fire from an airplane. He returned to the United States that year to teach flying.[12]

The Ashburn military installation was a short-lived; it fell victim to Chicago's weather. The Aero Club traditionally closed its airports between November and March because of the weather, and the army, finding it difficult to train pilots in Chicago during the cold months, packed its equipment onto a train and moved it to Memphis in early February 1917. All of the

civilian flight instructors, by then including Matty Laird and Elmer Partridge, moved as well.[13]

The Aero Club simply geared up a campaign to have the installation replaced, and on April 16, ten days after the United States declared war on Germany, the War Department decided that it would have to have an installation near Chicago after all. The government planned to ship as many as forty-eight Curtiss airplanes to Chicago to train up to seventy-five pilots, and the Aero Club lobbied to have Ashburn Field designated as the site of the facility.[14]

Chanute Field

The War Department was at first agreeable and attempted to buy additional land adjacent to Ashburn before discovering that the price was too high. That led to the decision to buy cheaper farmland somewhere outside the Chicago area. In May, the University of Illinois at Champaign-Urbana had been designated as one of six ground schools to give flight-preparatory training to potential pilots, and later that month the Signal Corps picked as the site

The largest collection of military aircraft near Chicago is at the Octave Chanute Aerospace Museum in Rantoul, Illinois. The museum occupies a hangar and taxiway of the former Chanute Air Force Base.

of the new base a mile-square tract of flat farmland alongside the Illinois Central Railroad main line near Rantoul, Illinois, just north of Champaign and about 110 miles south of Chicago. The War Department concurred in the selection on May 21 and negotiated a construction contract the next day.

The federal government had developed its air arm at a leisurely pace prior to hostilities, but the Rantoul project—establishing one of the twenty-seven military flying schools the War Department opened during World War I—was accomplished with celerity. Local business and civic groups provided options on the land, a common practice during wartime for base-construction projects, and Washington spent $1 million to develop the installation and equip it with fifty-nine buildings, including twelve hangars. The base was

named Chanute Field in honor of Chicago's aviation pioneer.[15]

The newly established 4th Aviation School Squadron began its work at Ashburn Field while construction continued on the new base. The transfer of the squadron to Rantoul on July 16 was something of an air show in itself—the largest movement of men and material by air attempted in the United States up to that time. Lieutenant W. W. Spain and civilian instructor E. A. Johnson flew to Rantoul from Ashburn on July 3 to plot the course the air fleet would take. Before the official opening of Chanute Field on July 16, twenty-two military planes, each carrying a passenger, took off at one-minute intervals from Ashburn and flew to Rantoul. The pilot of the twenty-third plane, Fred A. Hoover, got lost and finally landed in St. Joseph, Michigan, which was no mean feat considering that all each pilot had to do was follow the airplane in front of him or the Illinois Central Railroad tracks due south from Chicago to Rantoul.[16]

Training of prospective pilots began the next day, and the first class of twenty-four pilots was graduated in September. Within three months, trained squadrons of 150 men each were transferred east for assignment in Europe. Basic pilot training in those days typically took six to eight weeks, depending on the availability of equipment and instructors, the weather, and the rate of progress of the cadets, as the students were called. Advanced training included armament; aerial gunnery; signals, for there were no aircraft radios in those days; and aerial tactics. During the sixteen months of war remaining after the school's opening, thousands of military aviators got their training there. Many of them were among the 2,644 graduates of the University of Illinois military aviation school, and others were from the reserve officer training programs. Flying operations at the base, though not aircraft maintenance, were shut down between mid-December and February because of winter weather, and much of the staff was transferred to southern bases.[17]

During demobilization following the war, Chanute Field was almost closed, but the Illinois congressional delegation managed to keep it open and to find money for the construction of nine steel hangars in 1922. The airfield was a major training base during World War II, but it was permanently closed and its land sold in 1993 following the end of the Cold War.[18]

Reed Landis

Despite the rushed training of the aviators, the system at Chanute produced a number of successful combat pilots, including several aces who shot down five or more enemy aircraft. One, Reed G. Landis, who later commanded aviation units in World War II and the Korean War, was the nation's sixth-leading ace of the war with twelve enemy aircraft shot down. Other Chicago aces include William P. Erwin, with nine aircraft; Frank K. Hays, with six; and John J. Seerley, Duerson (Dewey) Knight, Lawrence K. Callahan, and Victor Strahm, each with five. Differing methods of assigning credit for enemy aircraft shot down have resulted in conflicting totals for many aviators in World War I. The confusion is compounded because many

The Curtiss JN-4 Jenny pictured here at Chanute Field was America's basic-training plane during World War I. After the war, surplus aircraft sold by the government were a common sight in the nation's skies. They carried mail, were used by stunt pilots and crop dusters, and appeared in exhibitions. (Octave Chanute Aerospace Museum)

American aviators served part of their war tour with British, French, or Italian units. The British system gave Landis twelve "kills," but he is credited with only ten by the American system. Other pilots had similar differences in scores.[19]

Reed Landis was the son of Kenesaw Mountain Landis, a federal judge and the commissioner of professional baseball after the Chicago Black Sox bribery scandal, in which Chicago White Sox players were accused of taking bribes to throw the 1919 World Series. Reed left home in 1916 at age nineteen to enlist in the First Illinois Cavalry and serve on the Mexican border. The following year the United States entered World War I, and Landis was accepted in the officers training program at Fort Sheridan, north of Chicago. From there he volunteered for the training programs at Champaign and Rantoul.

He was posted overseas in August 1917 for assignment to the British air service for additional training and went to the front in March 1918 with the 40th Squadron of the Royal Flying Corps. On his first day in combat the next month, he downed a German plane in a face-to-face shootout. Although his plane was heavily damaged, Landis managed to nurse it back to his base.[20]

Probably his most notable day of the war was August 8, 1918. While on patrol in the Douai sector, he became involved in a dogfight and shot down two enemy planes and a balloon in just twelve minutes. He had caught both planes by surprise, and he shot them down before they could return fire, then leisurely downed the reconnaissance balloon they were supposed to be protecting.

Somewhat later he almost lost his own life after a successful attack on a German reconnaissance plane. While Landis was pursuing the damaged aircraft downward to apply the coup de grâce, two ammunition drums in his plane rolled forward and jammed the rear rudder pedal bar, causing his aircraft to plunge uncontrollably until he was able to knock the drums loose using his signal pistol as a hammer. He was able to pull out of the dive with only two hundred feet to spare.

From March through September 15, 1918, when he was reassigned from the British forces to the newly formed U.S. 25th Aero Squadron, Landis shot down an additional five enemy planes and a balloon. He was later awarded the British Distinguished Flying Cross and American Distinguished Service Cross, albeit belatedly in 1934 because his service records had been lost. On February 7, 1919, Landis, by then a major, returned to Chicago and bashfully told reporters as he stepped off the train: "Really there is no story to tell. I just got them and that's all."[21]

After the war, Landis decided against a career in flying and went into the advertising business, although he continued to maintain an interest in aviation. He testified for the defense in the 1925 trial by court martial of General William (Billy) Mitchell, the nation's chief prophet of air power. Four years later he was appointed to a special Cook County coroner's jury investigating the deaths of four persons in a midair collision over suburban Northbrook.

Landis strongly criticized the practice, common at the time, of allowing the county sheriff, whose staff rarely had anyone with much aviation experience, to enforce federal and local air safety standards. On March 3, 1929, he wrote to Illinois governor Louis T. Emmerson urging the state to enforce air safety regulations strictly, despite a reluctance on the part of the state because it might impede the development of that industry. "With the enormous growth of aviation during the last year, however, it becomes necessary to have a set of ironclad rules governing the conduct of the industry," Landis wrote.[22]

Emmerson soon appointed him as a member of the newly formed Illinois Aerial Navigation Commission and, on August 31, 1931, as chairman of the Illinois Aeronautics Commission, an agency set up to regulate pilots and airports. In 1940, Landis was appointed regional vice president in Chicago for American Airlines, a post he held for only a year before taking a leave of absence to accept an appointment by New York mayor Fiorello La Guardia to organize the civil defense program being formed in anticipation of World War II. In that war he was commander of the Army Air Corps troop carrier unit, and in the Korean War, as a colonel, he commanded the 437th Reserve Troop Carrier Wing at O'Hare Field, a post he held until his retirement from the air force in 1953. He died on May 30, 1975, at age seventy-eight, in a lodge he owned near Hot Springs, Arkansas.[23]

The Navy's Millionaires Squadron

The Aero Club of Illinois was also instrumental in putting together a navy flying unit in the Chicago area during World War I, but the unit had little effect on the war effort. Many of the ranking members of the Aero Club were enamored with seaplanes, and in June 1917, the same month that Chanute Field opened, an unusual air squadron was formed at the Great Lakes Naval Training Center north of Chicago. William Wrigley Jr.—chewing gum magnate, Aero Club supporter, and aviation enthusiast—earlier that year had suggested to Captain William A. Moffett—Great Lakes commander and the man considered to be the father of naval aviation—that some sort of aviation training facility should be established at the base. The idea was enthusiastically supported by Pop Dickinson and the Aero Club. Wrigley and John J. Mitchell, president of the Illinois Trust and Savings Bank, then organized the Great Lakes Aeronautical Society to finance a flying and mechanics training school under Moffett's command.[24]

The new unit quickly became called "The Navy's Millionaire Squadron" because many of its members came from wealthy Chicago-area families. The group included Aero Club secretary Lee Hammond, Wrigley's son Philip, William Mitchell, Ellsworth Buck, Alfred Wolff, William McCormick Blair, Albert Dewey,

Allister McCormick, and early hydroplane enthusiast Logan A. (Jack) Vilas. Hammond was commissioned a lieutenant and was in charge of the training on the unit's three seaplanes. Although the mechanics school graduated 2,100 men during the war, the flying unit at Great Lakes was short-lived. It was transferred in October 1917, just a few months after being formed, to a navy base at Pensacola, Florida, ostensibly because Chicago's fierce winters caused the lake to freeze and rendered seaplane operations impossible.[25]

Perhaps the single most important product of the Great Lakes endeavor was Moffett, a product of the big-gun navy who had been a cruiser commander before his training assignment in Chicago. He became so enamored with the possibilities of aviation during his association with the Aero Club that he made it his personal cause during the remainder of his career. He was promoted to rear admiral in 1921 with the task of organizing the navy's Bureau of Aeronautics, a job he did so well that aviation historian William F. Trimble dubbed him the "architect of naval aviation." Moffett held that post until he was killed in the 1933 in the crash of the navy dirigible *Akron* in a storm in the Atlantic off New Jersey.[26]

Grant Park Field

Chicago had two major airports during World War I. Civil flying activity was greatly curtailed once the United States entered the hostilities because many of the pilots joined or went to work for the military, which also consumed the bulk of the aircraft production, but crowds still gathered to watch occasional wartime aerial promotions, and they were present at the start-up of the new federal air mail service. One airport was Ashburn Field, and Grant Park continued to be a part-time site for occasional extravaganzas, some sponsored by the Aero Club, as well as for war rallies. The park was used as a permanent airport site beginning in 1918, when the U.S. Air

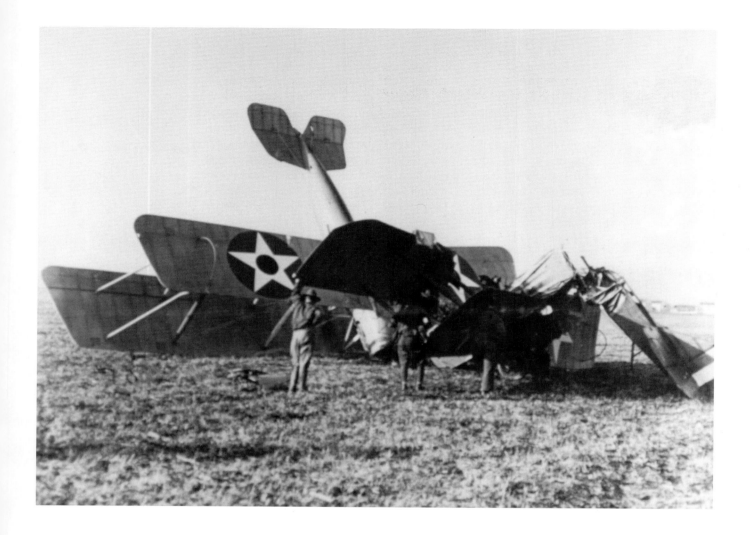

Midair collisions were relatively common for pilots learning to fly during World War I, when air traffic control was in its infancy and in many places nonexistent. Both aviators survived this November 1917 mishap at Chanute Field. (Octave Chanute Aerospace Museum)

Mail Service commenced operations.

Matty Laird and Katherine Stinson were among the aviators who drew large crowds to Grant Park for a six-day carnival on August 2–7, 1915, sponsored by the Chamber of Commerce. The event didn't get much attention in the press because reporters and editors were preoccupied with covering the *Eastland* disaster of July 24, 1915: the excursion steamship had capsized in the Chicago River, drowning the 844 persons aboard. At the carnival, Laird marked an aviation milestone when he became the first person to loop-the-loop with a passenger, Katherine Stinson's sister Marjorie.[27]

A number of air shows were staged in Grant Park in 1917 and 1918 to drum up support for the war effort. Ruth Law, who had taken off from Grant Park on a record-making flight to New York on November 19, 1916 (733 miles in six hours and thirty-two minutes between Chicago and Binghamton, New York), returned to the park in July 1917 and dropped enlistment "bombs" on a crowd watching a military parade. On September 4, 1918, pilots from Chanute Field staged a mock dogfight over the park as part of a week-long war exposition. Four months earlier, Katherine Stinson had flown a small load of mail to New York in one of the many demonstrations of the feasibility of air mail. She got as far as Binghamton, in upstate New York—783 miles in eleven hours and thirteen minutes in a Curtiss JN-4 Jenny—before she ran out of fuel. She completed the final hop the next day.[28]

The armistice did not bring an end to

the military air shows. As late as January 4, 1920, Chicago held a war show in Grant Park and the nearby Chicago Coliseum that was attended by a quarter of a million persons. The biggest stunt during the show was the setting of a world altitude record of 23,500 feet in a de Havilland with a military pilot at the controls and state senator Al Clark in the passenger seat. The show also featured three of the city's World War I aces—Reed Landis, Lawrence Callahan, and B. H. Pearson.[29]

Grant Park was designated as a permanent airport in 1918 when Benjamin B. Lipsner, superintendent of the U.S. Postal Aerial Mail, announced that he had selected it as the service's Chicago aerodrome and that a hangar and repair station would be built on the site. The Chicago–New York air mail route's test flight—in a Curtiss R-4, a larger and faster version of the Jenny, carrying pilot Max Miller and 490 pounds of mail—was greeted by a crowd estimated at several thousand persons when it arrived at 7:04 P.M. on September 6, 1918. Miller had gotten 150 miles off course because clouds obscured his view of the ground, and he discovered his error only after making an unscheduled landing in Jefferson County, Pennsylvania, to ask residents where he was.[30]

Continuous, scheduled air mail service to Grant Park began the following year and lasted into 1920, when the post office bowed to local pressure and moved its Chicago terminal to the suburbs. The Chicago business community, as well as some prominent conservationists who wanted the park kept as a park, were willing to suffer occasional air shows but didn't want a permanent airport there. Increased pressure by the city to prohibit flying over its downtown area in the wake of the July 21, 1919, *Wingfoot* disaster, in which a blimp caught fire and crashed through the skylight of a Loop bank, killing thirteen people, was also a factor (see chapter 1). In December of that year, the city banned flying without a special permit over the Loop

"and all thickly populated business and residential districts in the city limits." The regulation was probably unenforceable, but it was sufficient to convince the post office to head to the suburbs and the Aero Club to abandon plans to expand Ashburn Field, which club members had hoped would become the new air mail aerodrome for Chicago.[31]

Ashburn Field

Dickinson, the Aero Club's principal patron once McCormick began to withdraw from the scene, closed the deal for 640 acres at 83rd Street and Cicero Avenue near the Wabash Railroad's Ashburn station on April 17, 1916—the day after Cicero Field closed. The Aero Club at the same time let a contract for a thirty-by-fifty-foot building at Ashburn to house a wind tunnel and other aeronautical test apparatuses for use by members and hired Walter R. Brock, an aeronautical engineer who had won several air races in Europe, to manage the place. In the meantime, the pilots at Cicero had already transferred their aircraft to the Partridge-Keller aerodrome at 87th and Pulaski or to a vacant lot behind the Dickinson Seed Company at 35th Street and California Avenue.[32]

Although pilots began to dribble into the site all summer, the new airport wasn't officially dedicated until October 28, 1916, with an aerial show timed to coincide with the arrival of the first army flyers. Ashburn had enough traffic by December of that year that the club decided to build a tower there, the intended use for which was observation, not air traffic control. The tower's observation platform was fifty feet off the ground, high enough to give the observers an unobstructed view for two miles.[33]

Ashburn Field, it turned out, had a couple of major drawbacks. Despite the fact that it was within the city limits of Chicago and near a passenger station on the Wabash Railroad, it was relatively inaccessible. Poor drainage at the site made improvements expensive to build. Stout described the 1925 Ashburn as "the only operating field in Chicago . . . a small swampy place with a little shed in the middle where Jenny pilots used to congregate for their hangar talk. They would come with planes of all sorts, usually held together with bailing wire and pieces of fence."[34]

When regular air mail service was started by the U.S. Post Office Department in 1918, the mail planes used Grant Park as their regular airport because Ashburn was considered so remote, although maintenance on the planes was performed at Ashburn. In an unsuccessful attempt to induce the air mail service to relocate its operations there from Grant Park, the club built a hangar at Ashburn later in 1918 and lobbied the city for improvements to 63rd Street to give the public better access to the airfield. Cicero Avenue on the airport's western border was unpaved at the time.[35]

The club acquired a used water tank and a windmill to pump water into it from a well and moved them to the site. Dickinson continued to pour personal funds into the airport to upgrade it. The Aero Club files from the time contain numerous receipts for work to improve drainage on Ashburn's surface, to build an access road, and to construct a cinder runway. Dickinson paid all the bills by personal check.[36]

By 1919, the Aero Club was aggressively lobbying to have Ashburn assume Grant Park's functions as an airport. Competition had already appeared. Society Brand Field, later known as Checkerboard Field, at First Avenue and 12th Street (Roosevelt Road) in west-suburban Maywood opened on June 3, 1919, with a ceremony attended by Harry H. Merrick, president of the Chicago Chamber of Commerce. On July 18, 1919, Bion J. Arnold set up a meeting between Aero Club members and the Chicago Council Aviation Committee in the Congress Hotel to present a proposal by the club to improve Ashburn Field so it could replace Grant Park.[37]

Arnold made the Aero Club's case to the commission: "We should have a large landing field, plainly marked and equipped with sounding apparatus so that even on cloudy days when vision is impaired aviators would know where to land. The ideal field should be seen, felt, and heard. Grant Park, while not a bad field on a perfect day, is unsuited at present for that purpose." He was referring to the problem that plagued Chicago's lakefront airports throughout the twentieth century: they require north-south runways to clear downtown buildings, but the prevailing weather is west to east, requiring planes to frequently take off in strong crosswinds.[38]

Mindful of the effects thousands of miles of railroad tracks had on Chicago, city officials were concerned about what changes a growing aviation industry would bring to Grant Park and the city's central business district. "Despite the rapid progress of the airplane, it can still be considered in an elementary stage. We are apt to make plans without looking far enough ahead. In the years to come, when the airplane industry approaches the size of the rail transportation industry, we do not want Grant Park marred by airplane freight houses or large fields and hangars," E. H. Bennett, an engineer for the City Plan Commission, warned the meeting attendees.[39]

The aviation committee, convinced that Grant Park was too limited to remain an airport, for a time seemed interested in Ashburn, but the *Wingfoot* disaster in the Loop a few days later doomed the idea and soured the commission on the development of aviation in Chicago. The crash caused influential alderman Anton Cermak, who would later be mayor, to propose a ban on all flying over Chicago: "This accident shows we must stop flying over the city sooner or later, and we better do it sooner," Cermak told the newspapers.[40]

In the political furor that followed the crash of the blimp into a Loop bank, most Aero Club members temporarily backed away from the plan to expand Ashburn Field and spent their time defending aviation against its critics. Because of various proposals to restrict flying, the Aero Club adopted the position that federal safety regulation, not local, was what was needed, and James Stephens urged the Aero Club of America to assist in lobbying for such. Before the end of the month, the *Tribune* printed an op-ed piece by Stephens pointing out that Chicago was a transportation center and urging its citizens not to neglect the need for aviation facilities to sustain what was going to be a growing transportation industry. Early in 1920, the club predicted a rosy future for aviation—"the aerial ocean is the universal highway of the future."[41]

The club's appeals finally produced the desired effect. On January 22, 1920, the City Council Aviation Committee asked the Aero Club to help organize a general committee to promote commercial aviation in Chicago. But it was too late for Ashburn. The U.S. Air Mail Service shifted its operations to Checkerboard Field that month even though that airport was too small for its operations—its private operator was forced to hurriedly lease additional land. In July, Chicago made an unsuccessful bid to have the army's experimental aviation station shifted from Dayton to Ashburn.[42]

Despite the interest of the Chicago business community and some members of City Council in 1920 in building a municipal airport, the political establishment in Chicago did not again consider making a substantial

The British-designed de Havilland DH-4 bomber was the only warplane manufactured in the United States in appreciable numbers during World War I. It was known by air crews as the "flaming coffin" because of its propensity to catch fire. This DH-4 has British markings but was assigned to Chanute Field during the war. It was wrecked in a crash landing but did not catch fire. (Octave Chanute Aerospace Museum)

financial investment in aviation facilities for another six years. There was simply not enough air commerce to justify any sort of publicly owned airport, and airline passenger service in 1920 was only a dream.

Curiously, in 1929 Dickinson donated to the city sixty-five acres he had purchased on Lake Calumet on the far South Side for eventual development as an airport. A surprised City Council accepted the gift, but did nothing with the land. In the 1940s, the Lake Calumet area was considered as one of the sites for a new jet port for the city; however, it was too remote and lost out to Orchard Place Airport on the Northwest Side, which became O'Hare International Airport.[43]

Commercial Aviation in 1919

An account by a passenger aboard a converted British bomber on a November 8, 1919, nonstop test flight between New York and Chicago showed that aviation was still primitive despite the pronouncements of its advocates. The bomber was operated by Handley Page Transport, which had started scheduled service between London and Paris in June of that year and was testing the possibility of starting airline service in the United States.

According to the passenger, wet weather at the starting point in suburban Mineola, New York, had caused moisture to form on the magnetos, and the crew wasted considerable gasoline during the night just trying to get the engines started for the 7:05 A.M. takeoff. Cloud cover hid the earth for two hours, and the plane encountered turbulence and a strong headwind over the Catskill Mountains despite the fact that the crew climbed to eight thousand feet to smooth the flight. "The cold was intense, and eventually, at about 2:30, one of the water pipes split. . . . The water escaped and after the starboard engine heated up it was necessary to stop it. We considered it advisable on seeing a railway station, to look for a landing where we had a chance of getting what we required to repair the pipe, as preceding over some very uninvit-

ing country below us, we might have to make a landing where there was no chance of saving the machine in a crash," the passenger said.

The crew finally found a clear field large enough for a landing near Mt. Jewett, a small town in remote northwest Pennsylvania, and spent the night there. The water pipe was repaired, but the engines were once again balky, delaying the takeoff until 1:45 P.M. By that time there was only enough fuel left to make Cleveland. "The instructions we had received described Glenn Martin field at Cleveland as being rather to the west and south and four miles from the center of town. The visibility. . . was very bad, and added to this, as the Glenn Martin field was 16 miles from the point where we had been told it was, we naturally could not find it," the passenger wrote. The crew did spot a race track while they circled, looking for the designated field, and finally, with fuel running low and the sun setting, they landed there.

"We ran down the track, which being very hard did not bring the machine up for a considerable distance, and unfortunately, our wingspan was too great to go between the judge's and timekeeper's boxes on either side of the track." The plane hit them at about eight miles an hour, knocking off both wingtips and ending any chance that they would complete the rest of the flight to Chicago. The mishaps aside, the passenger reported that he was very optimistic about the future of airline service in the United States, despite the lack of proper aviation maps, aerodromes, and good flying weather.

> It is no good being pessimistic about this temporary setback. . . . It may be of interest to you to know that in England, since civilian flying and passenger carrying was allowed to commence on this first of May of this year (1919), that 63,000 passengers have been carried and a quantity of freight and that during these months in the summer, with a few Handley Page machines carrying passengers, 3,000 people went for flights without damaging a single person or plane."[45]

In the period between the world wars, Chanute Field abandoned pilot training and became a technical center to provide instruction in such skills as aircraft maintenance. The crew are shown working on Northrop A-17A light-attack bomber engines. (Octave Chanute Aerospace Museum)

In 1919, the United States, with few aerodromes, no surplus wartime bomber fleet that could be converted to commercial use, vast distances between cities, and several mountain ranges that challenged the primitive art of aviation, was still at least six years away from having any sort of reliable passenger airline service. However, small-scale freight operations began to pop up shortly after the war ended, and the federal government had started up its own airline to carry the mail—the single largest air freight market as the Roaring Twenties commenced.

The aviation enthusiasts in the Aero Club and local government correctly surmised that it was inevitable that Chicago, the nation's midcontinental transportation hub, would also become a commercial aviation center. It was simply a matter of time.

7 Early Commercial Aviation

In the 1930s, the terminal at Municipal Airport had the look of a neoclassical railroad or bus depot. Note the single boarding gate and the palm trees by the entrance to the restaurant. (Christopher Lynch Collection)

• Although the United States was remote from the battlegrounds of Europe, the war had a profound effect on the nation's transportation system. By 1916, the railroads, which had reached their maximum extent of 259,211 miles, quickly became bogged down with wartime traffic and had to be taken over by the federal government for the first and only time in history. Yet the reprivatized railroads emerged from the war looking nearly as dominant as they had twenty years earlier. In 1920 they carried a record 1.27 billion passengers.[1]

The river transportation system that in the nineteenth century was characterized by lines of steamboats chugging up and down the waterways was by 1917 extinct, a victim of competition from the railroads. It was rebuilt almost from scratch by the federal government during the war. The roads were also deplorable, so bad that the new motor-truck industry had to wait for the federal government to subsidize a hard-road program before it could begin hauling goods interstate with any efficiency.

Chicago in 1920 was the nation's largest

rail center, still had a healthy amount of Great Lakes traffic even though the cross-lake packet business was in decline, and was home to a growing motor-truck manufacturing industry. A prewar traffic count in 1913 indicated that over 200,000 trains used Chicago's six railroad stations, carrying more than 25 million passengers a year. In 1920, Chicago's International Harvester Company alone built 7,391 trucks.[2]

Air commerce was another matter, giving rise to a tongue-in-cheek saying that persisted throughout aviation's first century: "Air freight is a lot like Brazil. It has a lot of promise and probably always will." There had been plenty of demonstrations of the potential of air commerce in aviation's second decade. Eighteen-year-old pilot Farnum Fish flew from Cicero Field to Milwaukee on May 25, 1912, carrying four bolts of silk and 7,500 handbills advertising the Boston Store. He dumped the leaflets over Milwaukee before running out of gas and coasting to a landing in a park. There were assorted other one-shot handbill distributions and demonstration flights over the next few years, but all attempts to provide scheduled commercial air service—including McCormick's lakeshore commuter service in 1913 and the Lawson venture in 1919—were short-lived.[3]

Slightly more successful in that it lasted longer was the in-house airline established in 1919 at a cost of $50,000 by Alfred Decker & Cohn, makers of Society Brand clothes. The plan was for the airline to distribute the company's products to stores within five hundred miles of Chicago, although initial service was to Kankakee, Champaign, Danville, Valparaiso, and South Bend—a much smaller area. The company bought two war-surplus JN-4 Jenny biplanes, each capable of speeds of seventy-five miles an hour, and hired former Army Lieutenant David L. Behncke to manage the service. Its airfield was a forty-acre tract on the south side of 12th Street (later Roosevelt Road) between First Avenue and the Des Plaines River in suburban Maywood. On it the company built a hangar for its two planes, the wings of which were painted with the company's distinctive checkerboard logotype for high visibility. Because of that, the new airport quickly became known as Checkerboard Field.[4]

With few exceptions, privately owned airports like Checkerboard proved to be inadequate for the large-scale aerial commerce that developed in the 1920s, especially after the federal government turned over the business of carrying mail to commercial airlines and larger, passenger-carrying airplanes appeared. A major corporation like Ford Motor Company had the financial wherewithal to build a commercial airport in south-suburban Lansing, but the owners of most airfields didn't have the capital to buy sufficient land and build the hard-surface runways necessary to sustain the all-weather flying that commercial aviation would require, a condition that forced the post office to build and maintain some flying fields for its transcontinental route. The compromise that eventually emerged in the mid-1920s and that exists to this day was for the federal government to develop, maintain, and regulate the airways; local governments to build and maintain the airports; and private carriers to operate the airlines. This pattern of federal-state-local cooperation had been established more than a century earlier in the maritime industry. In Chicago, that meant Washington, D.C., was responsible for dredging Chicago's two rivers, providing lighthouses for navigation, and maintaining breakwaters to protect the harbors' mouths; the city had to build Municipal (later Navy) Pier; and the ships that used the pier were privately owned and operated.[5]

David Behncke

A native of a farm near Cambria, Wisconsin, David Behncke joined the army in 1915 and learned to fly at a base in San Diego. He spent much of World War I training pilots and testing and inspecting aircraft at Chanute Field. After the war he decided to

World War I–style biplanes were used to carry mail in the 1920s before the advent of passenger aircraft. The cargo was loaded into the space that would have been occupied by the second crew member in a military aircraft and was protected from the elements by a hatch cover that was closed during flight. (Christopher Lynch Collection)

make aviation a career, and after doing some barnstorming as Behncke's Flying Circus he was hired to run the Society Brand airline and manage Checkerboard Field. Behncke later went on to greater fame as a pilot for both Northwest and United Airlines and as the founder of the Air Line Pilots Association (ALPA), the union representing most of the nation's pilots.[6]

The Alfred Decker & Cohn service, typical of commercial aviation ventures of that time, was only marginally successful and lasted less than a year. One of Behncke's initial flights nearly ended in disaster when, on June 6, 1919, he ran into a heavy thunderstorm while making a delivery to Valparaiso, Indiana. Attempting to continue his flight to South Bend, Behncke nearly crashed on takeoff and had to fly part of the way only a few hundred feet above the ground to keep his bearings. Nevertheless, he reached South

Bend safely, and in a break in the storms, he dashed back to Maywood in just forty-five minutes.[7]

Alfred Decker & Cohn discontinued its aerial delivery service in early 1920, but Behncke bought the company's two airplanes and continued to operate Checkerboard as a commercial airport. Its principal business was Checkerboard Airplane Service, which offered airplane rides, exhibition flying, aerial photography, and air express service, but it was the 1920 decision by the U.S. Post Office Department to shift its Chicago base there from Grant Park that made Checkerboard Field a going concern. The transfer of the air mail service flights won Behncke enough revenue to make the small airport a profitable enterprise, lease an additional twenty acres for expansion, and hire Bert R. Blair as assistant manager and Louis E. Meyer as a mechanic.[8]

Although the post office expanded service later in 1920 from the single New York–Chicago route, adding service to Omaha (May 15), St. Louis (August 16), and Minneapolis (December 1), Congress refused to appropriate sufficient funds for the air mail service to operate anything but its transcontinental route in 1921. On June 30, 1921, the routes to Minneapolis and St. Louis were discontinued. When a fire destroyed most of Checkerboard's buildings later that year, the post office moved its air mail operations across First Avenue to government-owned land. That became Maywood Airport, the air mail terminal in Chicago until 1927.[9]

Behncke continued to operate Checkerboard Field with diminished revenues until 1923, when he sold out to Wilfred Alonzo (Tony) Yackey, a former air mail pilot who had founded Yackey Aircraft Company to specialize in the rebuilding of surplus military aircraft for commercial use, especially the French-built Brequet bombers. They were rebuilt and sold as Yackey Transports, and the company also built a two-seat biplane called the Yackey Sport. The airport was abandoned in 1928 after Yackey died in a plane crash.[10]

In 1926 Behncke was hired by Northwest Airways as its first pilot to get that operation started on the Chicago-Minneapolis route, and two years later he moved to Boeing Air Transport, one of United Air Lines' predecessor companies. In 1930, he began meeting secretly with other pilots to organize a union, which was finally chartered on April 1, 1931. Behncke was elected its first president, a post he held until 1951. The new union's first crisis occurred quickly in February 1932, during the depths of the depression. E. L. Cord, owner of Century Air Lines, began cutting salaries. The pilots struck, and Cord backed down.

By the following year, the airlines had formed an organization of their own and announced a lower pay scale and longer hours. Pilots would be expected to fly up to 140 hours a month. Behncke took what

he later described as a desperate gamble and announced a nationwide strike. "I figured it would cost $1,000 a day to conduct a strike, and our treasury had $5,000, so we would have lasted five days." He gambled that the administration of Democratic President Franklin Roosevelt would be more sympathetic to his union's cause than the Republican presidents had been in the 1920s and took his case to the National Labor Relations Board (NLRB). New York Supreme Court Judge Bernard Shintag's NLRB ruling of May 10, 1934, known in the industry as Decision 83, set a maximum of eighty-five hours a month flying time and established a system for determining pilot pay. The ruling was incorporated into the Air Mail Act of 1934 and the Civil Aeronautics Act of 1938.[11]

After World War II, opposition to Behncke's administration had begun to form within the union, and his health deteriorated. He survived a challenge to his leadership in 1947, but in 1951, while he was in New York arguing the union's case before an emergency board appointed by President Harry Truman to avert a strike against American Airlines, union representatives from other airlines were back at the organization's headquarters in Chicago agitating for his removal. They finally succeeded at a board of directors convention on July 16, 1951, although Behncke unsuccessfully fought his ouster in court for another year. He died in 1953.[12]

★ ★ ★ ★

Back in 1921, Behncke's only commercial competition in the Chicago area was an operation run by pilot Nimmo Black and several other aviators to carry film and photographs from news events to newspapers in time to make deadlines. They were part of a small but rapidly growing charter operator business—a segment of the aviation industry that continues to the present—willing to lease their services to sightseers and to individuals and companies that were in a hurry. Starting an in-house airline, as

Although largely out of sight of the flying public, fixed base operators, or FBOs as they are known in the trade, are an essential element of every airport. They provide fuel, maintenance, and weather information to pilots of small aircraft. Monarch Air Service was the FBO at Municipal/Midway Airport.

Henry Ford did in 1925, required considerable capital, so many firms with only occasional shipping deadlines resorted to charters. An early charter customer was Chicago's William Wrigley Company, which used aircraft in 1919 to deliver its spearmint gum to various cities as part of a nationwide promotion and advertising program.[13]

Black operated out of a small aerodrome in Chicago at Peterson and Lincoln Avenues. In May 1923, he rushed pictures of the Kentucky Derby from Louisville back to Chicago to meet the morning newspaper deadlines, a feat that required the ground crews to build bonfires on all four corners of the airport to enable him to find the field. Later that year, Black flew from Omaha and Marion, Ohio, to New York with photos of former president Warren Harding's funeral procession. In September 1923, the company hauled pictures of the Jack Dempsey–Louis Firpo fight in New York back to Chicago for the morning newspapers.[14]

In August 1919, when the Aero Club's James S. Stephens made his public appeal for aviation in the wake of the *Wingfoot* disaster, he was able to list only the air mail, Wrigley gum, and Society Brand clothes operations as examples of successful commercial aviation ventures. However, he claimed that 90 percent of the $2 million in orders for airplanes booked with the

Curtiss Airplane and Motor Corporation's office in Chicago since June 1 of that year were for "commercial purposes." Curtiss's sales represented 110 aircraft. The James Levy Aircraft Company, also of Chicago, purportedly sold another 155 planes during approximately the same period.

Octave Chanute's prediction, made nearly two decades earlier in 1904, barely three months after the Wrights' first flight, summarized the state of commercial aviation following World War I. His surprisingly pessimistic prophecy was that mail was aviation's potential market:

> Flying machines promise better results as to speed, but will be of limited commercial application. They may carry mail and reach inaccessible places, but they can't compete with railroads as carriers of passengers or freight. They will not fill the heavens with commerce, abolish custom houses, or revolutionize the world, for they will be too expensive for the loads which they carry, and subject to too many wind contingencies. Success, however, is probable.[15]

Aviation Finds a Market

As Chanute had predicted in 1894 and 1904, the commercial utility of the airplane was limited until such time as the government stepped in to provide the subsidies necessary to incubate the industry to the point that it could survive on its own. Just as World War I had created an instant market for larger, sturdier, and faster airplanes, the mail created a market for commercial air service as hostilities ended. The airplane in 1920 was still something on which a person could buy a thrill ride but not passage to a destination. It was certainly not a transportation mode that American industry could use as an alternative to express rail freight services. Air freight services existing in 1920 were largely novelties, and the largest such operation was run by the U.S. Post Office Department.

The department in its long history had proved willing to experiment with new modes of transportation—steamboats and the railroads, for example—to speed the mail. So it was only a matter of time before the post office took a serious look at aviation. There had been a number of local test flights around the country, beginning in 1911 when Earle Ovington carried fifteen pounds of mail daily for a week on short hops between Garden City and Mineola on Long Island.[16]

Chicago was the site of thirty-one such air mail demonstrations in 1912, including one in which Max Lillie flew the mail for a few days between Cicero Field, Elmhurst, and Wheaton, two suburbs farther to the west. The first mail flight, on Decoration Day (May 30), was an accidental one. Lillie became disoriented on a flight back to Cicero Field from Grant Park and inadvertently landed on a farm near Elmhurst, where the local postmaster, who had been summoned to the scene, handed him a sack of mail to haul back to Cicero. He dutifully complied, but the official demonstration, using three pilots, all deputized as assistant postmasters, was supposed to begin the next day because the post offices were closed on the holiday. When the demonstration officially began, Lillie hauled eighty pounds of mail from Cicero to the Elmhurst Golf Club, followed on June 1 and 2 by Paul Studensky and Marcel Tournier with a round trip from Cicero to Wheaton. A total of 458 pounds of mail had been hauled in four days.[17]

Although pilot William Robinson later made a flight between Des Moines and Chicago carrying mail, it wasn't until November 3, 1916, that the feasibility of long-distance air mail—in this case between Chicago and New York—was proved in yet another demonstration. Victor Carlstrom took off from Ashburn Field on November 2 to attempt a daytime flight, but was forced down by darkness in Hammondsport, New York, between Elmira and Buffalo, and he didn't complete the trip to Governor's Island until the next day. Flying time was eight hours and twenty-six

Nimmo Black was one of the pilots Pop Dickinson selected to fly his airplanes in his short-lived attempt to start an airline in 1926. After a succession of mishaps, Dickinson was forced to default on his air mail contract, and it was awarded to a group of investors from other cities, who formed what became Northwest Airlines.

The rapid growth in air travel forced Chicago to add parallel runways at Municipal Airport, doubling its size, just before World War II. The remnants of the railroad right-of-way that was relocated for the expansion project can still be seen bisecting the airport. (Christopher Lynch Collection)

The runway configuration at Midway, once it was expanded to its limits in the second half of the twentieth century, included parallel diagonal runways varying in length from 4,850 feet to 6,519 feet. Development that enveloped the airport meant that the clear zones beyond the runways were minimal. Cicero Avenue, shown at right, was bent to the east to allow for an expanded parking lot.

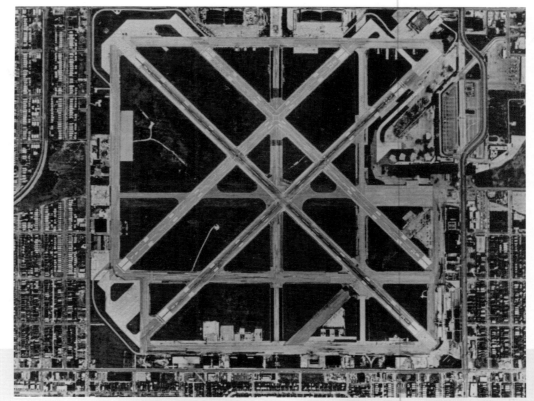

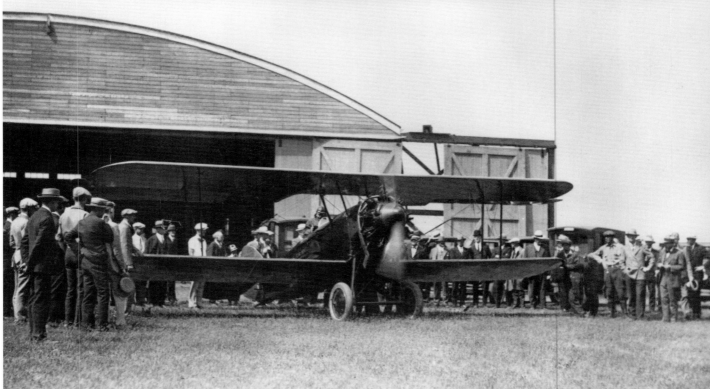

Throughout the 1920s, World War I–style aircraft were still being pressed into service by air carriers to fly the mail. This Laird Commercial—a two-seat, single-engine biplane—was rolled out of the hangar at Ashburn Field in 1926. It was an evolutionary successor to the wartime Jenny.

William A. (Pat) Patterson, a former banker, ran United Air Lines from 1934 through his retirement in 1966. (United Airlines)

minutes for the 850-mile trip, proving such a flight could be accomplished entirely by daylight. On the plane, he carried letters from Charles Dickinson and James Stephens to Alan Hawley, president of the Aero Club of America.[18]

Katherine Stinson repeated the journey two years later with a load of mail bound from Chicago to New York. Hers was also supposed to be a nonstop flight, but she was forced down on May 23, 1918, when she ran out of fuel 150 miles short of her goal. Stinson, who later in the year worked briefly as a pilot in the air mail service, completed the remaining hop to New York City the next day in her Curtiss JN-4 Jenny. The first nonstop mail flight between the two cities didn't occur until April 19, 1919, when Army Captain Earl E. White flew from Ashburn Field to Hazelhurst, Long Island, in a modified de Havilland DH-4 in six hours and fifty minutes.[19]

The standard procedure for most early air mail demonstrations was for the post office to provide some mail and for the sponsor to pay to fly it to a local airport. The "air mail" often was then put on a train bound for its final destination. Benjamin B. Lipsner, who later headed the air mail service for the government, described those early flights as "fine publicity" with "no utility." They planted in the mind of the public, and especially of Congress, that such service was feasible. Aside from the cost, the only question was reliability; it made no sense to fly mail at one hundred miles an hour between Chicago and New York if the planes were regularly grounded by darkness and inclement weather or if they crashed too frequently.[20]

It was Lipsner, a Chicagoan who was not an aviator but had a degree in mechanical engineering from Armour Institute and was an expert in fleet management and engine lubricants, who had the organizational skills to get the air mail service operating. He was one of the first of a new breed in civil aviation—an enterprise that until he came along was almost solely the province of adventurers, daredevils, entrepreneurs, inventors, and people rich enough to afford such expensive toys as airplanes. Lipsner was neither a pilot nor a tinkerer; his sole interest in aviation was that it was a new mode of transportation that potentially could be used, like motor trucks, to carry the commerce of the nation. He was a professional manager, and he applied his skills and the federal government's wealth toward making a success of aviation's first sustained commercial venture—the air mail.[21]

Ben Lipsner's Idea

On September 4, 1918, Lipsner returned to Chicago for an inspection of Grant Park, the field he had tentatively selected for the U.S. Post Office Department's first test air mail flight between Chicago and New York City the next day. He had been on hand the previous May 15 with President Woodrow Wilson at Washington's polo grounds to watch the inauguration of the air mail service between there, Philadelphia, and New York.

The New York to Chicago route—the crucial first leg of the transcontinental air mail line the post office was determined to establish between New York and San Francisco—was considered far riskier because of the longer distance involved and the necessity of flying over the Allegheny Mountains, known by pilots as the "graveyard" or "hell's stretch." Flying over those mountains was considered dangerous because of unusual air currents, downdrafts, unfavorable flying weather, a dearth of landmarks that could be used for visual navigation, and the absence of suitable emergency landing strips.[22]

It was obvious that the state of the art of aviation in 1918 would not permit nonstop flights. For months, Lipsner had planned the route of the experimental pathfinding flights from Belmont Park in New York with refueling stops in Lock Haven, Pennsylvania, and Cleveland and Bryan, Ohio, to Chicago's Grant Park. He had also hand picked the two pilots, Max Miller and Edward V. Gardner, to make the test runs. To justify the proposed service to the post office, Lipsner had computed that the mail could be carried by plane between New York and Chicago in about nine and a half hours, compared with the more than twenty-four hours necessary by train.[23]

The pathfinding flights had the usual problems. Miller, carrying 480 pounds of mail, was the first to take off from Belmont Park, at 7:08 A.M. Eastern time September 5 and Gardner followed. Both pilots ran into trouble with the weather over Pennsylvania. Gardner also was plagued with mechanical difficulties. The flights were to take twelve hours—time having been built into the schedule for such unforeseen contingencies as bad weather and mechanical problems—and Lipsner spent that long day anxiously sitting by a telephone at Chicago's central post office waiting for the pilots to call when they made their scheduled stops. Miller finally reached Chicago at 6:55 P.M., September 6, and Gardner,

who had been forced down by darkness in Westville, Indiana, arrived the next day. Both planes had been so battered by emergency landings that they needed two days of overhaul to make the return trip.[24]

Although the two flights took considerably longer than an express train between Chicago and New York, Lipsner was convinced that with proper organization the service would be successful. However, when scheduled service began on May 15, 1919, trains were used for portions of the trip: airplanes carried the mail between Cleveland and Chicago during daylight hours, and trains hauled it between Cleveland and New York at night. It was hardly a satisfactory arrangement, even by the standards of that day, but it did allow the air mail service to continue until the development of better aircraft permitted nonstop flights between Chicago and New York.[25]

For Lipsner, the air mail represented a surprising change in career, although he had had a brush with aviation as early as 1910, when he read in a Chicago newspaper about flying activities at Clearing Field, at 65th Street and Major Avenue, and went to see what they were all about. There he met Otto Brodie, a pilot, and R. W. (Shorty) Schroeder, a mechanic, and became so fascinated by flying machines that he spent much of his free time hanging around the field helping pilots and their ground crews in any way he could. He was too practical a man to think that the primitive airplanes of that day had any utilitarian value, although he later recalled that even then he was intrigued by the possibility of hauling mail by air.

A succession of jobs before World War I made Lipsner an expert on fleet maintenance and management. He was first hired to manage the fleet operated by Albert Pick & Company, a hotel supply firm, and discovered the importance of proper lubrication in keeping the fleet of assorted vehicles on the road. He later managed the vehicle fleets of two other large corporations, did some work in the oil industry, and in 1917 was called to Washington by one of his former employers to solve for the army the problem of lubricating airplanes. Airplane engines of that time were lubricated primarily with castor oil, an expensive and relatively scarce commodity. The army estimated that to maintain the anticipated numbers of aircraft it would have in Europe it would need five million gallons of castor oil annually—the entire U.S. production for three years. Lipsner's task was to find a substitute.[26]

Lipsner and his staff quickly accomplished that task, but to his regret he discovered that the army had nothing else for him to do. In his idle time, he began toying with the idea of delivering mail by airplane because, he thought, improvements made in aircraft since his acquaintance with the business in 1910 had made air mail a practical possibility. Furthermore, Congress in 1916 had appropriated $100,000 for air mail experiments, but the money had never been used, and the appropriation was to expire on June 30, 1918. Early that year, Lipsner went to Otto Praeger, second assistant postmaster general, and persuaded him that with proper maintenance and management an air mail service could succeed, especially after the war ended and large numbers of pilots and surplus military aircraft became available. Praeger was so impressed with the presentation that he had Lipsner detailed from the army to the Post Office Department and put in charge of establishing the initial air mail route between New York and Washington, a task Lipsner completed in a couple of months by using spare army pilots and planes.[27]

Lipsner then turned his attention to the possibility of establishing a longer route. The post office liked the idea of transcontinental mail service, and the Chicago to New York leg seemed the logical place to start. However, despite the fact that the pathfinding flights of Miller and Gardner in 1918 proved the service was feasible, the new agency had neither the planes nor the pilots to begin scheduled service while the war continued. The armistice on November 11, 1918, solved that problem.

Transcontinental Service

What emerged the next year was the plane-train compromise. On May 15, 1919, Gardner flew west from Cleveland and Trent C. Fry headed east from Chicago to inaugurate the service. It was only ten days old when the first fatality occurred. Pilot Frank McCusker's de Havilland DH-4, a plane known among the air mail pilots as the "flaming coffin," had caught fire just after takeoff, and he fell to his death when he attempted to bail out.[28]

By then, the new service was mired in a number of problems. Lipsner resigned on December 6, 1918, after a dispute with Praeger over political interference in the service, including the patronage hiring of unqualified pilots and plans to buy what Lipsner considered unneeded planes. After the resignation, the Post Office Department was embarrassed by several unsuccessful attempts to get the Chicago–New York route started in the winter of 1918–19.[29]

On May 25, 1919, the air mail pilots refused to work—the first such strike in U.S. aviation history—after one of them, E. Hamilton Lee of Chicago, was fired for refusing to take off in the fog. The post office backed down a few days later, announcing that local airport managers would be allowed to determine whether the weather was good enough to permit flying, and Lee was rehired. Then the *Chicago Tribune* published an article debunking the post office contention that the new service to New York saved sixteen hours over the railway postal service. The *Tribune* charged that although the airplanes reached Cleveland in five hours, the mail had to wait there for five hours for the train—a net saving of zero. The time saved on westbound mail was only three hours, the newspaper said.[30]

Despite the problems, the air mail service continued and with experience improved. On May 15, 1920, service was started between Chicago and Omaha and, on August 16, between Chicago and St. Louis. The last

gaps in the agency's long-awaited transcontinental service between New York and San Francisco via Chicago were closed on September 8 of that year. On November 7, Lee flew a test run between Chicago and Minneapolis to check that route, and regular service began December 1.[31]

Thus, by the end of 1920, Chicago had become the hub for the nation's fledgling air mail service, with routes to New York, Omaha, Minneapolis, and St. Louis. It was a short-lived role, but one that presaged the city's later position as hub for the nation's commercial airline system. Commercial aviation still could not survive without government subsidies, a reality made perfectly clear when an economy-minded postwar Congress reduced appropriations

for the service and the post office in 1921 dropped all but its transcontinental route.

That route was also plagued with trouble because the mail was flown by day and transferred to trains at night, a system that had proved inefficient on the Chicago–New York route two years earlier. Post office officials realized that if the transcontinental route were to avoid the fate of the others, mail would have to be flown at night to make the promised time savings. On February 22, 1921, the air mail service attempted coast-to-coast relay flights to prove to Congress that it could be done.

Two planes left New York and two others departed San Francisco, but they almost immediately ran into trouble. One westbound aircraft was forced down just

Government air mail contracts provided the profit motive for the earliest airlines, but with the development of larger and faster airplanes and the government's rebidding of contracts after the Spoils Conference scandal, the airlines discovered that passenger service could be more profitable. Here a crew unloads mail from a Boeing 80A. (United Airlines) after leaving New York, and the other plane made it as far as Chicago before being grounded by snow. The first plane from the West Coast crashed in Nevada, killing its pilot. Thus, within a few hours after the experiment began, only one of the four planes was still in the air, and it completed the trip only because of the heroics of one of its pilots in what became one of the epic flights in the history of American aviation.

The surviving airplane successfully negotiated the legs from San Francisco to Reno, Nevada; to Cheyenne, Wyoming; and to North Platte, Nebraska, where it was turned over to its next relay pilot, James H. (Jack) Knight. He headed east at 7:50 P.M. on the next, 276-mile leg to Omaha, where he was supposed to turn the plane over to another pilot, but upon landing there at 1:15 A.M., he learned that the pilot and plane that were supposed to meet him had been grounded by snow in Chicago. Knight decided to continue to Chicago, 435 miles farther east, despite the bitter cold and a snowstorm then in progress.

He discovered upon his arrival at the refueling station in Des Moines that there was too much snow on the ground to attempt a landing, so he continued to the alternate field at Iowa City, only to discover that it also was closed. The ground crew had gone home after assuming that because the flight from Chicago had been cancelled, the one from Omaha had been too. A night watchman guided Knight to a safe landing just as he ran out of fuel. They refueled the plane, and Knight gulped some coffee before continuing to Chicago despite the bad weather. Exhausted, he landed at Maywood Field at 8:40 A.M. during the snowstorm and turned the plane over to pilot J. O. Webster. The plane finally reached New York at 4:50 P.M. that day, thirty-three hours and twenty-one minutes after leaving San Francisco.[32]

Because of Knight's heroics, the flight had demonstrated once and for all the fea-

sibility of day-and-night service over the transcontinental route, although it was not until January 1, 1924, after signal beacons and airfield lights had been installed, that regular twenty-four-hour service was begun. Much of the credit for establishing it belonged to another Chicagoan, Colonel Paul Henderson, who was appointed to head the air mail service in January 1922. Lipsner complained that Henderson's appointment was political because he was the son-in-law of U.S. Representative Martin B. Madden of Chicago, but Henderson made much of the criticism moot by performing creditably in the job.[33]

The Search for an Airport

With the advances in aircraft that made scheduled air mail feasible, the major remaining problem for the post office was to develop a system of permanent airports that could handle its planes at night and in less-than-desirable weather, as well as serve as bases for such nongovernment aviators as student fliers, daredevils, and commercial operators. After three Chicago airports were tried in five years, it soon became obvious to the post office, the aviation community, and the City of Chicago that a large, all-weather, publicly owned airport would have to be built on a site large enough for continued expansion.

Because federal and state government were not in the commercial-airport-building business, the inevitable conclusion reached in Chicago and other cities was that any public airport would have to be a municipal venture. Private aviation in the 1920s had not developed to the point that it could raise the capital necessary to build a system of all-weather airports across the nation. With the postwar development of larger and more reliable aircraft, especially the Tri-Motors that appeared in the mid-1920s, the idea of a city-owned airport took on greater urgency. Airplanes, after all, could easily be rerouted far from Chicago to another city with adequate ground facilities, or even to a hub airport in a cornfield for that matter.

Despite the Aero Club's protestations to the contrary, Ashburn Field was suitable for general aviation but not for commercial operations on the scale that the nation's midcontinental transportation hub would need. The air mail service's Chicagoland airport was a small aerodrome in the suburb of Maywood. Despite the absence of air mail, Ashburn continued to flourish under Aero Club sponsorship. Elmer Partridge and Henry Keller continued to build their airplanes there. Ralph C. Diggins opened an aviation school at Ashburn in 1920 to train pilots and sold it in 1923 to the James Levy Aircraft Company, which kept the school there. Later that year, Matty Laird returned to Chicago from Wichita, Kansas, to start the E. M. Laird Airplane Company. Ashburn remained the home base for most of the private pilots in the Chicago area, as well as the Aero Club's center of activities.

Maywood Field was too small to survive long. It was adequate for the government's limited transcontinental air mail service but not for the rapid expansion of commercial activity that was expected to occur after 1926, when the Post Office Department was to begin awarding air mail contracts to private operators. By the time pilot Charles A. Lindbergh made his first air mail flight from Maywood in a Robertson Aircraft Corporation plane on April 15, 1926, it had already been concluded that Maywood was not the airport of the future, and Chicago had already acquired the rights to a huge tract on its Southwest Side.

The Air Commerce Act of 1926, approved by Congress and signed into law by President Calvin Coolidge on May 20 of that year, established that the federal government was responsible for the airways and aviation safety, but left airport building and operation to local jurisdictions. Congress was concerned that the building of a national system of airports was too expensive a burden for the federal treasury to bear. Several years before the act was passed, the Chicago City Council had concluded it would have to get into the business of building airports.[34]

The city's first aviation venture, largely the result of a lobbying effort by Dickinson to improve facilities available to private pilots, was an attempt to build several smaller airports around the city. Dickinson, in early 1922, had written to Dan Ryan, president of the Cook County Forest Preserve District, urging that the county use some of its recently acquired land for airports. Dickinson mentioned in his letter that there were already two airports on county land—apparently these were Cook County Airport, at Irving Park Road just east of River Road (not far from where O'Hare International Airport was ultimately built), and Cook County Airport Number Two, just south of Checkerboard Field in Maywood.[35]

The city's 1922 airport plan also called for building a number of flying fields at several sites on the fringes of the city—far north, northwest, southwest, and in Lincoln Park. Mayor William Hale Thompson, after attending the Detroit convention of the National Aeronautic Association in 1922, got carried away and also suggested a $10 million island airport in Lake Michigan just off the Field Museum and linked to the mainland by a tunnel.[36]

Only one of the municipal aerodromes was built as proposed, a flying field on a corner of a mile-square tract of open land 63rd Street and Cicero Avenue owned by the Chicago Board of Education and leased to truck farmers. It was dedicated by the city's aeronautical bureau on October 1, 1922, and was used initially for practice landings by pilots from Ashburn and Maywood until 1923, when it acquired its first tenant, Chicago Air Park Company, a firm offering flying lessons and aerial photography services.[37]

In the meantime, pressure from the U.S. Post Office Department to develop all-weather airports, especially for night flying, increased. By 1922, that agency was already deeply involved in planning the facilities

Mishaps were fairly common in the air mail service. This plane crashed at Maywood Field in 1921. (Chicago Historical Society)

necessary for a night route between New York and San Francisco through Chicago. To demonstrate the feasibility of night flying, on July 26, 1923, Dickinson, Eddie Stinson, and Art Gray made their nonstop all-night flight between Ashburn Field in Chicago and Curtiss Field in Garden City, New York, in an all-metal, single-engine Junkers plane. The flight, which began at 11:00 P.M., took eight hours.[38]

Regular, scheduled night flying would require a more elaborate navigation system than simply letting pilots chase the headlights of trains on the ground—a common practice that led to the later aviation joke:

IFR, which in contemporary terms means "instrument flight rules," in the old days meant "I Fly Railroads."

Under Henderson's direction, in 1923 the post office began installing the first of 289 gas-powered signal beacons at twenty-five-mile intervals between Chicago and Cheyenne, Wyoming, and renting emergency airstrips at strategic locations along the route. The fields were equipped with emergency lighting, rotating electric beacons, boundary markers, and telephones. The navigation beacons were, of course, available to anyone flying that route, not just air mail pilots. Thus began the policy, which continues to this day, that the federal government maintains the nation's air navigation system.

With most of the new equipment in place, on July 1, 1924, the post office began around-the-clock service between New York and San Francisco via Chicago on a thirty-day trial basis. The service proved reliable enough that it was continued at the end of the trial period, and the Aero Club sent a bulletin to members listing the location of six air mail boxes installed around the city. The success of the service, the continued expansion of aviation, the possibility that commercial airlines would be formed within the next few years, and the increasing pressure from the aviation community for an all-weather airport convinced many of Chicago's civic leaders that the city would have to build a large municipal airport, not just a number of small fields scattered around the city.[39]

Charles H. Wacker, chairman of the Chicago Plan Commission, on July 15, 1924—two weeks after the transcontinental test started—asked the Chicago City Council to lease from the Board of Education the truck farms bounded by Cicero Avenue, 55th Street, Central Avenue, and 63rd Street to be developed "as a Municipal Airplane Landing Field." The Plan Commission had endorsed the idea on June 24 because the tract "is practically the only remaining site of its size, kind, and availability within the City of Chicago," and the southwest corner of the tract included the earlier municipal aerodrome.[40]

Four months later, the City Council unanimously adopted a resolution offered by Alderman Dorsey Crowe to have the council's Committee on Public Works and Recreation find a location for a new public airport in Chicago. Ashburn, which had remained the area's most important airport, was probably never seriously considered as the site of the proposed new municipal field. That must have been obvious to Dickinson, because in 1925 he sold for subdivision all but eighty of the original 640 acres at Ashburn.[41]

The primitive conditions at Ashburn made Laird's airplane manufacturing operation especially difficult, and in 1925 he took the step that apparently forced the city's hand. He wrote to the Board of Education asking to lease the existing field at 63rd Street and Cicero Avenue so he could locate his aircraft factory there. The board turned down his request, forcing him to build his new factory at 4500 West 83rd Street, on the north edge of Ashburn Field. Within a month, Crowe introduced in the City Council an ordinance authorizing the city to negotiate with the Board of Education for the 63rd Street and Cicero Avenue site.[42]

A major factor in Crowe's decision to introduce the ordinance was the February 2, 1925, signing by President Calvin Coolidge of the Contract Air Mail Act (popularly known as the Kelly Act after its sponsor, Congressman Melville Clyde Kelly), turning over the transportation of air mail from the post office to private contractors. The Kelly Act authorized the postmaster general to grant air mail contracts to private companies on a low-bid basis, setting the stage for the modern airline industry. Enactment of the law was widely interpreted at the time to mean that Chicago would get additional air mail routes linking it to cities not then on the Post Office Department's transcontinental route.

The City Council approved Crowe's ordinance with unusual speed—within a week of its March 25, 1925, introduction. The April 1 ordinance authorized the city to sign a twenty-five year lease with the Board of Education for as much as six dollars an acre for the new airport. Two days later, Philip G. Kemp, chairman of Mayor William E. Dever's Aero Commission, reached an agreement with the Board of Education on a twenty-five-year lease on three hundred acres. Early the next year, the City Council approved $25,000 for improvements to the field and $1,560 in annual rent payments.[43]

The speed with which the Post Office Department implemented the Kelly Act also contributed to the city's haste in establishing a municipal airport. By October 2, 1925, about eight months after the act was signed into law, the post office awarded the first five air mail contracts, which included routes serving Chicago, Dallas, St. Louis, Detroit, and Cleveland. The first Chicago company to bid successfully on the new routes was National Air Transport (NAT), which had been formed the previous May 21 with the financial backing of a number of prominent Chicagoans. The airline promptly hired Henderson away from the air mail service to be its general manager.

However, Chicago could not build an airport as fast as the post office replaced its air mail service with private carriers, so Maywood remained the Chicago area's principal airport even after the new carriers started flying. The Ford Motor Company, which got the Chicago-Detroit-Cleveland route contract two weeks after the others were awarded, was in the best position to get into operation because it already operated an in-house freight airline between Dearborn, Michigan, and what was then known as Chicago-Hammond Airport in south-suburban Lansing, Illinois (now Lansing Municipal Airport). That operation began April 3, 1925, and enabled Ford to get its Detroit-Maywood air mail operation started somewhat before the new carriers began hauling mail. The first

Ford plane left Maywood Field at 1:45 P.M. on February 15, 1926, for Detroit. The first NAT aircraft to Chicago arrived at Maywood on February 21 en route to Kansas City from the Curtiss factory in Buffalo, New York. It carried no cargo, however.[44]

Although the official opening of Municipal Airport wasn't until the air mail flights were transferred there from Maywood on December 1, 1927, the city held a ceremony at the new airport nineteen months earlier, on May 8, 1926. Thus, Chicago's new airport had opened with a great deal of hoopla but very little business. The first airplane to land there was a Curtiss Carrier Pigeon owned by NAT and flown by Edmund Marucha from Maywood Field just for the ceremony. It was christened *Miss Chicago* during the festivities, but immediately afterward it was flown back to Maywood, where it took off on May 12 with a load of mail destined for Dallas.[45]

After the crowd left, Municipal Airport reverted to the sleepy field it had been since 1922, a place where pilots from other airports could practice their approaches, takeoffs, and touch-and-go procedures with little competition from other traffic. It was destined to become the busiest airport in the world, but not until after the fledgling U.S. airline industry became established and began to carry passengers in appreciable numbers, as well as sacks of mail.

8 Airlines Come to Chicago

• America's airlines for the most part began as a stepchild of government—carriers of the mail and package freight—and for that reason Chicago became the principal center of airline activity in the interior of the United States from the inception of commercial aviation. Although airplanes had a greater freedom of routing than any form of ground transportation because they could overfly topographical obstacles, the air mail routes dictated by the post office followed for the most part the railway postal routes because that is where population and commerce had concentrated. It was almost impossible in 1926 for an airline to survive without the steady revenues and the monopoly that the post office conferred on the successful bidders on its routes. Any change in political winds, as happened when the Hoover administration unilaterally determined there would be only three transcontinental carriers, could prove fatal to individual airlines.

As the nation's largest inland transportation center by virtue of its railroads and waterways, Chicago benefited greatly

Airline travel was expensive during the Great Depression, but air traffic at Municipal Airport grew sevenfold in the decade ending in 1940. That year 2.8 million passengers used the airport. (Christopher Lynch Collection)

The Ford 4-AT Tri-Motor, the first successful passenger plane built in the United States, continued in charter service long after the airlines abandoned it for faster and larger aircraft. This one based at Midway Airport regularly flew sightseers along the lakefront for an aerial view of the Loop. The now-abandoned Illinois Central Railroad yards and the outer drive's S-curve can be seen east of the Loop. (Christopher Lynch Collection)

from the postal era in aviation. It became the nexus of the early air mail routes, and it quickly eclipsed its early rivals, St. Louis and Detroit. For a time, it was necessary for residents of those cities to fly through Chicago to get to either coast. The limited range of early airplanes meant that everything traveling between the Atlantic and Pacific had to visit Chicago en route. It was inherently more efficient to fly westbound mail and passengers from Boston, New York, Philadelphia, Washington, and Baltimore to Chicago for consolidation on flights to the West Coast, and vice versa, than to maintain a dozen parallel routes serving smaller cities in less populated areas of the country.

The most apparent solution to the post office's economic tyranny over the new airline industry was to develop alternative markets—passenger or freight. Except in rare circumstances, freight never became

a reasonable alternative: the airlines collectively have never carried more than a tenth of a percent of the intercity tonnage in the United States in any year. As late as 1990, trucks carried 41 percent of freight; railroads, 26.8 percent; pipelines, 16.5 percent; waterways, 16.2 percent; and air, 0.1 percent.[1]

It became obvious almost from the start that passenger traffic was a potentially lucrative alternative to mail. It was also a form of traffic in which the government, at least initially, had little interest, and over which it exercised very little control, except in matters of safety. The earliest attempts at establishing airlines, most of them unsuccessful, usually involved passenger service. Although there is debate among aviation historians about which airline can be properly called the first, the earliest attempts to provide scheduled passenger service seem to date from 1913–1914, about a decade after the Wrights invented the flying machine. These early carriers' relatively short shuttle routes using primitive flying boats proved to be considerably ahead of the market for air travel.

Thomas Benoist established an aerial shuttle across Tampa Bay, the St. Petersburg–Tampa Airboat Line, that started service on January 1, 1914, a venture many aviation historians consider the first scheduled airline in America. At about the same time, Chicagoans Harold F. McCormick, James E. Plew, and Bion J. Arnold started Lake Shore Airline, a commuter operation using flying boats on Lake Michigan between downtown Chicago, South Shore Country Club on the South Side, and the northern suburb of Lake Forest. Neither survived more than a few months.[2]

More airlines were attempted in 1919, including one organized by William E. Boeing as an air mail shuttle between Seattle and Victoria, British Columbia, and the ill-fated attempt by Alfred W. Lawson to establish an airline between Chicago and New York. The evolution of successful airlines had to await government subsidies to incubate them and corporations with sufficient capital to buy and operate airplanes.[3]

That happened in 1925–1926. In the spring of 1925, Henry Ford joined with William B. Stout to start Ford Motor Company's in-house airline between Chicago and Detroit, and that was quickly followed in 1926 by subsidies in the form of air mail contracts. The Ford Freight Line was established on April 3, 1925, to fly freight between the company's main plants near the Detroit suburb of Dearborn, Michigan, and its assembly plant in the south suburbs of Chicago. The company built its own grass landing strip at nearby Lansing, Illinois, because the nearest commercial airport was Ashburn Field on the Southwest Side of Chicago. Stout had to await the awarding of government air mail contracts to start his Stout Air Services line between Detroit and Grand Rapids, Michigan, on August 2, 1926. It was the first airline to carry sub-

stantial numbers of passengers in addition to mail because the Ford Tri-Motors he used were considerably larger than the planes acquired by the other early airlines.[4]

Emergence of the Airlines

Once regular annual government subsidies were established, it took only a few years for modern airlines to emerge, initially as small local carriers and then, after a wave of consolidations, as truly national carriers. The post office awarded contracts to twelve airlines on fourteen routes in 1925–1926, four of them involving Chicago. From 1927 to 1930 it awarded contracts to another twelve airlines on twenty additional routes, five involving Chicago. Thus, by 1930 Chicago was the hub for nine of the thirty-four contract air mail, or CAM, routes and was linked by air to St. Louis, Detroit, Minneapolis, Dallas, New York, San Francisco, Cincinnati, Pontiac, and Atlanta.[5]

As is typical in American business, the consolidation of the industry began almost immediately. First, many of the original airlines were bought up by enterprises controlled by a handful of financiers. They were then integrated into vertical aviation conglomerates, and finally they were consolidated into four national trunk airlines, although a few independents survived. The entire process took less than a decade.

The first airlines, more often than not, were hastily assembled by aviators, entrepreneurs, local boosters, and civic leaders. Least typical of the 1926 carriers was a corporation assembled specifically for the purpose of operating as a freight airline to bid on air mail routes: National Air Transport (NAT) was organized by a consortium of well-to-do investors in Chicago, Detroit, and New York. Wealthy aviation buff Pop Dickinson underbid NAT for the Chicago-Minneapolis route, then threw together his makeshift airline of scrounged airplanes flown by his pilot friends from the Aero Club of Illinois.[6]

Dickinson's undercapitalized airline was doomed almost from the start. Challenging NAT, which had warned that he would never get the contract and had tried to prevent him from obtaining engines for his planes, the old man had submitted an unrealistically low bid. He borrowed three aircraft until new, Chicago-built Laird Speedwings could be acquired, and he hired some of the nation's best pilots—Elmer Partridge, Nimmo Black, Alfred O. Sporrer, David L. Behncke, Matty Laird, William Brock, Henry Keller, and Ervin E. Ballough. He refused to hire a young pilot named Charles A. Lindbergh because he was concerned about Lindbergh's flying habits.[7]

Dickinson launched his service on June 6, 1926, a day that turned out disastrously. High winds whipped up dust, making visibility poor. Dickinson wept when he got the news that his old friend Partridge, heading for Chicago, had been killed in a crash after taking off in Minneapolis. Meanwhile, Laird, Keller, and Black, flying from Chicago, had been forced down by the storm at La Crosse, Wisconsin. Only Black was able to continue on to Minneapolis.

The new airline never was able to recover. The pilots, probably instigated by Behncke, who later founded the Air Line Pilots Association (ALPA), refused to fly, contending that Dickinson had failed to provide safe planes. One pilot, Dan Kaiser of Milwaukee, charged that Dickinson had only one aircraft that met safety standards. The airline was nearly shut down for a week in August when Ballough was the only pilot willing to continue flying. For a while, Dickinson considered cutting back service from seven days a week to five because there wasn't enough mail to justify the service, then on August 17, after Ballough was forced down near La Crosse, he called it quits and gave the Post Office Department the requisite forty-five-day notice that he was halting service. Later in the month, the post office awarded the contract to a Detroit consortium, which took over the route as Northwest Airways on October 1.[8]

National Air Transport was considerably more successful. At that time, it was the only corporation in the nation that had been formed exclusively for the purpose of operating an airline. Among its incorporators were no aviation pioneers and no aviators: its board consisted of wealthy businessmen. Like the railroads that preceded it, NAT was made possible by New York venture capital, although its principal organizer, New York financier Clement Melville Keys, insisted that Chicago financial interests should provide a quarter of the initial subscription.

Uniting United

When it became obvious that the government was going to contract air mail services to private airlines, Keys in early 1925 approached Carl B. Fritsch, general manager of the Aircraft Development Corporation in Detroit, about the possibility of establishing an airline. Fritsch and his automobile-minded colleagues hoped to establish Detroit as an aviation hub as Chicago was a railroad hub. They decided to raise $2 million in venture capital, originally $1 million apiece in both New York and Detroit, but Keys insisted that Chicago be the western terminus of the airline because the CAM award was for the Chicago–New York route and that $500,000 of the capital be raised in Chicago. The decision ultimately became Keys's undoing because the Chicago group would eventually take control of the operation.[9]

Keys, Fritsch, and Colonel Paul Henderson, the former government air mail director, whom Keys had hired to run the proposed airline, arranged to have Chicago banker Rufus Dawes sponsor a luncheon of potential investors. The lunch was a failure, probably because the railroad industry was so dominant in Chicago; here was an ironic repeat of the problems William B. Ogden had raising local capital for Chicago's first railroad in 1847 when the town was dominated by the maritime industry. But the airline promoters noticed that many of the tycoons invited to the luncheon had sons who had served as pilots in World War I, and they changed their fundraising strategy accordingly: they sought out the sons instead of the fathers. The eventual subscribers from Chicago included John J. Mitchell (banking), Philip K. Wrigley (gum), Lester Armour (meat packing), Philip Swift (meat packing), Wayne Chatfield-Taylor, Earle J. Reynolds, John F. Gilkey Jr., Marshall Field III, and Robert P. Lamont.[10]

The resulting company, National Air Transport (NAT), was incorporated on May 21, 1925, with an authorized capitalization of $10 million, an unprecedented amount for that time. Its rapid development over the subsequent ten years into the nation's largest airline was the result not so much of any technological developments, but of

a lot of wheeling and dealing by aviation's money men, who were reminiscent of the so-called robber barons of the railroad industry in the nineteenth century. National Air Transport became United Air Lines as the result of the amalgamation, sometimes hostile, of a number of pioneer airlines.[11]

For the first few years, Keys remained in the background, although he held the post of chairman of the executive committee, and allowed the Detroit and Chicago investors to control most of the seats on the board. Howard E. Coffin of Detroit, a vice president of the Hudson Motor Car Company, was president. However, the relative position of the Detroit group eroded quickly, leaving the Chicago group in managing control of the airline when NAT successfully bid the Chicago-Dallas route in late 1925 and the Chicago–New York route

Before airport gates were developed, airplanes from various carriers formed a queue in front of a single terminal gate at Municipal Airport and awaited their turn to load passengers. (Christopher Lynch Collection)

the following year, bypassing Detroit.

NAT began service on May 12, 1926, with ten Curtiss Carrier Pigeons built by another Keys company, North American Aviation, which had been formed as a corporate apparatus to finance various aviation ventures, including several other airlines and airplane builders such as Curtiss. The following year, NAT shifted those planes to the Chicago–New York segment of the transcontinental route when it was awarded that contract. NAT had been underbid by Boeing Air Transport (BAT) on the Chicago–San Francisco segment. Curiously, NAT functioned in its early years almost exclusively as a mail and parcel carrier, discouraging passengers whenever possible by bumping them to make room for mail, and at one point doubling fares to $200. In the carrier's first year of operation, it carried only 168 passengers.[12]

Virtually all of the major airlines in the United States emerged as a result of consolidations of smaller carriers, but NAT's evolution into United Air Lines was a particular Byzantine affair involving a power struggle among some of the largest players in American aviation at the time. On one side was Keys and his North American Aviation holding company, and on the other was a combination of airplane builder William E. Boeing and industrialist Frederick W. Rentschler, who at the time was head of Pratt & Whitney, the manufacturer that made the engines for Boeing's commercial airplanes.

Until the practice was banned by federal law in 1934, vertical integration of aviation companies, with aircraft manufacturers controlling airlines as a captive market for their products, was common. Boeing and Rentschler had combined forces in 1927 to form United Aircraft and Transport Corporation, which included Boeing Air Transport, the carrier that held the air mail contract on the Chicago–San Francisco route, as well as Boeing's airplane factory and Rentschler's engine manufacturing operation. They then acquired several smaller aviation manufacturers and airlines.

At that point, Rentschler decided to form a transcontinental New York–to–San Francisco (via Chicago) airline by merging Boeing Air Transport with National Air Transport. BAT was considerably more oriented toward passenger traffic than was NAT, which often left BAT's New York–bound passengers stranded in Chicago. At one point in 1928, NAT withdrew entirely from the passenger business on its Chicago–New York route, largely because Keys was attempting to develop transcontinental traffic on another of his airlines, Transcontinental Air Transport (TAT), later TWA. Rentschler was concerned about Keys's attempt to establish TAT as a coast-to-coast carrier.[13]

The Struggle for Control of United

Rentschler proposed a merger to Keys in early 1930 but Keys was not interested. Rentschler then began plotting a takeover. First he approached the Chicago group which by then controlled a third of the outstanding shares and were in operating control of the airline. Earle Reynolds (by then president of NAT), John J. Mitchell, and Lawrence Armour—organizers of a financial group called Aviation Securities Corporation—alone held 100,000 shares; and Mitchell, as treasurer, held another 30,000 shares in escrow for employees buying stock on time payments. The Chicagoans, intrigued by the possibility of a transcontinental airline based in their city, joined him.

When the story broke in the newspapers that Rentschler had arranged for an exchange of stock agreement to enable him to try to take control of NAT at the April 10, 1930, shareholders meeting in Wilmington, Delaware, Keys called a board meeting to change the company's bylaws and issue an additional 300 shares to his North American Aviation holding company. Rentschler then sought an injunction preventing the stock from being transferred to Keys' holding company and set his agents to work buying up every

share they could find. By April 17 he announced he controlled 375,000 shares or 57 percent of the airline. Keys was beaten, and Rentschler was elected the new president and chairman.[14]

NAT's shareholders ratified the takeover on May 7, 1930, and the carrier became a subsidiary of United Aircraft and Transport as well as the nation's first transcontinental carrier. The pattern was set just five years after passage of the Kelly Act; the other aviation conglomerates to survive would have to become transcontinental airlines. Several carriers that failed to assemble strong transcontinental networks early in the game—most notably Braniff, Eastern, and Pan-American—failed to survive a shakeout in the industry later in the century.

Rentschler decided to create a separate management company for the four airlines—Boeing Air Transport, National Air Transport, Varney Airlines, and Stout Air Services—and United Air Lines Transport Corporation came into existence on July 1, 1931, with offices in downtown Chicago.

(The offices were moved to a building near Municipal Airport in 1939 and to Elk Grove Township near O'Hare International Airport in 1961.) William Boeing's long-time associate Philip G. Johnson was then installed as the president of the new airline.

The emergence of the nation's first transcontinental carrier coincided with and may have resulted from anticipation of the Hoover administration's plans to rationalize the entire U.S. airline system into three transcontinental networks. Three other major airline groups—Eastern Air Transport, Transcontinental and Western (TWA), and American Airways—also came into existence at about the same time as United, the result of consolidations of smaller carriers. In TWA's case, the merger was forced by the Commerce Department, which did not want two airlines—Keys's Transcontinental Air Transport and Harry Hanshue's Western Air Express—competing on the same transcontinental route. Thus, by the end of 1931, the four major carriers that were to dominate America's skies for the next half a century were in place.

The terminal at Municipal Airport and its parking facilities for both airplanes and automobiles, shown here in the 1930s, were expanded almost continuously through the end of the century. The control tower originally sat atop the terminal. (Christopher Lynch Collection)

The logotype on the fuselage of this Ford Tri-Motor shows the transition of National Air Transport (NAT) to United Air Lines as a result of NAT's merger with Boeing Air Transport in 1930. (Christopher Lynch Collection)

Continued attempts by the U.S. Department of Commerce under the Hoover administration to influence the development of transcontinental carriers, and the scandal that resulted, enabled another group of carriers to come into prominence in 1934. President Hoover appointed as postmaster general Walter Folger Brown, who had been an assistant when Hoover headed the Commerce Department under President Calvin Coolidge. Brown decided to rationalize the patchwork system of thirty-two air mail contracts then in existence. The first step was to amend the original Air Mail Act so payment would no longer be based on the weight of mail carried but on the space available for the mail whether or not it was used.

The amendment, known as the McNary-Watres Act, also empowered Brown to extend whatever routes he deemed necessary. His attempt to do that in 1930 by means of a series of private meetings with invited airlines that became known collectively as the Spoils Conferences resulted in five carriers, including United, getting all but two of the twenty-two contracts. Brown apparently had no nefarious agenda in consolidating the routes in the hands of a few carriers but acted out of a conviction that such a consolidation would result in a stronger domestic airline system. In fact, some aviation historians have argued that the progressive approach of Hoover and Brown was beneficial to the infant industry.[15]

The chosen carriers profited considerably from the arrangement. Airline historian R. E. G. Davies calculated that in the three-year period 1931–1933 the airlines realized $34 million in profits on $56 million in revenues from the Post Office Department. However, United lost some 40 percent of its revenues to the new competitors, TWA and American. The next blow followed when the Democrats came to power in 1933. They launched an investigation of the Spoils Conferences and in 1934 enacted legislation requiring that the routes be rebid, the big aviation holding companies divest themselves of their airlines, and participants in the Spoils Conferences be barred from management of any airline for five years.[16]

Philip Johnson left United and went to Canada. He was succeeded by his assistant, William A. (Pat) Patterson on April 13, 1934. United Aircraft and Transport Corporation, the holding company, dutifully spun off its management arm, United Air Lines Transport Corporation, as an independent corporation by issuing its shareholders a half share of airline stock for each share they had in the holding company. When the transaction was complete, the new United wound up with 34.5 percent of the predecessor corporation's assets, no outstanding debt, and $4 million in cash. The cushion proved to be crucial because United had been devastated by the federal intervention. Patterson decided to keep the airline running on a regular schedule despite the loss of the air mail business that had accounted for 45 percent of its revenues. The airline lost $850,000 in the first quarter of 1934 and $2 million for the entire year. Although it was successful in winning back its transcontinental route when the government rebid the air mail contracts, it lost the Chicago-Dallas route to the new Braniff Airways.[17]

Another new entrant and beneficiary of the Spoils Conferences was Pacific Seaboard Airlines, which was low bidder on the contract for the Mississippi Valley route. It promptly changed its name to Chicago & Southern Air Lines and merged with Delta Air Lines in 1953. Although C&S later began flying to Kansas City and Detroit, Chicago remained its principal northern connection, primarily because the transcontinental routes crossed there. By the 1930s, the Windy City, despite being challenged for a time by Detroit and to a lesser extent by other cities, was indisputably the midcontinental hub for the nation's airline industry, just as it had been for the railroads and waterways.[18]

The other airlines affected by the Spoils Conferences in 1934, like United, were also forced to reorganize to successfully rebid the air mail contracts they had lost. In some cases, a change in name sufficed. Thus Transcontinental & Western became TWA Inc. at that time, Eastern Air Transport became Eastern Airlines, and both American and Northwest changed their names from Airways to Airlines.

The Airplane Builders

Chicago, which had a thriving automobile and truck manufacturing business for two decades after those vehicles were developed, was never much of a center for airplane manufacture, for a variety of reasons. A number of bright young aviators who became manufacturers—men like Glenn Martin, Chance Vought, and William B. Stout—learned their trade in Chicago but went elsewhere to build airplanes. The Wright patent wars inhibited aircraft development in the United States until after World War I, but the culprit in Chicago's inability to build planes was probably its weather. The cold, snowy, and stormy winters shut down the early airports and severely inhibited the testing of aircraft that came off the production line between the end of October and the beginning of April. The manufacturers, who tended to congregate on either coast, preferred a milder, less variable climate.

While assorted companies came and went during the early decades of aviation in Chicago, two companies found specialized markets and were able to build airplanes with varying degrees of success until external events claimed them in the early 1930s. E. B. Heath's company did not survive as a builder of airplanes following the death of its founder, although the company did continue and prosper by manufacturing electronics equipment.

Matty Laird's company, which specialized in custom airplanes, often for racing, was a victim of the depression.

Heath and His Kits

Edward B. Heath, born in New York state in 1888, learned how to build things, including biplanes, in his family's machine shops. By 1909, he was in Chicago fabricating parts for machinery, and three years later he founded the E. B. Heath Aerial Vehicle Company that complained in a letter to the Aero Club about the lack of cooperation it was getting at Cicero Field. Unlike other aircraft builders, who ran afoul of the Wright patents and the fickle market in the early days of aviation, Heath built his business by concentrating on accessories, things such as propellers and wings.[19]

By 1913, he was advertising his accessories in national aviation publications, and his business at 3403 Southport Avenue was already something of a legend among local aviators. The place was known in the industry as Heath's Airplane Trading Post, and there they could cheaply buy everything from fabric paint for the wings to fuel tanks and rebuilt engines. If he didn't have a part, he designed and fabricated it in the shop. In 1913, he also designed his second flying machine, a hydroplane.[20]

Because in the prewar years flying was a costly hobby available mainly to the rich, Heath hoped to develop an inexpensive airplane affordable to the average American, but the war intervened and by the time he was ready in 1919 to introduce his Feather model—a lightweight, 270-pound aircraft powered by a motorcycle engine with only 7 horsepower—the market was flooded with cheap war-surplus planes. He had to wait until 1923 to produce the Feather, occupying himself in the meantime by adding flying and mechanics schools to his business and producing a lighted aircraft called the Favorite for night-time advertising.[21] He used that plane to fly four passengers to St. Louis in

1923 and win several air races there. The next year he built a monoplane, Tomboy, which he flew in the national air races in Philadelphia.

It was in 1926 that Heath produced the airplane that made his reputation—a build-it-yourself aircraft sold in kit form and called the Heath Parasol.[22] The Parasol weighed only 285 pounds, and its motorcycle engine was capable of driving it at speeds of up to eighty-five miles an hour for two hundred miles on just five gallons of gasoline. Heath sold ready-to-fly models for $999, but customers could buy the completed airframe for $690, a do-it-yourself kit for $199, or the blueprints for as little as $5. Sales of the kit took off, but in February 1931, Heath was killed in a crash of a new model he was developing. Without its founder, the company struggled through the depression. After World War II it moved to Benton Harbor, Michigan, and experienced a renaissance, offering electronic equipment and radio kits.[23]

Matty Laird

Like so many of Chicago's aviation pioneers, Laird claimed that he had gotten hooked on flying as a teenager. In 1910, at age fourteen, he glanced out of a window of a Loop bank in which he was working and saw pilot Walter Brookins flying over Grant Park. His father, a carpenter, had died a few years earlier, and Laird had quit school and gone to work for $4.50 a week at the First National Bank of Chicago to help support his mother and five siblings.[24]

Years later, Laird liked to recall to interviewers that at age fifteen he attached a set of wings to his bicycle and attempted to get it airborne by pedaling down Chicago's streets into the wind. He had better luck with models after joining the Aero Club's youth model club in 1912. He drew his first plans for a rubber band–powered model on butcher paper and soon was grinding out different designs to test for stability and balance. When he was

demonstrating a model in the lobby of the bank where he worked, the bank's president accosted him and instead of firing him ordered a copy for his son's Christmas present. Laird subsequently sold between thirty and forty models at five dollars apiece to help finance a real airplane he was cobbling together from what parts he could beg or buy at Cicero Field—barrel hoops, scraps of wood, and parts from automobiles and motorcycles.[25]

By September 15, 1913, he was ready to begin testing his *Baby Biplane,* as he called the flying machine. Laird had secured the use of a hangar at Cicero Field and managed to mount a four-cylinder, 12-horsepower engine on the aircraft. While making some test taxiing maneuvers, Laird

unexpectedly discovered he was airborne by ten feet. "I knew how to take off, but had never thought about how to land," he later recalled to an interviewer. He put the nose down, turned off the engine—the usual procedure in those days before aircraft brakes, spoilers, and variable-pitch propellers—and proceeded to break off a wing when he hit the ground. He was unhurt but a little wiser.[26]

He repaired the plane and kept trying, and by the spring of 1914 he was making regular hops at Cicero. The following year he was earning $350 a month barnstorming at county fairs in the *Baby Biplane.* By mid-1915 he and Katherine Stinson were performing together at various shows, and Stinson used the Laird-built *Bone Shaker* for

United Air Lines launched the Boeing 247, shown here at Municipal Airport, into service. United acquired the entire production run to obtain a competitive advantage over its rivals, but the plan backfired when the other airlines acquired the superior DC-3.

The Boeing 80A, one of the last trimotors to appear in commercial service, shown here flying over downtown Chicago, could carry eighteen passengers for about 450 miles at a speed of just over 120 miles an hour. The Wrigley Building is at the extreme left.

exhibitions after World War I. The nickname referred to the plane's vibrations.[27]

Laird had been changed from a barnstormer to a full-time plane builder by injuries he suffered in a wartime accident. In San Antonio, where he had been assigned to test Curtiss Jennies, one of his planes stalled in midair, and he crashed, crushing an elbow, breaking a leg, and seriously injuring a knee. The injuries hospitalized him for nine months, and it was after he returned to Chicago on crutches that he built his *Bone Shaker*.[28]

By 1919 Laird's reputation as a builder

of custom aircraft was so secure that a Wichita, Kansas, company that serviced airplanes, offered rides, and had bought four Laird-built aircraft proposed he move his manufacturing operation to Wichita. Wealthy oilman Jacob M. (Jake) Moellendick was part-owner of the firm and had the financial resources Laird needed for expansion. It was in Wichita between 1919 and 1923 that Laird established his national reputation in the aviation industry, and that city became the center for the manufacture of small, general-aviation aircraft. Clyde Cessna had already built a few small planes there, although he had withdrawn from the business by the time Laird arrived. Lloyd Stearman and Walter Beech, who later went on to found the Consolidated Aircraft and Beechcraft manufacturing companies, respectively, both got their start in the Laird plant.[29]

It was during his stint in Wichita that Laird developed his best-known type of aircraft, originally called the Wichita Tractor but later dubbed the Swallow after it went into production. A more advanced model of the Swallow was the aircraft flown by Walter T. Varney's airline when it first went into service on April 6, 1926. That airline was acquired by United in 1930.[30]

Laird and other partners had a falling out with Moellendick in 1923 over financial matters, primarily Moellendick's big-spending habits. Laird sold out and returned to Chicago with $1,500 and two aircraft to start another company at 23rd Street and Archer Avenue but later moved to Ashburn Field. The Wichita company he had left went into receivership in 1927, and Moellendick eventually died penniless.[31]

Laird's new company built the LC-B Commercial for airline service, but it proved to be a better racing plane, and gradually the firm shifted to producing custom-built racers. Dickinson bought two LC-Bs for his racing operation after his airline failed in 1926—a year before he subsidized the move of Laird's twenty-one-employee company to its new factory at Ashburn Field.[32]

As a builder of racers, Laird had some of the best customers in the business. Charles (Speed) Holman used a Commercial in the 1930 National Air Races and a Laird LC-DW Solution in the Thompson Trophy races the same year. Racing pilot James H. (Jimmy) Doolittle, the man who led the spectacular air raid on Tokyo in 1942, used a Laird LC-DW-300 Super Solution to win the Bendix Trophy in 1931 with an average speed of 217 miles an hour. He also built the wings for the Turner-Laird Special used in the 1938 and 1939 Thompson Trophy races.[33]

The weakness of the racing market during the depression finally caused Laird to get out of the business of building airplanes,

By the end of the 1930s, the DC-3 had become the dominant commercial airplane in the skies, as this lineup of DC-3s at Municipal Airport shows. The aircraft maintained its dominant position until after World War II ended and four-engine transports became available to the domestic airlines. The DC-3 cruised at nearly two hundred miles an hour and as high as twenty thousand feet and could carry twenty-one passengers. (Christopher Lynch Collection)

The December 13, 1950, fare from Youngstown through Cleveland to Chicago on United Air Lines was $24.96.

In 1949, Transcontinental & Western Air Inc. was better known as TWA, even though its name had not yet changed to Trans World Airlines.

Chicago & Southern Air Lines was absorbed by Delta Air Lines in 1953.

although during World War II he built B-24 bomber subassemblies in a plant in La-Porte, Indiana. He retired in 1945 and died in 1982. The airplane builders who were successful in the early years of the airline industry concentrated on building larger aircraft to haul people and mail, not necessarily the speedier planes.

The Airplanes

The air mail contracts had the practical effect of not only incubating the airlines but also subsidizing passenger service to the extent that the carriers were able to survive until it was possible to make a consistent profit on passenger traffic—an event aviation historians usually date at 1936, when the first DC-3 went into service. However, more than a decade before the DC-3 appeared, the industry was producing aircraft designed to handle passengers, not just mail sacks.[34]

The most successful of those early passenger aircraft was the Ford Tri-Motor. Originally designed in Stout's company as a larger version of his eight-passenger, single-engine, all-metal *Maiden Detroit,* the Tri-Motor was developed in 1926 to fly at a speed of 107 miles an hour with a range of 570 miles carrying ten or eleven passengers. Stout added the third engine as a safety feature; in the event one engine failed, the plane would still have two to enable it to find an airport. Although the Ford 4-AT Tri-Motor, as it was officially known, was noisy, drafty, and slow, Ford sold 194 of the model to U.S. airlines between its introduction and 1934 when it was replaced by the newer Boeing 247 and a series of Douglas aircraft culminating in the DC-3.[35]

The principal rival of the Tin Goose, as the 4-AT Tri-Motor was informally known, was the three-engine Fokker F-10, a commercial derivative of Anthony Fokker's original Tri-Motor, F-VIIa-3m, built in 1925 and made famous when Richard E. Byrd and Floyd Bennett used one to fly over the North Pole for the first time on May 9,

1926. Fokker later claimed that the Tin Goose, which first flew on June 11, 1926, was copied from his F-VIIa-3m during its visit to Detroit, but Stout in his memoirs wrote that many of the design features were already on the drawing board or had evolved from the *Maiden Detroit,* although the idea of suspending the engines beneath the wing to reduce landing speed had been borrowed from Fokker.[36]

Until technology overtook them in less than a decade, the two aircraft were the most successful commercial airliners in the sky, and each had a rendezvous with destiny. The 1931 crash of a Fokker that killed famous University of Notre Dame football coach Knute Rockne doomed that plane and raised some serious questions about the safety of air travel. A year later an American Airways Ford Tri-Motor carried New York governor Franklin Delano Roosevelt to the Democratic National Convention in Chicago to accept his party's nomination for president. The picture of Roosevelt and his family stepping off the plane at Chicago Municipal Airport to be greeted by a cheering crowd made the front page of newspapers around the world and did much to rehabilitate the public's perception of how safe it was to fly in an airplane.

Even before Rockne's and Roosevelt's flights, the airline industry had begun fishing around for better passenger planes. The Rockne crash had the effect of accelerating that search, and the aircraft industry, which at that time also dominated the airlines by means of holding companies, acquired some needed new blood and competition. The first partnership to act was Boeing-United, which in 1934 converted a two-engine army bomber to commercial production. The second actor was Donald Douglas, an airplane builder who had no ties to commercial aviation, but who was able in a few years to build a succession of airplanes that proved so economically and technologically successful that they came to dominate American aviation until well after World War II.

Chicago—Airport to a Nation

• It wasn't very long after airplanes began carrying mail that people began going along for the ride. The government had no interest in directly subsidizing a passenger market, but it was interested in developing larger aircraft to enable passenger service that would cross-subsidize the mail. The fledgling airlines, however, very quickly realized that revenues from the passenger market had the potential for dwarfing mail revenues, the subsidies for which were subject to the whims of Congress and the ever-changing administrations in Washington.[1]

The principal impediments to developing the passenger market were the cost of flying and John Q. Public's innate suspicion that if God had wanted him to fly he would have been born with wings. The publicity generated by every fatal airplane crash only reinforced this fear. It took the airline industry until the 1950s to solve both problems by offering cheaper tickets and by conquering most people's fear of flying. Again, war was a factor.

World War II resulted in the development of larger, faster, and more reliable airplanes that allowed thousands of Americans who would not otherwise have done so to travel by air as passengers aboard C-47 and C-54 military transports. Having survived the experience in the Spartan accommodations of military aircraft, they could certainly do so in the more comfortable accommodations of the DC-3 and DC-4 civil versions of those planes. Larger planes, especially the jets that came on line in the 1960s, meant lower seat-mile (an industry measure of efficiency) costs because the same flight-deck crew that could fly a twenty-seat airplane on a 200-mile flight could also handle one with four hundred seats on a 2,000-mile flight. The speedier jets got to their destinations faster and were ready for the next hop while their propeller-driven predecessors were

still in the air. Reliability both reduced maintenance costs and negated much of the fear-of-flying conundrum.

Competitiveness—a human characteristic raised to a high art in America's free enterprise system—solved the problem of the high cost of air travel. Having begun in 1926 with government-regulated mail-route monopolies, by 1955 the airlines were competing among themselves for passengers and offering ever more innovative fare packages despite heavy-handed regulation by the Civil Aeronautics Board and were in the process of driving the railroad passenger train toward extinction. There were casualties, to be sure, but the weaker airlines were absorbed by the stronger ones, which by the end of the century grew into international giants.

When World War II ended, air travel accounted for less than half a percent of the intercity travel mileage in America. The railroads, with 27.1 percent of the market, were still the favored common carriers, and buses accounted for 7.9 percent. The balance (63.8%) was by automobile. Within ten years the airlines, with 21.3 billion passenger miles, had nearly pulled even with the railroads, at 28.7 billion miles, and by 1960 travel by air dwarfed the declining railroad passenger system. The gap widened as the century wore on.[2] It was possible by the end of the century to hop a domestic carrier in Chicago for a nonstop flight to many of the capitals in Europe and Asia as well as to almost any city of any size in the United States. By then, railroad intercity passenger service subsisted only by virtue of generous government subsidies, and ocean liners were relegated to the status of recreational cruise ships.

Cities along the air routes joined the competition by building bigger and better airports the same way American ports on the East Coast more than a century earlier had dug canals westward to create economic satrapies in the American interior and the cities and states in that region had subsidized railroads to extend their economic influence at the expense of their rivals. Chicago had won the competition for canals and railroads in the 1850s and was not about to be left out of the race in the air.

Municipal/Midway Airport was a work in progress from its inception in 1922 until the city ran out of space to expand it. Then Chicago built O'Hare International Airport, which was continually expanded and improved through the end of the cen-tury. By that time, increased air traffic threatened to inundate both Midway and O'Hare, and public debate was about whether the state should build a third airport for the metropolitan area. The state had already rescued many of the area's smaller private airfields from oblivion by encouraging public ownership to prevent them from being transformed into shopping centers and by subsidizing their expansion to create homes for the private and corporate aircraft that were being driven out of O'Hare and Midway by the heavy commercial airline traffic.

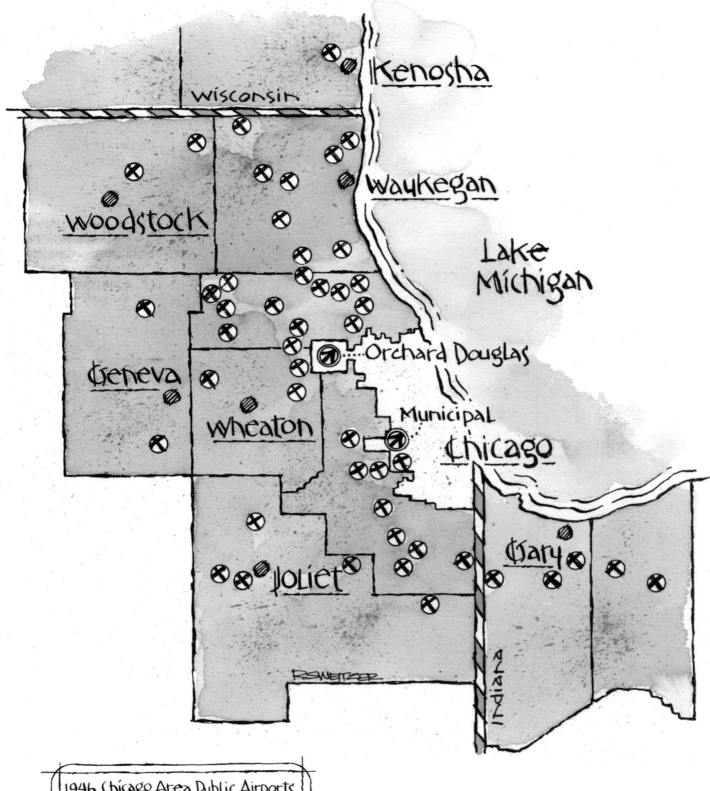

Wisconsin

Kenosha

Waukegan

Lake
Michigan

Woodstock

Geneva

Wheaton

Orchard Douglas

Municipal

Chicago

Gary

Joliet

Indiana

RSWEITZER

1946 Chicago Area Public Airports
⊕ Air Carriers
⊗ General Aviation Airports

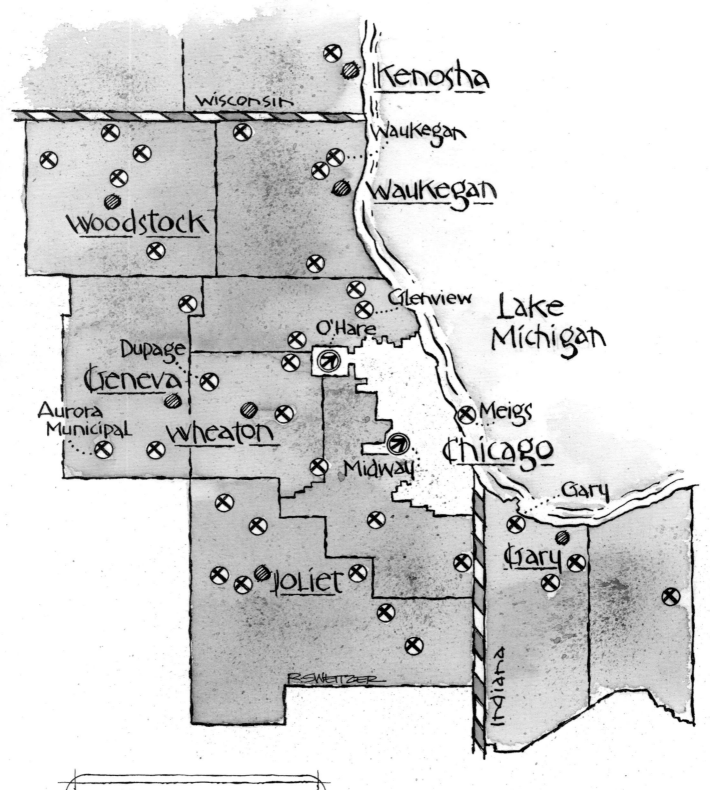

1960 Chicago Area Public Airports
✈ Air Carriers
⊗ General Aviation Airports

Air Disasters

Perhaps because humanity has always had an innate fear of flying, safety has been a concern of aeronauts and aviators from the inception of manned flight. Balloons, beginning in the eighteenth century, were often tethered to the ground to prevent them from being swept away by the wind; early aviators a century later often picked sandy beaches or pastures, open expanses bereft of obstructions, to test their flying machines. Yet the pastime by its very nature—the thrill of soaring like birds—

attracted more than its share of daredevils, with a resulting toll in human life.

Between 1890 and 1912, by one count, 182 people died as a result of aerial mishaps worldwide—an unexpectedly high toll considering how few aircraft there were. (By way of contrast, 324 people were killed in railroad accidents in 1910 alone.) During the three years (1911–1913) in which fewer than one hundred airplanes were being operated sporadically in and around Chicago, including the transients entered in the air

The eighteen passengers and three crew members aboard this TWA DC-3 that crash-landed on July 2, 1946, on some railroad tracks near 47th Street and Cicero Avenue all survived without serious injury. The plane went down after an engine failed following takeoff from Municipal Airport. (Chicago Historical Society) shows, crashes claimed six lives, and another five pilots who used Chicago facilities as their base were killed while barnstorming elsewhere. The toll included a few pilots on their first or second flights and such famous and experienced aviators as St. Croix Johnstone, Eugene Ely, Cal Rodgers, Otto Brodie, Andrew Drew, and Max Lillie.[1]

The high toll has caused some "speculation" that if the flying machine had been invented at the end of the twentieth century instead of the beginning, it would have been banned by the U.S. Occupational Safety and Health Administration. Although concerns over aviation safety periodically were stated publicly in the years before World War I, for the most part they did not result in government regulation of aviation because the vast majority of those who died were aviators who knew and accepted the risks of flying, not innocent victims of planes falling into crowds or crashing into houses; passengers were a rarity on early airplanes, although the first fatality in an airplane crash, which did not occur until 1908, was that of a passenger, Army Lieutenant Thomas Selfridge. It was another year before a crash claimed a pilot, Eugene Lefebvre in France. Occasional sport or exhibition flying had its risks, but attempting to maintain scheduled commercial service invariably meant flying in marginal weather, which increased the death toll even for experienced pilots. A total of 26 air mail pilots were killed in the line of duty in the two and a half years between late 1918, when service started, and mid-1921.[2]

Because the primitive planes were small, an early air mail crash typically claimed a single life, that of the pilot. It wasn't until after World War I that Chicago experienced its first crash that could be considered an aviation disaster (having a toll of ten or more lives): the flaming *Wingfoot* blimp plunged through the skylight of a Loop bank. The next local disaster did not occur for another twenty-one years, when

a DC-3 crash took ten lives. By then the federal government was regulating not only pilots but also airplanes and airlines, and the public was beginning to accept the risks of flying. (Appendix B lists Chicago area aviation disasters.)

The risk was well enough known by 1910 that the private associations governing aviation began to impose some rules. The Federation Aeronautique International (FAI) in Paris in October of that year adopted rules for issuing licenses to pilot not only flying machines but also balloons and dirigibles. The sixteen nations that were members of FAI were in charge of testing and licensing pilots, and the Aero Club of America delegated the testing and certification to local organizations like the Aero Club of Illinois. As a practical matter there was little the American organization could do to enforce its regulations except to ostracize from its sanctioned meets or airports unqualified pilots or those who violated the rules, which it did in 1912, when a number of pilots flew in an unsanctioned meet in Boston.[3]

The pilot's test was simple by modern standards: a candidate had to successfully complete two flights of fifty meters altitude and five kilometers length over a closed course that consisted of figure eights. The pilot also was required to land within fifty meters of a predesignated point and properly shut down the engine upon touchdown. In 1912, the national organization added an expert aviator license that required a fifty-mile round trip cross-country flight and for the first time required a physical examination of the candidate. The tests could be conducted at either Cicero Field or the national organization's Hempstead Field on Long Island.[4]

It was inevitable, because states were unable to effectively do so, that the federal government would eventually regulate airmen and their machines, just as it had been forced to regulate steamboats and their pilots and engineers beginning in 1853 and railroads somewhat later. As early as 1911, the Aeronautical Society of New York enlisted the help of the Aero Club of Illinois in lobbying for federal air safety regulations. The first federal legislation to appear was an outgrowth of World War I: in February 1918, President Wilson issued a proclamation prohibiting civilians to fly in the United States except with a license issued by the Joint Army and Navy Board of Aerial Recognizance. The measure was imposed for national security, not safety, reasons and was lifted in July 1919.[5]

The U.S. Department of War in 1919 and 1920 imposed some rudimentary specifications—actually little more than guidelines—for municipal landing fields, making such observations as: "An effort should be made to select a location in a place where the field is unlikely to be later surrounded by building operations." Unfortunately, it took several disasters to prod the government to impose safety regulations on aviation, despite pleas by the industry that such rules were needed.[6]

Local Safety Rules

After the *Wingfoot* crash, the City of Chicago, in late 1919, used its general public safety powers to authorize the police to ban flying over the Loop and other heavily populated areas of the city except by permit "for the reasonable and proper guarding of the public." In 1921, an ordinance banned pilots from performing aerobatics over the city, flying at altitudes below two thousand feet (this would enable airplanes to glide to airports or open areas should their engines fail), and dumping handbills or ballast except over designated areas. The ordinance also established midair passing rules and gave blimps, balloons, and dirigibles the right of way over heavier-than-air machines. However, the City Council clearly recognized that air safety was a federal issue: the Chicago ordinance stipulated that the rules were to remain in effect until superseded by federal law.[7]

The *Wingfoot* disaster also prodded the insurance industry into action. Insurance

Early airline pilots flew with their planes in conditions that would not be tolerated by modern pilots. Safety was a motive for the formation of the Air Line Pilots Association in the early 1930s. When Elmer Partridge took off from Minneapolis for Chicago in this Dickinson Airlines plane on June 6, 1926, the tire on the right wheel was missing. He died when the plane went down a few minutes later.

companies in those days were more of a regulator of safety than was government, and absent any federal regulation of air safety, coverage of airplanes was expensive to obtain. The Klee, Rogers, Wile & Loeb insurance agency in the Loop offered aviation insurance for fire, theft, and collision to the Aero Club of Illinois in 1920. Additional premiums were required to cover aerobatics, flight instruction, and demonstration flights. A year later the insurance companies hired Underwriters Laboratories of Chicago to begin a registration system for aircraft.[8]

In the public debate that followed the *Wingfoot* disaster, World War I ace Reed Landis proposed that the Aero Club appoint a committee to look into the need for state and municipal regulations. He suggested that as a start the regulations should ban aircraft that had not passed a safety inspection from flying over Chicago and that minimum flying altitudes be required over the city. Visibility permitting, higher altitudes are generally favored by pilots because of the time and distance given to recover should a malfunction occur. On early aircraft, a midair engine failure simply meant that the pilot would have to glide to a safe landing on the first available beach, pasture, or park—a procedure that would be difficult at low altitude because of the necessity of clearing obstacles like trees and buildings to reach an open area.[9]

The blimp disaster resulted in some debate on Capitol Hill in Washington on the advisability of aviation safety regulations, but the legislators were not ready to tackle the issue. Congress turned its attention to more pressing problems of a nation trying to make the transition from war to peace. The furor in Chicago also subsided under the crush of postwar problems and as a result of a public relations campaign by the Aero Club. Front-page stories about the *Wingfoot* disaster quickly yielded to accounts of a bitter streetcar strike, race riots, a sensational child murder case, the revolution in Mexico, and the Chicago White Sox winning the American League pennant.

Pressure for federal regulation, especially from the aviation community, continued to mount, although there was no grassroots movement to prod Congress. The American public seemed to think that if daredevils wanted to risk their own necks it was no business of Washington. Despite the support for such legislation by three successive presidents—Woodrow Wilson, Warren Harding, and Calvin Coolidge—it took a couple more disasters to spur Congress into action. It finally passed the Air Commerce Act of 1926.

By 1918, the National Advisory Commission for Aeronautics (NACA) had concluded that "federal legislation should be enacted governing the navigation of aircraft in the United States," and NACA's executive committee ultimately drafted a bill creating such a regulatory agency under the jurisdiction of the Department of Commerce. Wilson endorsed the bill in February 1919. Several bills based on that proposal were finally introduced in Congress in 1920, but the issue became lost in the dispute over suggestions by controversial Army Air Service Brigadier General Billy Mitchell that a separate cabinet-level aviation department be created with jurisdiction over civil and military aviation.

Meanwhile, a young former World War I aviator and Chicago attorney, William P. MacCracken Jr., had become interested in aviation law almost by accident: when a local club asked him to present a paper, he chose aviation law for lack of any other suitable topic, and to his surprise he discovered that almost nothing existed on the subject. He then induced the American Bar Association (ABA) to appoint a committee to conduct its own study, and it too found a vacuum. Undaunted, MacCracken worked through the ABA and the newly formed National Aeronautic Association, the successor to the Aero Club of America, to put together meaningful federal legislation on aviation. In the 1920s, MacCracken was probably the most significant figure in the nation in establishing a federal civil aviation policy and a federal regulatory system for aviation.[10]

Although the nation's political bodies usually respond with safety legislation only after a disaster, many members of Congress had become concerned with the high postwar death toll in barnstorming exhibitions. Typical was the case of eighteen-year-old daredevil Louis James, who was killed on July 3, 1922, while attempting to climb between airplanes in an exhibition over Ashburn Field. He had just grabbed a rope ladder suspended from one plane when the aircraft he had just left swerved into him and he was cut to pieces by the propeller. James was one of 353 persons to die in aviation accidents in the five-year period from 1921 to 1925.[11]

Federal Regulation

Congress continued to debate the issue but did not pass any legislation on the topic until 1925, when the Air Mail Act came up for a vote. The act would transfer the carriage of mail from the federal government to private contractors. It was by then obvious to a majority in Congress that some sort of regulation was needed, if for no other reason than to protect the mail. Still, nothing was accomplished until later that year, when two aerial crashes occurred within a week of each other. On August 31, a navy seaplane with a crew of five disappeared on a flight to Hawaii, and on September 3, the giant navy dirigible *Shenandoah* broke up during a storm over Ohio, and fourteen of her crew of forty-five died in the ensuing crash. The houses of Congress quickly passed differing aviation bills that required for the first time the licensing of pilots and federal registration of aircraft. The Senate version required such regulation only in the case of interstate commerce, and it was that version that ultimately emerged from the conference committee and was signed by President Calvin Coolidge on May 20, 1926.[12]

The law gave to the Department of Commerce the power to administer the new act as it applied to interstate commerce. Chicagoan Paul Henderson was

Secretary of Commerce Herbert Hoover's first choice as assistant secretary of commerce for aviation, but Henderson, who had resigned as head of the air mail service to help organize the new National Air Transport, declined. U.S. Representative Martin Madden, another Chicagoan and Henderson's father-in-law, insisted that the job go to a resident of his home town, so William MacCracken was offered the post, accepted it, and was instrumental in drafting the ensuing federal air regulations.[13]

MacCracken ultimately became a victim of the Spoils Conference scandal in 1934. He had left government service in 1929 to become an aviation attorney and lobbyist, had chaired the airlines' Spoils Conference, and was sentenced to ten days in jail in 1934 after the Senate cited him with contempt for refusing to turn over his papers during its investigation of the affair. He served the sentence after the U.S. Supreme Court rejected his claim of attorney-client privilege.[14]

Establishing air mail subsidies and effective federal safety regulation were the first two steps in creating a viable commercial aviation industry; manufacturing larger and more reliable airplanes was the third. But convincing the public that flying was safe was the greatest hurdle aviation faced. Aviation historian R. E. G. Davies contends that Charles Lindbergh's solo flight across the Atlantic Ocean on May 20–21, 1927, was the most important single event to jolt the public out of its reluctance to fly. Lindbergh, a former air mail pilot for Robertson Air Lines on the Chicago–St. Louis route, was the seventy-ninth person to cross the Atlantic by air, but the first person to do it solo, and the feat received worldwide publicity.[15]

The public perception of safety is an issue transportation historians have grappled with for generations, and public perception often influences legislatures as well as the travel market. The high incidence of explosions of high-pressure boilers on river steamboats between 1820 and 1852 resulted in federal safety legislation, and the increased likelihood of death in accidents involving wooden railroad cars caused the railroad industry in the late nineteenth century to begin to convert to steel passenger cars. The explosion of the *Hindenburg* was the last in a succession of disasters that doomed the dirigible industry in the late 1930s.[16]

The Rockne Crash and the Roosevelt Flight

Two trips involving Chicago were probably as influential as Lindbergh's feat. They had a profound influence on the public's acceptance of commercial aviation and indeed on its perception of flying as a safe method of travel. The two early airline trips, one beginning in Chicago and the other ending there, were made a year apart in the early 1930s during the infancy of commercial aviation. They provide a convenient boundary to delineate the shift in public perception of the safety of travel by air, although large numbers of Americans didn't begin to fly commercially until after World War II when air fares became more affordable. The first trip ended in 1931 in the crash of a Fokker Tri-Motor that killed Knute Rockne, shocking the nation. The other was the successful flight a year later by New York governor Franklin Delano Roosevelt to attend the Democratic National Convention in Chicago. The picture of Roosevelt and his family stepping off the plane at Chicago Municipal Airport made front-page news around the world.

Rockne, coach of the University of Notre Dame's national championship football teams in 1929 and 1930, had visited his mother in Chicago on March 30, 1931, before beginning a trip to Los Angeles to give some speeches and advise Hollywood about making a film on football. He took the train to Kansas City to catch Transcontinental and Western Air (later TWA) Flight 3 to the West Coast. At 10:22 A.M. on March 31, the crew of the Fokker F-010A Tri-Motor, flying over Kansas, reported that they were turning back because of the weather and a few

minutes later asked for a report on the weather at Wichita. Witnesses on the ground near Bazaar, Kansas, said they saw the plane emerge from the clouds then a heard loud bang as a section of the wing broke off. The plane plunged 1,500 feet to the ground, disintegrating as it fell and spilling out some of its passengers.[17]

No event has a more chilling effect on the public perception of aviation safety than the failure of an airframe in flight. Such failures caused the groundings of the Fokker in 1931, the de Havilland Comet in 1954, and the Douglas DC-10 in 1979, although the Lockheed Electra was not grounded after two spectacular crashes in 1959 in which portions of the wings fell off in midair. The Fokker crash occurred during the first generation of passenger aircraft, and because Rockne was a victim it received national notoriety.[18] The crashes of a Transcontinental Air Transport plane on September 3, 1929, near Mount Taylor, New Mexico, killing eight, and of another TAT plane, a Ford Tri-Motor, in January 1930 near Oceanside, California, killing fifteen, did not receive nearly the attention in the press as the Rockne crash, although they did lead to some debate in the federal government over whether the results of its crash investigations should be made public.[19]

The Air Commerce Act of 1926 gave the U.S. secretary of commerce the power "to investigate, record, and make public the causes of accidents in civil air navigation," and the spectacular nature of the crash over Kansas and the fact that Rockne had been killed in it caused the federal government to act quickly. Clarence Young, head of the commerce department's aeronautics branch, concerned that the incident would destroy the public's fragile perception of the safety of air travel, sent investigators to the scene immediately. After successively and wrongly attributing the crash to the pilot losing control in turbulence, a broken propeller blade, and ice, investigators finally determined that deterioration of the glue holding together the spars inside the wing was the cause.[20]

After considerable confusion on the part of investigators, Young ordered all Fokker aircraft of that type grounded until inspections could be conducted. The resulting bad publicity and the difficulty of inspecting the interior of the wing hastened the departure of Anthony Fokker's planes from America's skies. TAT assembled its fleet of Fokkers, removed the engines, and burned the airframes.[21]

The Roosevelt family's flight to Chicago fifteen months after the Rockne crash did a great deal to revive the public perception that flying was a safe method of travel, though few people would be able to afford to fly for another twenty years. In the 1930s, all of the fledgling airlines maintained on their staffs traffic representatives whose job it was to promote air travel; a vestige of this survived into the 1980s in the form of the airlines' public relations departments, which were huge compared to similar departments in other segments of the transportation industry. For much of the decade preceding World War II, the airlines actively promoted flying by publicizing celebrities' flights and obtaining

their endorsements, and by adding such amenities as flight attendants and meals.[22]

The Roosevelt flight was engineered by Max Pollet, a local traffic representative in Albany, New York, for the former Colonial Air Transport, which at the time was evolving into American Airlines. Although presidential candidates traditionally stayed at home and awaited the arrival of a delegation from the convention to offer the nomination, Roosevelt was convinced that he could make a dramatic start to his campaign if he appeared in person to accept the nomination, and that could be done only if he flew to Chicago. Roosevelt had flown a couple of times during World War I when he was an assistant secretary of the navy, and he agreed to Pollet's proposal to charter for $300 a Ford Tri-Motor operated by American, taking the plane off its normal Dallas–Los Angeles run for the occasion.[23]

Although the planning was secretive, the object of the flight was to generate maximum press coverage for Roosevelt. Once Roosevelt's allies in Chicago had secured him the nomination, Pollet began

The crash that killed the University of Notre Dame's famous football coach Knute Rockne near Bazaar, Kansas, in 1931 received widespread attention in the press and resulted in the nation's first full-scale federal investigation to determine the cause of an airplane accident. The practice of federal investigations of air crashes continues to the present day. (Kansas State Historical Society) calling the newspapers and radio stations at stops along the route to generate news coverage. The 783-mile flight, with extended stops in Buffalo and Cleveland to enable Roosevelt to grant interviews, pose for pictures, and greet supporters, took eight hours. When the Tri-Motor touched down at Municipal Airport in Chicago, a crowd of 25,000 and the national press was waiting. Photographs of Roosevelt and his family posing outside the plane made the front page of most newspapers in the country the next morning.[24]

The Chicago flight was probably the most publicized of scores of flights by government officials, celebrities, and politicians campaigning for the 1932 elections. Roosevelt's wife, Eleanor, flew several times during the campaigns that year, as did John Nance Garner, the Democratic vice presidential candidate; several members of President Hoover's cabinet; and scores of congressmen.[25]

The Fear of Flying

Fear of flying did not disappear with the Roosevelt trip; nor did the issue of aviation safety. In 1937, American Airlines president C. R. Smith took on the issue with a signed advertisement placed in newspapers across the country. In it he admitted there is risk to flying, but contended that the same could be said of any form of transportation:

Regrettable as it is, the records show there have been accidents and fatalities in every form of transportation. What we do not understand, is why some people associate danger with a transport plane more than they do with a train, a boat, a motor car, an interurban, or a bus. Is it because airline accidents have received more publicity?

Whether you fly or not, does not alter the fact that every form of transportation has one thing in common—risk! No form of transportation—on the ground, on the water, or in the air—can guarantee its passengers absolute immunity from danger.[26]

Despite the risks, by the middle of the twentieth century the American public was gradually beginning to accept flying as a means of transportation instead of a thrill ride. Still, the issue of aviation safety continues, most recently as a result of the September 11, 2001, terrorist attacks using four hijacked jets. Though crash frequency has decreased, they have continued to occur with a variety of causes even as the industry has learned to build safer airplanes, weather forecasting has become more accurate, and the federal government has steadily improved the air traffic control system under its jurisdiction as new technology has come on line. By the end of the twentieth century, several types of radar, transponders, and computers, both in the air and on the ground, were an integral part of aviation. Computers were used not only for running the air traffic control system but also for designing airplanes and flying them. Captains and first officers have become more cockpit managers than pilots.

Improvements have not come without a toll, however, and Chicago, as the nation's midcontinental aviation hub and site of the world's busiest airports, has had its share of crashes. Between 1940 and the end of the century, the Chicago area was the site of fifteen major commercial airplane crashes in which a total of 761 people died. Another thirty-two persons were killed in the crashes of two military aircraft, in 1943 and 1982.

A number of other crashes, like the high-altitude midair collision over the Grand Canyon on June 30, 1956, and the crash of a United Airlines DC-10 in Sioux City, Iowa, during an emergency landing in 1989 after an engine disintegrated in flight, involved airplanes headed for Chicago. The Sioux City crash, in which the flight was heading from Denver to Chicago, killed 112 of the 296 persons aboard. The collision that took 128 lives at 21,000 feet in uncontrolled airspace over a remote area of the Grand Canyon involved two flights from Los Angeles, a United DC-7 with 53 passengers and a crew of five

headed to Chicago and a TWA Super Constellation going to Kansas City. That accident is notable because it accelerated the federal government's program to build a nationwide system of controlled airspace.[27]

The Northwest Airlines Lockheed Electra crash of March 17, 1960, though it occurred far from Chicago on the southern border of Indiana, involved a flight bound from the Windy City to Florida. After portions of both of its wings failed, the plane plunged eighteen thousand feet into a farm field near Tell City, Indiana, killing all sixty-three persons aboard. The crash replicated a similar accident on September 29, 1959, in which the left wing of a Bran-

iff Airways Electra failed at fifteen thousand feet near Buffalo, Texas, and the plane crashed, killing thirty-four. The Tell City disaster was particularly grisly, even to veteran crash investigators. The plane had come down like a rocket from eighteen thousand feet and had hit the ground at a speed in excess of six hundred miles an hour. Its fuselage burrowed a hole and telescoped to a third of its original length. The crash was unusual in that no bodies were recovered; they had been crushed to a pulp in the crater, and only five of the victims were ultimately identified. The local coroner was so overcome that he wanted to bring in a bulldozer and

Franklin D. Roosevelt's well-publicized flight to Chicago aboard an American Airways Tri-Motor to accept the Democratic Party's nomination for president did much to dispel the nation's fear of flying, which had been exacerbated by the Knute Rockne crash in 1931. Roosevelt, then governor of New York, and his family were photographed before boarding the plane in Albany, New York. (FDR Presidential Library) cover the site, leaving the wreckage as a tomb, but officials of the Civil Aeronautics Board overruled him.[28]

Combined, these two disasters ended the turboprop Electra's marketability to airlines, although the existing planes continued to fly in commercial service for years, and the navy used them for reconnaissance. In May 1960, engineers for Lockheed determined that the cause of the accidents was a factor known as "whirl mode," in which an engine mount would become loose and under certain conditions cause the propeller to wobble, in

turn transmitting destructive vibrations to the wing. The temporary solution was to slow the plane's cruising speed to reduce the vibrations.[29]

The Great Lakes Triangle Myth

Mechanical difficulties, weather, and pilot error account for the bulk of the crashes involving Chicago, but two of the disasters were never fully explained even after lengthy investigations. The disappearance of two planes in Lake Michigan in 1950 and 1965 fueled a revival of a pop-

Roosevelt, who can be seen in a white hat just to the right of the word *Airways* painted on the side of the plane, was greeted by the press and a crowd of well wishers when he landed at Chicago's Municipal Airport.

ular legend about a Great Lakes triangle, similar to the Bermuda Triangle, in which aircraft and ships were swallowed by the lake, leaving no trace. The myth, originally spun by mariners, dated back to 1679 when the explorer LaSalle's *Griffon*, the first ship to sail the lakes, disappeared. During the ensuing centuries, sporadic unexplained disappearances of ships, balloons, and airplanes added to the yarn.[30]

The first airliner to disappear was a Northwest Airlines DC-4 with fifty-eight persons aboard that vanished at night in turbulent weather at 3,500 feet above the lake about eighteen miles northwest of Benton Harbor, Michigan, on June 23, 1950. The plane's logbook and some wreckage was found floating on the surface of the lake, but the airframe was never found. The cause of the crash was never officially determined.[31]

The second plane to disappear was a brand-new United Airlines 727 jet bound from New York to Chicago with thirty persons aboard that crashed into the lake for unknown reasons on August 16, 1965, also at night. The aircraft was descending for a landing at O'Hare International Airport when it hit the lake at high speed about 19.5 miles east of the suburb of Lake Forest. The cause was never officially determined, but the best theory was that the altimeters on the early 727s could be misread in increments of 10,000 feet, so an inattentive air crew cleared to descend from 14,000 feet to 6,000 feet on approach to Chicago could have assumed when they reached 6,000 feet that they were at 16,000 feet. The aircraft also had a deceptively high "sink rate," or rate of descent, that required additional pilot training.[32]

The triangle myth eventually fell victim to improved technology: better radar, emergency locator beacons, and the use of sonar to locate wreckage. By 1980, airplanes that thirty years earlier would have vanished without a trace were being found and the causes of their crashes determined. That year, in a case that re-ceived little attention in the press because it involved a small airplane and only four persons, the National Transportation Safety Board (NTSB), the Civil Aeronautics Board's successor in investigating crashes, made considerable progress in dissolving the triangle myth. The case was unusual because the NTSB, which typically hoarded its resources for major plane accidents, spent an exceptional amount of time and money on the crash of a small plane.[33]

The twin-engine Beechcraft E-90 in air taxi service had taken off from O'Hare on December 7, 1980, and was headed for Michigan City, Indiana, with the pilot and three passengers aboard when it disappeared from radar about six miles northeast of its destination. The rescue effort was slow to mobilize because of bungled communications. Four hours after the disappearance the Coast Guard located a fuel slick but none of the aircraft's occupants. Investigators then spent three and a half days searching with sonar for the airplane on the lake bottom before locating it in thirty-eight feet of water. They raised the wreckage on December 18. Only two of the four bodies were ever found.

The NTSB's conclusions at the end of a year-and-a-half-long investigation were startling in that they dealt not with the cause of the crash but with the subsequent search-and-rescue operation. For one thing, the four persons aboard survived the crash but died of hypothermia in the lake's cold waters while the search effort was being mobilized. The airplane was equipped with an emergency locator transmitter designed to transmit a distress signal for forty-eight hours to guide rescuers to the scene in case of an accident, but the device had been turned off. Twenty years earlier the disappearance of a small plane over the lake would have been dismissed as just another of the mysterious incidents in which men and machines were swallowed up by the lake without a trace.[34]

Weather-Related Crashes

Weather—the bugaboo of flyers in the air mail service era—continued to cause airline disasters in the last half of the twentieth century, but they became rarer as improved navigation, weather forecasting, radar, and instrument landing systems became available. Chicago's first airline disaster, the crash of a United DC-3 near Municipal Airport on December 4, 1940, killing ten of the sixteen persons aboard, was blamed on ice that had accumulated on the cockpit windshield, impairing visibility, and on the wings, causing the plane to stall. A patch of dense fog that momentarily disoriented the pilot was cited as the cause of the crash of a Braniff Airways Convair 340 after it hit a gasoline service station sign just beyond the boundary of Midway on July 17, 1955. Twenty-two of the forty-three persons aboard died in that crash.[35]

Fog was once again a factor in the runway collision of two planes at O'Hare on December 20, 1972, when poor communication between a tower controller and the pilot resulted in a Delta Air Lines Convair CV-880 taxiing across a runway that was being used by a North Central Airlines DC-9-31 for a takeoff. The dense fog hampered rescue crews' efforts to find the smoldering planes, but 128 of the 138 persons aboard the two aircraft were able to escape. Icing was the cause of Chicago's last major aviation disaster of the twentieth century—the October 31, 1994, crash of an American Eagle ATR-72 near Roseland, Indiana, while it was in a holding pattern for O'Hare. Ice had built up on the wings around eight thousand feet as the plane circled downward in the holding pattern, causing a change in air flow over the ailerons at the rear of the wing. That in turn caused the French-built turboprop plane to begin to roll, and the crew lost control. All sixty-eight persons aboard died in the crash.[36]

As airplanes became larger and more powerful, what can simplistically be described as manmade weather became a factor in crashes. The vortex of air thrown up in the wake of a jet, especially a wide-bodied jumbo jet, became a problem until the industry learned how to cope with it. The phenomenon tragically visited O'Hare on December 27, 1968, when a North Central Airlines Convair 580 crashed into a hangar while attempting to land, killing twenty-eight. Federal Aviation Administration (FAA) investigators concluded that heavy wingtip vortex turbulence from a jet that had just taken off had caused the pilot of the North Central plane to lose control just before touchdown.[37]

Although misjudgments by the pilots may have been a factor in some crashes, especially the 1965 United 727 accident for which official speculation centered on whether the crew had misread the altimeter and literally flown their jet into the lake, major crashes that can be blamed solely on pilot error have been a relative rarity in Chicago. This is probably due to the city's widespread reputation for heavy air traffic, a factor that heightens the alertness of crews over Chicago, and the long-standing FAA policy to assign only the most experienced and competent controllers to the Chicago area. The metropolitan area was one of the first in the nation to be designated by the FAA as a terminal control area (TCA) in which the airspace above the city and its suburbs is rigidly controlled. No pilot—military, commercial, or private—can fly through the forty-mile-diameter Chicago TCA without being under direct supervision of ground controllers. Planes flying through the TCA are also required to have a transponder that automatically transmits to controllers' radar the identification of the airplane, its speed, and its altitude.[38]

The Chicago airliner crash most clearly attributed to pilot error was also the subject of considerable speculation that it was somehow related to the Watergate scandal that toppled the Nixon administration.

One of the forty-five victims in the December 8, 1972, crash of a United Airlines Boeing 737 twin jet on approach to Midway Airport was Dorothy Hunt, wife of Watergate conspirator E. Howard Hunt, a former Central Intelligence Agency officer then under indictment for conspiracy to break into the Democratic National Committee headquarters offices in the Watergate Hotel in Washington on behalf of the committee to reelect Nixon. Mrs. Hunt's purse containing more than $10,000 in cash was found in the wreckage, giving rise to the unfounded speculation that she had been traveling around the country paying off potential witnesses against her husband. The inference was that the airplane had

been sabotaged to silence her so she could not reveal what her husband knew about the conspiracy.[39]

The NTSB's meticulous investigation of the crash produced a different conclusion. The agency's report, adopted a year and a half after the incident, said that no evidence of sabotage or foul play had been found. It blamed the crash, which occurred as the airplane was on final approach to Midway after an uneventful flight from Washington National Airport, on the pilot, Wendell Louis Whitehouse, who had made several errors on his non-precision-instrument approach, including the failure to retract the plane's spoilers, or air brakes, at a critical stage in the descent.

Before the advent of computers and video display terminals, air traffic controllers kept track of planes on slips of paper called "boats," which were lined up in order in front of them to show each aircraft's place in line and proximity to the airport. The maps in front of the controllers showed the air traffic routes, or aerial highways, and the radio beacons that guided planes.

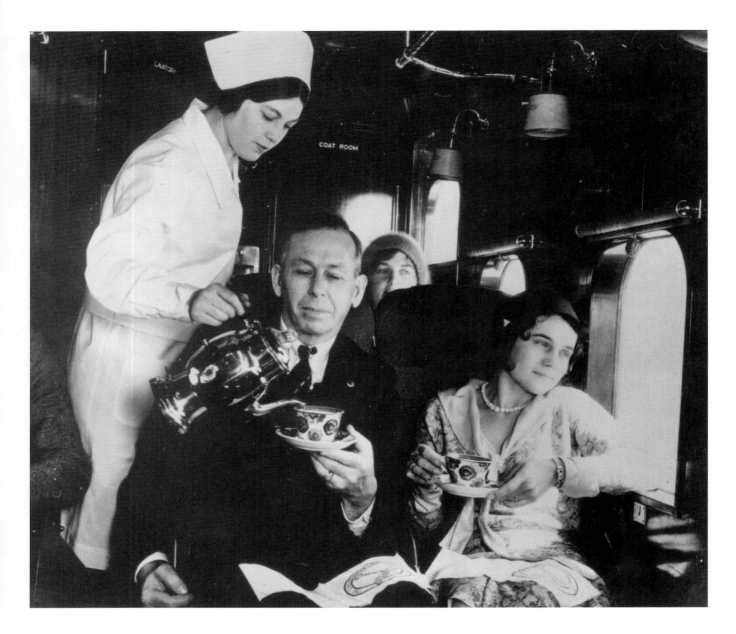

In an effort to ease apprehensions about flying, the airlines began hiring stewardesses instead of stewards to work the passenger cabins of their planes. Ellen Church, a nurse who had a pilot's license, suggested the idea of female flight attendants to Boeing Air Transport (later United Airlines) in 1930, and for a time the attendants were decked out in nurses' uniforms. (United Airlines)

The spoilers reduced the speed of the aircraft so much that it stalled and crashed in a residential area about a mile and a half from the runway.[40]

Mechanical Malfunctions

While pilot error continued to be the largest single cause of small-plane crashes, mechanical malfunctions became a far more common cause of commercial aircraft disasters in Chicago, including the complex 1979 crash of an American Airlines DC-10 that through the end of the century remained the worst single aviation disaster in United States history. Such terms as "metal fatigue" entered the public's vocabulary as a result of a series of spectacular crashes in the 1950s. The best-known such disasters involved the British de Havilland Comet, the world's first commercial jetliner, which was grounded in 1954 after three of them broke up in flight and crashed in less than twelve months between May 2, 1953, and April 8, 1954.[41]

Chicago's western suburb of Forest Park was the site of a commercial-helicopter crash on July 27, 1960, that was attributed to metal fatigue. The Sikorsky S-58C, on a seventeen-mile shuttle flight between Midway and O'Hare, crashed on the grounds of Forest Home Cemetery after one of the main rotor blades developed a fatigue fracture and broke apart 1,500 feet above the ground. The resulting severe shaking caused the tail cone and rotor to break off, and thirteen people died in the resulting crash—the first in the nation involving a helicopter in commercial air service. After the accident, the FAA limited the rotors to one thousand hours of service.[42]

The first Chicago disaster traced to mechanical problems occurred on March 10, 1948, when a Delta Air Lines DC-4 crashed on takeoff from Midway, killing twelve persons. The resulting Civil Aeronautics Board investigation never concluded what had caused the accident, but it did raise the possibility that the elevator gust lock mechanism, a system to prevent control surfaces on the tail from flapping in the wind when the airplane is on the ground, had somehow become locked on takeoff. On a DC-4, the pilot could inadvertently activate the gust lock with a floor pedal; such a scenario would have prevented the pilot from controlling the plane in flight. The plane was the only DC-4 in Delta's fleet that had not been modified, under provisions of a federal Civil Aeronautics Administration airworthiness directive, with a special handle in the cockpit to prevent the gust locks from being inadvertently kept in the locked position.[43]

As planes became larger and more complex in the 1950s, components that hadn't existed a few years earlier were suddenly being blamed for aircraft accidents. Boost assemblies, components pilots needed to transfer increased amounts of power to such things as ailerons, elevators, and rudders, replaced human-muscle-powered cable systems used on older planes. Boost assemblies were in turn replaced by complex hydraulic systems and electric motors as bigger and more powerful jetliners came into use.

A loose bolt in the elevator boost mech-

anism linkage in the tail was blamed for the September 1, 1961, loss of control and resulting crash of a Trans World Airlines Lockheed Constellation in a field near west-suburban Clarendon Hills shortly after takeoff from Midway. The crash killed all seventy-eight persons aboard the plane. Investigators were unable to determine why the bolt fell out. Slightly more than two weeks later, on September 17, 1961, thirty-seven persons died when a Northwest Airlines Lockheed Electra crashed after takeoff from O'Hare. The accident was blamed on the failure of an aileron boost assembly in the wing. The assembly had been improperly installed two months earlier by mechanics in Minneapolis, Civil Aeronautics Board investigators determined.[44]

The hydraulic system that controlled the slats on the leading edge of a DC-10 was a factor, though not the precipitating cause, in the spectacular crash of a DC-10-10 that was witnessed by hundreds of persons, and captured on film by one, at O'Hare on May 25, 1979. The disaster, which killed all 271 persons on the plane and two on the ground, occurred on an otherwise slow news day on a Memorial Day weekend and attracted the attention of the world press because of the model's prior problems. DC-10s had already suffered two accidents involving the loss of steering control after rear cargo doors blew out in midflight, causing the floor to collapse and severing the hydraulic lines to the tail. The pilot of one of them, an American Airlines DC-10, had managed to land his damaged plane in Detroit, but a Turkish Airlines DC-10 had crashed after takeoff from Paris's Orly Airport on March 3, 1974, killing 346, in what was to that time the world's worst aviation disaster.[45]

In Chicago, the DC-10's left engine fell off during takeoff, interrupting electrical power to the cockpit and severing the hydraulic lines that controlled the slats on the leading edge of the left wing. The slats, which reconfigure the aerodynamics of the wing to give the plane lift at slow speeds,

FLY TWA first

SAVE 25%

ON THE FINEST AIR TRANSPORTATION
NEW 15-DAY EXCURSION FARES OFFER
AIR TRAVEL AT STANDARD *RAIL* COSTS

The Lindbergh Line now offers you the first excursion fares in De Luxe air transportation. They bring the finest in air travel down to rail cost levels. Leave Saturday or Monday, return on any schedule any day within fifteen days. Tickets good on every flight, including famous overnight coast to coast SKY CHIEF. TWA operates the nation's finest planes, SKYCLUBS by day, SKYSLEEPERS by night. TWA complimentary meals en route save extra dollars.

TWA is the only major airline offering Excursion Fares

COMPARE THESE FARES

TWA Excursion Fares	(Round Trip)	Rail plus Pullman
$32.25	KANSAS CITY	$33.56
35.92	PITTSBURGH	34.20
67.42	NEW YORK	66.50

New low Los Angeles—San Francisco Fares only $157.50. Lowest Coast to Coast.

SCRIP CARDS May be used to charge these low excursion rates no *matter* what airline issued them.

CALL TWA
For All Airline Information
State 2433

TICKET OFFICE
Lobby Floor, Palmer House, or any Hotel, Travel Bureau, or Telegraph Office

SHORTEST—FASTEST TWA first COAST TO COAST

Airlines often avoided the safety issue in their advertisements, concentrating instead on plugging fares or amenities. In 1937, six years after the Rockne crash, TWA was comparing its fares to those of the railroads. (American Airlines)

retracted, causing the plane to roll to the left and crash into a field adjacent to a trailer park just north of the airport. The subsequent investigation showed that the loss of the engine was the result of a complex sequence of events beginning with the procedures used by the airline to maintain the pylons that held the engine to the wing. A maintenance crew at the American Airlines maintenance base in Tulsa, Oklahoma, contrary to the manufacturer's instructions, had improperly used a hydraulic lift to remove the left engine. The lift apparently lost some hydraulic pressure while it was left unattended during a

shift change, causing the engine assembly to shift backward, cracking the pylon. The crack worsened during subsequent flights until it gave way during takeoff two months later in Chicago.[46]

A few days after the disaster, a mechanic for United Airlines, which was preparing to resume operations after a strike, discovered a loose pylon on one of its planes in Chicago. That problem, it was later learned, was unrelated to the May 25 crash, but resulted from the improper installation of fasteners at the Douglas Aircraft factory, which weakened the pylons of an additional thirty DC-10-10 aircraft owned by several airlines. The discovery of the second problem caused FAA administrator Langhorne Bond to ground all DC-10-10s until the mess could be sorted out.[47]

The Public Embraces Flying

The public had lost its collective fear of flying long before the DC-10 went down in Chicago in 1979. The great increase in flying began after World War II, the result of reductions in airline fares. In 1979, 295.2 million passengers flew on domestic airlines that year, almost 47.5 million of them passing through O'Hare (see table 2). When declines in air travel occurred in the latter half of the twentieth century, as they did in 1969–1971, 1979–1981, and 1990–1991, they were more the result of downturns in the economy than of fear of flying.

Although the depression and World War II put a damper on flying by all but the wealthiest segment of the population, the introduction of coach class fares after the war resulted in a big jump in air travel. In 1930, all U.S. airlines combined flew only 32 million passenger miles; by 1940, they flew 1.2 billion passenger miles annually. By 1950, that number had increased nearly eightfold to 9.3 billion, with the biggest increase coming after the war. Over the next decade, as the airlines increasingly adopted coach fares, passenger travel nearly quadrupled to 42.2 billion. In 1960, the airlines still carried only half the num-

Railroads, in a struggle to preserve their passenger-market share in competition with the new airlines, sometimes referred to safety and reliability in their advertisements. This New York Central ad implies the trains still run when it is unsafe to fly.

But you're *sure* of your travel plans on New York Central!

You're at ease in mind and body aboard world's greatest fleet of new Diesel-electric streamliners and Dreamliners. 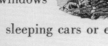 New coaches with lean-back seats, picture windows and modern dressing rooms. New, private-room sleeping cars or economical berths if you prefer. Famous New York Central meals, in smart new diners. 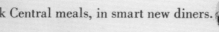 And for relaxation you'll find refreshments and good company in New York Central's new lounge cars. Best of all, neither stormy skies nor icy roads interfere with your plans. You go, *weather or no*, when you go New York Central!

NEW NEW YORK CENTRAL

NEW YORK CENTRAL SYSTEM

The Water Level Route — You Can Sleep

The air safety issue taxed the creativity of advertising copywriters into the 1950s, after which time the public had been assuaged and the carriers began to concentrate on amenities, comfort, and exotic destinations. This 1954 United ad shows a boy listening while a pilot explains how instrument landing systems enable the plane to get back to the ground safely in bad weather. (United Airlines)

Like going downstairs with your hand on the bannister

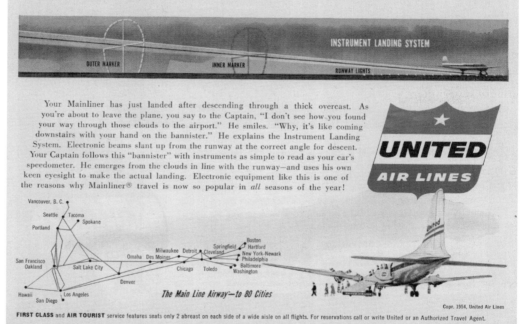

Your Mainliner has just landed after descending through a thick overcast. As you're about to leave the plane, you say to the Captain, "I don't see how you found your way through those clouds to the airport." He smiles. "Why, it's like coming downstairs with your hand on the bannister." He explains the Instrument Landing System. Electronic beams slant up from the runway at the correct angle for descent. Your Captain follows this "bannister" with instruments as simple to read as your car's speedometer. He emerges from the clouds in line with the runway—and uses his own keen eyesight to make the actual landing. Electronic equipment like this is one of the reasons why Mainliner® travel is now so popular in *all* seasons of the year!

UNITED
AIR LINES

The Main Line Airway—to 80 Cities

Copr. 1954, United Air Lines

FIRST CLASS and **AIR TOURIST** service features seats only 2 abreast on each side of a wide aisle on all flights. For reservations call or write United or an Authorized Travel Agent.

In the postwar era, most airline ads dealing with safety took an indirect approach. This 1950 American Airlines ad uses the example of flight insurance to get the safety message across. (American Airlines C. R. Smith Museum)

What other coin machine gives you **20,000-*to*-1 ODDS ?**

Americas Leading Airline **AMERICAN AIRLINES** INC.

THIS COIN MACHINE, strangely enough, sells life insurance. It is a familiar sight in airports all over the country where it offers 20,000-to-1 odds that you will complete your trip safely.

Machines like this, installed by one of the nation's leading life insurance companies, sell individual trip insurance at 25¢ for a $5,000 policy. Life insurance companies are known to be conservative-minded business organizations that base their policies on the law of averages. They do not gamble foolishly.

What better evidence could you seek that Flagships today are not only faster and finer but *safer* than ever before than this standing offer of 20,000-to-1 on every trip you take.

Table 2—U.S. Intercity Passengers by Common Carrier, 1979

(in millions of boardings)

Air	Bus	Rail
295.2	368.0	89.4

Source: Frank A. Smith, *Transportation in America: A Statistical Analysis of Transportation in the United States* (Washington, D.C.: ENO Transportation Foundation, Inc., 1992), 48.

ber of passengers as the intercity railroads—56.8 million compared to 122.7 million—but within a decade the airlines were hauling double the number of people as the railroads, a disparity that continued to increase as the century wore on. In 1990, the airlines carried 428.8 million passengers compared to only 22.2 million riding on the lone surviving intercity passenger railroad—government-subsidized Amtrak (see appendix C).[48]

Available data indicate that domestic airplane boardings, or enplanements as they are called in the industry, in the second half of the twentieth century were influenced more by the status of the economy than by any other factor. Declines in what was otherwise steady growth in air travel in the last three decades of the century occurred in both 1981 and 1991, when the United States was suffering the effects of re-

cessions. As would be expected at a major hub, passenger enplanements at Chicago's two large airports also declined in 1981, 1982, and 1991 (see appendix D).[49]

Air travel had softened considerably in 2001 because of an economic downturn even before September 11, when a group of Islamist terrorists commandeered four jetliners and crashed them into New York City's World Trade Center towers, the Pentagon in Washington, and a remote area in Pennsylvania. Air travel abruptly declined as a result of the disasters, the cancellation of flights in their aftermath, and the increase of security measures to counteract aerial terrorism. Enplanements dropped 34 percent on domestic flights and 27 percent on international flights in September 2001, and two months later they were still running about 20 percent below prior-year levels.[50]

10 Emergence of Modern Airlines

• The 1930s was the decade in which the airlines emerged in their modern form, and Chicago was transformed into the nation's busiest hub for the growing fleet of commercial planes and the headquarters for the two largest airlines in the nation, United and American. The Windy City was also the nation's railroad center and one of its busiest ports, and now Chicagoans, who had complained for years about the long waits at railroad crossings and the traffic congestion caused when bridges were raised to let ship traffic pass, faced a new source of annoyance: incessant airplane noise. Between sixty and ninety thousand airplanes a year took off from or landed at Municipal Airport during the decade.

Although an air show at the 1933 Century of Progress world's fair attracted a crowd, the city's golden age of aviation, when air exhibitions filled Grant Park with spectators, was gone, and the once-dominant Aero Club was in serious decline. During the 1930s, decisions about aviation were more likely to be made in corporate suites scattered around the country or in the halls of government in Washington than in once-a-month meetings in a Loop hotel by a handful of rich aviation enthusiasts. Aviation had become a business.

Chicago became a commercial aviation hub for many of the same reasons it had

After 1970, the development of wide-body jets, such as the Boeing 767, permitted a roomier interior and two aisles. Some were even equipped with passenger lounges. Many of the amenities of the bigger planes disappeared after deregulation of the industry in 1978 because airlines began squeezing in more seats and discounting tickets to pack them. (United Airlines)

The Boeing 247 cabin was noisy and drafty, and the plane's ride was rough by modern standards. The aisle was barely wide enough for a person to stand in. (United Airlines)

become a maritime and rail center earlier, principally geography. The city lay astride the rail routes between East and West, and the airlines flocked to it for the same reason the railroads did. Also, by the time the airlines came along, Chicago had become the nation's second largest city and was a ready market for air transportation. The planes in the 1930s did not have the range to overfly Chicago in their travels between the two coasts, so they set down in Chicago to refuel and swap passengers. A businessman traveling between Los Angeles and, say, Pittsburgh would switch planes and probably airlines in Chicago, just as he had switched trains and railroads in the Windy City a few years earlier.

Some of the early airlines, like Pop Dickinson's venture, had been entrepreneurial, but by the 1930s all the airlines had followed the example the railroads had set a century earlier and had become incorporated joint stock companies; the Big Four (at the time United, American, TWA, and Eastern) were primarily holding companies that controlled various smaller airlines they acquired. That meant whoever ran the airlines was expected to be a financial manager able to talk to investors, not an aviation pioneer capable of dashing out of his office and into the cockpit of a plane if the regular pilot called in sick. Besides the usual operating and maintenance departments typical of transportation corporations, the airlines also had substantial marketing departments in which route and fare strategy was plotted, as well as ways to induce the public to fly.[1]

Commercial aviation by 1935, a decade after the industry was founded, had emerged from its incubator and was rudely being weaned from federal mail subsidies. Passengers were becoming the industry's principal traffic, and the publicly held corporate structures that would direct the industry through the end of the century were in place, as were the unions. The Air Line Pilots Association (ALPA) was organized in 1931, and the Air Line Stewardesses Association was founded in 1945—sixteen years after the first stewardess was hired—and signed its first contract, with United Air Lines, a year later. Government economic regulation of the airlines began in the 1930s; it was the responsibility first of the Interstate Commerce Commission (ICC) and after 1938 of a new agency, the Civil Aeronautics Board (CAB).

The railroads, which had introduced the diesel-powered streamliner, were still the dominant mode of intercity transportation in 1935, although the federal and state governments' extensive highway-building programs in the 1920s and 1930s were making the automobile more competitive for intercity travel. By 1940, the automobile had captured 89 percent of the U.S. intercity travel market in terms of mileage, although trains and planes were faster. The railroads held 7.5 percent, buses 3.1 percent, and the airlines only four tenths of a percent. Population and commerce in the United States in 1935 was still concentrated along the railroad network of the Northeast and Midwest. Although the West Coast had begun its growth, the great dispersal of people and jobs to the South, Southwest, and West that favored auto and air travel over the capital-intensive railways did not occur until after World War II.[2]

In the middle 1930s, the airlines began an aggressive marketing campaign to attract high-profile, time-sensitive travelers, primarily celebrities, but the seats were still too expensive for anyone but the wealthy. It wasn't until larger and faster transports came on line after World War II and a two-tier fare structure was developed that the airlines cracked the middle-class market. Like the railroad industry before them, the airlines very early in their existence began to consolidate and merge their corporations and end-to-end routes systems into ever larger carriers offering transcontinental networks. By the time Roosevelt was elected in 1932, the populists in government were complaining about the Big Four airlines they had found necessary to regulate.[3]

Table 3—Airline Revenue Passengers, 1926–1940

Year	Chicago Municipal Airport Flights	Chicago Municipal Airport Boardings	U.S. Passenger Boardings
1926	——	——	6,000
1927	800	——	9,000
1928	41,660	15,498	43,000
1929	93,613	44,452	162,000
1930	58,688	62,456	385,000
1931	71,083	97,070	472,000
1932	60,947	100,847	476,000
1933	63,252	133,247	500,000
1934	80,492	175,538	472,000
1935	60,727	191,738	679,000
1936	73,345	260,863	929,000
1937	79,919	315,283	981,000
1938	69,604	352,563	1,197,000
1939	79,350	501,164	1,735,000
1940	88,201	704,846	2,803,000

Sources: Air Transport Association, Historical Statistics of U.S. Airlines by Carrier Group, Revenue Passenger Originations (table 46) (Washington, 1973); Chicago Department of Aviation, Chicago Municipal/Midway Airport statistics (Chicago, 1980).

Passenger traffic, which became the bread and butter of the airlines in the 1950s, was slow to develop in the 1930s. The depression and the relatively small size of the planes used by the airlines at the time were the two major factors. Most people couldn't afford the $160 coast-to-coast fare United charged in 1934 even if they had been willing to endure the noisy, drafty airplanes then in service. Traffic data for Municipal Airport, which almost from the beginning was a barometer for the U.S. airline industry, showed that in 1928 only 15,498 passengers used the airport—about one for every three airplanes that took off or landed. As late as 1935, the average passenger load was only three persons per plane, but by 1940, the average had reached almost eight. The statistics do not accurately reflect the load factors on commercial airliners to and from Chicago because all flights, including those by private pilots, are counted, but the data do give an indication of the rate of increase of passenger traffic.[4]

A major factor in Chicago's slow start was the fact that the hometown airline, National Air Transport (NAT), discouraged passenger traffic in its early years. Once it changed that policy, Municipal quickly developed as the single most important airport in the United States. About 16 percent of all airline passengers in the nation passed through Chicago's airport in 1930,

or 62,456 of the national total of 385,000. A decade later, Municipal handled 704,846 of the 2.8 million domestic airline passengers in the United States—about a quarter of the total (table 3).

NAT discouraged the carrying of passengers on its mail planes until after it was absorbed into United Air Lines in 1930 and that new carrier began to develop a New York–Chicago–San Francisco transcontinental route. Even then, the NAT fleet didn't have much passenger capacity, at least until it acquired some Ford Tri-Motors in 1930 and bought the ten-passenger Boeing 247D

The anticipation of four-engine transports and coach fares after World War II resulted in a substantial increase in air travel and hurried expansion projects for airports like Midway. Chicago was forced to add quickly built cement-block concourses to keep up with traffic. Passengers still had to walk outside to board.

in 1933. In the beginning, NAT flew Curtiss Carrier Pigeons, each of which had only one seat for a passenger, and then only if there wasn't enough mail to fill it. In 1927, NAT flew a total of only 168 passengers, most of them transferring from the West Coast route of Boeing Air Transport (BAT), and two years later, most of the 6,129 passengers BAT delivered to Chicago had to continue their trips east by train because NAT didn't have the planes to fly them.[5]

In Chicago, much of the history of aviation in the 1930s revolves around United Air Lines—as the name was spelled before 1974, when the last two words were merged into one in the title—and its principal rivals, American and TWA. United was so named because it was a holding company that came into being as a result of the merger of a number of aviation companies, including five airlines—National Air Transport, Boeing Air Transport, Varney Air Lines, Pacific Air Transport, and Stout Air Services. Because it was the first airline to operate a transcontinental route, it had the prime central route, which included not only New York, Chicago, and San Francisco, but also spurs to Seattle and Los Angeles from its San Francisco hub and to Dallas from its Chicago hub. TWA had a more southerly route, from Philadelphia through Cincinnati and St. Louis to Los Angeles, and American an even more southerly route, from New York through Buffalo, Cincinnati, Nashville, Dallas, El Paso, and Phoenix to Los Angeles. However, both had spurs to Chicago—TWA from Cincinnati and American over the old Robertson route flown by Lindbergh from St. Louis. Eastern was mainly a north-south carrier along the Atlantic seaboard between New York and Miami.[6]

Despite its geographical advantage, United had a tough decade in the 1930s, first because of the beating it took during and after the Spoils Conference and second because its president, William A. Patterson, only reluctantly accepted government regulation and paid a substantial

price for his recalcitrance. In 1934, Patterson dragged the airline into a prolonged legal struggle to prove that the government was unjustified in canceling the air mail contracts. That issue was not resolved until the U.S. Court of Claims ruled against him in 1942.

American, which was also an amalgamation of five airlines, traces its corporate roots to Lindbergh's first air mail flights between Chicago and St. Louis for Robertson Aircraft. Another of its predecessors was Universal Aviation Corporation, formed in Chicago on July 30, 1928, by a group of bankers to provide passenger-only service between the Windy City and Cleveland. Universal acquired Robertson and another small airline by the end of the year, and in 1929 it added more small carriers with the intention of creating a transcontinental route. It was in turn gobbled up by the Aviation Corporation (AVCO), a newly created holding company in New York that had $35 million in assets primarily because of the backing of investment bankers W. Averell Harriman and Robert Lehman.[7]

Harriman and Lehman began to force the consolidation of the subsidiaries, which had operated almost as independent companies, and in 1930, AVCO's new operating subsidiary was renamed American Airways. However, the new airline was hemorrhaging money, and board member Errett Lobban Cord—the owner of the Auburn and Dusenberg auto companies as well as Century Air Lines, Stinson Aircraft, and Lycoming Engines—became upset when other directors began to talk about an additional big acquisition that would dilute his 25 percent holdings in AVCO. He started a proxy fight to oust Harriman and Lehman, and in the resulting compromise he wound up as AVCO chairman in 1932. He promptly moved the airline's headquarters to Chicago and installed his own man, Lester Seymour, as American's president. When they had a falling out, Cord hired Cyrus Rowlett Smith, better known as C. R., to replace him. It was Smith who moved the company headquarters back to New York after 1939.[8]

Chicago's Rival Airlines

Long before Smith moved the headquarters, the Chicago-based lines got into a spirited rivalry, which persists to this day, over which of them would be the nation's largest airline. United was the largest until 1935, when it discovered that its three-year-old aircraft fleet had become obsolete almost overnight after its competitors introduced a newer and better airplane. The nature of the airline industry was—and is—such that carriers have used relatively small fleets of very expensive equipment. The entire U.S. commercial airline fleet as late as 1969 consisted of only about 2,600 planes, in contrast to 23,000 river barges and 4,000 towboats and tugs on American waters, 897,000 tractor-trailer trucks on the highways, and 1.3 million freight cars and 28,000 locomotives on the railroads. In the highly competitive aviation market, airplanes often became technologically or economically obsolete long before they wore out because a competitor bought a newer, faster, larger, more fuel efficient, or otherwise better airplane.[9]

The airlines had become painfully aware of the limitations of the Tri-Motors in the early 1930s, and because of the lucrative air mail contracts and government-imposed rationalization of the industry, they had the financial wherewithal to buy new aircraft even though the depression was in progress. United Aircraft, the Rentschler-Boeing holding company that controlled United Air Lines, launched what was to be the first of many airplane buying sprees in the industry when in 1933 it ordered a converted military bomber as its next-generation airplane. Boeing originally developed its B-247 in military specification in 1931 as a twin-engine medium bomber and in 1933 modified it into a commercial transport with a cruising speed of 189 miles an hour, a range of 745 miles, and a capacity of ten passengers. The B-247 enabled United to get its passengers from coast to coast in nineteen hours and forty-five minutes in 1933, contrasted to the twenty-six hours and forty-five minutes it took Transcontinental and Western (TWA) to fly the same passenger load the same distance in its Ford Tri-Motors.[10]

The all-metal B-247 was the first of the clean commercial airframes and is considered the first modern airliner. There were no structural protuberances outside the aircraft skin, and the landing gear was retractable. The first B-247 entered service on March 30, 1933, and by midyear United had thirty of them operating. Because United was still related to the airframe maker, it was able to buy out the entire production of sixty of the new planes, giving it a decided advantage over its competitors; for a time in the early 1930s, United was the largest and most profitable of the Big Four.[11]

The B-247 did not hold its competitive advantage for long. Other airlines, unhappy with their rival's monopoly on the new aircraft, immediately set to work to find a better plane. TWA already was under considerable pressure to replace its Fokker Tri-Motors after the Rockne crash in 1933. After being rebuffed by Boeing, TWA approached Donald Douglas to see if he could design a faster and more powerful machine. Douglas worked quickly. The resulting DC-1 prototype had its first test flight on July 1, 1933, three months after the B-247 entered service, and TWA put the production version, called the DC-2, into service in May 1934, a little less than a year after the B-247's debut. A week after taking delivery, TWA put the new plane onto the crucial New York–Chicago route in direct competition with United's B-247s. The DC-2 beat the B-247's 5.5 hour flying time on that route by thirty minutes and carried four additional passengers to boot.[12]

The successor DC-3 revolutionized air travel after its introduction in 1935. With a cruising speed of 192 miles an hour, almost twice that of the Ford Tri-Motor, and a capacity of twenty-one passengers, twice that of the B-247, the DC-3 in the period before World War II became the dominant civil aircraft in the world with sales of more than 430 planes. The DC-3s acquired by American's Smith enabled that carrier to eclipse United as the nation's largest. By 1938, American's revenues were double those of United. The negotiations for the new plane are something of a legend in the airline industry. Smith had told Douglas in a two-hour phone call that he wanted an improved version of the DC-2 that would enable the airline to make a profit carrying passengers and would wean the airline from the slavery of government mail subsidies. The plane also had to be able to cross the Rocky Mountains with one of its two engines shut down.[13]

American, United, and the other airlines had been hit hard by the Spoils Conference scandal, and especially by President Roosevelt's decision on February 9, 1934, to cancel all air mail contracts with the airlines and temporarily turn over the job of carrying mail to the Army Air Corps. The resulting military air mail service was nearly disastrous. The army took ten days to set up the replacement service then suspended it between March 10 and 19, 1934, because of a rash of accidents and bad weather. Using combat aircraft and a few bombers, the service then resumed, and it continued with improved consistency until its last flight on June 1 of that year. The post office meanwhile rebid the air mail contracts, and the same airlines submitted new bids; the resulting new route system looked much the same as the old one. The temporary cancellation of the contracts proved to be financially burdensome for the airlines. United, which reported a profit of $175,000 in 1933, lost $300,000 a month during the cancellations, and the struggling American Airways, which had posted a loss of $160,000 for 1933, hemor-rhaged money at the rate of $375,000 a month while the military flew the mail.[14]

The competition between the airlines involved more than just technology. Throughout the thirties, the carriers kept upstaging each other by adding such passenger amenities as flight attendants, onboard meals, and even sleeping accommodations. United's predecessor Boeing Air Transport claimed to have been the first to have flight attendants on board. BAT district manager Steve A. Stimpson had suggested to his superiors that the airline ought to hire cabin attendants. Ellen Church, a nurse by training who hoped to become a pilot, suggested, possibly during her February 23, 1930, job interview with Stimpson in San Francisco, that nurses like herself be hired for the role. She became the first flying nurse, or stewardess, and within a few years the other airlines picked up the idea for competitive reasons.[15]

Two of the principal competitors in the 1930s were Smith, who operated from American's headquarters at 20 North Wacker Drive, and United's William A. Patterson, who ran his airline from the LaSalle-Wacker building just down the street. Together with Juan Trippe, of Pan American, a Yale University graduate and investment banker who got hooked on aviation during a stint as a navy flier in the Great War; World War I ace E. V. (Eddie) Rickenbacker, of Eastern; and C. E. Woolman, a University of Illinois agricultural engineering graduate who fell in love with flying at the 1909 Rheims, France, air show and transformed a Mississippi crop-dusting business into Delta Air Lines, they rank as the men who transformed the rag-tag air mail charter business into the modern American airline industry. The other giant of the airline industry was the eccentric Howard Hughes, the wealthy heir to a tool-company fortune who acquired a controlling interest in TWA in 1938 but was forced out in 1965 after a long court fight.[16]

Neither Smith nor Patterson had any aviation background; Smith was an ac-

TEN O'CLOCK SHADOW

HEAD bowed into the norther, the shivering cowboy hears the hum of motors and sees a swift shadow race across the snow.

"Ten o'clock," he observes, checking with his watch. "The big ship's right on time."

His keen eye scans the winter sky and he marvels again at the glint of silver high in the air against the blue.

It's thirty below at ten thousand feet, yet inside the roomy cabin the thermometer registers a balmy seventy-two.

In their comfortable chairs twenty-one passengers are at their ease—reading, writing,

playing cards, dozing—as the great airliner speeds them on to their destination.

Once you have flown, you will realize that the time of year has little effect on the clock-like regularity of air travel.

In January as well as June, all the airlines maintain practically uninterrupted schedules.

Whenever and wherever you want to go, from city to city, across the continent, from farthest north to deepest south, overseas—you can travel faster, more comfortably, more economically by air. A few pleasant hours in passage against whole days and nights on the way!

Next time you leave home, on business or pleasure, take wings—go by air.

Then you'll understand why so many people are saying over and over again: *It Pays to Fly.*

Travel, Mail, Ship by Air

Air Passengers get there *first*—comfortably, economically, rested and refreshed.

Air Mail gets there *first*, and gets *first* attention—for only 6c an ounce.

Air Express packages get there *first*—low cost, world-wide. Call Air Express Division, Railway Express Agency.

AIR TRANSPORT ASSOCIATION
155 South LaSalle St., Chicago, Illinois

This educational campaign is sponsored jointly by the 16 major United States Airlines, and Manufacturers and Suppliers to the Air Transport Industry

Ask Your Travel Agent

It's *easy* to buy an air ticket to any place in the United States or the world. Simply phone or call at any Travel Bureau, Hotel Transportation Desk, Telegraph office or local Airline office, for airline schedules and fares or general information

IT PAYS TO FLY

The comfort and reliability of airline travel was the subject of this 1940 Air Transport Association advertisement. At the time, the trade group was based in Chicago; it later moved to Washington to better pursue its mission as the industry's lobbyist. (Air Transport Association)

countant who rose from a hardscrabble existence in the Texas panhandle, and Patterson was a banker from San Francisco. From age nine on, Smith worked at a variety of jobs to support his family after his father deserted them and finally worked his way through the University of Texas, earning a degree in business while moonlighting at

his one-man advertising agency and as a Federal Reserve Bank examiner. Patterson started his business career as an office boy at Wells Fargo Bank in San Francisco and worked his way up to teller.[17]

The entry of both men into aviation was fortuitous. Smith was an auditor for a utility when the president of that company

Airline food became something of a joke after 1980, and the deregulated budget carriers eliminated meals entirely, but in the 1950s the airlines aggressively promoted on-board meals. (United Airlines)

asked him to take a look at the books of a financially ailing airline he also owned. Within a year Smith was the general manager of the Southern Air Transport System, a post he continued to hold after the company was acquired by AVCO. That subsidiary was more successful than the others in the American system, a factor that caused Cord in 1934 to elevate Smith to president of American, charging him with bailing out the entire airline.[18]

Patterson was working as a loan officer at Wells Fargo in 1927 when Vern Gorst, the owner of Pacific Air Transport (PAT), a none-too-successful airline that operated between San Francisco and Seattle, approached him about a loan. The financial research Patterson performed made him something of an expert on airline finance, and after he suggested PAT be sold to the Boeing Airplane Company, William Boeing hired him in 1929 as an assistant. Patterson was managing Boeing's airline and three others when the United merger occurred, and in 1934 he was elevated to the carrier's top job when its president, Philip G. Johnson, was forced to resign in the wake of the Spoils Conference scandal.[19]

Patterson had a difficult time managing United after he became president, to some extent because of his own obstinacy in dealing with federal regulators. United was rapidly losing market share to its rivals because of the introduction of the DC-3 when in 1936 it petitioned the ICC for permission to acquire the ailing Pennsylvania Airlines to gain a route between Milwaukee, Detroit, Cleveland, Pittsburgh, and Washington. The ICC denied the petition, and Pennsylvania merged with another carrier to become Pennsylvania-Central (later Capital) Airlines.[20]

The situation continued to deteriorate for United. It had controlled 44 percent of the domestic passenger business in 1934, but that declined to 23 percent in 1937. By then, only seven of the largest cities in the nation were served by United, in contrast with sixteen by American Airlines and twelve by TWA; furthermore, its orientation to the sparsely populated West at a time when competitors were concentrating on the densely populated East contributed to its eclipse.

In 1938, United petitioned the new Civil Aeronautics Board—successor to the Interstate Commerce Commission as the economic regulator of the airlines—for a hostile merger with Western Air Express but was turned down.[21] United's troubles with the regulators continued after World War II. Although it was allowed to acquire financially troubled Capital Airlines in 1961 to avert a bankruptcy by that carrier, between that time and 1978, when the industry was deregulated, United

only once was granted authority for expansion into a new market. Such treatment at the hands of the regulators was certainly a major factor in United's president Richard Ferris's decision in the 1970s to support a law deregulating the industry.[22]

The Postwar Planes

By the late 1930s, Patterson was concerned enough about United's deteriorated financial position to take some innovative action. The downward financial trend had started when he refused to cut back schedules after the loss of mail contracts in 1934, apparently to preserve market share and maintain the airline's fragile credibility. In 1936, he approached Boeing about building a four-engine aircraft, but Boeing decided to concentrate on the four-engine flying boat that became the Pan American Clipper. Patterson then had his own staff draw up the specifications for a four-engine, forty-passenger transport capable of cruising at 175 miles an hour. Boeing wasn't interested, and Donald Douglas was dubious until Patterson agreed to underwrite half of the engineering costs—$300,000. In the days before sophisticated computers, airplane makers often built a prototype to be tested and debugged before designing the production model. The prototype DC-4 was completed in 1938, but by the time Douglas was able to complete the modifications the airlines wanted in the production model, World War II intervened and the army took over the DC-4 program to convert the plane to military production as the C-54 transport. Meanwhile, Patterson had bought DC-3s to remain competitive, and Boeing had developed the four-engine Model 307 Stratoliner.[23]

The lack of a new plane forced Patterson to try other things to keep his airline in business. In 1940, he decided to expand the flying market by offering coach fares to appeal to the middle class, although he later became an opponent of the two-tiered fare (first-class and coach) and as late as 1963 unilaterally and unsuccessfully tried to reestablish the one-class system. Also in 1940, Patterson inaugurated the first airline freighter service in the United States.[24]

Perhaps Patterson's biggest challenge was that the prime Chicago–New York route on which United once had a monopoly had become the most competitive route in the nation. Airline industry historian R. E. G. Davies takes particular note of that route in his definitive history of the industry, *Airlines of the United States:*

> New York–Chicago has always been the vital high density route of the United States, ever since the operation of the DC-3 showed that profits were possible over the 740-mile stage distance, without mail subsidy. Other routes have produced higher passenger fares or greater seat-mile productivity, but New York–Chicago has been subjected to the closest scrutiny by the participating airlines, each highly sensitive to the slightest penetration of their preserves by rival companies.[25]

For most of the first half of the twentieth century, the railroads were the dominant carriers of people on that route. The New York Central, Pennsylvania, Erie, and Lackawanna–Nickel Plate railroads, with such famous trains as the Twentieth Century Limited and the Broadway Limited, competed for traffic. By the 1930s, the airlines had begun to chip away at the most time-sensitive traffic, and after World War II, the Pennsylvania, Ohio, and Indiana turnpikes captured the cost-sensitive travelers who journeyed by automobile or bus.

National Air Transport (NAT) originally began operating a mail and parcel service on the Chicago–Cleveland–New York route in 1927, the latter in conjunction with the Railway Express Agency. By 1931, American Airways was offering an alternative to travelers with its Chicago–Buffalo–New York route, and TWA followed into the market shortly thereafter. The CAB in 1944 granted Pennsylvania-Central (later Capi-

tal) Airlines authority to fly the route via Pittsburgh and Detroit, and Northwest in 1955 became the fifth carrier in the market as a result of what has become known as the CAB's New York–Chicago Service case, a three-year deliberation by CAB over which airlines should be allowed to serve that route and intermediate cities. Since then, half a dozen other carriers, including Pan American, have been in and out of the market. At one point just after the industry was deregulated, there were more than sixty daily flights between the five airports in the two cities.

The competition for bigger and better piston planes continued after World War II even as the British were developing the jet Comet, and airlines continued to try to gain a monopoly on new planes despite what had happened to United and the B-247. This time it was Howard Hughes's TWA that got the upper hand. It backed Lockheed in the development of the Constellation, a four-engine pressurized aircraft capable of flying from coast to coast in eleven hours, two hours less than the DC-4 was capable of. United's entire fleet after World War II ended consisted of seventy-seven DC-3s, including twenty surplus models it leased from the War Department. To be able to compete in the transcontinental market with only a single stop in Chicago, United desperately needed a long-range aircraft. United and American both bought war-surplus DC-4s from the government at bargain-basement prices and retrofitted them for commercial passenger service. United was able to get its surplus DC-4s into service on its New York–San Francisco route on the same day TWA inaugurated the Constellation on its New York–Los Angeles route.[26]

In late 1946, Patterson ordered twenty of Douglas's new DC-6s for $49.5 million, but the plane was plagued with production and safety problems, as was TWA's Constellation, which was grounded in mid-1946 by the Civil Aeronautics Authority (predecessor of the Federal Aviation Administration [FAA]), after a series of fires and prob-

lems with the engine superchargers. On October 24, 1947, less than a year after going into service, a United DC-6 exploded in flight over Utah and crashed, killing fifty-two persons. Three weeks later, an American DC-6 caught fire near Gallup, New Mexico, but the pilot was able to land and safely evacuate the twenty-five passengers even though the cockpit filled with smoke. United, American, and another Douglas customer voluntarily grounded the plane until the airplane maker's engineers found and corrected the problem: fuel overflow was being ingested by an air scoop and ignited by the cabin heating system.[27]

The new-plane race went on. TWA acquired an upgraded version of the Constellation called the Super Constellation in 1952, and American responded by buying Douglas's new DC-7. United finally caved in and bought twenty-five DC-7s on June 1, 1954. Rapidly expanding Capital Airlines put its turbine-propeller, or turboprop, Vickers Viscount into service on the New York–Chicago route in 1955 in competition with United and American's piston-driven DC-6s and DC-7s, and American followed with the Lockheed Electra, also a turbo-

prop, in 1959. The effect of the plane race of the 1950s was to increase the speed of commercial airliners from 227 miles per hour in the case of the DC-4 in 1946 to more than 370 miles per hour in the case of the Electra in 1959, passenger loads from forty-four in a surplus DC-4 to approximately one hundred in the Douglas and Lockheed aircraft built in the 1950s, and cruising ranges from 2,500 miles in the DC-4 to more than 4,000 miles in the DC-7 and Super Constellation.[28]

Helicopter Airlines

At the same time the major airlines were buying ever larger airplanes for long-haul routes, they began to dabble with a relatively new invention, rotor craft, for use as shuttles in major metropolitan areas where airport space was at a premium. Experiments with rotor craft date to the infancy of aviation, but in the 1920s autogiros (autogyros), or gyro planes—aircraft equipped with a standard engine in front and unpowered rotating blades mounted over the fuselage to act as wings—began appearing. True helicopters, which have a powered

Rotor aircraft began to make their appearance in the 1930s, and the airlines became interested in them for short-haul shuttle service around metropolitan areas. This Kellet KD-1 autogyro in TWA livery was evaluated for use by the U.S. Army Air Corps as a reconnaissance vehicle. (Robert F. Zilinsky Collection)

By 1960, Chicago Helicopter Airways carried more than 300,000 passengers in its Sikorsky S-58s, one of which is shown here on its downwind leg to Meigs Field. Within two years, the abandonment of Midway Airport by the major airlines caused the helicopter shuttle business to evaporate. (Joshua Koppel Collection)

overhead rotor for propulsion and a tail rotor for stability, appeared in the late 1930s and were used in limited numbers during World War II. After hostilities ended and surplus pilots and machines became available, various local entrepreneurs began to look into the possibility of using helicopters for mail shuttle duty in the big metropolitan areas.[29]

The first such shuttle service to get off the ground, in 1947, was in the Los Angeles area. Helicopter Air Service of Chicago (known after 1956 as Chicago Helicopter Airways [CHA]) started service October 20, 1949, between Midway Airport, Chicago's central post office just west of the Loop, and thirty-four suburban heliports with small, bubble-cockpit Bell 47 choppers. The suburban facilities often were little

more than small fenced clearings on the edge of the suburbs; their only navigation aids were flapping wind socks to tell pilots which direction and with what intensity the wind was blowing. Although the Civil Aeronautics Board in Washington provided subsidies to keep the mail shuttle service flying, in the 1950s the helicopter airlines in Los Angeles, Chicago, and (after 1952) New York began developing passenger service to increase revenues.[30]

CHA in 1956 acquired three Sikorsky S-55 machines and flew them as passenger shuttles between Midway, the developing O'Hare Field to the northwest, and Meigs Field on the lakefront. The service was an instant success, carrying 55,000 passengers in its first full year of operation in 1957 and 108,911 the following year, when it

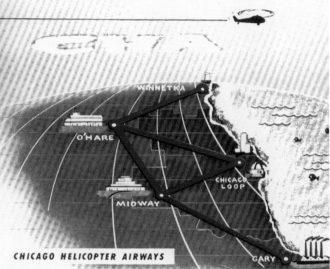

APRIL 1, 1963

CHICAGO HELICOPTER AIRWAYS

FREQUENT UP AND OVER SERVICE

O'HARE—DOWNTOWN CHICAGO
MIDWAY—O'HARE
DOWNTOWN CHICAGO—MIDWAY

PHOTO COURTESY CHICAGO DAILY NEWS

WORLD'S LARGEST SCHEDULED HELICOPTER AIRLINE

Fly CHA

CHICAGO HELICOPTER AIRWAYS

**PASSENGER — AIR MAIL — AIR EXPRESS
SWIFT LIFT AIR CARGO**

ONE DAY EXCURSION FARES

TAKE THE FAMILY HELICOPTER SIGHT-SEEING!
SKYTOURS START AT A LOW $2.50

ROUTE	Young Adults & Children Round-Trip One-Day Excursion Fares	Adult Round-Trip One-Day Excursion Fares
MIDWAY-MEIGS	$2.50	$5.00
O'HARE-WINNETKA	2.50	5.00
MIDWAY-O'HARE	3.00	6.00
MIDWAY-GARY	3.00	6.00
O'HARE-MEIGS	3.00	6.00
MIDWAY-WINNETKA	4.00	8.00
O'HARE-GARY	4.50	9.00

NOTES:
All excursion fares are sold on a stand-by basis . . . no advance reservations can be accepted.
All excursion fares are round trip fares and must be completed within one calendar day.
All Fares Subject to 5% Federal Transportation Tax.

CHICAGO

With the loss of most of its Midway-O'Hare shuttle business in 1962, Chicago Helicopter Airways the following year began to offer aerial sightseeing trips to drum up business. The ploy failed, as did CHA in 1966.

Chicago & Southern Air Lines, which came into existence in 1934 as a result of the Spoils Conference scandal, was never more than a marginally profitable regional carrier serving the Mississippi Valley corridor. It was merged into Delta Air Lines in 1952. The plane shown is a Lockheed Constellation. (Delta Air Lines)

acquired three twelve-passenger S-58 helicopters to keep up with demand. In just two years of operation, CHA had become the largest helicopter passenger airline in the world, although at 37 percent, load factors (percent of seats filled) were too low for the airline to make a profit and federal subsidies were still necessary to keep it flying. The phenomenal growth continued: in 1959 CHA carried 204,000 riders, and with a 51 percent load factor it was nearing the break-even point; in 1960 it handled 309,000 passengers despite a July 27 crash in which it lost an S-58C

with all thirteen aboard. By the end of the year, CHA was using eight helicopters to operate 158 flights daily.[31]

The end of the airline was abrupt. With the shift of airlines from Midway to O'Hare in 1961–1962, CHA disposed of most of its larger helicopters and leased the rest to charter operations. In 1962, it operated only thirty-four scheduled passenger flights. The end came in 1965 when the federal subsidies ended and the carrier could not find an airline willing to subsidize its operations the way United and American had made loan guarantees to the

This Chicago & Southern Air Lines advertisement from early in World War II (April 1, 1942) belies the severe restrictions that were placed on civilian travel during the war, primarily because the government pressed much of the commercial air fleet into military service, constraining capacity. (Delta Air Lines)

Los Angeles helicopter airline and Pan American World Airways had taken over the New York operation. Chicago Helicopter Airways shut down on January 1, 1966, and since then, despite a brief and unprofitable revival in 1969, Chicago, unlike cities on the East and West coasts, has not been a hospitable climate for helicopter operators. By the end of the twentieth century, only a handful of helicopters were in commercial service in the area, mainly in charter work.[32]

Chicago & Southern Air Lines

Inevitably, the cutthroat competition and high cost of new aircraft resulted in a shakeout in the U.S. airline industry, taking an especially heavy toll on the smaller trunks. The CAB was forced to sanction a number of route realignments and later some mergers both to strengthen the smaller trunks and prevent some bankruptcies. United bought the Denver–Los Angeles route from financially troubled Western, giving it its long-sought New York–Chicago–Los Angeles route via

Denver—a more direct journey for passengers than its earlier New York–Chicago–San Francisco–Los Angeles route. United also absorbed Capital to prevent its failure. That merger once against established United as the nation's largest airline. A smaller trunk with substantial operations in the Windy City, Chicago & Southern Air Lines (C&S), was absorbed by Delta.

C&S, which had been created in 1934 as a result of the Roosevelt administration's reform of the industry after the Spoils Conference, began as a regional airline serving mainly the Mississippi River Valley after it won the Chicago–New Orleans mail contract. An entrepreneur named Carleton Putnam, who only shortly before had founded a Los Angeles–San Francisco coastal airline called Pacific Seaboard Airlines, had successfully bid against Robertson Air Lines for the Mississippi Valley route between Chicago and New Orleans. He moved to the Midwest, began service with a couple of leased aircraft, and renamed his venture Chicago & Southern.[33]

The new airline was never more than marginally profitable. It lost $131,121 on

Turbine-propeller aircraft were already being displaced by jets when United Airlines in 1961 acquired a fleet of Vickers Viscount turbo-props as a result of its acquisition of the failing Capital Airlines. United replaced them with jets as quickly as it could. (Christopher Lynch Collection)

the Chicago–New Orleans route between the beginning of service in 1934 and May 1, 1937; not quite half of that loss ($58,391) occurred in the two years after the Interstate Commerce Commission, on March 11, 1935, fixed rates. In the fiscal year ending June 30, 1937, C&S lost $6,113 on revenues of $537,951; of those revenues, $331,220 were attributable to air mail, and $191,854 to passenger service. Nevertheless, Putnam believed by the end of 1939 that his airline was doing well enough to place a $700,000 order for six DC-3s. By the eve of World War II, C&S was employing not only its new DC-3s but also six Lockheed 10-B Electras over an extended route system that included its original Chicago–New Orleans spine as well as offshoots to Detroit, Kansas City, and Houston. C&S was also something of an

international carrier as the result of a joint venture with another airline with routes from New Orleans to Belize, Guatemala, and Panama.[34]

Beginning during World War II, C&S, like Capital, became an early beneficiary of the CAB policy to strengthen some of the smaller trunks to prevent them from being swallowed by the Big Four by giving them favorable treatment in new-route awards. Chicago & Southern's principal route awards were international, breaking Pan American's monopoly on service to the Caribbean. In 1946, the CAB awarded C&S the New Orleans–Havana route, which was extended to Caracas in 1948. By 1950, when C&S began operating Lockheed Constellations, it also served Kingston, San Juan, Ciudad Trujillo (later Santo Domingo), and Port au Prince.[35]

For most of its nineteen years of independent existence, Chicago & Southern was based in either St. Louis or Memphis, where the bulk of its operations and maintenance were conducted, but it briefly moved some of its corporate headquarters to Chicago after World War II. The airline's dependence on access to the Chicago transcontinental hub was crucial to its ability to feed traffic to its north-south spine and was cited in 1946 as the reason for its intended transfer of its corporate headquarters to the Windy City. "Chicago is fast becoming the center of the United States' growing airline industry. For this reason we deem it best to have our executive offices there, although our general offices and main operations base will continue in Memphis," Colonel N. Henry Jacobs, vice president of finance and administration, told a *Chicago Tribune* reporter. The airline acquired five floors of a building in downtown Chicago at Wabash Avenue and Monroe Street for that purpose; however, the high cost of remodeling the structure and financing a new $750,000 hangar at Municipal Airport, as well as the airline's continuing financial problems, doomed the move.[36]

Despite its possession of new routes, C&S remained in shaky financial condition after World War II, losing almost $800,000 on revenues of $8 million in 1947, losing $1 million on revenues of $8.2 million in 1948, and not paying its first postwar stock dividend until 1949. Even though it posted some modest profits in the early 1950s—net earnings of $856,035 on revenues of almost $12.9 million in 1950, earnings of $1,130,959 on revenues of $16.2 million in 1951, and earnings of $1,338,510 on revenues of $18.9 million in 1952—it was obvious to everyone in the industry that C&S could not long survive.[37]

C&S needed a partner to avoid being gobbled up by one of the Big Four, as did Delta Air Lines, another principally north-south carrier, which operated along the Chicago-Atlanta-Miami axis. The CAB had allowed Delta access to Chicago via Cincinnati in 1945. The two airlines began talks in early 1952, and the resulting merger was unusual at the time because it involved airlines of almost equal size, although Delta was the stronger of the two financially. C&S operated 9,388 route miles between thirty-three cities with eighteen major aircraft, and Delta operated 7,572 route miles between thirty-four cities with thirty aircraft.[38]

Delta had to borrow $10 million to cover the acquisition, but it did so by issuing that much in 5.5 percent debentures, which future revenues were pledged to repay, in return for 509,326 shares of C&S common stock. Each thirty-five dollars of debentures were convertible to a share of Delta common stock. Although Putnam became chairman of the new corporation after the CAB approved the merger in early 1953 and the name "Delta C&S" was painted on aircraft for a time, there was no doubt that Delta would be the surviving entity. Long before Delta absorbed Northeast Airlines in 1972 and Western Air Lines in 1987 and replaced Eastern as one of the Big Four, the name "Chicago & Southern" had disappeared from its aircraft livery.[39]

Pennsylvania-Central, which changed its name to Capital Airlines on April 24, 1948, was the biggest beneficiary of the CAB's postwar policy. The CAB, by virtue of the Civil Aeronautics Act of 1938, could control which airlines flew which routes, set their fares, regulate airline mergers, and to some extent oversee airline safety, at least until the safety function was transferred to the new FAA as a result of the Federal Aviation Act of 1958. But it was powerless to regulate schedules and equipment, and therefore could not regulate capacity. Since its creation, the CAB had never tried to rationalize the route system the way Walter Folger Brown had done in the Spoils Conference; instead, it considered each route award on a case-by-case basis as the airlines applied.[40]

Fare Wars

Although both Capital and United had experimented with the idea before World War II, in 1948 Capital introduced the industry to coach fares to gain an advantage on the highly competitive Chicago–New York route. Despite the skepticism of the CAB, the other airlines quickly followed its lead in order to remain competitive. Capital's original Nighthawk fares, inaugurated on November 4, 1948, were priced at two-thirds of first class, or $33.30 one way, and were justified to the CAB on the basis that the airline would use high-density seating and only offer the fares at night. However, by 1954 coach fares were standard in the industry.[41]

The resulting airline stampede to coach fares effectively nullified whatever advantage Capital had gained and caught the CAB's attention. The agency intervened in the 1950s and made Capital the nearly exclusive beneficiary of route awards in its 1952–1955 New York–Chicago Service case. The Big Four by that time accounted for half the seat miles flown in the United States, and the CAB used their increasing dominance to justify route awards to Delta in the Southeast and Braniff in the Southwest.

Capital then began searching for ways to effectively compete in its new markets, and mindful that the Big Four could quickly copy any attempt to discount fares as they had done after 1948, the airline decided to gain a competitive edge by ordering a new type of aircraft. The plane it selected was the British-built Vickers Viscount, a turboprop seating up to forty-seven passengers. Capital ordered sixty Viscounts on a liberal five-year credit arrangement offered by Vickers and in mid-1955 rushed them into service on the Washington-Chicago and New York–Chicago routes.

Although the airline increased its market share substantially, the added revenues were not sufficient to cover its debt service and operating costs. By 1957, Capital can-celled an order for additional planes and fell behind by $10 million in its payments to Vickers. As the airline's financial position continued to deteriorate despite new Florida route awards by the CAB, some stockholders attempted to oust the board of directors, and Vickers threatened to foreclose. United finally stepped in with an offer to buy Capital, and the CAB had no choice but to agree to the deal. None of the rest of the Big Four was interested. United absorbed Capital on July 1, 1961, in what was to that time the largest merger in U.S. airline history, and United was once again the nation's largest airline.[42]

At that point, United's only major success in getting the CAB to agree on new routes had occurred just after the war when it was awarded access to Hawaii from the West Coast in competition with Pan American. Patterson was convinced Hawaii eventually would be a big tour market—an aerial gold mine. Pan American had been serving Hawaii since 1935 with Glenn Martin's flying boats as a leg of its trans-Pacific route, but until long-range bombers were developed for World War II, it was impossible for land-based aircraft to serve the 2,400-mile, overwater route with no emergency fields along the way. After the CAB ruled on May 16, 1946, that United could fly between San Francisco and Hawaii, Patterson interrupted a long-standing relationship with Donald Douglas and ordered seven new planes from Boeing. The resulting Boeing 377 Stratocruiser, which had evolved from the wartime B-29 bomber through the C-29 and KC-29 military transport and tanker programs, was a disappointment. The planes were two years late in delivery and so full of bugs that United sold them in 1951 and went back to Douglas, eventually using DC-7s on the San Francisco–Hawaii run. By then it was also flying between Los Angeles and Hawaii.[43]

The Capital acquisition gave United more problems with its aircraft fleet, especially its plan to convert to jet-powered planes. Patterson realized during World

War II, when jet aircraft made their appearance in combat, that jets would eventually replace piston-powered planes. He commissioned one of his executives, J. A. (Jack) Herlihy, to look into the question. Patterson determined that the first commercial jet on the drawing board, the British Comet, was too small for United's needs. So even before the acquisition of Capital and its turboprop Viscounts, United had in 1955 been the launch customer for thirty Douglas DC-8 jets for long-haul service and had in 1960 placed an order for twenty midrange Sud Aviation Caravelles jets from France.[44]

However, the transformation to the jet age raised a new problem over which the airlines did not entirely have control. The early jets needed longer runways and larger terminals than were available at the older airports built during the propeller era. The rapid growth in commercial aviation after World War II was taxing the older airports like Municipal/Midway to their limits. The airports in smaller cities might have been adequate for commercial aviation for a few years, but a major hub like Midway needed immediate attention.

There was a domino effect. As Midway and later O'Hare became congested with commercial traffic, the smaller aircraft owners—not just private pilots, but also corporations that owned their own planes and had coexisted with the airlines for years—increasingly found they were being squeezed out. As early as 1944, the Civil Aeronautics Administration in its National Airport Plan warned Congress that a postwar increase in flying would require improvements to 1,625 of the 3,086 airports across the nation and the construction of 3,050 new ones. As suburban sprawl increasingly gobbled up the old flying fields scattered about metropolitan areas, there was no place for the private pilots to go. Safety was also an issue. About 46 percent of all accidents occurred during landing, although the spectacular midair disasters received the most attention in the press. Mixing slow-moving private aircraft and fast-moving but less maneuverable jets was a recipe for disaster.[45] Both Chicago and, somewhat later, the State of Illinois had reached the same conclusions during World War II, and after the end of hostilities they began to plan for the jet age.

The Airports

Meigs Field, the smallest of Chicago's three modern airports, was built on Northerly Island in Lake Michigan. Its fate became a political football in the 1990s when Chicago wanted to use the island for a park, but the state wanted to keep the field open as a reliever airport.

• The rapid development of the airlines in the 1930s and their expansion into the business of hauling passengers required a collateral improvement in the nation's airports. The grassy flying fields that were adequate for barnstormers giving occasional rides or Jenny biplanes carrying a few sacks of mail were hopelessly inadequate once paying passengers started to show up. The air mail terminals were no more than shacks for the offices of the carriers, or worse, a few desks in the corner of an unheated hangar. That might be

suitable for an old aviation buff like Charles Dickinson, but it would in no way be adequate for the glitterati on whom the airlines were increasingly becoming dependent for revenue.

The major airports of the 1930s required all-weather runways pointing in several different directions to enable planes to always take off into the wind to keep weather delays to a minimum, and they needed taxiways to get the airplanes from the runways to the terminals. Railroads had introduced the phenomenon of scheduling to American transportation; ships, the earlier form of mass transportation, had left when their holds or manifests were full and the weather was right. The tight schedules that inevitably developed as the airlines moved into the passenger business required that the airports have beacons and lighted runways so pilots could see them at night and in inclement weather. As the number of flights increased, the airports had to build towers, often mounted atop terminal buildings, to control traffic on the ground and in the immediate vicinity of the fields.

Airport planners very quickly adapted the design of railroad and bus depots to their own needs. They built waiting rooms with seats for passengers, and in some cases private lounges for the rich and famous who wanted privacy while they waited. The new terminals had ticket counters and often lunchrooms. However, instead of being protected by train sheds, early airline passengers walked outside onto the open tarmac and climbed a few steps to get on their airplane. Because the new airports were most frequently built in remote areas with plenty of cheap land, parking became a requirement. Cicero Field, which predated commercial aviation, was one of the few public airports with rail service.

The expansion of aviation into passenger service during the 1930s resulted in explosive growth in the number of airfields and in government involvement in building and operating them. The earliest fields were built by aviation organizations, such as the Aero Club or the Chicago Flying Club. Others were developed by entrepreneurs, like Nimmo Black and Roy Guthier, whose Guthier Flying Field survived the twentieth century but came under municipal ownership as Palwaukee Airport. Partridge and Keller and Edward B. Heath maintained independent airports for their aviation companies. When local governments first got into the airport business, they treated their new flying fields as recreational facilities. The Cook County Forest Preserve District operated a few airports, and Chicago's first municipal field, created in 1922 on the site of what would become Municipal/Midway Airport, was operated and maintained by the city's Bureau of Parks, Playgrounds, and Bathing Beaches.[1]

A map drawn in 1912 for the Aero Club showed four aerodrome sites in the Chicago metropolitan area—Cicero, Clearing, Maywood, and Skokie. Several unsanctioned flying fields also existed but didn't make the club's official map. By 1928, when Municipal Airport was in operation, a survey by the Chicago Regional Planning Association found twenty-eight civil-aircraft landing fields, including nine sites with aerial navigation beacons and four beacon-equipped facilities operated by the U.S. Department of Commerce as intermediate fields, the euphemism of the day for emergency landing strips. The growth continued despite the depression, and by the eve of World War II there were sixty airports of assorted quality in metropolitan Chicago, excluding private fields available only to their owners.[2]

The new airports required to sustain and nurture the fledgling airlines of the 1930s were too expensive for private industry. Henry Ford's one-thousand-acre company field in Lansing was a rarity in 1926. The Ford Motor Company used the airstrip to serve its nearby auto assembly plant, but once Ford's new airline started hauling mail on the Chicago-Detroit-Cleveland route, it had to shift its operations to Maywood to connect with the other air mail carriers. By then Ford had decided to get out of the airline business and to concentrate on building cars. In July 1928, the company relinquished its air mail contracts to William B. Stout, who in turn sold out the following year to a predecessor of United Airlines.[3]

By the early 1930s, the enormous amount of capital required to buy land for and to build passenger-carrier airports meant that they were becoming the exclusive domain of municipal government, not only in Chicago but across the nation.

Any city that wanted to remain on the map had to have an all-weather airport, and such facilities became continual works in progress, ever expanding and modernizing to meet the needs of the growing industry. By 1939, when the Civil Aeronautics Administration submitted its first national airport survey to Congress, there were 1,046 municipal airports in the country, 787 private, 42 state, and 22 federal-government operated.[4]

As the century progressed, the growth in commercial traffic at the big-city airports forced the smaller planes to private fields. Eventually the operators of those aerodromes, especially in metropolitan areas, found that they were becoming prohibitively expensive to operate, and they were forced to move them to the fringe of suburbia. The principal culprit after World War II was urban sprawl. As development crept outward from the city and reached the once-remote private airports one by one, their owners began to sell them to developers who built housing subdivisions and shopping centers. The residents of the new subdivisions that were built around the airports complained about airport noise and danger, and urban sprawl resulted in an increase in the value of the land beneath the airports, causing property taxes to rise to the point that it was uneconomical to operate the facilities as flying fields. As the private airport closings continued into the 1980s, the state became alarmed and began a program to subsidize the public acquisition and improvement of the surviving airports by suburban municipalities.

Municipal Airport

Municipal Airport in 1928, its first full year of operation, handled only 15,498 passengers on 41,660 aircraft operations, or one customer every third flight. Although Chicago officials began claiming as early as 1929 that Municipal Airport was the busiest in the world, it was not until 1930 that the number of passengers exceeded

the number of operations. Passenger traffic continued to grow through that decade despite the depression. By 1940, the number of flights at Municipal had increased by 50 percent over 1930, but the number of passengers had jumped elevenfold to more than 700,000 as a result of the introduction of larger, faster, and safer airplanes over the decade (see appendix D).[5]

The faster and larger twin-engine airliners introduced in the 1930s put pressure on the airports designed in the air mail era because they required longer and more substantial runways. Also, because passenger traffic required reliable schedules, all-weather, paved runways became a necessity. So did passenger terminals; mail could sit in an unheated hangar for hours awaiting the next plane, but paying passengers demanded comfortable terminals with such amenities as seats, lavatories, and restaurants.

The DH-4 of the air mail service weighed 3,720 pounds, had a cruising speed of 121 miles an hour, could carry one or two passengers, and was designed to use turf runways. The Ford Tri-Motor, designed to handle up to eleven passengers, was 10,100 pounds—still light enough for well-drained turf runways. However, the DC-3, with a capacity of twenty-one passengers, weighed 24,000 pounds and had a cruising speed of 192 miles an hour. It could land on grass runways, but hard surfaces were better in inclement weather. Plowing snow off a grass runway was an adventure, and the heavy beating grass took from frequent takeoffs and landings by heavy airplanes quickly destroyed it, leaving only mud. By the end of the 1930s, the prospect of four-engine Boeing 307 Stratoliners with a weight of 42,000 pounds and a passenger load of thirty-three, and the even larger DC-4s, at 73,000 pounds and carrying forty-four or more passengers, threatened to make almost every airport in the nation obsolete.[6]

As early as 1929, the Chicago Association of Commerce began a campaign to induce the city to enlarge Municipal, then

only three years old and 120 acres in size, by leasing an additional 160 acres to the west. At the time the runways were completed in 1928, two years after Municipal was officially opened for business, the airport occupied only the eastern half of a three-hundred-acre oblong tract. It had cinder runways, the longest of which was 3,600 feet, and a flagman stood near the end of the runway to direct air traffic. Close to the airport perimeter were the offices and hangars of the companies that did business there. Four airlines—NAT, BAT, Robertson, and Aviation Service and Transport Company—and an Illinois National Guard outfit had hangars along the southeast boundary. Four additional airlines shared two other hangars: Grey Goose Air Lines and Embry-Riddle in one hangar,

and Thompson Aeronautical Corporation and Interstate Air Lines in the other. In the earliest years of operation, passengers often went to the hangar to catch a flight, although a small passenger terminal was finally completed in 1931—a boxy structure whose most memorable interior feature was a couple of palm trees to remind passengers of their potential destinations. Cicero Avenue was served by a streetcar line that required at least one transfer from the Loop, so various parking areas were built around the site. Until a Chicago Transit Authority train line was built there from the Loop in 1993, access to Municipal/Midway was primarily by automobile.[7]

By 1936, a year in which Municipal still handled only 260,800 passengers, the airlines were warning that the airport

The relative proximity of Municipal/Midway Airport to the Loop—about ten miles—meant that propeller aircraft that were served by Midway, like this Constellation, were at lower altitude over the Loop than the jets bound for O'Hare International Airport seventeen miles away. (Christopher Lynch Collection) would be hopelessly inadequate for the four-engine aircraft expected to enter service within a few years. They recommended that the city acquire a mile-square site on which runways of 5,000 feet could be built. Some of Municipal's existing runways were only 2,600 feet. The airlines also warned in an article by the *Tribune*'s Wayne Thomis, aviation editor and himself a pilot, that they might have to begin bypassing Chicago.[8]

In the 1920s, the nation's airports were still primarily financed locally, but that began to change in the 1930s. Chicago established Municipal Airport in 1926 with a modest $1,560 per year investment, the cost of leasing the former federal land grant site from the city's school system. A federal study shows that as late as 1932 total capital expenditures on airports in the United States was $146.3 million, almost equally split between private sources and municipalities. The states had contributed only 2 percent and the federal government less than 1 percent of the total. Various depression-era, make-work projects increased the federal government's share of airport capital spending to 42.6 percent, with municipalities accounting for 31 percent and private sources slightly less than a quarter of the total.[9]

The CAA recommended that for national defense and air transport reasons the government begin a systematic program of subsidies to airports to enable their number to be increased by more than 50 percent and the airports in major cities to be enlarged. The agency also established 4,500 feet as the minimum runway length for major airports like Municipal. Congress dithered until after World War II began in Europe, when it became obvious that aviation was going to be an important part of national defense. The legislature then hurriedly approved $40 million to improve 250 airports considered vital to national defense.[10]

Long before that happened, both New York and Chicago proceeded with airport expansion programs on their own. With Works Progress Administration (WPA) as-

sistance, New York acquired and expanded what became LaGuardia Airport. It opened on October 15, 1939. Chicago reached an agreement in 1937 with the Chicago & Western Indiana Railroad to relocate the railroad's right-of-way, creating the mile-square site the airlines wanted so Municipal Airport could be enlarged. That was the first step in an $8.5 million modernization, completed in 1941, that included the construction of nine runways to meet federal standards. By the end of that year, the City Council had authorized $1.2 million for a new terminal.

World War II

Before the terminal could be built, the Japanese air raid on the U.S. fleet in Hawaii abruptly brought the nation into World War II, which interrupted commercial aviation development in the United States between 1941 and the end of 1945. Not only was aircraft production, including the twenty DC-4s United had ordered, diverted to the military, but also private flying was restricted in many areas, federal subsidies to civil airports were rerouted to purely military fields, and national defense traffic was given priority at the existing commercial airports. The Civil Aeronautics Administration also took over air traffic control at local airports and proved so effective at the job that it retained control of the system after the war ended. Strategic commercial airports like Municipal handled as much or more military traffic than civilian. The war's only aviation disaster in Chicago occurred on May 20, 1943, when an Army Air Corps Liberator bomber smashed into a giant gas storage tank southeast of Municipal, killing all twelve servicemen aboard.[11]

Despite the war, in 1944 an international convention was held in Chicago to negotiate the rules for international air traffic. Earlier such conventions in Paris in 1919 and Havana in 1928 had gotten the ball rolling on international cooperation on aviation but had failed to achieve the scope of what the fifty-two nations attending the Chicago Conference accomplished, including establishing American standards for such things as air traffic control, communications, operating personnel, aircraft specifications, and meteorology, as well as rules governing the handling of passengers on international routes. The rules of the Chicago Conference then became the global standard, or at least the basis from which bilateral aviation treaties were negotiated for the remainder of the century.[12]

Although the airline industry had averted nationalization by coming up with its own mobilization plan prior to the Pearl Harbor attack, much of its fleet was pressed into service for military charters, sometimes with such abruptness that aircraft made unscheduled stops and dumped puzzled civilian passengers at airports far from their destinations. The combined U.S. airline fleet as the war began was 363 airplanes, and Washington immediately acquired two hundred of them for military service. This effectively reduced United's

Civilian air traffic was restricted during World War II, but the reduced number of airline flights handled a considerable amount of wartime cargo. Railroads and cartage companies often painted their vehicles with patriotic slogans, like this plug for war bonds.

Soldiers, sailors, and other people involved in national defense made up a substantial percentage of airline traffic during World War II and into the 1950s. Municipal/Midway Airport's terminal dating from 1941 quickly became overcrowded.

fleet from sixty-nine to only thirty-three aircraft, all DC-3s. The military and people traveling on defense business had priority for the remaining seats, so nonessential customers had to fly standby if a seat became available or, most often, simply take the train. Despite the reduction of the fleet, the number of passengers handled by the airlines during the war jumped from 2.8 million in 1940 to 6.5 million in 1945, then nearly doubled to 12.1 million the year after the war ended. The numbers of passengers handled at Municipal Airport over the same span increased from 704,846 to 1,496,634, then shot up to 2,645,674 in 1946.[13]

Chanute Field, the army aviation base that had been deserted and was almost closed during demobilization in 1919 but had survived as an aviation technical training center, got a new lease on life. Beginning in 1938, it was rebuilt as a depression-era WPA project, not from the army budget. During the war, the Chanute schools graduated more than 200,000 Air Corps technicians, and at one time in 1943 the air base had as many as 25,000 trainees on site—so many that thousands of them lived in tents. Following the Japanese surrender, Chanute continued to expand and contract during the Korean, Vietnam, and cold wars, and for a time it was transformed into a training center for crews of Minuteman intercontinental ballistic missiles. It was finally closed permanently in 1993 following the end of the cold war.[14]

The navy had maintained a small aviation presence at north-suburban Great Lakes training center after World War I, essentially as a center for air reservists, but as the war clouds gathered over Europe, it decided it needed a larger air base to handle the high-performance aircraft then coming on line. The reservists were transferred to the existing three-hundred-acre Curtiss-Wright Airport in north-suburban Glenview in 1938, and two years later the navy bought the airport outright and an additional nine hundred acres nearby. The expanded base became Glenview Naval Air Station, a major training school for pilots during the war.[15]

Perhaps Glenview's best-known role during World War II was the training of thousands of navy combat pilots using two aircraft carriers on Lake Michigan—the *Wolverine* and *Sable,* both converted from paddle-wheel excursion steamships that had been used on the Great Lakes and requisitioned by the navy once war broke out. Crews removed much of the superstructure of the former *Seeandbee,* built a flight deck, and had the renamed *Wolverine* in service by August 12, 1942, just

eight months after the Pearl Harbor attack. The carrier *Sable,* which had been converted from the SS *Greater Buffalo,* joined the *Wolverine* on Lake Michigan the next year. Together they freed the nation's ocean-going carriers for combat duty. Among their graduates was Navy Ensign George Bush, who became the nation's forty-first president in 1989, six years before Glenview was declared a surplus base and permanently closed.[16]

The other major defense airfield in the Chicago area was Orchard Place Airport in northwest-suburban Park Ridge. It was there that Douglas Aircraft hurriedly built an airfield and factory beginning in 1942 to augment its Santa Monica, California, plant. At Orchard Place, Douglas manufactured C-54 transports for the army and R5D transports for the navy—the martial versions of the DC-4 and the airplane best known for its role in the cold war's Berlin Airlift of 1948–1949. The Chicago factory ultimately built 653 of the planes, 132 of them for the navy, before shutting down after the war.[17]

Orchard Place–Douglas Airport, or ORD as it became known in the aviation industry code used to identify airports, became an air reserve and national guard training center after the war and, in perhaps its most unusual role, was used as a temporary museum for World War II aircraft captured from the axis powers. An outfit called the 803rd Special Depot, commanded by Captain Robert C. Strobell, was used beginning in 1946 to store such enemy war birds as German Messerschmitt 262 jet fighters and a Japanese Nakajima C6NI-S Saiun night fighter, first for study and later for distribution to American museums. The special depot was closed in 1949.[18]

O'Hare's Beginnings

ORD became a surplus and underutilized military aerodrome at about the same time Chicago began looking for a site for a new airport to augment Municipal and to handle the boom in air travel

Urban sprawl that followed World War II took a heavy toll on general aviation flying fields. The Howell Airport at Illinois Highway 83 and Cicero Avenue near suburban Crestwood was still relatively isolated in 1953. (Octave Chanute Aerospace Museum)

By 1987, development had surrounded Howell Airport, increasing the value of its land and the amount of its property taxes to the point that it was no longer economical to use it as an airport. (Bill Howell Collection)

The Howell Airport was closed in 1989, and the Rivercrest Shopping Center was built on the site. (Octave Chanute Aerospace Museum)

that was expected in the postwar period. The new field had to be large enough to accommodate the next generation of commercial aircraft that in all probability would ascend from the ME-262 jets sitting at ORD's 803rd Special Depot awaiting placement in museums.

It didn't take long for the boom in air travel to develop, although commercial jetliners were still a decade away. Passenger traffic at Municipal nearly doubled to almost 2.6 million boardings the year after the war ended, and by 1950 it exceeded 3.8 million. By 1949, the first year for which reliable comparative data is available, Midway Airport, as Chicago Municipal had been renamed, was the most active airport in the nation in terms of aircraft operations, with 223,493 arrivals and departures, and was second only to New York's La-Guardia in passenger volume. That year the New York airport handled 3,215,961 air carrier passengers, while there were 2,842,378 at Midway, but by 1951 Midway led in passenger traffic as well.[19]

The clamor by business and aviation groups for additional airports to handle the anticipated growth had begun even before Municipal/Midway's prewar expansion program was completed. The Chicago Association of Commerce recommended in a report at the end of 1941 that Chicago build two additional airports by 1960 to relieve the pressure on Municipal/Midway. The association proposed that one be built near the Loop, possibly on an island in Lake Michigan, a site suggested twenty years earlier and several times thereafter, and the other somewhere on the northwest side of the city where large tracts of open land were still available. The Civil Aeronautics Administration, in its November 30, 1944, proposal to Congress for a $1 billion postwar airport building program, recommended that as many as three additional airports the size of Municipal be built in

188CHICAGOAVIATION

O'Hare International Airport was named to honor Lieutenant Commander Edward H. (Butch) O'Hare, a navy pilot from Chicago who won the Congressional Medal of Honor for intercepting a formation of nine Japanese bombers about to attack his carrier, the *Lexington*. He shot down five and seriously damaged a sixth in the February 20, 1942, aerial engagement. O'Hare was killed on November 26, 1943, in a dogfight over Tarawa.

the Chicago area, two of them in the suburbs. The prospect of receiving federal subsidies for a new airport that everyone agreed needed to be built and the thought of losing political control of the principal commercial aviation hub in the metropolitan area prompted Mayor Edward J. Kelly to appoint a committee to find a site for a new airport.[20]

The situation that Chicago found itself in at Municipal Airport was typical of similar predicaments in big cities across the nation well into the 1960s. The airports designed and built in the 1930s were magnets for various aviation-related commercial development on their borders—

motels, airline offices, restaurants, and cargo businesses—which ultimately ringed the airport sites, making expansion impossible. Expanding Municipal Airport as an alternative to building a new airport was rejected for that very reason: the development on its borders made land acquisition prohibitively expensive. Municipal also lacked adequate public transit and would have no easy access to the new expressway system that would be built in the 1950s and 1960s.[21]

As the size of aircraft grew rapidly as a result of the technology learned in long-range bomber development during World War II, Municipal Airport could handle additional numbers of passengers, but its air traffic control system was taxed once operational volumes exceeded 200,000 in 1947, and it lacked sufficient groundside capacity for such things as parking. Traffic congestion on Cicero Avenue, despite its widening to four lanes, became intolerable.

Despite the problems, the number of operations tripled between 1944 and the end of 1956, and passenger traffic increased ninefold. The peak was reached in 1959 when the airport handled more than 430,000 flights and 10 million passengers. By then, relief was on the way in the form of a new airport.

As early as 1945, a site selection committee appointed by the mayor had decided that Douglas's wartime aircraft factory and the adjacent Orchard Place–Douglas airfield near Mannheim and Higgins Roads northwest of the city was not only suitable as a site for a commercial airport, but also the best of the five alternatives, which included Municipal, the Clearing industrial district just to the south of Municipal, the Lake Calumet area, and an airport in the lake just east of the Loop. The original Orchard Place field was a small private aerodrome built by Douglas in 1943 with four concrete runways varying in length from 5,500 to 5,700 feet. The city acquired 1,081 acres of the site in 1946 from the War Assets Administration. That was larger than Municipal Airport's 640-acre site, but considerably less than would be needed for the airport of the future, so the city issued $46 million in general obligation bonds to buy an additional 6,000 acres and to relocate the Chicago & North Western Railway spur to the western edge of the site to clear it for aviation. In 1949, the city spent an additional $2.4 million to acquire enough additional land to bring the airport site up to 7,700 acres.[22]

In May of that year the airport was renamed O'Hare International Airport after Navy Lieutenant Commander Edward Henry "Butch" O'Hare, a fighter pilot who won the Congressional Medal of Honor for single-handedly attacking a formation of nine Japanese bombers approaching the aircraft carrier *Lexington,* shooting down five, and damaging a sixth on February 20, 1942. O'Hare later was reported missing and apparently killed in a dogfight on November 26, 1943, near Tarawa. Municipal Airport was renamed Midway later in 1949 after the World War II carrier battle of 1942, considered the turning point in the Pacific war against the Japanese.[23]

The new airport, which didn't officially open to domestic commercial traffic until October 1955, was not much of an improvement over Midway in terms of runways and terminals, and it was considerably less convenient to downtown Chicago, although traveling businesspeople in the northern, northwestern, and western suburbs found it more accessible. O'Hare was considerably less crowded than the older airport. The year it opened, it handled only 471,000 passengers, on average about 1,300 per day, whereas Midway reported 9.1 million boardings. That climbed to just over 10 million in 1959, Midway's busiest postwar year, by which time O'Hare was handling a fifth of that volume, serving principally travelers using the new commercial jet aircraft unable to land at Midway.

Financing O'Hare

To build an airport capable of handling the growing jet traffic, Chicago turned from the general obligation bond method of financing construction (bonds were backed by a property tax and the city's full faith and credit), to the revenue bond. At the time, it was an unusual system for financing local aviation improvements, and it became a model for other major airports across the nation. The theory behind revenue bonds was that the users of the airport would pay for it. It was not an entirely novel approach locally; Chicago had purchased its mass transit system in 1946 using revenue bonds to be paid off by riders' fares and over the years had defrayed portions of the capital and operating costs of Municipal Airport by imposing user fees based on the weight of aircraft. In 1937 such fees ranged from twenty dollars for a small aircraft of less than 15,000 pounds to seventy-five dollars for an aircraft of more than 200,000 pounds and generated less than $30,000 a year in revenue. The airlines simply passed along the fees to their customers in the price of tickets.[24]

In the case of O'Hare, the costs of land acquisition and construction were so great that the city decided almost from the beginning to recover all capital and operating costs from the airport users. A bargain was struck in 1955 in which the scheduled airlines agreed to adjust landing fees annually on the basis of the cost experience of the previous year and to finance most of the $120 million cost of O'Hare construction with the proceeds from revenue bonds underwritten by the airlines, in ef-

fect by pledging landing fees to repay the bonds. The minimum fee charged for each aircraft upon landing was six cents per thousand pounds of weight. In return, a committee of airline representatives was created to oversee operation of the airport and to approve all major capital projects.[25]

The city's initial plan was that O'Hare would relieve some of the congestion at Midway as well as handle the expected growth in air traffic. In the 1950s, not only were more Americans traveling, but they were traveling more frequently. The nation's population grew by slightly more than a third between 1940 and 1960, but intercity travel increased by nearly 75 percent. Annual per capita intercity travel increased from 2,499 miles in 1940 to 3,342 in 1950, and 4,355 in 1960 with no change to the trend in sight (see appendix C). To accommodate that growth, the airlines had begun to order first-generation jets, which were both larger and faster

By 1958, O'Hare Airport had been operating as a commercial airport for three years, and the aeronautical highway system controlling air traffic had evolved into a complex system that used radio transmitters to guide aircraft. This aeronautical map still shows for visual reference the Sanitary and Ship Canal, the Des Plaines River winding to the southwest, and assorted railroads fanning out through the metropolitan area. (Octave Chanute Aerospace Museum)

than propeller aircraft; they could not only carry more people on each trip but also make more trips each day.

Consultant Ralph H. Burke's 1948 master plan for O'Hare called for runways varying from 7,700 to 8,100 feet in length, conforming to the November 4, 1947, order by CAA administrator T. P. Wright establishing national standards for runways. But commercial jets would need longer runways to safely operate in all weather, and the first of them arrived within three years of O'Hare's opening, Boeing's 707 in 1958, and Douglas's DC-8 a year later. With those planes just over the horizon, Chicago in early 1958 was forced to revise its master plan for O'Hare, lengthening runways to eleven thousand feet. The new plan also abandoned the original idea of a star-shaped passenger terminal in midfield in favor of a U-shaped terminal that would permit additional ramp and apron space for the large jets as well as more space for the ticket counters and waiting rooms needed to handle the expected increase in the number of passengers.[26]

The airport planners were not disappointed. In 1947, planners had projected that O'Hare would handle 500,000 flights carrying 22 million people by 1970; instead, it handled 641,390 flights with 29.7 million passengers that year. The average passenger load per aircraft operation tripled from 15 in 1960 to 46 in 1970. Within a decade of its opening, O'Hare had become the largest hub in the nation's domestic airline network—a giant connecting center in which half of the travelers at any time were simply changing planes and thousands more were spending only a few hours in Chicago to attend business meetings with colleagues from around the nation in the scores of hotels and convention centers that had sprung up around the airport.

The growth meant O'Hare was almost continually under construction from 1970 through the end of the century as the city, the airlines, and the federal government expanded, remodeled, and rebuilt the air-

port to reduce congestion and remain competitive with other cities in the nation's air network. The year 1970 was when Chicago completed the relocation of Irving Park Road and the construction of a new 8,070-foot runway (4 Right–22 Left) at the southern border of the airport. Even before the concrete had been poured for the new runway, U.S. Secretary of Transportation Alan Boyd stepped in to impose temporary controls on air traffic for safety reasons. The result was the FAA's "high-density rule" restricting the number of operations at O'Hare, Washington National (now Reagan National), LaGuardia, Kennedy, and Newark airports. Newark was later exempted. O'Hare was assigned a limit of 155 operations (takeoffs and landings) per hour between 6:45 A.M. and 9:15 P.M.; that number was later increased to 163.[27]

Airport Expansion

As early as 1970, the airlines were agitating for a third airport to relieve overcrowding at O'Hare. The plea did not impress Chicago politicians, who noted that plenty of capacity was available at Midway Airport because the airlines abandoned it in 1961–1962 to move to O'Hare. Mayor Richard J. Daley's response was to urge the airlines to transfer 219 flights to Midway, where the traffic had dwindled from slightly fewer than 7 million passengers in 1960 to only 417,544 before reviving somewhat at the end of the decade. In 1970 it still handled only 1.4 million passengers and would not rebound, despite the city's best efforts, until after the airline industry was deregulated in the 1980s.[28]

An underlying issue was political control of Chicago's airports—it was the Chicago Democrats versus the suburban Republicans. The city was running out of available space for a new airport, but any new airport in the suburbs probably would be built and operated by either the state or a special taxing district controlled by the suburbs. A study commissioned by Mayor

Orchard Place–Douglas
Airport, the future O'Hare,
in this view looking south,
in 1948 sat amid truck farms
northwest of Chicago. The
Douglas Aircraft plant that
built wartime transports is at
the left along Mannheim
Road, and the village of
Bensenville can be seen in
the upper right-hand corner.

By 1958, when Chicago had
completed a small terminal
at O'Hare and two northwest-
southeast parallel runways
to handle the new jet traffic,
development was
beginning to occur along
the Northwest (top right)
and Tri-State (bottom right)
tollways. There were a few
complaints by neighbors
about jet noise in the 1950s,
mainly concerning military
aircraft.

O'Hare had eclipsed Midway as the region's major airport by 1961, when the airlines began transferring most of their flights there. Development, seen in this aerial photograph looking east, had begun to encircle the airport, and complaints by neighbors about aircraft noise accelerated.

Richard J. Daley in the 1960s had resurrected the proposal for an airport on an island in the lake after rejecting two suburban sites, but the idea was dropped in 1973 after conservationists armed with new federal environmental laws opposed it, the Republican administrations in Washington showed little interest in helping to finance it, and the new jumbo jets (Boeing 747, Douglas DC-10, and Lockheed L-1011) that were too large to use a lake airport were introduced into service. The oft-discussed proposal for an airport along Lake Calumet on the far South Side met a similar fate a few years later.[29]

The growth in aircraft and passenger traffic at O'Hare continued through the decade, and by 1978 ORD was handling more than 760,000 flights and almost 50 million passengers annually. The airport had become such a critical nexus of the nation's commercial air network that service disruptions at O'Hare, even those lasting only an hour, were likely to have a ripple effect across the nation's commercial air system despite the development of similar high-density hubs in Atlanta, Dallas, and Denver. The airlines could find a substitute for a single plane delayed at O'Hare, but twenty or more sitting on the ground in Chicago could disrupt much of an airline's national schedule.

On March 18, 1971, a day known among aviation historians as Black Thursday, a snowstorm and two minor accidents that forced the temporary closing of two of O'Hare's ten runways delayed 681 arriving aircraft, some for as long as an hour and a half, and at one time sixty-eight airplanes were circling the city waiting for slots to land. Hundreds of others were delayed or held on the ground in other cities. Severe thunderstorms on June 30, 1977, virtually closed O'Hare, trapping three hundred aircraft, or approximately a quarter of the nation's available civil aircraft fleet. Planes had to be parked on any available space on taxiways, run-up pads, and runways until the storm abated. By then the air traffic control system was strained to the limit, and it finally cracked in 1981 when air traffic controllers staged a nation-wide strike that disrupted the system before the FAA was able to replace them. Despite some improvements in such things as radar and traffic control, bad weather remained a sporadic problem for O'Hare and the national commercial aviation system through the end of the century. A slow-down by fifteen controllers on July 17, 2000, caused 155 flights to be cancelled and another 420 delayed at O'Hare; a storm on September 11, 2000, caused 368 flights to be cancelled there. Flight cancellations due to storms was a major reason O'Hare lost its title as the nation's busiest airport to Atlanta's Hartsfield International in both 1999 and 2000.[30]

The Federal Aviation Administration initially tried to cope with the aerial traffic jams by using holding patterns in which circling jets were stacked one above another and slowly circled downward 1,000 feet at a time until they were ready for the final approach to the airport. The holding patterns were abandoned in favor of a national flow control system after the oil crises of the 1970s caused the price of jet fuel to increase dramatically and the national strike by air traffic controllers forced the agency to restrict traffic while it rebuilt its manpower. Flow control meant that if delays were likely at O'Hare, the FAA simply held Chicago-bound aircraft on the ground in other cities or greatly reduced their cruising speed en route until the problem was cleared up. The continual addition of such things as improved instrument-landing systems for use in inclement weather, high-speed turnoffs to enable landing jets to clear the runways faster, and computer-controlled data on air traffic controllers' radar scopes helped relieve congestion somewhat.

On the ground, Chicago in 1982 began a $1 billion expansion and modernization program at O'Hare to keep up with growth. Before it was complete, the city had moved much of the air freight operations to the west side of the airfield to make room for a new international terminal. The old international terminal was demolished and rebuilt as a terminal for United Airlines. Remote parking lots were built east of the airport, and an elevated railway was installed linking the parking lots and all the terminals. The city in 1984 extended the Milwaukee Avenue rapid transit line from its terminal at Jefferson Park to O'Hare to provide for the first time elevated-subway rail service from the Loop to the airport.

Reliever Airports

With airport improvements, flow control, and the deregulation of the airline industry, which resulted in fare wars, O'Hare was handling in excess of 800,000 flights and 60 million passengers annually by 1990. Deregulation also revived Midway Airport, which in 1990 handled 320,247 aircraft operations and nearly 8.8 million passengers, its best year in three decades. However, the net effect of the increase in commercial traffic was to create another sort of airport crisis in metropolitan Chicago: small planes increasingly were being forced out of the two big airports and into the suburbs, where at the same time airports were disappearing at an alarming rate as their owners sold off to developers. The aircraft being displaced belonged not so much to recreational flyers but to a variety of business and private interests—corporations, assorted charter operators, flight schools, flying clubs, and individuals.

The situation was exacerbated late in the century when the city announced that it intended to close Meigs Field, the small, one-runway airport that had been built in 1948 on Northerly Island in the lake between Roosevelt and Cermak Roads (12th and 22nd Streets). Over the years, the airfield, because of its proximity to the Loop, had become a favorite for assorted commuter airlines, State of Illinois shuttles to Springfield, businesspeople attending conventions at nearby McCormick Place, and some individuals wealthy enough to commute by their own airplanes to work in downtown Chicago. It handled as many as 91,452 flights in 1968, and in 1980 passenger traffic hit a record 468,933 before beginning a long decline. In 1994, the city announced that it intended to close the airport and convert it into a park as part of the museum campus it was developing nearby. Although the state objected and negotiated a delay, Mayor Richard M. Daley (the son of Richard J. Daley) stuck to his guns and ruled that the airport must close in 2002. That decision lasted only a few months. Meigs had become a bargaining chip in the dispute between city and state over the expansion of O'Hare and the construction of a third airport. The city agreed to continue operation of Meigs Field until 2006 in return for the state's withdrawal of objections to construction of a third east-west runway at O'Hare.[31]

As Midway and O'Hare increasingly became dominated by the large air carriers, the major concern of the aviation community was where to handle the business aircraft, including the corporate jets used to shuttle executives around the nation. By 1980, the decentralization of American manufacturing to the suburbs and to rural areas of states in the Southeast and Southwest with relatively low land and labor costs had created a demand for corporate aircraft to fly to cities not conveniently served by scheduled carriers. The dwindling numbers of privately owned airports in the suburbs didn't have the financial resources to expand and build the long concrete runways needed by the high performance corporate jets; a 3,000-foot asphalt strip was adequate for most pleasure aircraft, but corporate aviators wanted concrete runways at least 5,000 feet long and equipped with instrument landing systems so they could be used in all weather.[32]

The land beneath privately owned airports, which usually consisted of cleared tracts of one hundred acres or more, was valuable to developers as urban sprawl crept into the suburbs after World War II. The sprawl-induced increases in property taxes reached the point that aviation revenues could no longer cover the tax bills, and many private-airport owners decided to sell out, but for the most part, suburban governments were unwilling or financially unable to buy the airfields. The attrition began abruptly after World War II. Of the sixty airports operating within a fifty-mile radius of Chicago's Loop in 1940, eight did not survive until the end of 1946; some of them were undoubtedly casualties of the wartime restrictions on private flying. In the four years between 1946 and 1950, twenty-four of the surviving airports closed, and only ten new ones were built, usually in even more remote locations. So by 1950 the average distance between the general aviation airports and the Loop was 30.2 miles, an increase of a mile a year since the war ended.[33]

The attrition and outward migration continued for the next three decades. By 1980, only thirty-one airports remained in northeastern Illinois at an average distance of 38.4 miles from the Loop. Worse, only three of those suburban airports were publicly owned. The closing of Chicagoland Airport in Lincolnshire in 1978 and Elgin Airport in 1983 and the threatened sale of privately owned Palwaukee Airport shortly thereafter forced the state to act to preserve the remaining general aviation airports by subsidizing their acquisition by local governments and upgrading their facilities to handle corporate jets. Palwaukee Airport was acquired by the two adjacent municipalities of Mount Prospect and Wheeling in 1986, but only after the federal and state governments agreed to pay the entire $40 million required for the purchase. A state effort to save Chicagoland Airport failed because no local government would agree to sponsor it. Both federal and state laws prevented subsidies to private airports, although grants were provided to

The Chicago terminal control area (TCA) has been likened to an upside-down wedding cake extending from the ground to an altitude of seven thousand feet. In the first five-mile-radius ring, or "A" ring, around O'Hare, all planes have to be under positive control, and in the second ring planes between 1,900 and seven thousand feet have to be under positive control. In the "C" ring, ten to fifteen miles from O'Hare, planes are restricted to positive control between three thousand and seven thousand feet. Outside the TCA, pilots can travel by visual flight rules, meaning it is their responsibility to watch for other aircraft to avoid collisions. (Illinois Aeronautical Chart, 1990, Illinois Division of Aeronautics)

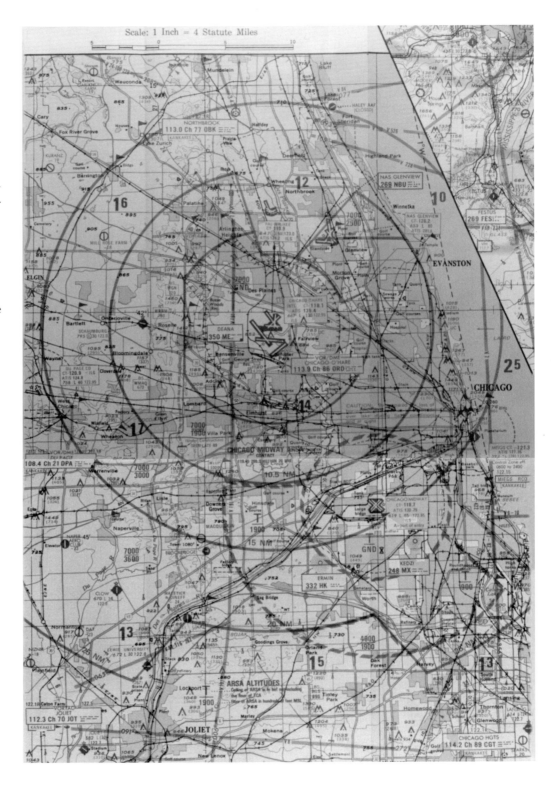

allow local governments to buy the airports, which could then be subsidized.[34]

By 1991, ten of the twenty-two surviving fields were publicly owned by a motley collection of suburban jurisdictions that included park districts, port agencies, airport districts, counties, and municipalities. Many of those newly public fields became reliever airports that were to relieve pressure on O'Hare and Midway by allowing corporate aircraft to move to new bases. Of the seven reliever airports—Lansing Airport in the south suburbs, Lewis University Airport in Lockport, Aurora Airport in Sugar Grove, Waukegan Airport in Waukegan, DuPage Airport in West Chicago, and Palwaukee Airport in Wheeling—two were among the busiest aerodromes in the state, trailing only O'Hare and Midway in volume of flights. Palwaukee with 210,000 operations in 1990 and DuPage with 218,000 the same year each handled roughly two-thirds the volume of aircraft at Midway, but no airline traffic.[35]

However, even public ownership did not ensure that a suburban airport would be upgraded. West-suburban DuPage County acquired a war surplus airport on its border with Kane County just after World War II, but squabbling by various municipalities prevented its expansion as a reliever airport. Its principal, 4,000-foot runway was at least a thousand feet short of the minimum requirement for a reliever airport and lacked a sophisticated instrument landing system that would permit all-weather operations by corporate jets. To prevent expansion, various municipalities in Kane County in 1974 used an all-but-forgotten state law, the Municipal Airport Authorities Act, to create a special airport district, the Fox Valley Airport Authority, which then took control of the field from DuPage County after a long court battle.[36]

When the new agency continued to balk at expansion, the state legislature intervened in 1985, amending the law to allow the chairman of the DuPage County board to appoint a majority of the members of the airport authority board. That failed to resolve the impasse on expansion, and the legislature in 1987 again amended the law, creating the DuPage Airport Authority, which included all of that county, to take over the airport. The amendment also gave the new agency the authority to issue general obligation bonds to expand the airport and a property tax to pay off the bonds. That precipitated another court battle, which wasn't resolved in favor of expansion until 1990, by which time the airport authority had issued $65 million in bonds for expansion.[37] The irony of the situation was that many of the same DuPage County politicians who were in favor of expanding that county's airport on its western border were adamantly opposed to expansion of another airport in the county's northeastern corner—O'Hare.

The arrival of the jet plane and deregulation of the airlines were the defining events in American commercial aviation in the last quarter of the twentieth century. The airlines had difficulty adjusting to both changes, and there were casualties. TWA, Eastern, and Pan American, three of the most familiar names in U.S. aviation, did not survive the shakeout. American Airlines and United Airlines both struggled for a while but continued to maintain the positions they held in the 1930s as the nation's two largest airlines.

The most controversial issue in Chicago during the period was airport noise. As more jets roared overhead to serve the market for increasingly affordable air travel, substantial areas of neighboring suburbia rose up in protest of the accompanying noise and congestion. The resulting dispute pitted the city versus the suburbs, Democrats against Republicans, and, in some cases, the pillars of the Chicago business community who lived on the North Shore against their employees who resided in more modest housing underneath the flight paths to O'Hare.

The Jet Age

Traffic at O'Hare was so heavy by the 1970s that planes waiting to take off had to queue up on taxiways to await their turn, and the Federal Aviation Administration imposed its high-density rule limiting traffic to 155 operations (takeoffs and landings) an hour during peak daytime periods.

• When Pat Patterson retired as head of United Airlines in 1966, he did so with the satisfaction that in his more than three decades of stewardship the airline had successfully made the transition from the air mail era to the jet age and had reclaimed its position as what was then called the free world's largest carrier. Only Aeroflot, the state-owned Soviet airline, was larger. Patterson had had a fleet of three hundred airplanes under his command, an exceedingly strong position in the Chicago hub that still dominated the nation's transcontinental routes, although rival-city hubs were appearing; a near monopoly on the growing Hawaiian vacation market; and plenty of cash, despite huge outlays for the

new jets that were appearing on the scene.

However, he had not had international service or particularly good relations with the federal regulators who kept a tight rein on fares and routes. The succession of six men who followed him into the executive suite at United in the final third of the century were more successful at getting into the international markets and ending the stifling regulation than Patterson had been, but less successful at mollifying United's board of directors, investors, and unions. Four of Patterson's successors left the company abruptly. Deregulation of the airline industry in the final quarter of the century was a major factor in the turmoil in the executive suite; pressure on the airline to both diversify and keep fares low to remain competitive in the new deregulated environment got United in trouble with its unions, which at one point demanded and got seats on the company board of directors.

Deregulation also resulted in a variety of new airlines being formed to compete with United and the other large trunks. Most failed within a few years of their inaugural flights, however, taking with them some of the carriers that had been pioneers in the airline industry—Pan American, Eastern, and TWA. One of those new carriers, Midway Airlines, survived for more than a decade and failed only after it tried unsuccessfully to transform itself from a budget carrier to a trunk airline. As the name implies, Midway Airlines was based at Chicago's Midway Airport, which had a renaissance as a result of deregulation. By the end of the twentieth century, the once moribund facility was handling more passengers as the city's second airport than it ever did when it claimed to be the world's busiest, and the city's two airports combined were handling considerably more than a million flights a year, carrying almost 88 million passengers (see appendix D).

Long before that happened, the overriding aviation issue in Chicago had become the noise, congestion, and pollution all those jets were producing. Chicago's airports had become the center of a political brouhaha that reached all the way to Capitol Hill in Washington. The suburbs were agitating for a third airport in a remote south suburban exurb called Peotone to relieve some of the traffic at O'Hare, and the city was resisting because it would lose political control of a major segment of the region's commercial air traffic if such a facility were built. Chicago, its downtown business community, and the airlines wanted to expand O'Hare. Then, as the twenty-first century dawned, two U.S. senators from Iowa suggested that if the local politicians couldn't settle their differences, the federal government might have to step

in and expand O'Hare. Their announcement was a statement that as an aviation hub Chicago was too important to the nation's increasingly congested air transport system to allow local political squabbling to interfere with progress.

United's Jets

United placed its first order for jet aircraft in 1955 when it ordered thirty DC-8s even though the delivery time was longer than Boeing was offering for its 707; the Douglas plane was about a year behind the Boeing jet in development. The airline had approached Boeing first, but the Seattle company was reluctant to modify its design to fit United's specifications for six-abreast seating. Boeing also was unable to develop a medium-range jet to meet United's timetable, so in 1960 the airline ordered twenty twin-engine Sud Aviation Caravelles from France—its first order for new foreign-built aircraft. The Caravelle first went into service in 1961 on the crucial Chicago–New York route, but it never proved very popular with the flying public after the initial excitement. It was retired in 1970 after the twin-jet Boeing 737s became available.[1]

The ability of aircraft to operate on the New York–Chicago route, specifically on LaGuardia Airport's limited runways, became one of the most important design criteria for the new generation of medium-range jets that appeared in the 1960s. In the case of the three-engine Boeing 727 trijet, which first went into service in 1964, that meant the ability to operate off of LaGuardia Airport's controlling 4,860-foot Runway 4-22. United in 1960, even before its first Caravelles were delivered, placed an order for forty 727s. Douglas's two-engine DC-9, introduced in 1965, and the Boeing 737 twin-jet, which went into service two years later, were also able to use LaGuardia (see appendix E).[2]

Patterson retired during a winning streak. United had spent $1.3 billion in more than a decade to purchase 270 new

MAIL PLANE PROG.
6-7-27

By the late 1920s, aircraft companies had adopted the assembly-line techniques pioneered by Henry Ford for construction of automobiles. The Boeing factory produced the Monomail (foreground), a single-seat, single-wing mail plane, and the Series 80 (top center), a trimotor biplane. (United Airlines)

aircraft, converting its fleet to jets. Its last piston-powered airplane was retired in 1970. The airline had been consistently profitable since it acquired its first jets and was becoming more so. Its earnings, or profits, per share of common stock increased from 31 cents in 1961 to $2.03 at Patterson's retirement in 1966, and its assets over the same span increased from $658,685 to $1.3 billion even though the CAB's policy of keeping fares low had caused the airline's yield (revenue per passenger mile) to decline from 6.2 cents to 5.5 cents. When Patterson retired, he turned

the airline over to George Keck, a mechanical engineer and career airline employee.[3]

Despite United's size, the technological, economic, and competitive pressures facing the company in the jet age were substantial. The twenty French Caravelles that United added to its fleet in 1961, for example, lasted only nine years before reaching economic obsolescence. They were replaced by Boeing 737s, which in the early years turned out to be an unfortunate choice. Keck was unable to get the Air Line Pilots Association (ALPA) to allow United's 737s to be flown by two-man cockpit crews

To reduce weight, the wings and fuselage of an aircraft are built as fenestrated networks of wood or metal components and covered with a skin, originally of fabric but later of sheet metal. (United Airlines)

By the 1930s, wings were tested for strength by piling sandbags on them, as in the case of this Boeing 247. Later, complex hydraulic machines took over that function. (United Airlines)

By the 1980s, assembly of jetliners like these twin-engine Boeing 767s had become a complex undertaking involving design by computers and a battalion of industrial engineers to make sure all the components arrived at the proper sequence in the production cycle. (United Airlines)

(pilot and copilot) like the rival DC-9s used by other carriers. The crew-size factor cost the airline an estimated $100 million a year in additional operating costs because a flight engineer was required on the 737s after United lost the case in arbitration.[4]

Flush with cash, United in the late 1960s decided to join the diversification trend in the airline industry. The decision was made that the hotel industry was a natural extension of the air travel business, and Western International Hotels was ultimately selected as the merger partner, in

part because 78 percent of its rooms were in cities served by United. The first step was to create, in 1969, a holding company, UAL Inc., with the airline as its sole subsidiary. The merger with the seventy-one-hotel Seattle chain was negotiated shortly thereafter. Much to the surprise of the rest of the airline industry, the hotel people were running the airline within twelve months.[5]

The United directors allied with the Western International subsidiary, in a coup engineered by Seattle banker Thomas F. Gleed, attempted to push Keck

THE JET AGE 203

upstairs in order to bring new management to the airline, but Keck resigned abruptly, apparently surprising everyone. Edward E. Carlson, a hotel man with no experience in the airline business, was then installed in 1970 as UAL's president and chief executive officer after a series of stormy board meetings at corporate headquarters in Elk Grove Township near O'Hare, where the company had moved in 1961 from Midway. Carlson's most immediate task was to restore the company to profitability. He did that within three years using the tried-and-true business method of lopping heads, reducing the payroll from 52,000 to 48,000.[6]

One of the most important factors contributing to Keck's downfall was the loss of United's dominant position in the Hawaii market. In its 1969 decision on the trans-Pacific route case, the CAB had allowed five additional carriers into the market between the mainland and Hawaii, effectively maiming United's cash cow. United saw its $19 million 1969 profit on that route become a $17 million loss in 1970. That loss coincided with a cyclic softening of air travel and the arrival of the first of the expensive new jumbo jets, meaning the industry was faced with substantial overcapacity.[7]

The general conclusion among aviation historians is that the jumbo jets arrived on the scene too early, before the airlines had the opportunity to absorb the extra capacity made possible by standard-size jets. For competitive reasons, the airlines stampeded into buying them in large numbers and were then forced into the cannibalistic practice of discounting fares to fill empty seats. The theory in the airlines' marketing departments at the time (as it is now) was that it was better to get some revenue from a seat than to allow it to go empty at full fare. During the 1970s, load factors (the percentage of seats filled) varied between 50 and 60 percent in the industry; in United's case, they had deteriorated from a high of 59.8 percent in 1967 to only 51.9 percent in 1970.[8]

United was an early contributor to the discounted fare wars when in 1966 it introduced the Discover America fare—a 25 percent discount on tourist coach fares to holiday markets in the off-season. The arrival of the jumbo jets in the 1970s made discounting a necessity even before the deregulatory movement picked up steam in Washington. The Boeing 747 (introduced in 1969), Douglas DC-10 (1971), Lockheed L-1011 (1972), and Airbus Industries A-300 (1973) in many cases had double the number of seats of the older aircraft they were intended to replace; air travel was not growing that quickly. The dam burst in 1977 when American Airlines inaugurated its Supersaver fare with discounts of up to 45 percent on as many as 35 percent of the seats on a given flight as long as the tickets were purchased thirty days in advance. The other airlines, United included, matched the fare to stay competitive. Coupled with deregulation the following year, the Supersaver precipitated almost continual fare wars, which lasted into the 1990s and seriously undermined the profitability of even the largest airlines.

The hotel era at United lasted until the mid-1980s. It resulted in the acceleration of the policy, begun in the 1960s, to diversify the corporation to offset cyclic downturns in the aviation business and expand the airline into international markets where it could use its huge domestic hubs, including Chicago, to feed traffic onto its own overseas flights. In 1981, United and American were the dominant airlines at O'Hare, accounting for nearly 37 percent of the scheduled flights at that airport.[9]

United Goes International

Carlson and his handpicked successor, Richard J. Ferris, another hotel man, were among the few executives of major carriers to realize that the deregulation of the airline industry then being considered in Washington could be of great benefit to a carrier the size of United, especially with its history of regulatory problems. Although

United's executives in the beginning went along with the other major trunk airlines in opposing the move, they eventually broke from the ranks and supported government efforts in 1977 to broaden the deregulation of the railroad industry to include the airlines. The decision was influenced by the CAB's policy of keeping United under control by refusing to grant it new routes; United had received authority from the CAB to serve only one new market in the prior seventeen years. Carlson and Ferris also felt that reform was necessary for the financial health of the industry generally, and specifically to allow United to move into international markets, using its huge domestic network as a feed to the overseas routes it hoped to establish, and to raise substantial capital in future years.[10]

Still fresh in the mind of United executives was the CAB's trans-Pacific route case, a regulatory morass that contributed to a large extent to Congress's decision to pass the Airline Deregulation Act of 1978. The case, which involved route authority to Hawaii and the Far East, had begun in 1959, but was remanded to the CAB by President Dwight Eisenhower and ended without resolution in 1963. It was then reopened in 1965 and approved by President Lyndon Johnson in 1968, but was reversed and remanded to the CAB by President Richard Nixon in 1969. After the CAB reopened the case in 1965, United applied for authority to fly from Honolulu west to Australia, New Zealand (later withdrawn), and Japan. The CAB ultimately decided not only that it would deny United any of the routes to the Far East, but that the carrier was large enough to withstand competition in the Hawaii market.[11]

Federal deregulation of the airlines was parallel to a similar program deregulating the railroad industry that began in 1970 with the creation of the National Rail Passenger Corporation (Amtrak) to take over the nation's failing intercity passenger train operations and culminated in 1980 with the Staggers Act, which abolished many of the ICC's powers to regulate freight traffic. One factor that led to deregulation was increased dissatisfaction with the CAB policies that had resulted in an inefficient point-to-point route structure and high airline operating costs that were passed on to travelers in higher ticket prices. The other was general satisfaction with the operation of and lower fares charged by two unregulated intrastate carriers: Pacific Southwest Airlines in California and Southwest Airlines in Texas. Although the CAB began to loosen its grip on the interstate airlines in the mid-1970s, Congress in 1978 passed the Airline Deregulation Act, which stripped it of its powers over domestic routes and fares. The agency was phased out of existence beginning in 1983.[12]

Once the industry was deregulated, United moved quickly to acquire some international routes even though they had traditionally been determined by bilateral treaties between nations, not by the regulatory agencies. Ferris was the driving force behind United's attempt to serve the Far East, which was chosen as the target over Europe because the two principal U.S. competitors for routes to Asia (Pan American and Northwest) were both relatively weak; the Pacific Basin was growing in importance; and United was relatively strong in San Francisco and Seattle, the jumping off points for the service. The European routes, on the other hand, had a dozen strong national carriers competing for traffic.[13]

United began service between Seattle and Tokyo in 1983, and a week later between Seattle and Hong Kong. Pan American Airways had begun San Francisco–Hong Kong trans-Pacific service in 1935 using flying boats with stops at Hawaii, Midway Island, Wake Island, Guam, and Manila. By the time United entered the picture forty-eight years later, Pan American was still flying the central Pacific route, and Northwest was flying the great circle route over the northern Pacific. Any significant expansion by United would have to come at the expense of those two carriers because U.S. bilateral treaties with

the major Far East powers had been written to protect those nations' flag carriers from overcompetition with domestic U.S. airlines. Three years after it received its first limited routes to the Far East, United bought for $750 million the entire Pacific division of the by then dying Pan American Airways.[14]

Ferris did not survive long enough to direct his airline's expansion to Europe. He was as much a victim of the turbulent early years of a deregulated environment as he was of what his detractors described as an autocratic and arrogant management style. His attempts to further diversify UAL by buying the Hilton Hotel and the Hertz rental car chains, by undertaking a joint

venture in credit cards, and by changing the corporate name from UAL to Allegis—a name that spawned the joke about "Alleged Airlines"—undermined his position with the UAL board. The diversification resulted in attempted takeovers by a group of investors in New York headed by Coniston Partners as well as the Air Line Pilots Association, the union representing United's cockpit crews. Ferris sold $700 million in notes to Boeing to avert the Coniston takeover, but the ALPA offer—to buy UAL, sell off the various nonairline subsidiaries, and turn the airline over to employees to operate—was potentially more damaging.[15]

Ferris's efforts to cut costs to be competitive with various new deregulated airlines

By the 1970s, one pattern for many of the nation's large commercial connecting airports had been established. Fields like O'Hare included long parallel runways, winglike terminal concourses at which jetliners docked so passengers could board or disembark without going outdoors, and huge parking lots. The terminals were built so connecting passengers, who at times accounted for half the traffic at O'Hare, could walk between flights.

was the underlying cause of his problem with the pilots. An effort by the airline to obtain a two-tier wage system, with new pilots getting considerably less than the veterans, resulted in a twenty-nine-day strike by ALPA in 1985. After forcing Ferris's resignation two years later, the United board agreed to sell the hotel and rental car subsidiaries and proposed that the airline's three major unions, ALPA, the International Association of Machinists, and the Association of Flight Attendants, be given partial ownership of the carrier and seats on its board in return for wage concessions.[16]

UAL, as the holding company was once again renamed, late in 1987 hired as its chief executive Stephen M. Wolf, an experienced airline executive who had most recently headed Tiger International's Flying Tiger Line, a freight carrier. He continued the airline's two-pronged deregulation strategy of cutting costs and expanding overseas. In 1990, United entered the trans-Atlantic market with service between Chicago, Washington, and Frankfurt, Germany, and a few weeks later between Chicago and Paris. An even larger expansion occurred a year later when United started flying to London from six U.S. cities, and in 1992 the airline acquired from Pan American various routes between the United States and Central and South America. By the end of that year, foreign routes accounted for 38 percent of the airline's revenues, and Wolf was coming under increased criticism for neglecting the airline's domestic system.[17]

Wolf, too, became a victim of the airline's union troubles in 1994. The pilots, which had failed in 1987 to acquire the airline after Ferris was forced to resign, two years later attempted again to buy United, offering wage concessions in return for stock. It wasn't until 1993 that two of United's unions, the machinists and the pilots, were able to negotiate an agreement giving their members up to 53 percent of the stock in the carrier and two seats on its

corporate board in return for wage and work rules concessions and the decision on the next chief executive. Wolf and several of his staff resigned, and Wolf was replaced as chief executive by Gerald Greenwald, an auto industry executive with a reputation for good labor relations. He retired in 1999, only the third chief executive in the airline's seventy-three-year history to voluntarily leave, and was succeeded by James E. Goodwin, an accountant and only the second career employee of UAL to get the top job at the airline. He was forced to resign in 2001; again, the airline's continuing labor troubles and resulting high labor costs were underlying causes.[18]

As the twentieth century ended, United Airlines, despite the turbulence in its executive suite over the preceding three decades, had been transformed into a truly multinational airline with 604 jet aircraft ranging in size from the 368-seat Boeing 747-400 down to the 120-seat Airbus A319-100, which was capable in the average day of doing the work of eight of the DC-3s United had in service on the eve of World War II (see appendix E). On December 31, 2000, the airline offered flights to 133 cities in twenty-eight countries from Singapore to Frankfurt—444 daily domestic and international flights out of Chicago alone. Approximately a third of the carrier's revenues came from international operations to Asia, Europe, and Latin America.[19]

However, United was experiencing another of its periodic financial downturns. The economy was already softening, resulting in a decline of profitability from $1.2 billion (on revenues of just over $18 billion) in 1999 to $50 million (on revenues of nearly $17 billion) in 2000. Then the attacks by Arab terrorists destroyed four U.S. domestic flights (two of them United planes) on September 11, 2001, and disrupted the nation's airline system. United posted a $2.14 billion loss in 2001 on revenues of $13.79 billion. In early 2002 the airline's interim chairman, John

W. Creighton, announced that he would seek concessions from the unions to cut costs. Labor accounted for 38 percent of those costs.[20] United's sheer size, however, masked underlying problems that would impel the carrier into bankruptcy court. The underlying problem was its ultimate inability to adjust to the deregulated environment that existed within the airline industry in the last quarter of the twentieth century.

Deregulation

Deregulation did not wreak as much havoc on the trunk airlines as they had predicted before the passage of the act in 1978. When deregulation began, the four largest U.S. airlines accounted for 54 percent of the total revenue-passenger miles flown in the United States, and by 1995 they controlled 64 percent of the traffic using that standard. By the end of that year, the big carriers controlled 90 percent of the market as a result of a number of mergers. By one count, a total of 182 new jet airline ventures were announced between 1978 and 1989. Eighty-two of them were able to start service but ultimately failed. A few, including Southwest, an unregulated intrastate airline serving Texas that expanded nationwide; American Trans Air (ATA), a charter operator that transformed itself into a scheduled carrier in 1986; and Midwest Express, an in-house carrier operated by Kimberly-Clark Corporation in Wisconsin that in 1982 became a common carrier operating solely from Milwaukee, survived the end of the century. Midwest Express actively marketed its Milwaukee Mitchell Field–based service in the Chicago metropolitan area as an alternative to O'Hare, and both Southwest and ATA had substantial operations at Midway Airport.[21]

Midway Airlines was one of the group of new carriers started from scratch following deregulation. Almost all of them began as so-called budget carriers, which hoped to undersell the existing trunk carriers and survive by virtue of their relatively low operating costs. Plenty used second-hand jets, and unemployed air crews were available as a result of cutbacks in the industry. In the case of Midway Airlines, the strategic plan was to create a niche in the market by operating a hub-spoke system solely from the then largely abandoned Midway Airport and charging fares substantially lower than those offered by the trunks serving O'Hare. Originally financed by venture capital provided for the most part by eastern investors, Midway began operations on November 12, 1979, with three leased DC-9 jets on routes from Chicago to Kansas City, Detroit, and Cleveland and by 1981 was able to show an operating profit of almost $9 million on revenues of $73.9 million. By that time, its fleet had grown to thirteen aircraft, all DC-9s, and the airline had expanded operations to thirteen cities.[22]

Midway Airlines lost money during 1983 and 1984 on essentially the same route structure, to some extent because of the recession, which hit the Midwest particularly hard, and because TWA, American, and United started a price war at O'Hare. The board in 1982 replaced President Gordon Linkon, a Frontier Airlines veteran, with Arthur Bass from Federal Express, the package delivery carrier. Bass decided that the airline could not survive as a discount carrier and should seek out the business travelers who were the bread and butter of the trunk airlines at O'Hare. A new one-class service called Midway Metrolink was introduced in 1983 and was instantly unprofitable. Bass then acquired some of the assets of Air Florida, one of a number of new budget airlines that had failed after expanding too rapidly, and by the end of the year Midway Airlines was serving twenty-two cities from Midway Airport with twenty-seven aircraft.[23]

Bass was forced out in 1985 and replaced with David Hinson. Midway Airlines remained modestly profitable for a three-year period beginning in 1986, although its property, capital, and equipment-lease obligations tripled over the same span and

Chicago-based Midway Airlines, which flew DC-9s, was the first new carrier started after the industry was deregulated in 1978. It folded in 1991, although the name continued in use by another carrier based in Indianapolis.

its long-term obligations increased 139 percent. By the end of 1988, on the eve of its next big expansion, the carrier had sixty-one aircraft serving fifty-one cities. The airline's effect on the airport after which it was named was substantial. Passenger traffic at Midway Airport had declined to less than 600,000 in the mid-1970s, and in 1978, on the eve of the founding of Midway Airlines, the airport handled fewer passengers (726,352) than O'Hare had flights (760,606). By 1980, Midway Airport reported handling 1,265,208 passengers, 464,521 of them attributable to Midway Airlines; by 1986, the number of boardings at the airport had increased to 3.9 million, 2,768,481 of them attributable to Midway Airlines; and by 1989, airport boardings exceeded 8.5 million.[24]

By that time, the entire U.S. airline industry had begun to drift into another of its periodic financial shakeouts. Ten years of almost continual fare wars had taken their toll, and the problems in the industry accelerated as the United States slid into a recession. In the fall of 1989, Hinson decided to lead Midway Airlines into another major expansion, paying $213 million to the failing Eastern Airlines for its gates, facilities, and landing slots at Philadelphia International Airport. The transaction also included the acquisition of sixteen DC-9 aircraft and international route authority between Philadelphia and Toronto and Montreal in Canada. Midway Airlines reached its greatest size as an immediate result of the Philadelphia venture—eighty-four aircraft serving fifty-six cities and carrying 7,135,906 passengers—but the deal proved to be lethal.[25]

Substantial competition from entrenched carriers in the eastern market and increases in the price of jet fuel as a result of turmoil in the Near East after Iraq invaded Kuwait overtaxed Midway's already extended financial resources. It was forced to sell the Philadelphia operation to USAir (formerly Allegheny Airlines) at a loss within twelve months of acquiring it just to get enough cash to continue to operate. The sale price was $64.5 million in cash and the assumption of $3 million in liabilities. By then Midway Airlines was hemorrhaging money. Its corporate net loss increased from $26.9 million during the expansion in 1989 to $86.1 million in 1990. On February 7, 1991, just under four months after it abandoned the Philadelphia venture, Midway suspended payment on all leases and loans. On March 25, 1991, it filed for bankruptcy, listing assets of $330.8 million and liabilities of $359.4 million. The airline was shut down and liquidated before the end of the year after a proposed acquisition by Northwest Airlines failed to materialize.[26]

The demise of Midway Airlines caused a substantial decline in traffic at Midway Airport: from nearly 8.8 million passengers in 1990 to slightly more than half that number two years later. However, the decision by a number of discount carriers, principally Southwest and ATA, to fill a vacuum quickly reversed the decline. Southwest began limited service to Midway Airport in 1985, and by the end of century it was operating 121 flights every day from the airport to twenty-five cities. ATA, which began limited service there in 1992, by the end of 2000 had an average of fifty-three daily flights from the airport. In the eight years between the demise of Midway Airlines and the end of the century, aircraft operations at Midway Airport increased from 177,009 annually to nearly 300,000, and passenger traffic more than tripled to almost 15.7 million (see appendix D).[27]

The big traffic increases at both Chicago airports in the final decade of the century were not entirely without problems. Traffic at the two airports combined grew by 177,000 flights and 20 million passengers between 1991 and 2000, and complaints about overcrowding and congestion caused flight delays grew correspondingly. Thunderstorms and snow were a cause of many of the snarls that delayed passengers and caused flight delays, but slowdowns by disgruntled United pilots, the airlines' scheduling of too many flights, an insufficient number of runways at major airports like O'Hare, and inadequacy of the FAA's air traffic control system were cited in other cases. The *Chicago Tribune* began ranting editorially about the lack of progress in eliminating the delays and won the Pulitzer Prize for its series. The situation had grown serious enough by 2000 that James Goodwin, United's new chief executive, found it necessary to discuss the problems in the company's annual report to shareholders that year.[28]

The Third-Airport Controversy

In Chicago, the dissension over the deterioration of airline service added fuel to another controversy, which had been building for more than thirty years—whether the region needed to build a third air-carrier airport to relieve congestion at the other two—an issue pitting the city against its suburbs. Chicago's position, and that of much of its business community, was that O'Hare needed to be expanded to accommodate growth and nurture the economic vitality of not only the Midwest but also the nation. On the other hand, the northwestern suburbs argued that they were unduly impacted by noise and congestion at O'Hare and wanted relief in the form of a third airport at a location remote from their subdivisions. Wisconsin and Indiana joined the fray because they thought their existing airports, on the south side of Milwaukee and in Gary, respectively, were underutilized and were available to relieve congestion at O'Hare.

Milwaukee aggressively promoted Mitchell Field as an alternative to O'Hare for the residents of Chicago's northern suburbs.[29]

To a large extent, the dispute over whether to build a third airport grew over the issue of airplane noise. Residents of the northwest suburbs, which were at first sparsely populated, had been complaining about noise from O'Hare since the 1950s, and as the suburbs and O'Hare both grew, the complaints increased accordingly. But it was not until 1970, when Chicago, without consulting the suburbs, opened the new 8,070-foot runway 4 Right–22 Left (indicating in aviation terminology that the runway was aligned in a 40-degree northeast and 220-degree southwest direction), positioning large numbers of flights directly over older, established suburbs in DuPage County, that the airport noise affected sufficient numbers of suburban residents to become a major political issue. The northeastern approach was rarely employed because traffic using it would have to cross traffic using the parallel 9-27 (east-west) runways, but the takeoffs to and landings from the southwest put large numbers of aircraft directly over DuPage County's residential suburbs.[30]

Bensenville, the suburb adjacent to O'Hare on the southwest, was the home of William Redmond, a Democrat and speaker of the Illinois House of Representatives from 1976 to 1981. Elmhurst, the next suburb to the south, was home to James (Pate) Philip, Illinois Senate Republican minority leader from 1981 to 1993 and president of that body since 1993, and to Lee A. Daniels, House Republican minority leader from 1983 to 1995 and since 1997 and House speaker from 1995 to 1997. Thus the opening of 4R-22L unintentionally gave the anti-noise factions in northwest Cook County some powerful political allies on both sides of the aisle.

The same year that 4R-22L opened, the suburbs collectively became more populous than Chicago, so their representation in the Illinois General Assembly increased considerably during the subsequent legislative reapportionment. Although the suburbs were a disparate group of communities spread over an area sixty miles long and thirty miles wide and for the most part lacked a unified political agenda, by the 1980s they were beginning to assert themselves in the state capitol in Springfield. The new runway gave the residents of the west and northwest Cook County suburbs a common agenda with the residents of DuPage County, abetted by the fact that the runway was used predominantly by the older, shorter-range, and noisier jets.[31]

Ultimately, Illinois attorney general William Scott, a Republican and an early champion of environmental causes, filed a suit in federal district court on August 23, 1974, charging that the FAA, in failing to mandate noise abatement procedures at O'Hare, was in violation of the 1969 National Environmental Protection Act. The suit was resolved on October 14, 1982, with a consent decree in which the City of Chicago, which had replaced the FAA as the principal defendant, agreed to conduct an environmental impact study of the $1 billion expansion of the airport then planned. The FAA approved the impact statement in 1984 but suggested that the state take a look at the need for a third airport as part of its airport planning process.[32]

The State of Illinois, which from 1977 through the end of the century had three successive Republican governors (James R. Thompson, Jim Edgar, and George Ryan), all beholden to the suburbs for political support, waded into the controversy and produced a plan of its own for a third airport in the far suburbs. Indiana, Wisconsin, and the City of Chicago also produced plans to relieve O'Hare congestion. The various federal, state, and local governments managed during the final two decades of the twentieth century to produce a mountain of studies but no airport. The three states completed a Chicago airport capacity study, and two years later Chicago produced a study for a new airport to be built within the city limits. The only sites large enough for such an airport were a proposed artificial island in Lake Michigan, an idea that had run afoul of

environmentalists earlier, and at Lake Calumet on the city's far south side. The airlines, the FAA, and Chicago then did a study of delays at O'Hare, which was followed by a study by Chicago and the States of Illinois and Indiana on the site of a new airport somewhere in the southern half of the metropolitan area. Illinois in 1997 produced an engineering study for a south-suburban airport near Peotone in Will County, followed by an environmental assessment of that site in 1998.[33]

The gist of the various aviation traffic projections contained or implied in the studies was that O'Hare would need some relief early in the twenty-first century, in the form of either expansion or a new airport to supplement it. There was little disagreement that congestion at both Midway and O'Hare would get worse. The state's consultants, TAMS Consulting Inc. of New York, opined in a 1998 report that O'Hare had a total operating capacity of 868,000 flights annually, but that number had already been exceeded every year since 1993. TAMS projected that because

Midway and O'Hare had both reached their limit, the proposed Peotone airport would handle 775,000 flights and 30.7 million passenger boardings by the year 2020. Landrum & Brown Inc., Chicago's aviation consultants, had said seven years earlier in its Chicago Delay Task Force report that by 1988 flight delays at O'Hare had already exceeded 100,000 hours annually—the highest of any airport in the nation. Midway had experienced only 7,800 hours of delays, but that was projected to increase to 58,000 hours annually by the year 2000. Two-thirds of the delays at both airports were related to weather.[34]

Despite the agreement that relief was needed, the discussions of a third airport quickly became a turf war. The Chicago Airport Capacity Study of 1988—the collective venture between Wisconsin, Illinois, and Indiana—concluded that a new airport was needed and focused on four in a list of fifteen potential sites—the existing Gary Regional and General Mitchell International Airports, a joint two-state airport on the Illinois-Indiana line south of the

O'Hare International Airport, shown here with downtown Chicago on the horizon, by the end of the twentieth century was handling more than 900,000 flights and 72 million passengers annually. (United Airlines)

metropolitan area, and a site near Peotone and Kankakee, Illinois. The study dropped the Wisconsin airport from consideration because it already functioned as a supplemental airport for the region. Illinois, Indiana, and Chicago then began a study to evaluate four surviving sites, having added Lake Calumet to the list because Chicago already had it under study, and in 1992 selected Lake Calumet as the winner. The participants in the study then agreed to create a Bi-State Airport Authority to build the new airport as well as to operate it, Midway, and O'Hare, but the enabling legislation failed by five votes to pass the Illinois Senate in Springfield, primarily because of suburban Republican opposition.[35]

That vote evoked an angry response from Chicago mayor Richard M. Daley, who on July 2, 1992, announced he was pulling the plug on the Lake Calumet airport and blamed Senate Republican minority leader Pate Philip for sabotaging the project. "They can go to green grass, blue grass, or anywhere they want. We're not going to participate," Daley said publicly. He was referring to the fact that consultants commonly referred to the proposed third-airport sites in the suburbs as "green

The terminal that architect Helmut Jahn designed for United Airlines at O'Hare had the fenestrated look of an aircraft skeleton. (United Airlines)

grass" sites because they were on farmland. Daley's pronouncement effectively committed Chicago to the expansion of O'Hare instead of a new airport. At that point, the State of Illinois decided to proceed on its own with a plan for an airport at Peotone, and Indiana governor Evan Bayh said his state would go ahead with a study on Gary.[36]

O'Hare Becomes a Federal Case

Although Illinois had taken an active role, indeed the major role, in the creation of general-aviation reliever airports in the suburbs to take some of the pressure off Midway and O'Hare, had prevented Chicago from closing Midway in the early 1970s, and had been instrumental in the development of MidAmerica Airport in Mascoutah, Illinois, twenty-four miles east of St. Louis, it had never before gotten involved in the development of an air-carrier airport in the Chicago area. Aside from the Midway case, the state's lone prior incursion into the Chicago airport system had ended in failure when it was unsuccessful in preventing the city from wavering in its plan to close Meigs Field on the lakefront, although it did obtain several delays. Chicago and its business community and aviation boosters had been responsible for building Municipal Airport in 1927. The business community, the city, and the airlines had been primarily responsible for the expansion of Midway just before World War II and the building of O'Hare after the war.

In the case of the third-airport dispute, the business community, the city, and the airlines lined up in favor of expanding O'Hare, but the suburbs and state were in favor of a new airport. The Civic Committee of the Commercial Club of Chicago, the organization largely responsible for architect Daniel Burnham's influential Chicago Plan of 1909, which determined much of the course the city would take for the rest of the century, in 2001 ran as an advertisement in the *Chicago Tribune* an

open letter to state officials endorsing the expansion of O'Hare by the addition of at least one runway. "O'Hare has become the primary economic engine of the region," said the letter signed by the executives of sixty major corporations in the metropolitan area, thirteen of them in the suburbs.

> Our companies employ over 1 million people who live and work throughout the six-county region or who use O'Hare airport for business or personal travel. We pay hundreds of millions of dollars annually in taxes to our home communities and the state of Illinois. We have a huge stake in the future economic health of our region.

The letter also said that neither a new airport at Peotone nor the expansion of Gary Airport would be an adequate substitute for expanding O'Hare. As might be expected, the letter drew a quick response from the suburbs. The mayors of four communities (Bensenville, Elmhurst, Elk Grove Village, and Park Ridge) that were members of an anti-noise organization called the Suburban O'Hare Commission threatened to pull their municipal funds from four metropolitan banks whose executives had signed the Commercial Club letter.[37]

The airlines, which paid landing fees that provided much of the financing for the terminal facilities at Midway and O'Hare, were also opposed to a third airport and were in favor of the expansion of O'Hare, but on different grounds. In a 1995 letter to Governor Jim Edgar, the Air Transport Association pointed out that its members had spent billions of dollars in facilities at Midway and O'Hare and did not want to spend more by duplicating the facilities at Peotone. The association also disputed some studies' suggestion that the airlines could efficiently split their operations between two or more airports. It repeated that position in 1997 during a public hearing on the Peotone environmental assessment and in a letter to the Illinois Department of Transportation shortly thereafter.[38]

The airlines that opposed the building

of a third airport included both the discount carriers using Midway and the trunks at O'Hare. Although George Mikelson, chairman and chief executive of American Trans Air (ATA), was a signer of the Air Transport Association's 1995 letter, Chicago aviation commissioner Mary Rose Loney was the discount airlines' principal spokesperson on the issue. "Midway's low-fare carriers, unlikely to invest in a financially risky Peotone airport, could disappear from Chicago," Loney warned in 1997.[39]

The underlying issue for the airlines was that in addition to necessitating expenditures for building and staffing new terminals and maintenance facilities, a third airport threatened to disrupt Chicago's position as an aviation hub, which it has held since the air mail era. The hub depends on connecting traffic that would be at risk of being diverted to other cities to avoid inter-airport transfers. A 1969 study indicates that more than 48 percent of the passengers using O'Hare were connecting between flights. Calculations from 1981 indicate that fewer than 38 percent of the passengers using O'Hare were simply changing planes, a decline attributable to the development of hubs in other cities.[40]

By the end of the twentieth century, the political stalemate over airport expansion in Chicago had become a national issue. The FAA has traditionally steered clear of local disputes over airports, but Congress began to tackle the political issue because many of its members connected through O'Hare on their way to and from their districts and were affected by the delays there. Iowa senators Charles E. Grassley, a Republican, and Tom Harkin, a Democrat, were the first to take the issue public with a joint letter to their colleagues on Capitol Hill:

> On a blue-sky day, there is no better or more efficient airport in this country. However, when the rain, high winds, or fog rolls in, O'Hare can be a gigantic obstruction in the middle of the American air transport system. The ripple effect on the rest of the system is tremendous, leading to delays at airports across the country.[41]

Although Congress in 2000 had granted O'Hare relief from the slot system imposed by the high-density rule, the airport needed two new runways to handle increased traffic, the senators said. They recommended that Congress expedite funding for two new runways in the fiscal 2002 appropriations and that Chicago be allowed to proceed with construction without further interference from the state on this "urgent national project. Simply put, the time for study and local conflict is past."[42] The letter by the two gentlemen from Iowa was a more succinct and eloquent a statement on the status of aviation in Chicago at the dawn of the twenty-first century than anything put forward in the reams of studies done over the prior thirty years and perhaps since Octave Chanute published his *Progress in Flying Machines* more than a century earlier.[43]

In the short term, the airport dispute may have been resolved inadvertently by the voters when they went to the polls November 5, 2002. Control of the governor's office and both houses of the state legislature was handed to the Democrats, who for the most part favor O'Hare expansion and the continued operation of Midway. The issue of whether to build a new airport at Peotone or expand O'Hare was subordinated to other controversies during the gubernatorial election campaign won by Chicago Democrat Rod Blagojevich. Republican governor George Ryan, who did not run for reelection because of a scandal, had been a staunch supporter of the proposed airport in Peotone near his home town of Kankakee. The outcome of the state elections likely means that for the foreseeable future, O'Hare and Midway will continue to dominate Chicago aviation.

Epilogue

• Aviation transformed itself entirely within the twentieth century from a sport played by daring young men in their flying machines to a big business filling the heavens with commerce. The young aviators who performed at the Chicago international air show of 1911 would probably be able to recognize the O'Hare of 2000 as an aerodrome, but it might take a few moments. Octave Chanute would probably puzzle for a while over the slats, flaps, rudder, and horizontal stabilizers on a modern jet before concluding that someone had finally solved the problem of aerial stability he had pondered in 1894. But a supercritical wing would most likely baffle him. Pop Dickinson, who liked to collect inaugural flight tickets in the 1930s, could go absolutely bonkers sitting before a computer terminal and surfing the Internet for destinations all over the world to which he could fly from Chicago.

United, though it was in financial difficulty that would eventually force it into bankruptcy, had transformed itself by the end of the twentieth century from an air mail line that discouraged the carrying of passengers into a global airline with flights spanning the seven seas. The entire aerial flotilla that performed in Chicago in 1911, which at the time probably represented a third to a half of the world's operational aircraft, could have been dismantled and placed inside one of United's Boeing 747s, with enough room in the third-deck passenger cabin for all the 1911 show pilots.

By the end of the century, United had also become involved in one of the alliances being formed by airlines around the world to better position themselves for the growing international-travel market. United's Star Alliance is a global cooperative of fifteen airlines created to exchange passengers and freight. The alliance, begun in 1997 with five carriers (United, Lufthansa, Scandinavian Airlines System [SAS]), Air Canada, and Thai Airways), has the potential for evolving into a truly multinational airline under single ownership the way corporations in other industries have done. Indeed, Airbus Industries, the European plane builder, was founded in 1969 as a multinational venture although its subsumed business units in each nation were separately owned.

United Bankruptcy

United's apparent strength was illusory, however. The effects of the deregulation of U.S. airlines more than two decades earlier were taking their toll. Deregulation did not immediately wreak as much havoc on the trunk airlines as they had predicted before the passage of the act in 1978; however, the predicted shakeout began to occur more than a decade later. The trauma of moving from a highly regulated market to one in which economic regulation was minimal was probably the first in a chain of events that in slightly more than a decade began forcing the bankruptcies and eventually the demise of a number of the nation's established airlines.

Despite its relatively high costs, strained relations with employees, and revolving door management, the sheer size of United enabled it to survive the malaise somewhat longer than its weaker rivals; however, it eventually succumbed in late 2002. By then Trans World Airlines, which was forced to file for bankruptcy protection in 1992, 1995, and 2001; Pan American, which filed in 1991; and Eastern Airlines, which filed in 1989, had all ceased to exist. U.S. Airways was forced into bankruptcy four months before United in 2002 after an attempted merger between the two failed to materialize.[1]

Although it was not immediately apparent to the public during the boom in air travel in the 1990s, the aborted merger was an attempt at survival by two carriers that were having difficulty adjusting to the changes that deregulation had brought to the airline industry. As the century came to a close, competition from the low-cost, deregulated carriers and the softening economy that resulted in a decline in travel combined to take their toll on United's weakening financial condition. United's parent UAL Corporation company after a succession of reasonably profitable years during the booming 1990s reported it earned a paltry profit of only $50 million on revenues of $10.35 billion in 2000. In the first six months of 2001, the red ink began to flow and it lost $605 million.[2]

The September 11, 2001, Islamist attacks on the Pentagon in Washington and World Trade Center in New York using hijacked jetliners, two of them operated by United, was the final blow. From that time, United's financial losses became alarming. Within a month of the attack, which caused a substantial decline in air travel, James E. Goodwin warned his employees in a letter that "Now we're in a struggle just to survive. . . . Today we are literally hemorrhaging money." Unless they made some substantial concessions, "United will perish sometime next year," Goodwin added.[3]

Goodwin's letter carried a prophetic message that no one wanted to hear, and the messenger was promptly shot. The "perish" letter as it became known got wide attention, and the carrier's unions publicly demanded his resignation. He complied within two weeks, but the corporation reported losses of $2.1 billion in 2001 and estimated at more than $3 billion in 2002 as its board searched for a replacement and a strategy to avert bankruptcy. The strategy that the board, interim chairman and chief executive John W. E. Creighton, and Goodwin's permanent replacement, Glenn F. Tilton, a former oil company executive, eventually de-

cided on was to simultaneously ask its unions for $5.2 billion in collective pay cuts and the federal government's Air Transportation Stabilization Board for $1.8 billion in loan guarantees.[4]

Although the pilots and fight attendants agreed to the wage cuts, the mechanics (International Association of Machinists and Aerospace Workers) on November 27, 2002, voted against the proposal. Then the following December 2 the Air Transportation Stabilization Board, which had been created in Washington to administer a $15 billion fund to help airlines with losses resulting from the September 11, 2001, disasters, turned down United's request for loan guarantees.[5]

As is often the case in bankruptcies, the repayment deadline on a large loan is the precipitating factor. In United's case, the company on December 2, 2002, defaulted on repayment of $375 million in equipment trust certificates, $500 million in bank loans, and $45 million in other debts. By the time UAL on December 9, 2002, filed for protection under Chapter 11 of the United States Bankruptcy Code in Federal District Court in Chicago, the airline's executives said it was losing money at the rate of $22 million a day. In the filings with the court and the SEC, Tilton stated he hoped to reorganize the company and emerge from bankruptcy within eighteen months.[6]

Airports

In the first half of the twentieth century, the automobile and the airlines demolished the one-time railroad monopoly on intercity passenger travel, and in the second half, aviation began to chip away at the auto's market share, especially on long trips. Deregulation of the airlines in the final quarter of the century resulted in budget fares that attracted people making long journeys that were too time-consuming by car and people of modest means who a few years earlier wouldn't even have considered a vacation to France or a visit to Aunt Grace in California. Air fare had become the cheapest element of a vacation's expenses for many travelers, and Americans responded by traveling more. Per capita intercity travel, which had been only 3,342 miles annually in 1950, increased to 5,808 miles by 1970 and to 8,800 miles by 1999, an average increase of 111 miles a year (see appendix C).

The numbers of persons traveling by air in the United States doubled between the deregulation of the airlines in 1978 and the end of the century, by which time the airplane accounted for more than a fifth of the intercity travel market in terms of miles traveled. In 1977, the airlines accounted for 11.6 percent of that market and cars almost 85 percent, but by 1999 airplanes accounted for 22.4 percent and autos 77.1 percent. The jump in air travel put a great deal of stress on the aviation system, including the airports. New replacement airports had been built or existing airports greatly expanded in Houston, Dallas, Denver, Atlanta, and Washington, but not in Chicago. The Windy City relied on the once largely unused Midway Airport to take up the slack O'Hare couldn't handle after its last new runway opened in 1970, but by the end of the century Midway was at or near capacity, and the only option left was to build new runways at O'Hare or a new airport to supplement it.

It was a dilemma for both the city and the airlines: no midcontinental airline hub in the United States had more than two airports—one for point-to-point budget flights and the other a connecting complex for the global trunk airlines. New York and Los Angeles, the sprawling metropolises on either coast, might have three or more airports, but the bulk of their passengers were not connecting between airplanes. A fifty-mile cab ride on the Tri-State Tollway and Highway 57 between O'Hare and Peotone to change planes was out of the question, so any new air-carrier airport in Peotone would have to be a small facility servicing the south-suburban market, a budget field competing with Midway, or a hub competing with O'Hare.

Two events occurring just after the turn of the century reinforced the notion that Chicago was still the nation's most important aviation hub. One was the announced intention of the Congress to intervene in the O'Hare-Peotone controversy in the national interest of preserving a viable air transport system. The other was the decision by the Boeing Company to move its corporate headquarters to Chicago from Seattle, where it had been since its founding and where many of its large aircraft manufacturing operations are located.

The Islamist terrorist attacks using hijacked jetliners on September 11, 2001, if anything accelerated Congress's resolve to move on the O'Hare expansion project. Senator John D. Rockefeller IV, a Democrat from West Virginia and chair of the Senate Aviation Subcommittee, in early 2002 announced that he would seek early approval of a $6.6 billion proposal to expand O'Hare: "Everything has got to be speeded up on aviation runways, and O'Hare is the place to start, because it just happens to be the busiest airport in the country," Rockefeller said during a meeting of his subcommittee.[7] The success of the Illinois Democrats in taking control of the governor's office and both houses of the state legislature in the 2002 general election seemed to be a ratification of Congress's interest in making progress on the O'Hare project.

Although U.S. air traffic declined dramatically after the September 11 crashes of two jets into New York's World Trade Center towers, a third into the Pentagon, and a fourth in a rural area of Pennsylvania, O'Hare reported an increase in the number of operations for the year 2001, the only major airport in the nation to do so. The airport reported 911,861 takeoffs and landings in 2001, an increase of 2,872 over the 908,989 flights it handled in 2000, enabling O'Hare to reclaim from Atlanta its status as world's busiest airport. Atlanta's Hartsfield

International Airport, which surpassed O'Hare in flight operations in 1999 and 2000, suffered a decline of 26,046 flights in 2001. The increase in traffic at O'Hare was attributed to relative labor peace at United and American, its two largest users, as well as good flying weather in 2001 after two consecutive stormy summers.[8]

The reasons for Boeing's move are particularly instructive. The three metropolitan areas in the running for the corporate headquarters were Dallas–Ft. Worth, Denver, and Chicago—all home to major aviation connecting complexes. Boeing, which had virtually no presence in Chicago or its suburbs, was looking for a culturally diverse city that offered ready access to global markets, had a strong probusiness environment, and allowed easy access to the company's far-flung operations and customers. In the end, the factor that turned out to be most important was the ability of Boeing customers from around the world to easily visit the company. O'Hare International Airport, despite its problems, filled the bill, reinforcing Chicago's place as the heartland of American aviation.[9]

1911 International Air Show

Winnings of Principal Pilots

(Includes $250 stipend for expenses)

Pilot	Team	Winnings
T. O. M. Sopwith		$14,020
L. Beachey	(Curtiss)	$11,667
C. P. Rodgers	(Wright)	$11,285
G. W. Beatty	(Wright)	$7,125
A. L. Welsh	(Wright)	$6,121
E. L. Ovington	(Curtiss)	$5,900
R. Simon	(Bleriot)	$5,050
E. Ely	(Curtiss)	$4,672
P. O. Parmalee	(Wright)	$4,451

Twenty-five other pilots earned between $250 and $3,413 apiece.

Flying Records

The records set at Chicago's 1911 international air meet, though arcane by contemporary standards, are indicative of the status of aviation at that time. The data include the event, the record, the pilot (and airplane), and the date.

Event	Record	Pilot	Airplane	Date
*Altitude	11,642 feet	Lincoln Beachey	Curtiss 50	August 20
*Two-Man Duration	3:42:22.2	G. W. Beatty	Wright 30	August 19
*Climbing Speed	500 meters (1,640 feet) in 0:03:25 (8 feet per sec.)	T. O. M. Sopwith; Rene Simon	Bleriot 70; Bleriot 50	August 19
Two-Man Speed	57.785 mph (0:07:50 for 10 km.)	T. O. M. Sopwith	Bleriot 70	August 17
Three-Man Speed	54.6 mph (0:06:56.4 for 5 km.)	T. O. M. Sopwith	Wright 30	August 15
Three-Man Duration	1:18:22	G. W. Beatty	Wright 30	August 13
Weight Carrying	458 pounds	P. O. Parmalee	Wright 30	August 19
Two-Man Altitude	3,080 feet	G. W. Beatty	Wright 30	August 15

Records with an asterisk are world records; the others are records for the United States.

Major Air Disasters in the Chicago Area

• The Chicago area, by virtue of its position as the nation's midcontinental hub, has suffered more transportation disasters than other cities, a trend that lasted through the twentieth century as the airplane was developed as a commercial carrier. From the wreck of the schooner *Hercules* in 1816 with the loss of all aboard to the 1999 crash of a truck and an Amtrak passenger train in Bourbonnais, Illinois, the region has suffered some of the worst disasters in U.S. history. They include the nation's first railroad disaster in 1853 when two trains collided at a crossing, the capsizing of the steamship *Eastland* in the Chicago River in 1915, and the 1979 crash of a DC-10 at O'Hare International Airport. The definition of a disaster is subjective. Robert B. Shaw in his epic work, *A History of Railroad Accidents, Safety Precautions, and Operating Practices,* 2d ed. (Potsdam, N.Y., 1978), defines a disaster as an accident causing the loss of ten or more lives. That definition is used here.

Wingfoot Blimp, Fire over Loop

JULY 21, 1919—The Goodyear Tire and Rubber Company commercial blimp *Wingfoot Air Express,* with five persons aboard, caught fire and crashed through a skylight of the Illinois Trust and Savings Bank in the Loop, killing thirteen persons and injuring twenty-eight. The pilot and a crewman survived by parachuting, but the death toll included ten bank employees who were immolated when the fuel for the blimp's engines exploded on the bank's main floor. It was Chicago's first aviation disaster and the first civil aviation disaster in the United States.

The cause of the accident was never officially determined, but various Goodyear officials attributed the ignition of the volatile hydrogen that gave the airship lift to static electricity, hot oil from the engines, or sparks from the engines.

Goodyear switched to inert helium to inflate its blimps after the accident.[1]

United DC-3, Icing on Windshield and Wings

DECEMBER 4, 1940—A United Air Lines DC-3 bound from New York to Chicago became impaired with an accumulation of ice and crashed two blocks southeast of Chicago Municipal (Midway) Airport, killing ten. Six passengers survived. So much ice had accumulated on the windshield during the descent through overcast skies that the crew's vision was impaired and pilot Phillip C. Scott had to go around for a second landing attempt.

The Civil Aeronautics Board, in its report on the accident, criticized Scott's judgment during the second approach: he had declined to use a longer east-west runway and had attempted to land on a shorter northwest-southeast runway. An accumulation of ice on the leading edges of the wing caused the plane to stall, and it crashed on approach. The board recommended the installation of stall-warning devices on commercial aircraft, better windshield wipers, and research into ways to reduce icing hazards.[2]

Liberator Bomber, Hit Gas Tank

MAY 20, 1943—An Army Air Corps Liberator bomber struck a gas storage tank southeast of Municipal Airport, killing all twelve servicemen aboard.

Delta DC-4, Tail Elevators Left Locked

MARCH 10, 1948—A Delta Air Lines DC-4 crashed and burned on takeoff from Midway Airport, killing twelve. One passenger survived. Although the Civil Aeronautics Board was unable to determine the cause, it raised the possibility in its report on the accident that the elevator gust lock mechanism, a device to prevent the control surfaces on the tail from becoming damaged in high winds when the plane is on the ground, had been left locked on takeoff, preventing the crew from controlling the aircraft.

The plane was the only DC-4 in Delta's fleet that had not been modified, under provisions of a federal Civil Aeronautics Administration airworthiness directive, with a special handle in the cockpit to prevent the gust locks from being inadvertently kept in the locked position. The sole survivor was awarded a $132,000 settlement by the airline and its insurance carrier for her injuries.[3]

Northwest DC-4, Disappeared over Lake

JUNE 23, 1950—At about 11:00 P.M., Northwest Airlines Flight 2501, a DC-4 bound from New York to Seattle with fifty-eight passengers and crew aboard, disappeared in turbulent weather at 3,500 feet over Lake Michigan about eighteen miles northwest of Benton Harbor, Michigan. The cause of the crash was never officially determined by the Civil Aeronautics Board, although there was speculation that the pilot may have inadvertently activated the gust locks, that the plane suffered a structural failure, or that the crew lost control when it hit a squall line (weather front) over the lake. A search of the area produced no bodies, but the plane's log and some wreckage indicating a high-speed impact were found floating near the scene.[4]

Braniff Convair, Hit Sign at Midway

JULY 17, 1955—A Braniff Airways twin-engine Convair 340 plane struck a gasoline service station sign just beyond the northwest corner of Midway Airport while attempting to land, killing twenty-two and injuring twenty-one. The Civil Aeronautics Board concluded that the pilot, who was killed, had become momentarily disoriented by a small patch of dense fog just beyond the airport boundary and came in too low to miss the sign just across 55th Street (at Central Avenue) from the airport. The accident sparked the renewal of a public debate over the existence of obstructions to aerial navigation around the airport, which had been built in the 1920s when the surrounding area was largely undeveloped.[5]

TWA Freighter, Crash Landing

NOVEMBER 24, 1959—A Trans World Airlines Constellation in cargo service crashed in a residential area southeast of Midway Airport while attempting an emergency landing. Three crew members and eleven persons on the ground were killed.

Northwest Electra, Fell from Sky

MARCH 17, 1960—A Northwest Airlines Lockheed Electra on a flight from Chicago to Florida dove eighteen thousand feet into a farm field near Tell City, Indiana, after its wings disintegrated in flight. All sixty-three persons aboard were killed.

The crash followed a similar disaster on September 29, 1959, in which thirty-four died after the left wing fell off a Braniff Airways Electra at fifteen thousand feet near Buffalo, Texas. In May 1960, engineers for Lockheed determined that the cause was a factor known as "whirl mode" in which an engine in a loosened mount under certain conditions caused the propeller to wobble, in turn transmitting destructive vibrations to the wing.[6]

Sikorsky S-58C Helicopter, Rotor Broke

JULY 27, 1960—A Sikorsky S-58C helicopter operated by Chicago Helicopter Airways on a scheduled, seventeen-mile shuttle flight between Midway and O'Hare airports crashed onto the grounds of the Forest Home Cemetery in the western suburb of Forest Park, killing the two crewmen and eleven passengers on board.

This was the first disaster involving a helicopter in commercial air service in the U.S. The accident occurred when one of the main rotor blades developed a fatigue fracture and broke apart in flight fifteen hundred feet above the ground. The severe shaking that resulted caused the tail cone and rotor to break off, and the aircraft crashed and burned. After the accident, the Federal Aviation Administration limited the rotors to one thousand hours of service.[7]

TWA Constellation, Crash near Clarendon Hills

SEPTEMBER 1, 1961—A Trans World Airlines Lockheed Constellation crashed in a field near west-suburban Clarendon Hills shortly after takeoff from Midway Airport, killing all seventy-eight aboard.

Investigation disclosed that a nickel-steel bolt from the elevator boost mechanism linkage in the tail had come loose sometime after takeoff, causing the crew to lose control. As the name implies, the mechanism is designed to hydraulically boost the power necessary to manipulate the tail elevator under pressure in flight. Civil Aeronautics Board crash investigators were unable to determine why the bolt fell out.[8]

Northwest Electra, Crash at O'Hare

SEPTEMBER 17, 1961—A Northwest Airlines Lockheed Electra crashed after takeoff from O'Hare International Airport, killing thirty-seven. The crash was O'Hare's first.

Although the factors in this incident were in no way related to those that resulted in the two high-altitude crashes of Electras in 1959 and 1960, the O'Hare accident further hastened the departure of the turboprop Electra from commercial service. Like the TWA crash after takeoff from Midway less than three weeks earlier, the O'Hare disaster was caused by the failure of a boost assembly, in this case for the ailerons on the wing. Civil Aeronautics Board investigators opined that the assembly had been improperly installed on July 11, 1961, during maintenance in Minneapolis after previous crews complained eight times of aileron control discrepancies.[9]

United 727, Crash into Lake

AUGUST 16, 1965—A United Air Lines Boeing 727 designated as Flight 389 between New York and Chicago crashed into Lake Michigan about 19.5 miles east of Lake Forest at 9:21 P.M., killing all thirty aboard.

Although the cause of the nighttime crash of the eleven-week-old tri-jet airplane was never determined, official speculation centered on whether the crew misread the altimeter by an increment of ten thousand feet and flew the plan into the lake believing they were descending from sixteen thousand feet when in fact they were lower. They had been cleared to descend to six thousand feet on approach to Chicago.[10]

Convair 580, Wake Turbulence on Landing at O'Hare

DECEMBER 27, 1968—A North Central Airlines Convair 580 crashed into a hangar while attempting to land at O'Hare International Airport, killing twenty-eight.

Federal Aviation Administration investigators concluded that heavy vortex turbulence from the wingtips of a jet that had just taken off caused the pilot of the North Central plane to lose control within one hundred feet of the ground during an otherwise normal descent. The left wing hit the ground and broke off, and the remainder of the plane crashed through the doors of a Braniff Airways hangar near the northwest corner of the airport.[11]

United 737, Pilot Error on Descent

DECEMBER 8, 1972—The crash of a United Air Lines Boeing 737 into some homes on approach to Midway Airport killed forty-five, including forty-three of the sixty-one passengers and crew aboard.

The crash received a great deal of notoriety nationally because one of the victims was Dorothy Hunt, wife of a Nixon administration official who was involved in the Watergate conspiracy. Mrs. Hunt was carrying ten thousand dollars in cash in a valise at the time of the crash. The National

Transportation Safety Board said it found no evidence of sabotage or foul play but blamed the crash on errors made by pilot Wendell Lewis Whitehouse on approach to the airport, including the failure to retract the spoilers, or air brakes, at a critical stage of the descent. The spoilers reduced the speed of the aircraft to the point that it stalled and crashed in a residential area about 1.5 miles from the runway.[12]

Delta Convair and North Central DC-9, O'Hare Runway Collision in Fog

DECEMBER 20, 1972—The collision of two aircraft in the fog on a runway at O'Hare International Airport killed ten of the 138 persons aboard the two planes. The casualties were unusual in that none of the victims was killed by the impact. All succumbed to smoke and fumes from the burning DC-9 jet before they could reach the exits.

The crew was criticized for leaving the aircraft before the passengers had been evacuated. The subsequent investigation placed the blame for the accident on poor communication between the air traffic controller in the O'Hare tower and the crew of the Delta Air Lines Convair CV-880, which caused them to taxi across a runway that a North Central Airlines DC-9-31 jet was using for a takeoff. The heavy fog also impeded rescue operations.[13]

American DC-10, Engine Loss on Takeoff at O'Hare

MAY 25, 1979—An American Airlines DC-10-10 crashed in a field near O'Hare International Airport after its left engine fell off on takeoff, killing 273 persons, including everyone on the aircraft and two on the ground in what to that time was the worst aviation accident in U.S. history.

The accident was the result of a complex sequence of events involving procedures used to maintain the pylons that hold the engines to the wings of the airplane. The incidents leading up to the crash began when a maintenance crew at the American Airlines base in Tulsa, Oklahoma, contrary to the manufacturer's instructions, improperly used a hydraulic lift to remove the left wing engine. The lift apparently lost some hydraulic pressure during a shift change, causing the engine assembly to shift backward, cracking the pylon. The crack worsened during subsequent flights to the point that the pylon gave way during takeoff two months later in Chicago, severing critical hydraulic and electronic lines in the wing. The severing of the electrical lines caused a blackout in the cockpit, contributing to the crew's inability to reestablish control of the plane, and the rupture of the hydraulic lines caused the leading edge slats on the left wing to retract and the plane to stall, or fall below the minimum flying speed. The accident investigation also led to the discovery of improperly installed fasteners that weakened pylons on an additional thirty DC-10-10 aircraft owned by other airlines.[14]

KC-135 Military Tanker, Exploded

MARCH 19, 1982—An Air National Guard KC-135 tanker, the military version of the Boeing 707, broke apart with twenty persons aboard at fifteen thousand feet above the tiny village of Greenwood in northwest suburban McHenry County. It crashed, killing everyone aboard. A subsequent investigation by the air force concluded that an explosion in one of the aircraft's fuel tanks, possibly caused by an electric spark, was the probable cause.[15]

American Eagle ATR-72, Wing Icing over Indiana

OCTOBER 31, 1994—A Simmons Airlines French-built ATR-72 operated as an American Eagle commuter flight from Indianapolis to O'Hare International Airport crashed near Roseland, Indiana, while in a holding pattern for O'Hare. The crash killed all sixty-eight crew and passengers.

The NTSB in its final report opined that ice had built up on the wings at eight thousand feet as the plane circled downward in the holding pattern, causing a change in air flow over the ailerons at the rear of the wing. That, in turn, caused the turboprop plane to roll uncontrollably and eventually crash.[16]

APPENDIX   C

Intercity Travel Mileage in the United States, 1940–1999

Year	Per Capita Miles	BREAKDOWN BY MODE			
		Auto	Air	Bus	Rail
1940	2,499	89.0%	0.4%	3.1%	7.5%
1950	3,342	87.2	1.8	4.5	6.5
1960	4,355	90.4	4.1	2.5	2.8
1970	5,808	86.9	9.3	2.1	0.9
1980	6,877	83.5	13.1	1.8	0.7
1990	8,276	81.0	16.6	1.1	0.7
1999	8,800	77.6	22.4	1.4	0.6

Source: *Transportation in America: A Statistical Analysis of Transportation in the United States,* 9th and 18th eds. (Washington, D.C., 1991 and 2000).

Chicago Airport Traffic, 1940–2000

| Year | MUNICIPAL/MIDWAY | | ORCHARD/O'HARE | |
	Operations	Passengers	Operations	Passengers
1940	88,201	704,846		
1941	87,837	804,461		
1942	88,349	720,746		
1943	118,477	802,490		
1944	120,783	1,089,553		
1945	153,007	1,496,634		
1946	190,338	2,598,418		
1947	206,140	2,645,674	108,704	217,412[b]
1948	221,552	2,564,103	121,416	238,314[b]
1949	223,493	3,246,693	124,519	259,402[b]
1950	234,331	3,820,165	94,682	176,902[b]
1951	263,737	4,953,160	80,519	146,278[b]
1952	295,456	5,945,438	70,958	127,796[b]
1953	331,297	7,151,474	90,940	201,968[b]
1954	348,909	7,935,879	117,461	311,530[b]
1955	380,996	9,134,483	142,912	471,170
1956	368,580	9,174,930	156,043	723,296
1957	408,128	9,709,633	207,498	1,030,346
1958	420,193	9,667,696	231,412	1,263,147
1959	431,400	10,040,353	231,636	2,156,755
1960	376,168	6,981,667	252,799	5,691,446
1961	249,852	3,565,561	322,054	9,615,480
1962	107,778	659,550	416,991	13,525,955
1963	126,959	417,544	426,098	16,163,464
1964	217,037	823,676	458,460	18,394,126
1965	216,043	882,349	509,621	20,998,325
1966	258,491	1,094,878	543,500	23,589,683
1967	261,068	1,077,666	643,787	27,552,816
1968	243,142	900,1968	690,810	30,124,534
1969	194,923	1,205,546	676,473	31,443,218
1970	182,348	1,437,481	641,390	29,689,105
1971	204,245	1,909,489	641,429	30,119,151
1972	187,447	1,667,388	670,737	33,454,981

Year	MUNICIPAL/MIDWAY		ORCHARD/O'HARE	
	Operations	Passengers	Operations	Passengers
1973	195,400	1,500,000	695,306	35,548,039
1974	170,677	765,156	694,572	37,893,449
1975	177,515	585,261	666,584	37,296,362
1976	177,346	547,303	718,147	41,735,454
1977	183,929	703,972	741,329	44,238,019
1978	176,094	726,352	760,606	49,151,449
1979	189,698	896,048	735,245	47,482,510
1980	211,496	1,265,208	724,144	43,653,167
1981	192,889	1,773,218	645,614	37,992,151
1982	212,853	2,089,411	604,383	37,748,598
1983	211,132	2,301,998	667,967	42,873,953
1984	190,862	2,455,105	731,742	45,725,939
1985	268,202	2,482,575	746,376	49,954,362
1986	211,820	3,905,340	795,026	54,770,673
1987	243,172	5,887,675	792,897	57,543,865
1988	311,313	7,486,606	803,453	58,860,349
1989	320,202	8,506,452	794,546	59,215,032
1990	320,247	8,794,256	810,865	60,010,234
1991	281,110	7,245,709	813,896	59,852,330
1992	177,009	4,624,224	841,013	64,441,087
1993	201,410	6,762,093	859,208	65,091,168
1994	271,804	9,561,983	883,062	66,468,269
1995	257,216	9,922,216	900,279	67,253,358
1996	255,713	9,812,859	909,593	69,153,528
1997	265,572	9,829,151	883,761	70,385,073
1998	278,919	11,419,528	897,354	72,485,218
1999	297,136	13,585,262	896,228	72,609,191
2000	298,115	15,672,688	908,989	72,144,244

[a] For prior years, see table 3 in chapter 10.

[b] Orchard/O'Hare figures for 1947–1954 represent primarily general and military aviation, not scheduled air-carrier operations.

Source: Chicago Department of Aviation and Federal Aviation Administration.

United Airlines Fleet, 1942–2000

1942	
B-247	13
DC-3	49
TOTAL	**62**

1958	
DC-6	90
DC-7	55
CV-440	53
TOTAL	**198**

1969	
B-720	29
B-727	150
B-737	73
DC-8	114
Caravelle	20
TOTAL	**386**

1980	
DC-8	109*
DC-10	42
B-727	173
B-737	48
B-747	18
TOTAL	**390**

1991	
DC-10	54
B-727	115
B-737	196
B-747	50
B-757	47
B-767	24
TOTAL	**486**

2000	
A-319	32
A-320	68
B-727	75
B-737	182
B-747	44
B-757	98
B-767	54
B-777	48
DC-10	3
TOTAL	**604**

*Includes 23 grounded and awaiting sale

A=Airbus   B=Boeing   CV=Convair   DC=Douglas

Source: United Airlines annual reports to shareholders for the years indicated.

Notes

Part I: Chicago at the Dawn of Powered Flight

1. Fred C. Kelly, *The Wright Brothers: A Biography Authorized by Wilbur Wright* (New York, 1943), 10; H. A. Thompson, *Our Bishops* (Dayton, Ohio, 1903), 529; Tom D. Crouch, *The Bishop's Boys: A Life of Wilbur and Orville Wright* (New York, 1989), 182.

1: The Balloons

1. Society of Philatelic Associations bulletin, October 1949; Howard L. Scamehorn, *Balloons to Jets: A Century of Aeronautics in Illinois* (Chicago, 1957), 5–9.

2. Tom D. Crouch, *The Eagle Aloft: Two Centuries of Ballooning in America* (Washington, D.C., 1983), 15–16, 24–25.

3. Carl Van Doren, *Benjamin Franklin* (New York, 1938), 700; I. Bernard Cohen, "Benjamin Franklin and Aeronautics," *Journal of the Franklin Institute* (August 1941): 103–4; Crouch, *Eagle Aloft,* 16.

4. Donald Dale Jackson, *The Aeronauts* (Alexandria, Va., 1980), 36–41, 43.

5. Crouch, *Eagle Aloft,* 64–68.

6. Christopher Chant, *The Zeppelin: The History of German Airships from 1900 to 1937* (London, 2000), 11–15; Crouch, *Eagle Aloft,* 283.

7. *Illinois State Journal,* July 3, 1858; Crouch, *Eagle Aloft,* 450–51.

8. *Chicago Tribune,* November 5, 1899.

9. *New York Times,* August 4, 1875; *Chicago Tribune,* November 5, 1899.

10. *Chicago Tribune,* September 30 and October 26, 1879; Crouch, *Eagle Aloft,* 449.

11. Crouch, *Eagle Aloft,* 531–34.

12. *Chicago Tribune,* May 9, 1917; August 11, 1920; August 17, 1920; and March 15, 1924.

13. *Chicago Tribune* and *Chicago Daily News,* July 5–8, 1908; Crouch, *Bishop's Boys,* 301–26.

14. *Aeronautics,* August 1908, 19; and September 1908, 45.

15. Zenon Hansen, *The Goodyear Airships* (Bloomington, Ill., 1977), 1.

16. Ward T. Van Orman, *The Wizard of the Winds* (St. Cloud, Minn., 1978), 584–87.

17. Crouch, *Eagle Aloft,* 591–603.

18. Ibid., 604–14.

19. Eric Norgaard, *The Book of Balloons* (New York, 1971), 118–20; Robert Jackson, *Airships: A Popular History of Dirigibles, Zeppelins, Blimps, and Other Lighter-Than-Air Craft* (New York, 1973), 43–47.

20. Peter W. Brooks, *Zeppelin: Rigid Airships* (Washington, D.C., 1992), 176–77.

21. Jackson, *Aeronauts,* 12.

22. Chant, *Zeppelin: The History,* 80–81; James L. Shock, *American Airship Bases and Facilities,* unpublished manuscript in the collection of Zenon Hansen, 1979.

23. Shock, *American Airship Bases.*

24. Hansen, *Goodyear Airships,* 1.

25. Chant, *Zeppelin: The History,* 32–33, 37; Hansen, *Goodyear Airships,* 1.

26. Don Glassman, *Jump: Tales of the Caterpillar Club* (New York, 1930), 31–32.

27. John A. Boettner, transcript of testimony to coroner's jury (Cook County Coroner's office, Chicago, July 23, 1919).

28. Ibid., 33–36; *Chicago Tribune,* July 22–24, 1919; Glassman, *Jump,* 45.

29. *Chicago Herald and Examiner,* July 22–25, 1919.

30. *Chicago Tribune,* July 22–29 and August 1–3, 1919.

31. Hansen, *Goodyear Airships,* 1.

32. Jackson, *Airships,* 155–66; Brooks, *Zeppelin: Rigid Airships,* 168; Chant, *Zeppelin: The History,* 96–97; Hanson, *Goodyear Airships,* 21.

33. Brooks, *Zeppelin: Rigid Airships,* 7–8.

34. William F. Althoff, *Sky Ships: A History of the Airship in the United States Navy* (New York, 1990), 27–28; Brooks, *Zeppelin: Rigid Airships,* 174–76.

35. Althoff, *Sky Ships,* 48–58, 102–4, 121–22.

36. Jackson, *Aeronauts,* 144–46.

2: Octave Chanute

1. Tom D. Crouch, *A Dream of Wings: Americans and the Airplane, 1875–1905* (New York, 1981), 21–22.

2. Octave Chanute, "Opening Address," *Proceedings of the International Conference on Aerial Navigation Held in Chicago, August 2, 3, and 4, 1893.* (New York, 1894).

3. Crouch, *Dream of Wings,* 80–81.

4. Pearl I. Young, *Octave Chanute: 1832–1910* (San Francisco, 1963), 1; Alicia Chanute Boyd, *Some Memories of My Father Octave Chanute with an Account of His Trip to New Orleans,* unpublished manuscript, c. 1915, National Air and Space Museum library, Washington, D.C., 1.

5. Boyd, *Some Memories of My Father,* 2–3.

6. Young, *Octave Chanute,* 1–2; Boyd, *Some Memories of My Father,* 3; "Memoir on Octave Chanute," *Western Society of Engineers Journal,* May 1911.

7. "A Voyage to New Orleans and the Actual Condition of the South," *L'Opinion Nationale* (Paris, January 17, 1862), translation in Chanute files, National Air and Space Museum library, Washington, D.C. The article was published anonymously during the Civil War and probably originated as a letter Chanute wrote to a friend in France.

8. Boyd, *Some Memories of My Father,* 5.

9. Ibid.

10. Young, *Octave Chanute,* 2. Simine Short, in "Octave Chanute, A Civil Engineer Turns to Aeronautics: A Documentary History," unpublished manuscript outline and bibliography (Lemont, Illinois), notes on the basis of her examination of the Chanute research collection at the University of Chicago's Crerar Library that the earliest article he collected was M. Bescherelle Aine, ed., "Histoire des ballons et des locomotives aeriennes depuis Dedale jusqu'a Petin" (Paris, 1852). Crouch, in *Dream of Wings,* 25–27, bases his opinion on Chanute's own writings, specifically an abstract, titled "Resistance in Air to Inclined Planes in Motion," of a presentation given at the American Association for the Advancement of Science conference in Toronto in August 1889 (Box 9, Chanute collection, Library of Congress, 198–99).

11. Octave Chanute, "Scientific Invention," address before the American Association for the Advancement of Science, American Association for the Advancement of Science Proceedings, *Science* 35 (August 27, 1886): 165–82.

12. Octave Chanute, "Note sur la resistence de l'air aux plans oblique," a speech given on August 1, 1889, to the Congrès International d'Aéronautique, *L'Aéronaute* 22 (September 1889): 202–14, and "Resistance to Air in Inclined Planes in Motion," a paper presented at Section D, Mechanical Science Engineering, American Association for the Advancement of Science Proceedings, *Science* (August 1889): 198–99, were similar in content.

13. Octave Chanute, "Aerial Navigation," speech to the Cornell University Sibley College of Engineering, Ithaca, N.Y., May 2, 1890, serialized in *The Railroad and Engineering Journal* 64, no. 7 (July 1890): 316–18; 64, no. 8 (August 1890): 365–67; 64, no. 9 (September 1890): 395–97; 64, no. 10 (October 1890): 442–44; and 64, no. 11 (November 1890): 498–501.

14. Ibid.

15. Octave Chanute, *Progress in Flying Machines* (1894; reprint, Long Beach, Calif., 1976), 264–69.

16. Chanute, *Progress in Flying Machines,* 250, lists ten requisites (or problems to be solved) for flying machines to be successful:

1. The resistance and supporting power of air.
2. The motor, its character and energy.
3. The instrument for obtaining propulsion.
4. The form and kind of the apparatus.
5. The extent of the sustaining surfaces.
6. The material and texture of the apparatus.
7. The maintenance of the equilibrium.
8. The guidance in any desired direction.
9. The starting up under all conditions.
10. The alighting safely anywhere.

17. David M. Young and Neal Callahan, *Fill the Heavens with Commerce: Chicago Aviation, 1855–1926* (Chicago, 1981), 13; Crouch, *Dream of Wings,* 177–79.

18. Octave Chanute, "Chanute's Diary of His Glides in 1896," Chanute papers, Manuscript Division, Library of Con-

gress, June 22–July 4, 1896, and later published in Marvin W. McFarland, ed., *The Papers of Wilbur and Orville Wright, 1899–1948* (New York, 1953), 1:641–54. Hereafter, this source will be referred to as the Wright Papers.

19. "Men Fly in Mid Air," *Chicago Tribune,* June 24, 1896.

20. Octave Chanute, "Diary," June 25–July 2, 1896.

21. Octave Chanute, "Gliding Experiments," October 20, 1897, address to the Western Society of Engineers, published in the *Journal of the Western Society of Engineers* (November 1897): 601.

22. Crouch, *Dream of Wings,* 192–93.

23. *Chicago Inter Ocean,* August 27, 1896; *Chicago Tribune,* September 8 and 14, 1896; *Chicago Record,* September 28, 1896; Chanute, "Diary," September 8, 1896.

24. Chanute, "Diary," September 14 and 26, 1896.

25. Ibid., August 31 and September 4 and 11, 1896.

26. Octave Chanute, "Gliding Experiments," *Journal of Western Society of Engineers* 2, no. 5 (October 1897): 593–628.

27. Wilbur Wright, letter to Octave Chanute, May 13, 1900, and Octave Chanute, letter to Wilbur Wright, May 17, 1900, Wright Papers, 1:15–21.

28. Wilbur Wright, letter to Chanute, November 26, 1900, Wright Papers, 1:45, and Chanute, letters to Wilbur Wright, November 23 and 29, 1900, Wright Papers, 1:44 and 47; Crouch, *Bishop's Boys,* 202.

29. Crouch, *Bishop's Boys,* 218, 230–33.

30. Ibid., 249–52.

31. Robert Wohl, *A Passion for Wings: Aviation and the Western Imagination, 1908–1918* (New Haven, Conn., 1994), 17; *L'Aerophile,* April 1903, 82.

32. Octave Chanute, "Aerial Navigation," paper read December 30, 1903, before Section D, American Association for the Advancement of Science, St. Louis; *St. Louis Post-Dispatch,* December 30, 1903; *Popular Science Monthly* 64 (March 1904): 385–93.

33. Wilbur Wright, letter to Chanute, April 28, 1910, Wright Papers, 2:991.

34. *New York Times,* July 9, 1910; *Chicago Tribune,* July 18, 1910; *Chicago Record Herald,* October 30, 1910.

35. *Western Society of Engineers Journal,* May 1911.

3: The Flying Machine Comes to Chicago

1. *Chicago Tribune* and *Chicago Daily News,* July 5 and 6, 1908; *Chicago Tribune,* July 5, 1910; *Chicago Record Herald,* September 27, 1910.

2. Crouch, *Bishop's Boys,* 278; Scamehorn, *Balloons to Jets,* 44.

3. Octave Chanute, letter to Wilbur Wright, January 23, 1910, Wright Papers, 1:980–81.

4. *Chicago Evening Post,* May 31, 1910; *Chicago Record Herald,* September 28, 1910.

5. David M. Young, *Chicago Transit* (DeKalb, Ill., 1998), 154.

6. *Chicago Tribune,* January 7, 1951, based on an interview with race driver Ray Harroun, who said he sold Scott an engine for four hundred dollars but never saw him fly the airplane. J. E. Scully is quoted in the same article as saying that Scott managed

to fly his airplane for short hops of 150 to three hundred feet on the infield of the Harlem race track. *Chicago Daily News,* May 29, 1975; Scamehorn, *Balloons to Jets,* 47–48.

7. Scamehorn, *Balloons to Jets,* 49–50.

8. *Aeronautics Magazine,* January 1909.

9. Emil M. (Matty) Laird, interview with author, September 1979; *Aeronautics Magazine,* January 1909; Scamehorn, *Balloons to Jets,* 45–47.

10. *Chicago Daily News, Chicago Tribune,* and *Chicago Record Herald,* October 16–17, 1909.

11. *Chicago Tribune,* July 5, 1910.

12. *Chicago Daily News* and *Chicago Tribune,* September 28, 1910.

13. *Chicago Tribune,* September 29, 1910.

14. *Chicago Record Herald* and *Chicago Tribune,* September 30, 1910.

15. Scamehorn, *Balloons to Jets,* 76–77.

16. *Chicago Record Herald* and *Chicago Tribune,* October 10, 11, and 12, 1910; Scamehorn, *Balloons to Jets,* 79–80.

17. Aero Club of Illinois, minutes of board of directors meeting of March 6, 1911, Aero Club of Illinois files. The records from 1911 to 1948, hereafter cited as the Aero Club files, are in the possession of the Chicago Historical Society.

18. Invitation dated April 1, 1911, and text of Harold F. McCormick's speech of April 6, 1911, in Aero Club files.

19. Harold F. McCormick, form letter of April 28, 1911, and Grover Sexton, Aero Club secretary, letter of August 18, 1911, in Aero Club files.

20. Rodney K. Worrel, "The Wright Brothers' Pioneer Patent," *American Bar Association Journal* (October 1979): 1512–18.

21. Anne Millbrooke, *Aviation History* (Englewood, Colo., 1999), 1.28–31, contains a concise synopsis of the Wrights' patent battles.

22. Telegram dated April 14, 1911, in Aero Club files; John T. McCutcheon, *Drawn from Memory* (Indianapolis, 1950), 239–41.

23. Harold F. McCormick report to Aero Club, June 23, 1911, in Aero Club files; *Aeronautics Magazine,* December 1909; Aero Club meeting minutes, June 1911, in Aero Club files; Harold F. McCormick, letter to Bernard Mullaney, general manager of IAMA, July 1, 1911, in Aero Club files.

24. Minutes of June 1, 1911, meeting of IAMA executive committee held in the Auditorium Hotel, and Frank X. Mudd, chairman of the IAMA contest committee, letter to James E. Plew, June 5, 1911, in Aero Club files.

25. Bernard Mullaney, letter to Adam Claflin of Boston, July 6, 1911, in Aero Club files; *New York Herald,* July 9, 1911; George M. Guy, New York Electrical Society, letter to Harold McCormick, July 10, 1911, in Aero Club files; Charles J. Strobel, Toledo, Ohio, aviator, letter to James E. Plew, July 11, 1911, in Aero Club files.

26. F. H. Russell, manager of the Wright Company, letter to Bernard Mullaney, IAMA, July 5, 1911, in Aero Club files.

27. *Aeronautics Magazine,* September 1911; minutes of IAMA executive committee meeting of September 8, 1911, in Aero Club files. Guy Campbell Wood, secretary of the Aero Club of America, letter to James E. Plew, July 28, 1911, in Aero Club files.

28. The descriptions of the meet described hereafter were culled from *Aeronautics Magazine,* September 1911; from Chicago newspaper accounts for the period August 12–21, 1911, principally in the *Chicago Tribune, Chicago Daily News,* and *Chicago Evening Post;* and from the "Report of the International Aviation Meet Association," November 1, 1911, in the Aero Club files.

29. William Bushnell Stout, *So Away I Went* (Indianapolis, 1951), 203–10.

30. McCutcheon, *Drawn from Memory,* 239.

31. Ibid., 240.

32. Ibid.

33. "Report of the International Aviation Meet Association," November 1, 1911, in Aero Club files.

4: The Aero Club

1. Katherine Stinson, application for pilot's license, May 24, 1912; Chauncey M. Vought, application for pilot's license, June 25, 1912; James Drew, manager of Cicero Field, report, August 16, 1912; all in Aero Club files. *Chicago Tribune,* September 13, 1912, and July 23, 1913.

2. James J. Flink, *The Automobile Age* (Cambridge, Mass., 1988), 27–28, 37; Beverly Rae Kimes, *The Standard Catalogue of American Cars, 1805–1942,* 3rd ed. (Iola, Wis., 1996), 304, 575–76, 770; Frederick W. Crismon, *International Trucks* (Osceola, Wis., 1995), 12, 14–23.

3. The Lockheed name is the subject of confusion. It was originally Loughead, but pronounced Lockheed. After brothers Allan and Malcolm founded their aircraft manufacturing company, they changed their name and the name of their company from Loughead to Lockheed in 1926. However, older stepbrother Victor, a writer, decided to spell his name Lougheed.

4. June Skinner Sawyers, *Chicago Portraits* (Chicago, 1991), 30, 97.

5. L. M. Howland, letter to Harold F. McCormick, November 9, 1901, in Aero Club files.

6. Grover Sexton, letter to Victor Lougheed, August 8, 1911, in Aero Club files.

7. *Chicago Tribune,* July 3, 1911.

8. *Chicago Tribune,* July 16, 1913; Grover Sexton, letter to Percy Noel, July 17, 1911, in Aero Club files.

9. *Flying,* May 1913; McCutcheon, *Drawn from Memory,* 240–41.

10. *Chicago Tribune,* July 16, 1913.

11. *Chicago Tribune,* January 25, 1914; Harold F. McCormick, "From My Experiences Concerning Aviation," speeches of December 1 and 8, 1917, before the Psychological Club of Zurich, Switzerland, McCormick Collection, State Historical Society of Wisconsin, Madison.

12. Harold F. McCormick, letter to Aero Club of Illinois, July 15, 1922, in Aero Club files.

13. Wayne Andrews, *Battle for Chicago* (New York, 1946),

205, 257–59, 261, 275; Barbara Marsh, *A Corporate Tragedy: The Agony of International Harvester Company* (New York, 1985), 50–51, 62.

14. Aero Club of Illinois bulletin of March 18, 1913, and announcement of January 1, 1914, in Aero Club files.

15. *Flying,* August 1915.

16. V. L. A. Farrell, *Lawson: From Bootblack to Emancipator* (Detroit: Humanity Benefactor Foundation, 1934), 6–7, 39, 55.

17. Alfred W. Lawson, letter to James Stephens, July 23, 1919, in Aero Club files; *Chicago Tribune,* September 1, 1919; Alfred W. Lawson, *A Two Thousand Mile Trip in the First Airliner* (Detroit: Humanity Benefactor Foundation, n.d.), 2–12. In his account of the flight, Lawson does not mention any financial involvement on Dickinson's part; he makes no reference to any damage on the landing near Toledo, although the *Chicago Tribune* account by reporter Morrow Krum gives the details of the incident; and he identifies the crash landing site of Connellsville as "Collinsville."

18. Charles Dickinson, telegram, July 27, 1923, in Aero Club files; *Chicago Tribune,* July 27, 1923.

19. *Chicago Tribune,* December 30, 1923.

20. Walter J. Boyne, *Beyond the Horizons: The Lockheed Story* (New York, 1998), 1–16.

21. Crouch, *Bishop's Boys,* 445, citing a November 8, 1911, letter from Orville Wright to T. S. Baldwin, Wright Papers, 2:1029; Victor Lougheed, letter to Grover Sexton, August 12, 1911, in Aero Club files.

22. Boyne, *Beyond the Horizons,* 1–16.

23. Maurice Holland, *Architects of Aviation* (New York, 1951), 127–35.

24. William B. Stout, letter of April 19, 1912, in Aero Club files; *Aerial Age,* June 1912.

25. Holland, *Architects of Aviation,* 135–39; Enzo Angelucci, *World Encyclopedia of Civil Aircraft* (New York, 1981), 113–14, 116.

26. Holland, *Architects of Aviation,* 139–44; John H. White Jr., *The American Railroad Passenger Car* (Baltimore, 1978), 2:612–13.

27. Mignon Rittenhouse, *The Amazing Nellie Bly* (New York, 1956), 141–215. Nellie Bly's trip was mainly by ship but did conclude with a train trip across the United States with the obligatory stop in Chicago to change trains.

28. Aero Club of America Bulletin, August 1912; Doris L. Rich, *Queen Bess: Daredevil Aviator* (Washington, D.C., 1993), 15–32, 107–20; Elizabeth A. H. Freydberg, *Bessie Coleman: The Brownskin Lady Bird* (New York, 1994).

29. Katherine Stinson, May 24, 1912, application for pilot's license, Aero Club files. Stinson indicated that she was born in Jackson, Mississippi, on February 14, 1895, which would have made her only seventeen years old when she arrived in Chicago. A July 11, 1977, article in the *New York Times* indicates that she was born on February 14, 1891, in Fort Payne, DeKalb County, Alabama. Andrew Drew, in a July 19, 1912, report in the Aero Club files, noted that Stinson completed the requisite altitude test for a pilot's license on July 19,

1912, at Cicero Field with a flight 350 feet above the ground.

30. Katherine Stinson, letter to James B. Stephens, August 31, 1912, in Aero Cub files; U.S. Postal Service announcement of September 23, 1914; *Flying,* August, 1915. Judy Lomax, *Women of the Air* (New York, 1987), says Ruth Law was also acclaimed as the first woman to do the loop-the-loop. *Chicago Tribune,* May 24, 1918.

31. Stout, *So Away I Went,* 97.

32. John W. Underwood, *The Stinsons* (Glendale, Calif., 1969), 5–18, 49.

33. Lomax, *Women of the Air,* 34–39.

Part II: Chicago as a Growing Air Center

5: The First Airports

1. Crouch, *Bishop's Boys,* 278–79.

2. Scamehorn, *Balloons to Jets,* 45–46.

3. Benjamin B. Lipsner, *The Airmail: Jennies to Jets* (Chicago, 1951), 51–52; Scamehorn, *Balloons to Jets,* 194.

4. December 1911 notice in Aero Club files.

5. Andrew Drew report of October 20, 1912, on the operation of Cicero Field, in Aero Club files; Federal Aviation Administration, report on flight operations of Midway Airport for 1959 and O'Hare International Airport for 2000; Grover F. Sexton, Aero Club of Illinois secretary, in an article published in the August 1912 *Aero Club of America* bulletin, claimed that Cicero Field was the world's busiest airport with operations that nearly equaled the activity "on almost all other American Fields together."

6. *Aeronautics,* August 1911.

7. Grover F. Sexton, letter to *Aero Magazine,* St. Louis, June 9, 1911, in Aero Club files.

8. *Aeronautics,* August 1911.

9. Report of July 14, 1911, in Aero Club files; *Chicago Tribune* and *Chicago Daily News,* July 14, 1911.

10. Charles Dickinson, waiver dated August 26, 1911, in Aero Club files.

11. Edward Wilder, letter to Harold F. McCormick, May 4, 1912, in Aero Club files.

12. Andrew Drew, report, May 19, 1912, in Aero Club files.

13. Curtiss Aeroplane Company, letter to Aero Club, May 7, 1912, and undated Aero Club announcement, both in Aero Club files.

14. Agreement between the Wright Company and the Aero Club of America, April 29, 1912, in Aero Club files.

15. Harold F. McCormick, letter to Glenn Curtiss, April 30, 1912; Curtiss, letter to McCormick, May 21, 1912; James Stephens, letter to McCormick, June 12, 1912; and Norman Prince, letter to Aero Club of Illinois, August 6, 1912, all in Aero Club files.

16. Unsigned letter of August 5, 1912, believed to have been written by James Stephens to Harold F. McCormick, in Aero Club files.

17. Agreement of September 7, 1912, between the Wright Company and the International Aviation Meet Association, the Aero Club of Illinois, and the Aero Club of America, in Aero Club files.

18. *Chicago Tribune*, May 26, 1912.

19. Millbrooke, *Aviation History*, 3.26–27, has a concise history of the Gordon Bennett races, which were suspended during World War I and discontinued after 1920.

20. Grover Sexton, letter to G. F. Campbell Wood, secretary of the Aero Club of America, July 8, 1911, in Aero Club files.

21. Harold F. McCormick, letter to club membership, June 12, 1912; James Stephens, letter to McCormick, June 25, 1912; McCormick, letter to Stephens, July 2, 1912, all in Aero Club files.

22. Minutes of Aero Club of Illinois meeting of March 18, 1912, in Aero Club files.

23. Aero Club of Illinois, letter to Windes & Marsh, civil engineers in Winnetka, March 21, 1912; and James Stephens, telegram to McCormick, July 17, 1912, both in Aero Club files.

24. Robert Wohl, "Aviation's Belle Epoque," *Air & Space Magazine* (April/May 1996), 5–6.

25. Orville Wright, letter to Harold Robbins, secretary of Aero Club of Illinois, February 21, 1912, in Aero Club files. Wright quoted the $5,000 price for a flyer with a four-cyclinder engine and landing wheels. He offered the club pontoons for an extra five hundred dollars, a six-cylinder engine for an additional seven hundred dollars, and flight school at a discounted rate of twenty-five dollars an hour below the normal rate of five hundred dollars for a four-hour course. Angelucci, *World Encyclopedia of Civil Aircraft,* 67–68; Henry Woodhouse, "The 1912 Gordon Bennett Cup Race," *Flying* (October 1912).

26. Angelucci, *World Encyclopedia of Civil Aircraft,* 75.

27. Aero Club announcement of April 19, 1912, in Aero Club files.

28. Harold F. McCormick, telegram to James Stephens, September 2, 1912, in Aero Club files.

29. Earle L. Ovington, letter to the Aero Club of Illinois, July 19, 1912, in Aero Club files; Young and Callahan, *Fill the Heavens with Commerce,* 68n.

30. Young and Callahan, *Fill the Heavens with Commerce,* 90.

31. Woodhouse, "1912 Gordon Bennett Cup Race"; Oliver Jensen, *The American Heritage History of Railroads in America* (New York, 1975), 264; Philip Van Doren Stern, *A Pictorial History of the Automobile as Seen in Motor Magazine, 1903–1953* (New York, 1953), 252–53.

32. Woodhouse, "1912 Gordon Bennett Cup Race."

33. *Chicago Daily News* and *Chicago Tribune,* September 22 and 23, 1912.

34. *Chicago Tribune,* September 13 and 16, 1912.

35. Andrew Drew, report of September 14, 1912, in Aero Club files; *Chicago Tribune,* September 21, 1912; Report of the Inquest of the Cook County Coroner, September 28, 1912, author's collection.

36. *Chicago Tribune,* September 19–20, 1912.

37. *Chicago Tribune,* September 21, 1912; Audit Company of Illinois, audit of the Aero Club of Illinois, January 21, 1913, and audit of the International Aviation Meet Association, November 1, 1911, both in the Aero Club files.

38. Aero Club of Illinois form letter of January 23, 1912, in Aero Club files; Laird interview, September 1979; Stout, *So Away I Went,* 190–94.

39. Stout, *So Away I Went,* 190–94.

40. Aero Club of Illinois, minutes of March 14, 1913, in Aero Club files; *Flying,* May 1913.

41. *Aero and Hydro,* March 22, 1913.

42. Aero Club, letter to W. H. Williamson of the *Chicago Tribune,* April 10, 1913, in Aero Club files.

43. Attachment to Aero Club letter of June 28, 1913, in Aero Club files.

44. *Chicago Tribune,* July 6, 1913; *Flying,* May 13, 1913.

45. Andrew Drew report of May 25, 1912, in Aero Club files; John P. V. Heinmuller, *Man's Fight to Fly: Famous World Record Flights and a Chronology of Aviation* (New York, 1944), 288. On September 23, 1913, Garros made what was an astounding over-water flight for the time—558 miles from Cannes, France, to Bizerte, Tunisia.

46. *Chicago Tribune,* July 2, 1913, and July 2, 1948.

47. *Chicago Tribune,* July 2, 1948, and May 16, 1976.

48. *Chicago Tribune,* July 6–8, 1913.

49. *Flying,* August, 1913.

50. *Chicago Tribune,* May 17–19, 1914.

51. *Chicago Tribune,* March 10, 1915.

52. William T. Block, secretary and treasurer of the Grant Land Association, letter to James Stephens, January 26, 1914.

53. Harold F. McCormick, letter of January 24, 1916, in Aero Club files; Emil (Matty) Laird, interviews with author, June and September 1979.

6: The Changes that War Brought

1. Chanute, *Progress in Flying Machines,* 268.

2. Francis X. Mudd, letters to Bernard J. Mullaney, June 27 and July 24, 1911, in Aero Club files.

3. Millbrooke, *Aviation History,* 4.40–41.

4. Ibid.

5. Army Major Samuel Reber, letter to Harold F. McCormick, May 16, 1911; James Stephens, letter to U.S. Representative Claude Stone, June 2, 1911, and letter to President William Howard Taft, July 2, 1912; Aero Club of Illinois, form letter to members, April 20, 1914; Lee Hammond, aircraft inventory report, April 30, 1914; Charles Dickinson, form letter to various businesspeople, May 17, 1915, all in Aero Club files. Charles Dickinson, *Flying,* June 1915.

6. National Aeroplane Fund letter of July 20, 1915, in Aero Club files.

7. Aero Club press release of July 6, 1916, in Aero Club files; *Chicago Tribune,* July 7, 1916; Aero Club of Illinois minutes of September 11, 1916, in Aero Club files.

8. *Aero and Hydro,* March 22, 1913, quoting an announcement by the Aero Club.

9. *Chicago Tribune,* October 15 and 16, 1916.

10. *Chicago Tribune,* October 29, 1916.

11. McCutcheon, *Drawn from Memory,* 241.

12. *Chicago Tribune,* October 29, 1916.

13. U.S. Army notice of February 17, 1917, in Aero Club files.

14. *Chicago Tribune,* April 16, 1917; Charles Dickinson, telegram to U.S. Representative James R. Mann, April 26, 1917, in Aero Club files.

15. Scamehorn, *Balloons to Jets,* 116.

16. Aero Club of Illinois notations of July 1917, in Aero Club files; Scamehorn, *Balloons to Jets,* 116–17.

17. Scamehorn, *Balloons to Jets,* 117–19.

18. Octave Chanute Aerospace Museum, history brochure (Rantoul, Illinois, 1997), also at <www.aeromuseum.org>.

19. *U.S. Air Service Victory Credit,* USAF Historical Study-N. (Aerospace Studies Institute, Historical Research Division, Maxwell Air Force Base, Alabama, June 1969), 133.

20. *Chicago Herald and Examiner,* January 29, 1928.

21. *Chicago Tribune,* February 8, 1919.

22. Reed G. Landis, letter to Governor Louis T. Emmerson, March 30, 1929, in Aero Club files.

23. *Chicago Tribune, Chicago Sun-Times,* May 31, 1975.

24. William F. Trimble, *Admiral William A. Moffett: Architect of Naval Aviation* (Washington, D.C., 1994), 55.

25. Alfred Wolff interview in February 1979; Trimble, *Admiral William A. Moffett,* 57.

26. Althoff, *Sky Ships,* 103–5; Trimble, *Admiral William A. Moffett,* 59, 255–76.

27. *Chicago Daily News,* August 3–8, 1915; *Chicago Tribune,* August 7, 1915.

28. *Chicago Tribune,* May 24–25, September 4, and November 20, 1918; Aero Club of Illinois memoranda of May 1918, in Aero Club files; James Stephens, report of November 21, 1916, in Aero Club files.

29. *Chicago Tribune,* January 5, 1920.

30. William M. Leary, *Aerial Pioneers: The U.S. Air Mail Service, 1918–1927* (Washington, D.C., 1985), 40–41, 58–61; *Chicago Tribune,* September 4–7, 1918.

31. Young and Callahan, *Fill the Heavens with Commerce,* 75, 118; memorandum of December 1919, in Aero Club files; Leary, in *Aerial Pioneers,* 97, notes that the post office had concluded that Grant Park was barely adequate for the operation of its airplanes and wanted to relocate to a larger facility.

32. Aero Club of Illinois, news release, April 17, 1916; Aero Club of Illinois, letter to members, May 8, 1916; Charles Dickinson, telegram to Newton D. Baker, U.S. secretary of war, June 28, 1916, all in Aero Club files.

33. Aero Club of Illinois, press release, December 1916, in Aero Club files.

34. Stout, *So Away I Went,* 182–83.

35. Charles Dickinson, letters to L. A. Busby, president of the Chicago City Road Commission, January 29 and March 24, 1919, in Aero Club files.

36. Aero Club of Illinois, news release, July 1917; assorted receipts, June–August 1917, in Aero Club files.

37. *Chicago Tribune,* June 4, 1919; photo caption of June 3, 1919, in files of Chicago Historical Society aviation collection.

38. *Chicago Tribune,* July 19, 1919.

39. Ibid.

40. *Chicago Tribune,* July 22, 1919.

41. James S. Stephens, letter to the Aero Club of America, August 1, 1919, and op-ed article, August 1919; Aero Club of Illinois, press release, January 5, 1920, for publication in *Flying,* all in Aero Club files.

42. Aldermen Frank J. Link, George M. Maypole, John H. Lyle, Dorsey Crowe, and Guy Guernsey, letter to Aero Club, January 22, 1920, and U.S. Post Office announcement, January 8, 1920, in Aero Club files; David L. Behncke, lease agreement with Herman A. Schultz, May 19, 1920, in Aero Club files; Bion J. Arnold, chairman of the Air Board of Chicago, letter to Major General Charles T. Menoher, director of the Army Air Service, July 23, 1920, in Aero Club files.

43. *Chicago Tribune,* October 1, 1929.

44. This account is believed to have been written by W. W. Workman about a November 4, 1919, flight of a Handley Page aircraft, in Chicago Historical Society files.

7: Early Commercial Aviation

1. *Historical Studies of the United States* (Washington, D.C., 1975), 2:729.

2. Bion J. Arnold, *Report on Steam Railroad Terminals* (Chicago, 1913); Frederick W. Crismon, *International Trucks* (Osceola, Wis., 1995), 38.

3. Andrew Drew, report, May 25, 1912, in Aero Club files.

4. James S. Stephens, op-ed piece of August 1919, in the *Chicago Tribune;* Scamehorn, *Balloons to Jets,* 137; photo caption, June 3, 1919, Chicago Historical Society aviation files.

5. Nick A. Kommons, *Bonfires to Beacons: Federal Civil Aviation Policy under the Air Commerce Act, 1926–1938* (Washington, D.C., 1978), 80–87.

6. Wisconsin Aviation Hall of Fame, sketch of David L. Behncke, April 29, 2001.

7. Society Brand clothes advertisement dated June 2, 1919, in Aero Club files.

8. David L. Behncke lease of May 19, 1920, with Herman A. Schultz and related documents in Chicago Historical Society files.

9. U.S. Post Office Department press releases of May 15, August 16, and December 1, 1920.

10. Young and Callahan, *Fill the Heavens with Commerce,* 141–42.

11. Allied Pilots Association pamphlet, *The Beginnings,* Fort Worth, Tex., March 5, 1997, 2.

12. Ibid., 3, 5–6; Isaac L. Cohen, "The Airline Pilots and the New Deal: The Struggle for Federal Labor Legislation," *Labor History* 41 (Washington, D.C., February 2000), 1:47–62; George E. Hopkins, "David L. Behncke," in William M. Leary, ed., *Ency-*

clopedia of American Business History and Biography: The Airline Industry (New York, 1992), 52–57.

13. James S. Stephens, op-ed piece of August 1919, in the *Chicago Tribune*.

14. Scamehorn, *Balloons to Jets*, 137–38.

15. Octave Chanute, *Popular Science Monthly*, March 1904.

16. Benjamin B. Lipsner, *The Airmail: Jennies to Jets* (Chicago, 1951), 55.

17. Untitled document of May 30–June 2, 1912, in Aero Club files.

18. *Chicago Tribune*, November 2–4, 1916.

19. *Chicago Tribune*, April 20, 1919.

20. Lipsner, *Airmail*, 55.

21. Ibid., 47–71.

22. *Chicago Tribune*, September 4–6, 1918; Lipsner, *Airmail*, 104; General Otto Praeger, U.S. second assistant postmaster general, prepared statement of January 4, 1919, U.S. Post Office Department, Washington.

23. Lipsner, *Airmail*, 100 (table).

24. *Chicago Tribune*, September 7–8, 1918; Lipsner, *Airmail*, 133.

25. Lipsner, *Airmail*, 151.

26. Ibid., 58–61.

27. William M. Leary, "Otto Praeger," in Leary, *Encyclopedia of American Business History and Biography*, 373–77, credits Praeger as the "father of Air Mail."

28. *Chicago Tribune*, May 26, 1919.

29. *New York Herald*, December 7, 1918; Lipsner, *Airmail*, 172–91.

30. Young and Callahan, *Fill the Heavens with Commerce*, 133, 139ff; *Chicago Tribune*, June 3, 1919.

31. *Chicago Tribune*, September 8 and November 8, 1920.

32. *Chicago Tribune*, February 23, 1921; Millbrooke, *Aviation History*, 4.5–46; Heinmuller, *Man's Fight to Fly*, 311.

33. Lipsner, *Airmail*, 32.

34. Kommons, *Bonfires to Beacons*, 80–87.

35. Charles Dickinson, letter to Daniel Ryan, February 20, 1922, in Aero Club files.

36. *Greater Chicago Magazine*, November 1922.

37. W. W. Fuller, secretary of Chicago Air Park Company, letter, July 9, 1923, in Aero Club files.

38. Charles Dickinson telegram of July 27, 1923, in Aero Club files; *Chicago Tribune*, July 27, 1923.

39. U.S. Post Office Department, press release, July 1, 1924; Aero Club of Illinois bulletin, July 1, 1924, in Aero Club files.

40. Charles H. Wacker, letter to the mayor and City Council of Chicago, July 15, 1924, in Chicago's *City Council Journal*.

41. *City Council Journal*, October 22, 1924.

42. Emil (Matty) Laird, interview, December 1977; *City Council Journal*, March 25, 1925.

43. *City Council Journal*, March 25 and April 1, 1925, and January 16, 1926; *Chicago Tribune*, April 4, 1925.

44. *Chicago Tribune*, February 16 and 22, 1926; R. E. G. Davies, *Airlines of the United States since 1914* (Washington, D.C., 1972), 39, 585 (table).

45. *Chicago Tribune*, May 9, 1926.

8: Airlines Come to Chicago

1. Frank A. Smith, ed., *Transportation in America: A Statistical Analysis of Transportation in the United States* (Washington, D.C.: ENO Transportation Foundation, Inc., 1992), 43.

2. Roger E. Bilstein, *Flight in America: From the Wrights to the Astronauts* (Baltimore, 1994), 26–28, notes that Silas Christofferson started a passenger shuttle across the bay between San Francisco and Oakland in about 1913, the year before the St. Petersburg–Tampa and McCormick's Lake Michigan commuter shuttles began.

3. Davies, *Airlines of the United States*, 1–3; *Chicago Tribune*, January 22, 1914; Young and Callahan, *Fill the Heavens with Commerce*, 79.

4. Stout, *So Away I Went*, 200; Davies, *Airlines of the United States*, 39, 52.

5. Davies, *Airlines of the United States*, 585 (table).

6. Stout, *So Away I Went*, 192–93, 203–10.

7. Young and Callahan, *Fill the Heavens with Commerce*, 94–97.

8. *Chicago Tribune*, June 7 and August 18, 1926; Laird interview with author, September 1979; Geoff Jones, *Northwest Airlines* (Vergennes, Vt., 1998), 5.

9. Frank J. Taylor, *High Horizons: Daredevil Flying Postmen to Modern Magic Carpet: The United Airlines Story* (New York, 1955), 36.

10. Ibid., 38. Taylor credits Thomas Wolfe, head of the new business department of the Chicago Association of Commerce, with suggesting the shift in strategy.

11. Davies, *Airlines of the United States*, 52.

12. Ibid., 62.

13. Taylor, *High Horizons*, 41–50.

14. Davies, *Airlines of the United States*, 75.

15. F. Robert van der Linden, "Progressives and the Post Office: Walter Folger Brown and the Creation of United States Air Transportation," in William F. Trimble, ed., *From Airships to Airbus: The History of Civil and Commercial Aviation*, vol. 2, *Pioneers and Operations*, Proceedings of the International Conference on the History of Civil and Commercial Aviation (Washington, D.C., 1995), 245–60; Millbrooke, *Aviation History*, 6.38–39; Don Bedwell, *Silverbird: The American Airlines Story* (Sandpoint, Idaho, 1999), 28–29; Kommons, *From Bonfires to Beacons*, 202–16; Davies, *Airlines of the United States*, 110–16.

16. Davies, *Airlines of the United States*, 161; Oliver E. Allen, *The Airline Builders* (Alexandria, Va., 1981) 90.

17. Taylor, *High Horizons*, 83; Allen, *Airline Builders*, 90, 95.

18. A second and unrelated airline with the name Chicago & Southern later existed briefly as an intrastate commuter carrier. It was abandoned after its president and pilot, Frank Hansen, was killed in an October 21, 1971, crash in Peoria that took sixteen lives.

19. Bjorn Heyning, *Heath Stories* (Benton Harbor, Mich., date unknown), an anthology of Heath Company employees' recollections, privately published over a period of years and bound in two volumes, and published on the Internet at

<www.members.aol.com/wwheco2>, no. 41; Edward B. Heath, letter to Aero Club of Illinois, September 3, 1912, in Aero Club files.

20. *Aerial Age,* July 1913; Heyning, *Heath Stories,* no. 41.

21. Heath Company announcement, summer 1922, in Aero Club files; Heyning, *Heath Stories,* no. 41.

22. Heath Company announcement of October 1, 1923, in Aero Club files; Heyning, *Heath Stories,* nos. 8 and 41.

23. Heyning, *Heath Stories,* nos. 8 and 41.

24. Emil (Matty) Laird, interview with author, September 1979; *The Wichita Eagle,* November 5, 1984; *Midwest Flyer,* June–July 1999, 3–5.

25. Laird, interview with author, September 1979; *The Wichita Eagle,* November 5, 1984.

26. George Bindbeutel, letter to Emil Laird, September 11, 1913, in Aero Club files; Laird, interview with author, September 1979.

27. *Chicago Tribune,* August 7, 1915; Underwood, *The Stinsons,* 5–18, 49.

28. Laird, interview with author, September 1979; *The Wichita Eagle,* November 5, 1984.

29. *The Wichita Eagle,* November 5, 1984; *Midwest Flyer,* June–July 1999, 3.

30. Laird letter of March 6, 1920, to James Stephens, in Aero Club files. Davies, *Airlines of the United States,* 42, 78.

31. Laird, interview with author, September 1979; *The Wichita Eagle,* November 5, 1984.

32. Aero Club of Illinois annual reports for the years 1924 and 1925, in Aero Club files.

33. E. M. Laird Airplane Company, advertising brochure in author's files (Chicago ca. 1930), 1–16; *AeroFiles,* an Internet encyclopedia of individual aircraft at <www.aerofiles.com>; *The Wichita Eagle,* November 5, 1984; *Midwest Flyer,* June–July 1999, 3.

34. Davies, *Airlines of the United States,* 191; Edward Jablonski, *Man with Wings: A Pictorial History of Aviation* (New York, 1980), 245; Angelucci, *World Encyclopedia of Civil Aircraft,* 240–41.

35. Marc Dierikx, *Fokker: A Transatlantic Biography* (Washington, D.C., 1997), 95–97, 122, 130, 138, 140; Stout, *So Away I Went,* 176–80, 203–10; Jablonski, *Man with Wings,* 225–27.

36. Angelucci, *World Encyclopedia of Civil Aircraft,* 114–17; Stout, *So Away I Went,* 203–5.

Part III: Chicago—Airport to a Nation

1. F. Robert van der Linden, *The Boeing 247: The First Modern Airliner* (Seattle, 1991), 20–21, noted that the Air Mail Act amendments of 1930, commonly called the McNary-Watres Act, or Watres Act, changed the method of paying airlines for hauling mail from weight to volume of space available ($1.25 per cubic foot per mile) a modification that encouraged the airlines to fill unused space with passengers and develop larger aircraft that would earn higher subsidies because of their greater payload.

2. Smith, *Transportation in America,* 47, table.

9: Air Disasters

1. *Chicago Tribune,* September 16, 1912. Data for 1911–1913 culled from Aero Club files for those years.

2. U.S. Post Office Department announcement of June 4, 1921, in Aero Club files.

3. Aero Club of Illinois, letter to Aero Club of America, July 17, 1912; Major Samuel Reber, chairman of Aero Club of America's contest committee, letter to James B. Stephens, August 30, 1912, both in Aero Club files.

4. Aero Club of America, "Rules and Regulations for the Issue of Pilots Licenses," received June 21, 1911, by Grover S. Sexton; Aero Club of Illinois bulletin of August 19, 1912, both in Aero Club files.

5. Arnold Kruckman, general secretary of the Aeronautical Society of New York, letter to James E. Plew, president of the Aero Club of Illinois, June 28, 1911, in Aero Club files; Kommons, *From Bonfires to Beacons,* 26.

6. U.S. Department of War announcement of January 1, 1920, in Aero Club files.

7. Kommons, *Bonfires to Beacons,* 20–21; City of Chicago, directive to the general superintendent of police, December 1919, in Aero Club files; "Rules and Regulations Governing the Operation of Aircraft in Chicago," *City Council Journal,* February 4, 1921.

8. Klee, Rogers, Wile & Loeb, 175 W. Jackson Boulevard, Chicago, letter to James S. Stephens, January 20, 1920, and Underwriters Laboratories, document of January 1, 1922, both in Aero Club files; Kommons, *Bonfires to Beacons,* 29.

9. Reed G. Landis, letter to Aero Club of Illinois, August 1, 1919, in Aero Club files.

10. Kommons, *Bonfires to Beacons,* 48–49.

11. *Chicago Tribune,* July 4, 1922.

12. Kommons, *Bonfires to Beacons,* 86; *Congressional Record,* 69th Congress, First Session, 9356, 9391, 9811.

13. Kommons, *Bonfires to Beacons,* 87.

14. David D. Lee, "William P. MacCracken Jr.," in Leary, *Encyclopedia of American Business History and Biography,* 285–89.

15. Davies, *Airlines of the United States,* 55.

16. Louis C. Hunter, *Steamboats on the Western Rivers* (New York, 1993), 520–46; White, *American Railroad Passenger Car,* 1:117, 130–31; Althoff, *Sky Ships,* 141. In addition to the *Hindenburg* and *Wingfoot Air Express* explosions, the airship disasters included the explosions of a British ZR-2 over Hull, England, in 1921 that killed forty-three; a British R-101 crash in France in 1930 that killed forty-six; and the U.S. *Akron* crash in a storm in the Atlantic Ocean in 1933, killing seventy-three.

17. Dominick Pisano, *Air & Space,* December 1991/January 1992, 89; Kommons, *Bonfires to Beacons,* 183–89. Davies, *Airlines of the United States,* 92–93, notes that TWA was formed on July 19, 1930, by a merger of Transcontinental Air Transport and Western Air Express, under pressure from the commerce department and over the objection of Western Air Express. It made its first flight under the new name on October 25 of the same year.

18. Jablonski, *Man with Wings,* 416–17; Stuart I. Rochester,

Takeoff at Mid-Century: Federal Civil Aviation Policy in the Eisenhower Years, 1953–1961 (Washington, D.C., 1976), 102–7, 234, 280, 284, 298; Robert J. Serling, *Loud and Clear* (New York, 1969), 184–250; *Chicago Tribune,* May 26–30, June 1–5, August 12, 1979.

19. Kommons, *Bonfires to Beacons,* 178–83.

20. Pisano, *Air & Space,* 89; Kommons, *Bonfires to Beacons,* 183–89.

21. Dierikx, *Fokker,* 140–45.

22. Barbara Bean, *Of Magic Sails* (Chicago, 1975), 37–40; Davies, *Airlines of the United States,* 336–38.

23. Richard Sanders Allen, "Charter to Chicago," *Aviation Quarterly* 8, no. 4 (Fall 1988), 318–31.

24. Ibid., 322. The Federal Aviation Administration Record Center in Oklahoma City indicates that the aircraft, NC 415H, had been built at the Ford-Stout plant in Dearborn, Michigan, in 1929 for Firestone Tire and Rubber Company as an executive aircraft. American Airlines bought it on October 31, 1931, and flew the plane until 1935. After that, it was successively used in Honduras, Nicaragua, and Mexico until it was damaged beyond repair in an accident on August 16, 1949, at Putla, Oaxaca, Mexico.

25. *Aircraft Yearbook* (New York: Aeronautical Chamber of Commerce, 1933), 49–51.

26. American Airlines newspaper advertisement of April 19, 1937, reprinted in Bedwell, *Silverbird,* 36.

27. Rochester, *Takeoff at Mid-Century,* 126–31; *Chicago Tribune,* July 20–26, 1989.

28. Serling, *Loud and Clear,* 200–4; John Cyrocki, Great Lakes regional director for the Federal Aviation Administration and, at the time of the crash, an investigator for the Civil Aeronautics Board, interview with author, 1977.

29. Serling, *Loud and Clear,* 184–250.

30. Jay Gourley, *The Great Lakes Triangle* (Greenwich, Conn., 1977), 8–10, 120–26; William Ratigan, *Great Lakes Shipwrecks and Survivals* (Grand Rapids, Michigan, 1960), 36–37.

31. *Chicago Tribune,* June 25, 1950. Civil Aeronautics Board Accident Investigation Report, SA-215, File No. 1-0081 (Washington, D.C., January 18, 1951).

32. Serling, *Loud and Clear,* 256–59.

33. Ed McAvoy, investigator for the National Transportation Safety Board, interview with author, August 1981.

34. National Transportation Safety Board, Special Investigation Report: Search and Rescue Procedures and Arming of Emergency Locator Transmitter: Aircraft Accident near Michigan City, Indiana, December 7, 1980, NTSB-SIR-81-2 (Washington, D.C., August 11, 1981).

35. Civil Aeronautics Board, Accident Investigation Report, March 28, 1941; *Chicago Tribune,* March 29, 1941, and November 16, 1955.

36. National Transportation Safety Board, Aircraft Accident Report NTSB-AAR-73-16 (Washington, D.C., August 29, 1973); National Transportation Safety Board, Aircraft Accident Report NTSB-AAR-96-01 (Washington, D.C., July 9, 1996), 1:vii–viii, 76, 91–93, 158–59, 203–9.

37. *Chicago Tribune,* January 18, 1969.

38. The conclusions are the author's, based on interviews with numerous air crews and observations made during many jump seat cockpit rides in commercial and private planes to and from Chicago during the period 1975–1984.

39. *Chicago Tribune* and *Chicago Sun-Times,* February 28, 1973, and June 14 and 15, 1973; Associated Press dispatches, February 28, 1973, and June 14 and 15, 1973. The conspiracy theories were first advanced by Sherman H. Skolnick, a Chicago legal researcher who appeared at the NTSB hearings.

40. National Transportation Safety Board, Aircraft Accident Report: United Air Lines Inc., Boeing 737, N9021u, Chicago Midway Airport, December 8, 1972, NTSB-AAR-73-6 (Washington, D.C., August 29, 1973).

41. Rochester, *Takeoff at Mid-Century,* 104–8; Angelucci, *World Encyclopedia of Civil Aircraft,* 344–45; Millbrooke, *Aviation History,* 8.22–23.

42. Civil Aeronautics Board, Aircraft Accident Report SA-357, File No. 1-0054, Aug. 14, 1961, 1–11.

43. Civil Aeronautics Board, Accident Investigation Report SA-167, File No. 1-0023, June 13, 1949; *Chicago Tribune,* February 25, 1949.

44. Civil Aeronautics Board, Aircraft Accident Report SA-363, File No. 1-0011, December 11, 1962; Civil Aeronautics Board, Aircraft Accident Report SA-364, File No. 1-0018, December 10, 1962, 1–36.

45. *Chicago Tribune,* May 26–29, 1979; August 12–13, 1979.

46. National Transportation Safety Board, Aircraft Accident Report NTSB-AAR-79-17 (Washington, D.C., December 21, 1979).

47. *Chicago Tribune,* May 28–29, 1979.

48. Smith, *Transportation in America,* 47–48, tables.

49. Rosalyn W. Wilson, ed., *Transportation in America: Statistical Analysis of Transportation in the United States* (Lansdowne, Va.: Transportation Foundation, 1997), 48.

50. U.S. Department of Transportation, Bureau of Transportation Statistics (Washington, D.C.), press release of January 9, 2002; Historical Air Traffic Data Monthly, years 1999, 2000, and 2001, available online at <www.bts.gov> for 1999; append the appropriate year to the URL for subsequent reports.

10: Emergence of Modern Airlines

1. James E. Vance Jr., *Capturing the Horizon: The Historical Geography of Transportation since the Sixteenth Century* (Baltimore, 1990), 547–48.

2. Georgia Panter Nielsen, *From Sky Girl to Flight Attendant* (Ithaca, New York), 24–49; Smith, *Transportation in America,* 47.

3. Davies, *Airlines of the United States,* 89, 495.

4. Air Transport Association, Historical Statistics of U.S. Airlines by Carrier Group, Revenue Passenger Originations (Table 46) (Washington, D.C., 1973); Chicago Department of Aviation, Chicago Municipal/Midway Airport statistics (Chicago, 1980).

5. Taylor, *High Horizons,* 38–41, 50.

6. Vance, *Capturing the Horizon,* 547–49; Davies, *Airlines of the United States,* 70–79.

7. Bedwell, *Silverbird,* 22–26.

8. George E. Hopkins, "E. L. Cord," in Leary, *Encyclopedia of American Business and Biography,* 123–25; Bedwell, *Silverbird,* 27–29, 35.

9. Data from the individual trade groups, including the Air Transport Association, American Waterway Operators, American Trucking Association, and Association of American Railroads; Vance, *Capturing the Horizon,* 555.

10. van der Linden, *Boeing 247,* 34–52; Davies, *Airlines of the United States,* 181.

11. Angelucci, *World Encyclopedia of Civil Aircraft,* 234; Allen, *Airline Builders,* 95–96; van der Linden, *Boeing 247,* 70–87.

12. Davies, *Airlines of the United States,* 186.

13. Bedwell, *Silverbird,* 39.

14. Davies, *Airlines of the United States,* 155–64.

15. Nielsen, *From Sky Girl to Flight Attendant,* 1–25.

16. Davies, *Airlines of the United States,* 532–39.

17. Bedwell, *Silverbird,* 33–35; Taylor, *High Horizons,* 56–57; National Aviation Hall of Fame (NAHF) biographies of C. R. Smith (Dayton, Ohio, 1974) and William A. Patterson (Dayton, Ohio, 1976) (Internet versions are available at <www.nationalaviation.org>); Frank J. Taylor, *"Pat" Patterson* (Menlo Park, Calif., 1967); F. Robert van der Linden, "William Allan Patterson," in Leary, *Encyclopedia of American Business and Biography,* 351–63.

18. Bedwell, *Silverbird,* 33–35.

19. Taylor, *High Horizons,* 83; NAHF biography of Patterson.

20. Taylor, *High Horizons,* 102–4.

21. The ICC had been given the task of airline regulation in 1934 in the wake of the Spoils Conference scandal, but that overburdened agency, which also handled the railroads and the new trucking industry, suggested a new agency be created. The other federal aviation agency at the time was the Civil Aeronautics Authority (CAA), created in 1938 to replace the Commerce Department's Aeronautics Branch, which dated from 1926. Those two agencies successively regulated aviation safety by such means as licensing pilots, building airway beacons, and setting airport standards. The CAA was renamed the Civil Aeronautics Administration in 1940, and in 1958 it became the Federal Aviation Administration. The Civil Aeronautics Board (CAB), which also investigated commercial airplane crashes to determine the cause and made safety recommendations to the CAA/FAA, in 1966 lost that function to the newly created National Transportation Safety Board (NTSB). The CAB, whose sole function remained the economic regulation of airlines, was abolished beginning in 1983. Thus the two federal agencies involved with aviation as the twentieth century ended were the FAA, which regulated safety, and the NTSB, which investigated crashes and made safety recommendations. The proposed merger between United and US Airways in 2001 was not subject to review by any of the surviving federal aviation agencies, but it was aborted by both carriers after the U.S. Justice Department, citing antitrust concerns, threatened that summer to file suit to block the merger (Donald R. Whitnah, "Civil Aeronautics Board"; Nick A. Kommons, "Civil Aeronautics Administration"; Edmund Preston, "Federal Aviation Administration"; and Robert Burkhardt, "National Transportation Safety Board," in Leary, *Encyclopedia of American Business History and Biography,* 105–107, 101–104, 170–72, and 306–309; Kommons, *From Bonfires to Beacons,* 91–124, 347–79; John R. M. Wilson, *Turbulence Aloft: The Civil Aeronautics Administration amid Wars and Rumors of Wars* [Washington, D.C., 1979], 9–42 and 49–52; Rochester, *Takeoff at Mid-Century,* 189–219; U.S. Department of Justice, press release of July 27, 2001).

22. Elizabeth E. Bailey, David R. Graham, and Daniel P. Kaplan, *Deregulating the Airlines* (Cambridge, Mass., 1985), 33; Allen, *Airline Builders,* 95–96; Richard Ferris, interviews with the author, 1977–1978.

23. Allen, *Airline Builders,* 95; Taylor, *High Horizons,* 112–14.

24. Robert E. Johnson, *Airway One* (Chicago, 1974), 54.

25. Davies, *Airlines of the United States,* 338.

26. Taylor, *High Horizons,* 148–53; Davies, *Airlines of the United States,* 329.

27. Wilson, *Turbulence Aloft,* 245–47.

28. Angelucci, *World Encyclopedia of Civil Aircraft,* 300, 306–7, 310, 316.

29. Bilstein, *Flight in America,* 116–17, 202, 260; Jablonski, *Man with Wings,* 271–72.

30. A. Gerald Peters and Donald F. Wood, "Helicopter Airlines in the United States, 1945–1975," *Journal of Transportation History* 4, no. 1 (February 1977): 9–11; William M. Leary, "Helicopter Airlines," in Leary, *Encyclopedia of American Business and Biography,* 208–11.

31. Chicago Helicopter Airways, annual reports for the years 1958–1960, author's collection; Peters and Wood, "Helicopter Airlines in the United States," 9, 11; Leary, *Encyclopedia of American Business and Biography,* 209.

32. *Chicago Tribune,* August 20, 1999; Peters and Wood, "Helicopter Airlines in the United States," 11; Leary, *Encyclopedia of American Business and Biography,* 210; Los Angeles Airways ceased operation in 1970 following two fatal accidents, San Francisco–Oakland Helicopter Airlines was shut down in 1976 by a mechanics' strike, and New York Airways fell into bankruptcy in 1979 after two fatal crashes.

33. Carleton Putnam, *High Journey* (New York, 1945).

34. *Chicago Tribune,* June 2, 1937, based on a Chicago & Southern filing before the Interstate Commerce Commission; Chicago & Southern press release of September 12, 1937; R. E. G. Davies, *Delta: An Airline and Its Aircraft* (Miami, Fla., 1990), 44–58; *Chicago Tribune,* November 11, 1940.

35. Davies, *Delta: An Airline,* 51.

36. W. David Lewis and Wesley Phillips Newton, *Delta: The History of an Airline* (Athens, Ga., 1979), 204; *Chicago Tribune,* January 9, 1940; February 20, 1946; and January 1, 1953.

37. Chicago & Southern Air Lines, Memphis, annual financial reports to the Civil Aeronautics Board for fiscal years 1950, 1951, and 1952.

38. Lewis and Newton, *Delta: The History,* 211–28.

39. Davies, *Delta: An Airline,* 44–58.

40. Bailey, Graham, and Kaplan, *Deregulating the Airlines,* 1–13.

41. Davies, *Airlines of the United States,* 336. Capital had introduced a fare called Sky Coach on April 10, 1940, on its San Francisco–Los Angeles route as a way to fill its old but fully depreciated B-247s, but the experiment was discontinued during World War II, and the airline lost interest in the idea.

42. Johnson, *Airway One,* 70–81.

43. Davies, *Airlines of the United States,* 251–52; Angelucci, *World Encyclopedia of Civil Aircraft,* 340; Johnson, *Airway One,* 66–70.

44. Johnson, *Airway One,* 86.

45. Richard J. Kent Jr., *Safe, Separated, and Soaring: A History of Federal Aviation Policy, 1961–1972* (Washington, D.C., 1980), 22–23, 38, 212–16; Wilson, *Turbulence Aloft,* 171–75.

11: The Airports

1. Scamehorn, *Balloons to Jets,* 172–73.

2. Aero Club of Illinois, Aerodrome Sites, Chicago and Vicinity (Winnetka, 1912), in Aero Club files; Chicago Regional Planning Association, Aircraft Landing Fields and Paved Highways in the Region of Chicago (Chicago, March 1928), in Aero Club files; Division of Aeronautics, Illinois Department of Transportation, *Metro-Chicago Airports 2000* (Springfield, Illinois, 1989).

3. *Chicago Herald & Examiner,* February 4, 1926; Davies, *Airlines of the United States,* 72.

4. Wilson, *Turbulence Aloft,* 31.

5. *Chicago Tribune,* November 3, 1929.

6. Angelucci, *World Encyclopedia of Civil Aircraft,* 98, 106, 214, 300.

7. Scamehorn, *Balloons to Jets,* 174.

8. *Chicago Tribune,* June 13, 1929; January 24, 1936; and May 6, 1936.

9. Wilson, *Turbulence Aloft,* 28–31.

10. Ibid., 32–34.

11. Wilson, *Turbulence Aloft,* 113–29; Neal Callahan, *Significant Aviation Disasters,* an unpublished and incomplete chronology of aviation disasters from 1908 to 1977, in author's collection (Chicago, 1978), 2.

12. Wilson, *Turbulence Aloft,* 193–202.

13. Bedwell, *Silverbird,* 66–67; Taylor, *High Horizons,* 125–26; Bean, *Of Magic Sails,* 54; Air Transport Association, Traffic Summary, 1926–1972 (Washington, D.C., 1973); Chicago Department of Aviation, Chicago Municipal Airport Statistics, 1927–1950.

14. Scamehorn, *Balloons to Jets,* 128–29; Octave Chanute Aerospace Museum (Rantoul, Illinois), History of Chanute Field.

15. Scamehorn, *Balloons to Jets,* 132.

16. U.S. Navy, Naval Reserve Force, New Orleans, Louisiana, press release of September 14, 1995.

17. Boeing, Inc., corporate histories of acquired companies, Douglas Aircraft Company, *C-54 Skymaster,* (Seattle, Washington, 2000). Richard P. Doherty, "The Origin and Development of Chicago-O'Hare International Airport" (Ph.D. diss., Ball State University, Muncie, Indiana, 1970), contains the most complete history of the selection of the site and early development of O'Hare.

18. Smithsonian Institution, National Air and Space Museum, roster of collections (Washington, D.C., 2001).

19. Civil Aeronautics Authority, *CAA Statistical Handbook of Civil Aviation* (Washington, D.C., 1956), 14–23, lists traffic at LaGuardia (LGA) and Midway (MDW) as follows:

Year	Airport	Scheduled Air Carrier Passengers	Aircraft Arrivals and Departures	
			Total	Scheduled Air Carrier
1949	MDW	2,842,376	223,943	137,735
	LGA	3,215,961	159,465	138,715
1950	MDW	3,502,716	234,331	150,442
	LGA	3,512,411	156,470	135,349
1951	MDW	4,507,881	263,737	177,428
	LGA	4,277,995	183,243	151,222
1952	MDW	5,488,549	295,456	203,531
	LGA	3,999,875	185,622	158,822
1953	MDW	6,736,224	331,297	250,246
	LGA	4,496,678	199,407	166,359

Note that the CAA statistics for passenger traffic pertain only to scheduled air carrier operations and do not include such operations and aircraft as nonscheduled flights, charters, air taxis, commuter and sightseeing aircraft, and shuttles. Port Authority of New York and New Jersey, *LaGuardia Air Traffic Statistics* (New York, 2000), 4, indicates that a total of 3,284,214 passengers used that airport in 1949. The Chicago Department of Aviation, *Midway Airport Traffic* (Chicago, 2001), table, indicates a total of 3,246,693 at that airport in 1949.

20. *Chicago American,* December 8, 1941; Harold M. Meyer and Richard C. Wade, *Chicago: Growth of a Metropolis* (Chicago, 1969), 448–49; Ralph J. Burke, *Master Plan of Chicago Orchard (Douglas) Airport,* consultant's report (Chicago, 1948), 2–3.

21. Burke, *Master Plan,* 4.

22. City of Chicago, Department of Aviation, *Brief History of Chicago-O'Hare International Airport,* 1–2; Philip Handleman, *Chicago O'Hare: The World's Busiest Airport* (Osceola, Wis., 1998), 12.

23. Charles B. Cannon, *The O'Hare Story* (New York, 1980), 2–12; Steve Ewing and John B. Lundstrom, *Fateful Rendezvous: The Life of Butch O'Hare* (Annapolis, 1997).

24. William E. Downes Jr., commissioner of aviation, untitled and undated memorandum on airport finances and their legal ramifications (Chicago, Department of Aviation, ca. 1975).

25. Ibid.

26. *Chicago Tribune,* March 2–6, 1958.

27. Federal Aviation Administration, Washington, D.C., press release of May 16, 1968; Kent, *Safe, Separated, and Soaring,* 164, 22, 239; *U.S. Transportation Department, Report to Congress: A*

Study of the High Density Rule (Washington, D.C., May 1995), executive summary, 1–2.

28. *Chicago Tribune,* February 4, 1970; Chicago Department of Aviation, Chicago Municipal Airport statistics, 1960–1970, and Chicago-O'Hare International Airport statistics, 1960–1970.

29. Illinois Department of Transportation, "South Suburban Airport Environmental Assessment" (Chicago, 1998), 5 vols., 1:1.

30. Federal Aviation Administration, "Operational Analysis: Chicago-O'Hare International Airport: Thursday, 18 March 1971," FAA files, Chicago, 1972; Federal Aviation Administration, assorted internal communications of June 30, 1977; *Chicago Tribune,* July 18, September 12 and 21, and November 19, 2000; and January 18, 2002.

31. *Chicago Tribune,* December 6, 2001.

32. Roger C. Marquardt, director of the Illinois Division of Aeronautics, interview with author, August 28, 1991; *Chicago Tribune,* September 7, 1991.

33. Illinois Department of Transportation, Division of Aeronautics, *Metro-Chicago Airports 2000* (Springfield, 1989).

34. *The City of Geneva et al.* v. *The DuPage County Airport Authority et al.,* Illinois Appellate Court, Second District, 2-89-0303, January 25, 1990, 6–8.

35. Illinois Department of Transportation, Division of Aeronautics, *Illinois Airport Inventory Report* (Springfield, 1991), 28, 47; *Chicago Tribune,* September 7, 1991; James V. Bildilli, engineer for planning and programming, Illinois Division of Aeronautics, interview with author, August 28, 1991.

36. *The City of Geneva et al.* v. *The DuPage County Airport Authority et al.,* 3–7.

37. *Chicago Tribune,* February 23, 1987; October 26, 1988; and June 5, 1990.

12: The Jet Age

1. Johnson, *Airway One,* 87–88.

2. The controlling runway had the shortest length of the major runways at the airport; any plane designed to use it would be able to use all the other major runways. J. E. Steiner, *Requirements and Major Decision Outline,* Boeing Commercial Airplane Co. (Seattle, 1978), and subsequent interview with author.

3. UAL, Inc., "Ten-Year Comparative Statistics," in *Annual Report* (Chicago, 1970), 26–27.

4. Johnson, *Airway One,* 149.

5. Ibid., 127.

6. Ibid., 147–57.

7. UAL, Inc., "Management Statement to Shareholders," in *Annual Report* (Chicago, 1970), 2–3; UAL, Inc., "Ten-Year Statement of Consolidated Financial Position" (Chicago, 1972), 28; Johnson, *Airway One,* 118.

8. UAL, Inc., "Ten-Year Comparative Statistics," in *Annual Report* (Chicago, 1970), 26–27; Bailey, Graham, and Kaplan, *Deregulating the Airlines,* appendix, table A, 206; Johnson, *Airway One,* 109; and Davies, *Airlines of the United States,* 576–77.

9. Bailey, Graham, and Kaplan, *Deregulating the Airlines,* 215.

10. Edward E. Carlson and Richard J. Ferris various conversations with the author in 1977–1979. Bailey, Graham, and Kaplan, *Deregulating the Airlines,* 33.

11. Johnson, *Airway One,* 117–18.

12. Donald R. Whitnah, "Civil Aeronautics Board," in Leary, *Encyclopedia of American Business and Biography,* 107.

13. Richard J. Ferris, interviews with author, 1982–1983.

14. UAL Corporation, Form 10K annual report to the Securities and Exchange Commission for the year ending December 31, 1986, 3–4.

15. *Chicago Tribune,* June 11, 1987.

16. *Chicago Tribune,* April 12, 1987; June 12, 1987; and June 14, 1987.

17. UAL Corporation, Form 10K annual report to the Securities and Exchange Commission for the year ending December 31, 1992, 3–4; UAL Corporation, *Annual Report* (to stockholders, Chicago, 1992), 1.

18. *Chicago Tribune,* September, 6, 7, and 17, 1989, and July 13, 1994; UAL Corporation, Form 8-K report filed with the U.S. Securities and Exchange Commission, December 22, 1993, 10.1–10; *New York Times,* October 29, 2001.

19. UAL Corporation, *2000 Annual Report* (to shareholders, Chicago, 2001), 8, 28–31, 34, 50.

20. UAL Corporation, fourth quarter financial press releases of January 21, 1999; January 19, 2000; January 18, 2001; and February 1, 2002, summarized the corporation's annual financial results (in millions of dollars) as follows:

Year	Revenues	Net Income (Loss)
2001	13,788	(2,145)
2000	16,932	50
1999	18,027	1,235
1998	17,561	821
1997	17,378	949

21. Tom W. Norwood, *Deregulation Knockouts: Round One* (Sandpoint, Idaho, 1996), foreword and introduction, 118–19; *Chicago Tribune,* March 15, 1992.

22. Midway Airlines Inc. stock prospectus of December 4, 1980, on file with the Securities and Exchange Commission; Irving Tague, Midway Airlines chairman, interviews with the author in 1979 and 1980; Norwood, *Deregulation Knockouts,* introduction.

23. Norwood, *Deregulation Knockouts,* 24–25.

24. Chicago Department of Aviation operating statistics, Midway Airport, 1978–1989; Midway Airlines Inc., "Ten Year Summary of Selected Financial and Operating Data," in *Annual Report* (to stockholders, Chicago, December 31, 1989), 34–35; *Chicago Tribune,* March 29, 1987; January 15, 1989; and November 19, 1989.

25. *Chicago Tribune,* March 27, 1991; Midway Airlines, press release of March 26, 1991.

26. Annual financial statements and 10K forms filed by Midway Airlines Inc. with the Securities and Exchange Com-

mission for the period 1980 through 1991; Midway Airlines Inc., bankruptcy petition 91B06449, filed March 26, 1991, in the U.S. Bankruptcy Court for the Northern District of Illinois; Midway Airlines, press releases of October 19, 1990, and March 26, 1991.

27. Mary Rose Loney, Chicago commissioner of aviation, letter published in the *Chicago Sun-Times,* November 20, 1997; Southwest Airlines press release of August 10, 2000; ATA press release of May 31, 2001; Chicago Department of Aviation operating statistics, Midway Airport, 1990–2000.

28. *Chicago Tribune,* September 12 and 21 and November 20–22, 2000; UAL Corporation, *2000 Annual Report,* 5.

29. *Chicago Tribune,* February 10, 1985; *Crain's Chicago Business,* February 24, 1992.

30. Lou Yates, director of the airport district office for the Federal Aviation Administration, Great Lakes region, interview with author, December 7, 1992.

31. Samuel K. Gove and James D. Nowland, *Illinois Politics and Government: The Expanding Metropolitan Frontier* (Lincoln, Nebraska, 1996) 21–39, 163.

32. *Chicago Tribune* and *Chicago Sun-Times,* August 24, 1974, and October 14, 1982; TAMS Consultants Inc. (aviation consults to the Illinois Department of Transportation), South Suburban Airport Environmental Assessment (Chicago, 1998), 5 vols., 1:1.

33. Landrum & Brown Inc. (aviation consultants to Chicago), *Chicago Delay Task Force, Delay Reduction/Efficiency Enhancement, Final Report* (Chicago, April 1991); TAMS Consultants Inc., *Phased Development of a Greenfield Airport* (New York, 1992); Federal Aviation Administration, *Aviation Capacity Enhancement Plan* (Washington, D.C., 1995); TAMS Consultants Inc., *South Suburban Airport Master Plan and Environmental Assessment* (Chicago, July 6, 1994); TAMS Consultants Inc., *South Suburban Airport Environmental Assessment* (Chicago, 1998).

34. TAMS Consultants Inc., *South Suburban Airport Environmental Assessment,* 2:19 (table 2.8); Landrum & Brown, *Chicago Delay Task Force,* 4–5.

35. *Chicago Sun-Times,* July 2, 1992; Landrum & Brown, *Lake Calumet Airport Feasibility Study* (Chicago, June 1991); TAMS Consultants Inc., *South Suburban Airport Environmental Assessment,* 1:2–5.

36. *Chicago Tribune,* July 2 and 7, 1992; *Southtown Economist,* July 8, 1992.

37. Harold M. Mayer and Richard C. Wade, *Chicago: Growth of a Metropolis* (Chicago, 1969), 274–76; *Chicago Tribune,* May 14, 2001, and June 14, 2001; *Daily Herald,* June 14, 2001.

38. Raymond J. Vecci et al., Air Transport Association, letter to James Edgar, governor of Illinois, January 17, 1995; Roger Cohen, Air Transport Association representative, testimony at a public hearing on the South Suburban Airport Draft Environmental Assessment, October 29, 1997; TAMS Consultants Inc., Phase 1 Engineering Study, *South Suburban Airport Environmental Assessment* (Chicago, 1998), 5:24–27 (appendix Q); Thomas J. Brown, managing director, airports, Air Transport Association, letter to Robert L. York, third-airport project manager, Illinois Department of Transportation, November 6, 1997.

39. *Chicago Sun-Times,* November 27, 1997.

40. Ralph M. Parsons Company, *Northeastern Illinois Airport Requirements Study* (Los Angeles, 1973), 1–9; Bailey, Graham, and Kaplan, *Deregulating the Airlines,* 215, appendix, table E.

41. Charles E. Grassley and Tom Harkin, letter to colleagues in Congress, April 6, 2001; Grassley and Harkin, letter to Senator Patty Murray, chair of the Senate Appropriations Subcommittee on Transportation, June 18, 2001.

42. Ibid.

43. Chanute, *Progress in Flying Machines.*

Epilogue

1. *Chicago Tribune*, December 8, 9, and 10, 2002; *Wall Street Journal,* December 10, 2002; *New York Times,* December 10, 2002.

2. UAL Corporation, Form 10-K annual report filed with the U.S. Securities and Exchange Commission on March 16, 2001, Item 6, Selected Financial Data and Operating Statistics, and Form 8-K quarterly report filed with the U.S. Securities and Exchange Commission on July 18, 2001, press release included as an amendment to the filing.

3. James E. Goodwin, chairman and chief executive officer, UAL Corporation, letter of October 18, 2001, to UAL employees and filed as an amendment to Form 8-K with the U.S. Securities and Exchange Commission on October 17, 2001.

4. *Chicago Tribune,* October 28, 2001, and December 8 and 31, 2002; *Wall Street Journal,* October 28, 2001; UAL Inc. press releases of February 1, 2002, and October 18, 2002.

5. *Chicago Tribune,* November 28 and December 3 and 8, 2002.

6. UAL Corporation, Form 8-K filed with the U.S. Securities and Exchange Commission on December 2, 2002. In re: UAL Corporation, et al., 02-48191 through 02-48218 filed in United States Bankruptcy Court, Northern District of Illinois, December 9, 2002. (The case numbers were assigned to UAL and twenty-seven of its subsidiaries, including United Air Lines, that simultaneously filed for bankruptcy protection.) UAL Corporation press release filed as an amendment to Form 8-K filed with the U.S. Securities and Exchange Commission on December 9, 2002.

7. *Chicago Tribune,* January 25, 2002.

8. *Chicago Tribune,* January 18, 2002. The Federal Aviation Administration reported the number of flight operations for the nation's ten busiest airports in 2001 (with the declines or gains) as O'Hare, 911,861 (+0.3%); Atlanta Hartsfield, 887,403 (-2.9%); Dallas/Ft. Worth, 802,587 (-7.3%); Los Angeles International, 738,679 (-5.7%); Phoenix Sky Harbor, 606,666 (-5.0%); Detroit Metropolitan, 523,039 (-5.7%); Denver International, 507,840 (-3.9%); Las Vegas McCarran, 501,846 (-3.7%); Minneapolis–St. Paul, 501,252 (-4.0%); and Lambert–St. Louis, 478,947 (-1.1%). The FAA also reported that Midway Airport had 276,520 flight operations in 2001, a decline of 7.3 percent.

9. Boeing Company press releases of March 21 and May 10, 2001.

Appendix B: Major Air Disasters in Chicago

1. Synopsis of testimony to Cook County Coroner's Jury, July 23, 1919; *Chicago Tribune,* July 22–25, 1919; *Chicago Herald and Examiner,* July 22–25, 1919; Glassman, *Jump,* 31–32, 45; Hansen, *Goodyear Airships,* 1.

2. Civil Aeronautics Board, Accident Investigation Report, March 28, 1941; *Chicago Tribune,* March 29, 1941.

3. Civil Aeronautics Board, Accident Investigation Report SA-167, File No. 1-0023, June 13, 1949; *Chicago Tribune,* February 25, 1949.

4. Civil Aeronautics Board, Accident Investigation Report SA-215, File No. 1-0081, January 18, 1951.

5. *Chicago Tribune,* November 16, 1955.

6. Serling, *Loud and Clear,* 184–250.

7. Civil Aeronautics Board, Aircraft Accident Report SA-357, File No. 1-0054, August 14, 1961, 1–11.

8. Civil Aeronautics Board, Aircraft Accident Report SA-363, File No. 1-0011, December 11, 1962.

9. Civil Aeronautics Board, Aircraft Accident Report SA-364, File No. 1-0018, December 10, 1962, 1–36.

10. National Transportation Safety Board, Aircraft Accident Report, File No. 1-0030 (Washington, D.C., December 19, 1967); Serling, *Loud and Clear,* 256–263.

11. *Chicago Tribune,* January 18, 1969.

12. National Transportation Safety Board, Aircraft Accident Report NTSB-AAR-73-16 (Washington, D.C., August 29, 1973).

13. National Transportation Safety Board, Aircraft Accident Report NTSB-AAR-73-15 (Washington, D.C., July 5, 1973).

14. National Transportation Safety Board, Aircraft Accident Report NTSB-AAR-79-17 (Washington, D.C., December 21, 1979).

15. *Chicago Tribune,* March 20, 1982.

16. National Transportation Safety Board, Aircraft Accident Report NTSB-AAR-96-01 (Washington, D.C., July 9, 1996).

Select Bibliography

• The following is not a complete bibliography on the subject of aeronautics and aviation or even a compendium of all the works consulted in the preparation of *Chicago Aviation* but is limited to books in general circulation that have some bearing on aviation in Chicago. Statistical summaries, interviews, periodical articles, dissertations, and government reports are cited in the notes.

Allen, Oliver E. *The Airline Builders.* Alexandria, Va., 1981.

Althoff, William F. *Sky Ships: A History of the Airship in the United States Navy.* New York, 1990.

Andrews, Wayne. *Battle for Chicago.* New York, 1946.

Angelucci, Enzo. *World Encyclopedia of Civil Aircraft from Leonardo da Vinci to the Present.* New York, 1982. Originally published as *Atlante Enciclopedico degli Aerei Civili del Mondo da Leonardo a oggi.* Milan, 1981.

Bailey, Elizabeth E., David R. Graham, and Daniel P. Kaplan. *Deregulating the Airlines.* Cambridge, Mass., 1985.

Bean, Barbara. *Of Magic Sails.* Chicago, 1975.

Bedwell, Don. *Silverbird: The American Airlines Story.* Sandpoint, Idaho, 1999.

Bilstein, Roger E. *Flight in America: From the Wrights to the Astronauts.* Baltimore, 1994.

Boyne, Walter J. *Beyond the Horizons: The Lockheed Story.* New York, 1998.

Brooks, Peter, W. *Zeppelin: Rigid Airships.* Washington, D.C., 1992.

Cannon, Charles B. *The O'Hare Story.* New York, 1980.

Chant, Christopher. *The Zeppelin: The History of German Airships from 1900 to 1937.* London, 2000.

Chanute, Octave. *Progress in Flying Machines.* 1894. Reprint, Long Beach, Calif., 1976.

Crouch, Tom D. *The Bishop's Boys: A Life of Wilbur and Orville Wright.* New York, 1989.

———. *A Dream of Wings: Americans and the Airplane, 1975–1905.* New York, 1981.

———. *The Eagle Aloft: Two Centuries of Ballooning in America.* Washington, D.C., 1983.

Davies, R. E. G. *Airlines of the United States since 1914.* Washington, D.C., 1972.

———. *Delta: An Airline and Its Aircraft.* Miami, Fla., 1990.

Dierikx, Marc. *Fokker: A Transatlantic Biography.* Washington, D.C., 1997.

Ewing, Steve, and John B. Lundstrom. *Fateful Rendezvous: The Life of Butch O'Hare.* Annapolis, 1997.

Farrell, V. L. A. *Lawson: From Bootblack to Emancipator.* Detroit, 1934.

Flink, James J. *The Automobile Age.* Cambridge, Mass., 1988.

Freudenthal, Elsbeth E. *The Aviation Business: From Kitty Hawk to Wall Street.* New York, 1940.

Freydberg, Elizabeth A. H. *Bessie Coleman: The Brownskin Lady Bird.* New York, 1994.

Garvey, William, and David Fisher. *The Age of Flight: A History of America's Pioneering Airline.* Greensboro, N.C., 2001.

Glassman, Don. *Jump: Tales of the Caterpillar Club.* New York, 1930.

Gourley, Jay. *The Great Lakes Triangle.* Greenwich, Conn., 1977.

Gove, Samuel K., and James D. Nowland. *Illinois Politics and Government: The Expanding Metropolitan Frontier.* Lincoln, Nebraska, 1996.

Handleman, Philip. *Chicago O'Hare: The World's Busiest Airport.* Osceola, Wis., 1988.

Hansen, Zenon. *The Goodyear Airships.* Bloomington, Ill., 1977.

Heinmuller, John P. V. *Man's Fight to Fly: Famous World Record Flights and a Chronology of Aviation.* New York, 1944.

Holland, Maurice. *Architects of Aviation.* New York, 1951.

Jablonski, Edward. *Man with Wings: A Pictorial History of Aviation.* New York, 1980.

Jackson, Donald Dale. *The Aeronauts.* Alexandria, Va., 1980.

Jackson, Robert. *Airships: A Popular History of Dirigibles, Zeppelins, Blimps, and Other Lighter-Than-Air Craft.* New York, 1973.

Johnson, Robert E. *Airway One.* Chicago, 1974.

Jones, Geoff. *Northwest Airlines.* Vergennes, Vt., 1998.

———. *U.S. Airways.* Surrey, England, 1999.

Kamin, Blair. *Why Architecture Matters: Lessons from Chicago.* Chicago, 2001.

Kelly, Fred C. *The Wright Brothers: A Biography Authorized by Wilbur Wright.* New York, 1943.

Kent, Richard J., Jr. *Safe, Separated, and Soaring: A History of Federal Civil Aviation Policy, 1961–1972.* Washington, D.C., 1980.

Kimes, Beverly Rae. *The Standard Catalogue of American Cars, 1805–1942,* 3rd ed. Iola, Wis., 1996.

Kommons, Nick A. *From Bonfires to Beacons: Federal Civil Aviation Policy under the Commerce Act, 1926–1938.* Washington, D.C., 1978.

Leary, William M., ed. *Encyclopedia of American Business History and Biography: The Airline Industry.* New York, 1992.

———. *Aerial Pioneers: The U.S. Air Mail Service, 1918–1927.* Washington, D.C., 1985.

———, ed. *From Airships to Airbus: The History of Civil and Commercial Aviation.* Proceedings of the International Conference on the History of Civil and Commercial Aviation. Vol. 1, Infrastructure and Environment. Washington, D.C., 1995.

Lewis, W. David, and Wesley Phillips Newton. *Delta: The History of an Airline.* Athens, Ga., 1979.

Lomax, Judy. *Women of the Air.* New York, 1987.

Lynch, Christopher. *Chicago's Midway Airport: The First Seventy-Five Years.* Chicago, 2002.

McCutcheon, John T. *Drawn from Memory.* Indianapolis, 1950.

Marsh, Barbara. *A Corporate Tragedy: The Agony of International Harvester Company.* New York, 1985.

Mayer, Harold M., and Richard C. Wade. *Chicago: Growth of a Metropolis.* Chicago, 1969.

Millbrooke, Anne. *Aviation History.* Englewood, Colo., 1999.

Modley, Rudolph. *Aviation Facts and Figures 1945.* New York, 1945.

Newhouse, John. *The Sporty Game.* New York, 1982.

Nielsen, Georgia Panter. *From Sky Girl to Flight Attendant: Women and the Making of a Union.* Ithaca, N.Y., 1982.

Norgaard, Eric. *The Book of Balloons.* New York, 1971.

Norwood, Tom W. *Deregulation Knockouts: Round One.* Sandpoint, Idaho, 1996.

Pisano, Dominick A. "The Crash that Killed Knute Rockne." *Air & Space,* December 1991/January 1992, pp. 88–93.

Preston, Edmund. *Troubled Passage: The Federal Aviation Administration during the Nixon-Ford Term.* Washington, D.C., 1987.

Putnam, Carleton. *High Journey.* New York, 1945.

Ratigan, William. *Great Lakes Shipwrecks and Survivals.* Grand Rapids, Mich., 1960.

Rich, Doris. *Queen Bess: Daredevil Aviator.* Washington, D.C., 1993.

Rittenhouse, Mignon. *The Amazing Nellie Bly.* New York, 1956.

Rochester, Stuart I. *Takeoff at Mid-Century: Federal Civil Aviation Policy in the Eisenhower Years, 1953–1961.* Washington, D.C., 1976.

Scamehorn, Howard L. *Balloons to Jets: A Century of Aeronautics in Illinois.* Chicago, 1957.

Serling, Robert J. *Loud and Clear.* New York, 1969.

———. *The Electra Story.* New York, 1963.

Shaw, Robert B. *A History of Railway Accidents, Safety Precautions,* *and Operating Practices,* 2d ed. Potsdam, N.Y., 1978.

Smith, Frank A., ed. *Transportation in America: A Statistical Analysis of Transportation in the United States.* Washington, D.C.: ENO Transportation Foundation, Inc., published annually.

Stout, William Bushnell. *So Away I Went.* Indianapolis, 1951.

Taylor, Frank J. *High Horizons: Daredevil Flying Postmen to Modern Magic Carpet: The United Airlines Story.* New York, 1951.

———. *"Pat" Patterson.* Menlo Park, Calif., 1967.

Thompson, H. A. *Our Bishops.* Dayton, Ohio, 1903.

Trimble, William F. *Admiral William A. Moffett: Architect of Naval Aviation.* Washington, D.C., 1994.

———, ed. *From Airships to Airbus: The History of Civil and Commercial Aviation.* Proceedings of the International Conference on the History of Civil and Commercial Aviation. Vol. 2, Pioneers and Operations. Washington, D.C., 1995.

Underwood, John. *The Stinsons.* Glendale, Calif., 1969.

Vance, James E., Jr. *Capturing the Horizon: The Historical Geography of Transportation since the Sixteenth Century.* Baltimore, 1990.

van der Linden, F. Robert. *The Boeing 247: The First Modern Airliner.* Seattle, 1991.

Van Orman, Ward T. *The Wizard of the Winds.* St. Cloud, Minn., 1978.

White, John H., Jr. *The American Railroad Passenger Car.* Baltimore, 1978.

Wilson, John R. M. *Turbulence Aloft: The Civil Aeronautics Administration amid Wars and Rumors of Wars.* Washington, D.C., 1979.

Wohl, Robert. *A Passion for Wings: Aviation and the Western Imagination, 1908–1918.* New Haven, Conn., 1994.

Young, David, and Neal Callahan. *Fill the Heavens with Commerce: Chicago Aviation, 1855–1926.* Chicago, 1981.

Young, Pearl I. *Octave Chanute: 1832–1910.* San Francisco, 1963.

Index